The Civil Rights Movement

D0061391

William T. Martin Riches

The Civil Rights Movement

Struggle and Resistance

Fourth Edition

© William T. Martin Riches 1997, 2004, 2010, 2017

All rights reserved. No reproduction, copy or transmission of this publication may be made without written permission.

No portion of this publication may be reproduced, copied or transmitted save with written permission or in accordance with the provisions of the Copyright, Designs and Patents Act 1988, or under the terms of any licence permitting limited copying issued by the Copyright Licensing Agency, Saffron House, 6–10 Kirby Street, London EC1N 8TS.

Any person who does any unauthorized act in relation to this publication may be liable to criminal prosecution and civil claims for damages.

The author has asserted his rights to be identified as the author of this work in accordance with the Copyright, Designs and Patents Act 1988.

First published 2017 by
PALGRAVE

Palgrave in the UK is an imprint of Macmillan Publishers Limited, registered in England, company number 785998, of 4 Crinan Street, London, N1 9XW.

Palgrave® and Macmillan® are registered trademarks in the United States, the United Kingdom, Europe and other countries.

ISBN 978–1–137–56482–5 hardback
ISBN 978–1–137–56481–8 paperback

This book is printed on paper suitable for recycling and made from fully managed and sustained forest sources. Logging, pulping and manufacturing processes are expected to conform to the environmental regulations of the country of origin.

A catalogue record for this book is available from the British Library.

A catalog record for this book is available from the Library of Congress.

For
Lilla
A Very Special Person

Contents

Preface

A friend at Harvard University in 1964 asked my wife and I where we planned to visit during our travels in the United States from our home in Canada. We told him we were going to the southern states, including Mississippi and Alabama, and he was very concerned about our safety and pressed us to put a Canadian flag in the windscreen of the car because we would be mistaken for civil rights 'outside agitators'. He said the locals would not know that our Ontario licence plate proved we were from Canada but would assume it was just another Yankee state. We did as he suggested.

As foreigners we were naive about the dangers we faced and more importantly equally unaware of the 'etiquette of segregation'. This became apparent as we approached the town of Biloxi, Mississippi. We were thirsty and just after crossing the city limits we stopped at a restaurant for a drink. It was crowded and we sat at the counter and I ordered two coffees. The woman did not answer. I asked for a second time. No response. I assumed it was my foreign accent and with a slightly raised voice I repeated my order but she just stared at me. Speaking slowly and distinctly, I asked again and she turned and fled. Before we could leave a man appeared and politely enquired what we wanted and I told him. He looked at the woman and told her to serve us. Throughout this surreal exchange we were aware that the conversation of the other customers had stopped and there was an oppressive silence. Looking around the restaurant we realised why – we were the only white people in the place. With my long hair and beard it must have seemed that I was one of those civil rights 'trouble makers' and by integrating that café we had endangered the man and his wife, and even his customers. Inadvertently, we had defied segregation etiquette.

Our Harvard friend assured us race relations were better in the North. But three years later, in 1967, when returning from a visit to Canada, we were caught in a snowstorm in Buffalo, New York and were forced to stop at a motel. As we checked in, the woman held her rosary and stared at the television. She cursed. We looked up to see a white priest leading a group of black men and women in a protest march. She did not speak to us but to the screen and muttered, 'You're no priest, you're a nigger lover, the Devil's agent. The Pope will destroy you. You'll burn in hell.' The weather dictated that we had to stay. Later I discovered that the priest she hated so vehemently was Father Groppi of Milwaukee.

In later years as graduate students at the University of Tennessee, Knoxville our defiance of the South and its customs was never accidental. What we did not appreciate at the time was how we had been met with gracious politeness by the owner of that café and the fact that we were served. If they had made the mistake that we had made in a white coffee bar, the white folks' reaction would have been very different.

The desire by many white Americans to exclude or 'disappear' African Americans – captured by Ralph Ellison's wonderful title, *The Invisible Man* – has shaped much of the history of the nation. It was highlighted by those, black and white, who fought against slavery and all forms of poverty and discrimination in the cities and rural America. Anti-colonialism profoundly influenced the struggle and some wanted to escape and return to Africa and a few still do. But for the overwhelming majority this was and still is not desirable. They want to be Americans. It remains their aspiration and it is bitterly contested by a significant number of white people.

For many, African Americans are 'the other', aliens and not true citizens as amply demonstrated during the campaign and election of Barack Obama as the first black president and the persistent belief that he is not a US citizen but Kenyan and a Muslim not a Christian. Although many of the barriers have gradually eroded over the years, it would be a mistake to be swept away by the obvious joy of almost two million people standing in the bitter cold on inauguration day in 2008. Post-racialism is an illusion. Race hatred has exploded in these years fuelled by the awareness that white folks will soon be the minority and eventually Spanish, not English, will be the first language. In this crisis for white America they are making a last stand and their fear and hatred is fed by politicians. In large parts of the country many feel the same weight of poverty and oppression that they felt in 1964. Some see Spanish moss as part of the romantic antebellum South, but for others it is a curtain that conceals the past and present violence and deprivation. And here I must make it clear that race is a purely social construct, that it has no scientific basis, but equally I know that people continue to believe in 'races' and these beliefs shape their behaviour.

The freedom struggle can be dated back to escaping enslaved people, but all historians periodise history and as Glenda Gilmore in *Defying Dixie* cogently argues there were important radicals fighting for civil rights after World War One and who wanted radical economic change. However, this underestimates the same goals after World War Two and diminishes the radical economic reforms agenda of the Movement and the role of pre-war radicals and tends to overstate the 'conservatism' of the National Association for the Advancement of Colored People (NAACP) and the black church. The demands of the Movement were, and continue to be, for widespread economic reform as well as social and political change. The Movement may have often failed in its economic goals but it was not for want of trying or to deny the continued fight. The United States in the 20th and 21st century has seen changes that I never thought possible as we travelled the United States in 1964 – or in our lifetime. This is one reason why my periodisation of events from 1945 is justified.

Some would argue that the challenge of writing contemporary history makes considered judgement impossible. In my case it is even more difficult in that I was also a participant in a very small way in some of these events. However, this is not a participant's history, but rather seeks objectively to analyse the civil rights struggle of African Americans after World War Two. I believe that my training as a historian, the intervening years and my views as an outsider living in Ireland and England, as well as the United States, have helped me in my quest for objectivity. I agree with Alan Dawley that 'the destiny of modern America was in the hands of the meek as well as the mighty'. As he points out: 'The struggle for racial justice and sexual equality were not simply a matter of good versus the bad guys but there is no doubt that good and evil hung in the balance. In comprehending what happened, I have aspired to objectivity. But objectivity does not mean indifference. It matters very much how things turned out' (Dawley, 1991).

I am well aware of the vital role played by Martin Luther King Jr in the struggle for civil rights and radical economic change which was the root of inequality and discrimination and I am very conscious of the tragic consequences of his assassination in Memphis. Other leaders played crucial roles in the fight such as A. Philip Randolph, Bayard Rustin, Ella Baker, E. D. Nixon and Fanny Lou Hamer to name a few. In the 2008 primary campaign for the Democratic nomination, Hillary Clinton was criticised unfairly for stressing the importance of President Lyndon Johnson in winning civil rights for the oppressed in the United States and belittling the work of Dr. King. However, the important thing is that King knew he had to work with Johnson and did so until the war in Vietnam endangered the War on Poverty. Johnson predicted that if other administrations did not join the struggle, his beloved child – the Great Society – would starve and many of the civil rights achievements would be lost.

I approach the struggle as an interaction of grass-root groups and individuals working through black institutions created by segregation. The work stresses the role of congregations, the often underestimated role of preachers and teachers, students, workers and unions who interacted with those who held political power at federal, state and local level – men and women who joined the struggle and organised despite massive resistance. I emphasis the role of the 'meek' who did so much to help the Movement from the bottom up; it is important to see and understand the extraordinary courage and sacrifices of hundreds of thousands who ensured the successes of the Movement. This does not diminish the later role of the men and women who held political power at the local, state and federal levels; this is especially true with the organisation of the Congressional Black Caucus in Washington.

It may well be argued that the chapter on the New South neglects massive resistance but that features throughout this book. My response is that the change in the attitudes of a significant number of white southerners has not been sufficiently acknowledged; they joined or assisted in the struggle when it would have been easier to ally with resisters and bigots. During my years as a graduate student in the South I taught, and studied and witnessed, these extraordinary changes in racial attitudes of many students from all over the South. They rejected the ways of many of their peers. They were, and are, well aware that in freeing black folks they free themselves too. The groups they established and those who worked in them have done much to fight to preserve the gains and many of my friends did, and still do, make the stand for justice. Many people view them as a tiny minority but virtually all activists in the nation were also in the minority. I strongly disagree with those who argue that the struggle ended in the 1970s.

I explore the coalitions formed by civil rights activists with environmentalists, lesbians, gays, bisexuals and transgender people, the disabled, and peace movements, who continually combatted a reinvigorated conservative political environment and a hostile judiciary. For example, the anti-Vietnam and anti-Iraq war teach-ins were a tactic copied by the Freedom Schools and were often led by women and men who had worked in the South. The battle against toxic pollution, that affects all races, uses protest marches, mobilisation of churches and pressure groups organised by politicians and others. I examine the debate in the black community about the benefit of coalition politics or the need to focus solely on black issues as well as the strains within and between various coalitions. There are other coalitions that I have not explored owing to limitations of space, especially the American Indian Movement.

I have revised all the chapters in the light of my own research and recent scholarship, I have introduced the important part played by music in creating a sense of community and the debate on Black Power has been extensively revised and extended. To keep this book at a reasonable length I discuss briefly African American literature and include some discussion on film. The northern struggle and resistance, especially in Milwaukee and Detroit, has been given greater consideration.

With the election of Richard Nixon in 1968, with civil right groups and their allies divided and on the defensive, it seemed all the gains of the previous years would be wiped out. A white friend, who was a doctor in Tennessee and whose father had been an illiterate Alabama sharecropper, invited me and my wife to a dinner with friends, black and white, who were active in the civil rights and the anti-Vietnam war movements. We reminisced about the years that had passed and were fearful about the years ahead. Before we left he insisted that we all sit listen and always remember when we were to separate to never forget these words. He left the room and returned shortly. On that hot summer evening in East Tennessee the group of southerners – academics, ministers, atheists and a couple from the United Kingdom – sat and listened to the speech given by Martin Luther King Jr at the Washington rally of 1963:

> So I say to you, my friends, that even though we must face the difficulties of today and tomorrow, I still have a dream. It is the dream deeply rooted in the American Dream that one day this nation will rise up and live out the true meaning of its creed – we hold these truths to be self evident, that all men are created equal.

However, there must be a warning. Many Americans, regardless of age, gender and ethnicity, are forgetting the history of racial segregation and discrimination. Others believe they have been overcome and the persistence of inequality is the fault of the black and poor themselves. Unlike King, Malcolm X and others, they fail to recognise that the widening gulf of economic inequality and persistent denigration of minorities, even by national parties, endangers the whole society. By their actions and in their forgetting much might well be lost. One can only hope that after the 2016 elections Dan Carter is right that 'the unfinished music of the movement still lingers in our collective memory to inspire the efforts of a new generation in a third symphony of reconstruction.'

Acknowledgements

I appreciate the invaluable advice given by my daughter Dr. Julia Riches and my son Dr. Theo Riches who have read and commented on this work. When I was lecturing, my students always reminded me of the wider struggle of those who fought for civil rights and I hope I have done justice to these activists. Also, I would like to say how much I appreciate the assistance of Dr. Simon Topping and David McAree who shared valuable sources. My graduate students, Dr. Mark Fannin, Dr. Stephen Milligen and Dr. Matthew McKee, contributed much and this brief acknowledgement does not do justice to their honest criticism and continued friendship.

And there are those who showed me that there is a more complex, more generous South, not remotely like Hollywood's stereotypical Gothic horror. My friends Oscar and Mary Allen, faculty and fellow graduate students at the University of Tennessee, Knoxville, Dr. John Thomas, Dr. Tom Wilson, Dan Pomeroy and the late O. C. Richardson were native southerners and introduced me to the variety and complexity of the region they were so proud of. My best friend, Professor David Bowen, was killed in a car accident. It is impossible to say how much I owe him, a poet, historian and fellow lover of Dylan Thomas. He had great courage in his fight against bigotry in his native and his beloved South. He inspired many – especially his students.

Not wishing to offend anyone, I will just say that many scholars in Britain, Ireland and the United States have helped in this work and I would like to thank the international scholars of the Milan-Montpellier Group for the Study of American History when ideas and research findings were combined with good food and wine. I must add that any errors in this book are not theirs but solely my responsibility.

Also, I want to acknowledge my friends the late Professors Tony Hepburn, whom I met in graduate school and worked with at the Ulster University, and Richard Marius – great teachers and scholars who did so much for me. Richard best described my relationship with him when he inscribed in one of his books: 'To a colleague in courses, comrade in causes and to Judy who endures all this.'

I am deeply indebted to my editors at Palgrave Macmillan. Elizabeth Holmes for her patience and for helping me through those moments when the manuscript almost ended up in the trash. Our 'conversations' taught me that emails are not necessarily impersonal. All authors wish that they will have an excellent editor. Rachel Bridgewater did so much to ensure my work was completed on time. They generously allowed me all sorts of latitude and ensured that I could make observations on the 2016 campaign and the early months of the Trump presidency.

The 73 magnificent villagers of Stacciola, Italy have continually proved their kindness and patience with the Englishman. Perhaps it is not fair to select four of them but I feel I must say a special thank you to Moro, Mimi, Nicola and Alessandra. But above all I owe everything to my wife, Judy, my sternest critic and my most loyal supporter. I dedicate this book to her and my family and especially to my buddy and granddaughter Lilla.

Acronyms

ACHR	Alabama Council on Human Rights
ACLU	American Civil Liberties Union
ACMHR	Alabama Christian Movement for Human Rights
ADA	Americans for Democratic Action
AFDC	Aid to Families with Dependent Children
AFL-CIO	American Federation of Labor and Congress of Industrial Organizations
AFSC	American Friends Service Committee
AME	African Methodist Episcopal
BLM	Black Lives Matter
BSCP	Brotherhood of Sleeping Car Porters
CBC	Congressional Black Caucus
CEEO	Commission for Equal Employment Opportunity
CIA	Central Intelligence Agency
CIO	Congress of Industrial Organizations
COFO	Council of Federated Organizations
CORE	Congress of Racial Equality
CRRA	Civil Rights Restoration Act
EEOC	Equal Employment Opportunity Commission
EPA	Environmental Protection Agency
ERA	Equal Rights Amendment
FBI	Federal Bureau of Investigation
FDR	Franklin Delano Roosevelt
FEPC	Fair Employment Practices Commission
FOR	Fellowship of Reconciliation
FSAM	Free South Africa Movement
HEW	Health, Education and Welfare
HUAC	House Un-American Activities Committee
IRS	Internal Revenue Service
JFK	John Fitzgerald Kennedy
KKK	Ku Klux Klan

LBJ	Lyndon Baines Johnson
LCFO	Lowndes County Freedom Organization
LGBT	Lesbians, Gays, Bisexuals and Transgender
MFDP	Mississippi Freedom Democratic Party
MIA	Montgomery Improvement Association
NAACP	National Association for the Advancement of Colored People
NOI	Nation of Islam
NOW	National Organization for Women
PAC	Political Action Committee
PMRC	Parents' Music Resource Center
PUSH	People United to Save Humanity
ROAR	Restore Our Alienated Rights
SCEF	Southern Conference Education Fund
SCLC	Southern Christian Leadership Conference
SDS	Students for a Democratic Society
SNCC	Student Nonviolent (changed in 1965 to National) Coordinating Committee
SPLC	Southern Poverty Law Centre
SSOC	Southern Student Organizing Committee
UAW	United Auto Workers
UCMI	United Christian Movement Incorporated
UNIA	Universal Negro Improvement Association
UPHWA	United Packing House Workers of America
USCC	United States Civil Rights Commission
UT	University of Tennessee
WCC	White Citizens Council
WPC	Women's Political Council

Introduction

John Rolfe described the arrival of the first Africans in North America. They came by accident. A Dutch ship exchanged '19 and odd' (odd meaning 'more') for food and supplies. Historians have argued ever since about the status of these first Africans in North America but most agree that *de facto* slavery did not emerge until 1640 and was not codified into law to become *de jure* slavery until 1660. After that most Africans were classified as property, and despite the existence of a small free black population, increased by manumissions after American independence, nine out of ten were held as slaves by 1860 (Riches, 1999). But well into the 19th century the lines between black and white were often breached (Hodes, 1997; Sandweiss, 2009).

White American colonists may have fought against the 'slavery' and 'tyranny' of George III but the vast majority of African Americans remained enslaved people, something the British were quick to point out. Some blacks who opposed the colonists were fortunate enough to get to Canada or Britain, and gained their freedom, but those who went to the West Indies were not so fortunate. Although slaves in the North were given either immediate emancipation (as in Massachusetts) or gradual freedom (as in New York State), the situation for most African Americans declined rapidly in the South, with emancipation virtually impossible and the American Colonization Society seeking to return the few free blacks to Africa (Davis, 2006; Piketty, 2014).

The Constitution drawn up by the leading intellectuals in America avoided the use of the word 'slave'; instead African Americans held in slavery were deemed to be three-fifths of a white man. According to Article 1, Section 2, representatives and direct taxes in each state were determined 'by adding the whole number of free persons, including those bound to service for a term of years and excluding Indians not taxed, and three-fifths of other persons'. These 'other persons' were in fact African American slaves. For many American historians this 'Great Compromise' between representatives of the North and the South personified the wisdom of the Founding Fathers in their search for a stable government. What they ignore is that it was achieved at the expense of African Americans and only delayed the confrontation which led to four years of Civil War and the destruction of slavery.

Slavery and the Civil War

The growing dispute between North and South over the institution of slavery as the nation expanded westwards was about the issue of free labour, not the ending of slavery. For northerners, free men were far more efficient as workers than slaves and those who wanted to limit the expansion of the institution were more worried about the corrupting influence of slavery than the plight of the slaves (Foner, 1970). Even some abolitionists, led by William Lloyd Garrison, argued that the North should secede from the Union to prevent the corruption of its democratic institutions by slaveholders. Former slave and leading abolitionist Frederick Douglass was quick to point out that this might protect free labour but it did nothing for the enslaved (Douglass, 1962).

These attacks on slavery heightened slaveowners' fear of slave rebellion in its many forms; for example, James Henry Hammond, senator and governor of South Carolina, was so fearful of the autonomous black church built by his slaves – a free space for them with their own black preacher – that he had it torn down and forced them to attend his church sitting in the balcony. What he never discovered was that they defied him and held their own services and sang their gospels with their own preacher (Faust, 1982). And Hammond was not the only one concerned about the slave church. After all, the emphasis on the Old Testament, with its stories of the flight from slavery, crossing the River Jordan to freedom and Jericho's walls tumbling down, was repeated over and over in sung sermons and spirituals (Smith, 2004).

Increasingly, southerners saw themselves as a beleaguered minority in the Union in which their 'peculiar institution' was in danger of being swept away by the tyranny of the majority. Under the leadership of John C. Calhoun, a former vice president and senator from South Carolina, they claimed that the Union was a compact of sovereign states, not of the people, and it was the duty of state governments to protect the citizens of the state from overbearing federal authority. If a state convention deemed a federal law to be unconstitutional, it was the duty of state officers to raise troops to nullify the law and to interpose their authority between the state and the federal government. The first attempt to practice nullification and interposition was by South Carolina during a dispute over tariffs in 1832. It failed. These arguments in favour of state sovereignty, nullification and interposition were defeated when the southern Confederacy was overwhelmed by Union troops. However, this did not stop southerners from trying to breathe life into these arguments when they resisted the civil rights movement of the 1950s and 1960s.

Lincoln and the recently founded Republican Party argued that they only favoured barring slavery from the territories and not abolition. With the outbreak of the Civil War, and as late as 1862, Lincoln assured Horace Greeley, a leading Republican and editor of the New York *Tribune,* in a letter that was made public, his only interest was to save the Union (Goodwin, 2006). Even if the majority of whites in the North opposed emancipation, African Americans in the North and slaves in the South knew the war was about freedom. Southerners who had lulled themselves into the belief that their slaves would be loyal, were shocked and then angered that their 'happy darkies' fled the plantation and sought to join the Union army. Despite the frequently hostile reception by Union officers, slaves continued to flood past the Union lines. Abolishing slavery was inevitable and Lincoln knew it. Even as he was writing to Greeley, the Emancipation Proclamation, which freed slaves in Confederate held territory, had already been drawn up. The president, in part responding to pressure from black abolitionists, agreed that African Americans could volunteer for the army. 'Totalling 140,313, they composed, by the last year of the war, well over 10 percent of the Union army, and in some departments close to half of it' (Hahn, 2003). The long tradition of African Americans fighting in America's wars was continued and this time they had greater incentive because they were not fighting for the freedom of white Americans but for all Americans.

The willingness of African Americans to take up arms to defend the Union had a dramatic effect on northern attitudes. This was reflected in the cover of the most popular northern journal, *Harper's Weekly*, which in 1863 had a cover of three dead Union soldiers on a hill. They had fallen with their arms around each other and the Stars and Stripes streams in the sky above. What is unusual about the picture is two of the men are white but the central soldier is African American. As Peter Parish has written: 'Millions of black Americans gained pride and self-respect from the knowledge that their own menfolk had shared in the fight for freedom' (Parish, 1975). And the South that had gone to war to defend slavery ensured its abolition with the Thirteenth Amendment adopted in 1865.

The assassination of Lincoln, the first president to be murdered, horrified the North. The anger and dismay was expressed not only by his friends and members of the Republican Party, but even by those who had opposed him and his policies. A Union soldier in Tennessee on hearing the news of the president's death wrote in his diary 'that the black flag of extermination' should be raised over the South. Lincoln's place was taken by his vice president, Andrew Johnson, who, like his fellow white Unionists of Tennessee, believed that 'the government of the United States and the governments of the states erected under the Constitution thereof are governments of free white men, to be controlled and administered by him [*sic*] and the negroes must assume that status of the laws of an enlightened, moral and high-toned civilization shall assign him' (Nashville *Daily Union*, 1 June 1864). Unlike the southern members of the Unionist [Republican] Party, Johnson before the war had vigorously defended slavery as a positive good for blacks and whites and necessary for the maintenance of civilisation. His passion had been the unity of the country and now the war was over nothing else needed to be done.

Reconstruction

Many northern Unionists were conservative, often racist, but none of them had ever argued as Johnson did and it was this difference in the matter of racism that would lead to the conflict between moderates and radicals in the National Union Party (Republican). The legislatures of the former Confederate states passed 'Black Codes' that virtually returned the freed slaves to servitude. Johnson's refusal to prevent this and his support for the South alienated him from the Party he was supposed to represent. The extent of this alienation is seen in Johnson's veto of the Freedman's Bureau Bill and the Civil Rights Bill. In the latter veto Johnson used an argument that would be used in the 1990s and into the 21st century, ironically by Republicans in their assault on affirmative action. Andrew Johnson argued that the Civil Rights Bill established 'for the security of the colored race safeguards which go infinitely beyond any that the General Government has provided for the white race. In fact, the distinction of race and color by the bill is made to operate in favor of the colored race against the white race.' What Johnson did not even consider was the fact that African Americans had been subjected to laws for over 200 years which not only safeguarded the white race but also held them as chattel with no rights in law.

Johnson's obduracy benefited the freedmen in the long term. By alienating northern sentiment and the Republican Party with attacks on the leadership as traitors, Johnson ensured the ratification of the Fourteenth Amendment in 1868 making all the former slaves citizens of the United States. In addition, Section 1 gave the country its first national law of due process stipulating that 'nor shall any State deprive any person of life, liberty, or property without due process of the law; nor deny any person within its jurisdiction the equal protection of the laws.' In 1870, with the aid of Radical Republican governments in the South, the Fifteenth Amendment declared that a citizen's right to vote 'shall not be abridged by the United States or any State on account of race, color, or any previous condition of servitude'. It is important to remember that the modern civil rights movement and the vital legislative victories – the Civil Rights Acts of 1957, 1964 and 1968 and the Voting Rights Act of 1965 – would not have been possible without these Amendments.

Although Reconstruction was not the unmitigated disaster that some historians have portrayed, the legacy of the Radical Republican governments was to unify the white South in the fight against what they believed was corrupt carpetbagger rule made possible by the votes of freedmen. The South lost the war and slavery and now they had to tolerate 'Negro domination'. African Americans did not dominate the white South; the highest state office held by a black man was lieutenant governor of Louisiana. All the governors were white, as were the majority of elected officials in the South at state and federal level. But the legend of black rule had disastrous consequences for black southerners until well into the 20th century (Blight, 2001). Whites of all classes turned to violence and paramilitary organisations. The Ku Klux Klan (KKK) was in effect the armed wing of the Democratic Party. Radical Republicans were driven from office, and despite the assurances of the Fifteenth Amendment, African Americans were virtually stripped of their right to vote, first through violence and then, starting in Mississippi, through a series of devices, such as literacy tests and poll taxes. These did not deny the vote for poor illiterate whites. By these means white southerners proclaimed that the South was redeemed (Foner, 1988). Ironically it was the Christian language of redemption that would be used by African Americans in their struggle for justice 80 years later.

Freedmen Abandoned

Increasingly the Republican Party was unwilling to oblige the South to obey the Constitution. In order to ensure one-party control of the South the Democrats, after the disputed election of 1876, virtually conceded the federal executive power to the Republican Party. In return the Republicans ignored the virtual re-enslavement of freedmen in the South through the peonage sharecrop system and forced unpaid industrial labour (Blight, 2001; Daniel, 1972). With power in the hands of the Democratic Party, most black Americans sought accommodation with the dominant southern whites. Booker T. Washington, president of the all-black Tuskegee College, reassured a large white audience in Atlanta in 1895: 'In all things social we can be separate as the fingers, yet one as the hand in all things essential to mutual progress.' And he assured the business listeners that he would advise his fellow blacks to 'cast down your bucket where you are … Cast it down in agriculture, mechanics, in commerce, in domestic service and in the professions. Black men worked in the fields, the mines, built railroads and cities and never withheld their labour. If the white man supported the education of his race then the white man could 'live with the most patient, faithful, law-abiding, and unresentful people that the world has seen' (Blight, 2001).

One year later the Supreme Court accepted Washington's view of social relations between the races when by a vote of eight to one in *Plessy v. Ferguson* (1896) they upheld the right of the South to segregate its facilities, transport and education on the basis of race so long as they were separate but equal. Justice Harlan, from the border state of Kentucky, dissented; the very act of segregation was a denial of equality and his opinion would profoundly affect the Movement in the next century. But the Jim Crow system became the touchstone of the southern way of life which would not be challenged seriously until the 1950s (Litwack, 1998). However, black and white intellectuals started the Niagara Movement and when this failed they set up the National Association of Colored People (NAACP) in 1909. W. E. B. Du Bois edited its magazine *Crisis*. Harvard educated, Du Bois in *The Souls of Black Folk* attacked Washington and wrote of the African Americans' 'double consciousness': 'It is a peculiar sensation, this double-consciousness, this way of looking at one self through the eyes of others, of measuring one's soul by the tape of the world that looks on in contempt and pity.' He called for a 'Talented Tenth' of blacks to challenge segregation and warned that the greatest problem of the 20th century would be the colour line. But he did not simply seek intellectual leadership but urged northern blacks to take pride in their own culture, in their spirituals and sorrow songs (Du Bois, 1903).

Washington's plea to white southern business leaders for mutual understanding failed. From 1885 to 1917 inclusively, there were 3740 lynchings in the United States. Although 997 of the victims were white, 2734 were black men and women. The NAACP pointed out in its 1918 report, the number of white victims had declined sharply in the years between 1900 and 1917 (186 or 13.3 percent) but the number of blacks murdered by lynch mobs did not show a similar decline with 1241 (or 86.7 percent) victims. According to the Association, while African Americans were serving their country, 63 black men were lynched. The worst states were Georgia, Texas and Mississippi. Fourteen were murdered because they were alleged to have attacked white women or, as in one case, a black man and a white woman were in a consensual relationship. Many victims were tortured before death (Bracey et al., 1972). It is important that the barbarity of these acts is known because there have been too many attempts by Americans to deny them. Those involved in the struggle of the 1950s and 1960s were always aware of this violent past and that they could easily be the next victims.

Civil rights workers did not have to rely on their collective memory of white violence against black Americans because such violence remained a characteristic of the southern way of life throughout the 1950s and 1960s and even into the 21st century. For example, in August 1955 a young boy's mutilated body was dragged from a river. The defence counsel told the all-white jury that Emmett Till had violated southern etiquette and 'every last Anglo-Saxon man of you has the courage to free these men' (Whitfield, 1988). They did. And almost 40 years later a Mississippi Democrat used the same arguments defending attacks on the lesbian commune, Camp Sister Spirit, because they violated the southern code. It was not until 2008 that Congress passed the Emmett Till Unresolved Crimes Act to re-open cold cases involving the murder of civil rights workers up to 1970 (Senatus.com, accessed January 2009). Two sponsors of the Bill were Senators Barack Obama and Joe Biden. Unfortunately, the good intentions have not always been fulfilled as in the case of Louis Allen murdered in Liberty County, Mississippi in 1965 (CBS, 60 Minutes, accessed 15 April 2015). The FBI have admitted their failings but they are still deeply distrusted in the black community.

Millions of African Americans from the 1890s onwards responded to the poverty, segregation, humiliation and violence by seeking a better place in northern cities – the Great Migration. In Chicago by the 1930s the black population reached 7 percent and continued to rise rapidly to 38 percent by 1970. According to the 1910 census, Detroit's black population was 6,000 but by 1920 it was 278,000. In New York's Harlem, later called the Black Capital of America, between 1920 and 1932 African Americans and West Indians were over 32 percent of the population, but for central Harlem it was 70 percent. As more moved into Harlem there was a literary renaissance often supported by wealthy white women and men who found the area and its people fascinating and even viewed the residents as noble primitives. This attitude is brilliantly conveyed by Langston Hughes' short stories, *Ways of the White Folks* (1934). It also led to interracial marriages and relationships (Kaplan, 2013; Wilkerson, 2010). But this migration did not affect every northern city; Milwaukee would not see significant numbers of black people until after World War Two (Jones, 2010).

Between 1910 and 1930, 1.6 million African Americans had migrated North and between 1940 and 1970 they were followed by another 5 million. When they headed North from the Delta to Memphis and on to Chicago and New York, they brought with them their unique gift to American and world culture: religious and secular spirituals, soul songs, shouts, blues and jazz and unique labour songs from slavery and after, such as the railroad repair men known as the Gandy Dancers. Bill Ferris writes that the urban and rural blues share the emphasis on place. 'B. B. King in *Why I Sing the Blues* describes Chicago's ghetto, the rats and cockroaches in tenements, and the inadequate schools' (Ferris, 1978). As Neil Brand points out the blues were aural and, without the recording and William Handy's notating, they would not have spread out of the South. Urban life and industrial labour changed their music. In a rare film, Bessie Smith is acting drunkenly as she leans on the counter of a bar singing *The St Louis Blues*. She uses the same call and response typical of African American spirituals but exaggerates the drawn-out phrasing. The patrons respond with dancing as close-holding couples not separated as they would have been in the church (Brand, 2014). Other black singers profoundly affected the 1960s and 1970s protest movement. Vera Hall Ward recorded the pre-Civil war slave gospel *Free at Last* and it became one of the anthems of the Movement. The Reverend Gary Davies was recorded in 1935 and influenced singer-songwriters such as Bob Dylan and Jerry Garcia. Davies' combined recitation with singing may have had an impact on hip-hop and black blues men who profoundly influenced white artists including Josh White as well as Doc Reed (Spottswood and Wolfe, 2003).

They had not escaped racism, but at least there was no *de jure* segregation and, although only able to compete for the menial jobs, earnings in the stockyards of Chicago were far in excess of anything they could have earned as sharecroppers in the South (Halpern, 1997). When the United States entered World War One white workers were drafted into the army and European immigration almost ceased; this meant it was necessary to recruit black workers from the South. The competition for jobs and housing led to serious racial violence such as in East St. Louis in 1917 (Rudwick, 1964). During the Red Scare of 1919, many northern cities were wracked by white riots against communists and African Americans. One of the worst was in Chicago where ethnic minorities, especially Irish and Polish, attacked the black ghetto. They were joined by the police and military and carried out appalling atrocities. They set an example for Birmingham, Alabama after World War Two, when they dynamited black homes – 25 bombs between March 1918 and August 1919 (Philpott, 1983).

Another explanation for this white rage is political. African Americans, simply by leaving the South with its literacy tests and poll taxes, were no longer denied the franchise. During the war the black vote decided two Chicago mayoralty elections and even saw three African Americans elected as aldermen. 'Black people paid a high price for their victories, however, in several significant ways it was instrumental in precipitating and maintaining the Chicago race riot' (Tuttle, 1980).

At the same time as President Woodrow Wilson campaigned under the slogan 'The World Must be Made Safe for Democracy', he segregated the federal government, praised the KKK for its part in redeeming the South (the first movie shown in the White House was D. W. Griffiths' racist *The Birth of a Nation* in which the white women are plagued by insatiable black rapists) and he did nothing about the revival of the Klan and its so-called Invisible Empire. The Klan attacked not only blacks but also Roman Catholics, Jews and radicals. It was no longer confined to the South but had widespread appeal in the northern states and in northern and southern cities. At its height in 1923 the Klan boasted that it had 5 million members, even in the far west, and effectively controlled states such as Indiana (Chalmers, 1965; Jackson, 1992). However, it was not only whites who were enraged; black anger at the abuse spilled over into passionate anti-white feeling as is demonstrated in the character of Bigger Thomas in Richard Wright's existentialist novel *Native Son* set in Chicago and published in 1940. Bigger finds freedom through the murder and dismembering of a young white woman and in his efforts to escape white power. When his Marxist lawyer says he is a victim of the system, Bigger throws coffee in his face (Riches, 1980). Bigger's sense of desperate anger is brilliantly captured by Billie Holiday in *Strange Fruit* (1939) when she sings about lynching – 'Southern trees bear strange fruit / Blood on the leaves / and blood on the root / Black bodies swingin' in the southern breeze / Strange fruit on southern poplar trees'.

Black Nationalism

Just as there were African Americans in the 19th century who fought for civil rights within the United States, there were also strong advocates of black nationalism or those who supported the return to Africa. Black delegates at a convention in 1854 called on the 'colored inhabitants of the United States to leave the country and settle in the West Indies, Central and South America or western Canada if that country should remain under British control' (Braccy et al., 1972). Edwin McCabe, a black man from Kansas, urged African Americans to move into Oklahoma territory and create an all-black state. McCabe failed, but several black towns were established. Others turned to Bishop Henry McNeal Turner and his plans to establish a nation in Africa (Redkey, 1969).

By far the largest black nationalist movement was the Universal Negro Improvement Association founded by a Jamaican, Marcus Garvey, who came to New York City in 1916 with the aim of setting up 'a new ambitious political movement'. He established his base in Harlem and appealed to the poor and working class. He was concerned with the communities' lack of self-respect, and their need for educational, religious and cultural institutions. He espoused Washington's self-help and established numerous businesses with his African Communities League, the most well known was a shipping business, the Black Star Line. In order to instil pride, he awarded titles and formed a Black Legion with their own national anthem and flag – green for the earth, black for skin colour and red for the blood of slavery. His Pan-Africanism is evident in that these colours are part of the many flags of independent former colonies in Africa (Stein, 1986).

Despite Garvey's popularity, the collapse of the Black Star Line and his authoritarianism led to a split in the movement. This combined with federal administration harassment led to his conviction for fraud, five years in prison and permanent deportation. But one man who remained a fervent Garveyite was Earl Little and his partner, the parents of Malcolm X, who converted to the Nation of Islam (NOI) in 1952 (Marable, 2011).

The NOI was founded in Detroit by a man who called himself W. F. Muhammad and whose real name was W. D. Fard. Some scholars are sure he was a white man seeking to exploit gullible people or that he was a drug pusher and poor restaurant owner. Fard claimed he was God and that the original people were all created black but a scientist, Yakub, 6000 years earlier had worked on the genes of the people to try to make them paler. After Yakub's death, his students created white people who were devils and who after wandering and mating with canines eventually enslaved the remaining black people. Christianity was the invention of whites and the only true religion was Islam. The NOI remained a small group even though it attracted some disillusioned Garvey followers. Fard disappeared (Essien Udom, 1964; Ogbar, 2005). All these black national-ist groups depended on segregation and sought to maintain it. As Redkey points out, black nationalism 'shares many attributes of other nation-alisms ... Afro-Americans had a political past of slavery, oppression, and isolation by whites who took special pains to exclude them from American life. As a result, blacks had overflowing recollections of collec-tive humiliations and regret.' But he argues also that these movements were not based solely on these negative experiences but also 'stressed the glories of their African heritage and the American rhetoric which claimed that all men are created equal' (Redkey, 1969).

But the vast majority of African Americans in the 19th century and to the present time want to be full American citizens and their views were represented by the NAACP whose first success came in 1915 when the new state of Oklahoma sought to deny blacks the franchise if their grandfathers had not been eligible to vote – that is, they were enslaved. The Supreme Court ruled that this 'Grandfather Clause' was unconstitutional because it violated the Fifteenth Amendment (Meier and Rudwick, 1970). This willingness to use the courts for redress was encouraged after the Court had lost its battle against Franklin Delano Roosevelt's (FDR's) New Deal legislation and the more liberal envi-ronment of the 1930s. The NAACP sought equal opportunity without demanding integration but rather exploited the ruling of separate but equal laid down in *Plessy v. Ferguson* (1896). They set out to prove that the facilities were not equal. The Supreme Court upheld their view and ordered that graduate and law schools such as Maryland and Missouri must be integrated or equal ones must be provided. It was cheaper for the states to desegregate.

The Depression and New Deal

Many white Americans experienced the poverty known by millions of African Americans during the Depression years of the 1930s. White southerners and westerners faced with the Dust Bowl followed black southerners into the cities of the North or trekked further west to California. Mississippi by 1932 was literally bankrupt with barely $1000 in the treasury and with debts of $14 million. As a historian of the South points out, Mississippi was not untypical: 'the shrinking tax base throughout the South resulted in cutbacks in state services, and schools closed, more workers were laid off. Low commodity prices and farm failures made a shambles of the South's economy' (Daniel, 1986).

Despite many benefits from FDR's New Deal, such as the social security scheme, many African Americans either faced discrimination in hiring and pay on the many employment schemes or were forced from the land because of the workings of the Agricultural Adjustment Administration (AAA). Commodity prices could only be raised by restricting the supply and farmers were paid to plough under crops such as cotton. The result was the forced dismissal of sharecroppers on a massive scale. The structure of the AAA 'made it well-nigh impossible for a sharecropper to appeal eviction' (Daniel, 1986). FDR did nothing to support an anti-lynching Bill that failed to pass Congress. Angry with their treatment, African Americans, led by A. Philip Randolph, the leader of the Brotherhood of Sleeping Car Porters Union (BSCPU), threatened a protest march on Washington in 1941 unless job discrimination was abolished.

The Swedish sociologist Gunnar Myrdal, in collaboration with black and white American scholars, produced a massive report (1438 pages) called *The American Dilemma*. They studied the status of African Americans between 1938 and 1940. The report, published in 1944, admits that the New Deal had helped some blacks but harmed many more. The American Creed – that all are created equal with the rights to life, liberty and the pursuit of happiness – was not a reality for African Americans but only the American Deed which was segregation, racism and inequality. 'From the point of view of the American Creed the status accorded the Negro in America represents nothing less than a century-long lag of public morals. In principle the Negro problem was settled long ago; but in practice the solution is not effectuated' (Myrdal ed., 1964). He doubted that African Americans would ever share in the benefits of the American Creed. Although there was, and is, much truth in his analysis it underestimates the determination of African Americans to struggle for their rights.

But even in the darkest days of the Depression, many black and white sharecroppers, meeting in black and white churches, formed the Southern Tenant Farmers Union (STFU) in an effort to protect their rights and their land and even conducted a successful strike in 1935. The STFU union members proved that interracial unionism in the South was possible just as it had with the Brotherhood of Timber Workers Union in the 1890s. STFU members, inspired by the timber workers and other radicals, influenced the later civil rights movement (Fannin, 2003). They shared churches in their battle for their rights as tenants and sharecroppers. They were mainly Baptist and Pentecostal fundamentalists with similar gospels, speaking in tongues and shouts. And they sang about poverty, lost love and cheating women in their blues and country music – music that was saved thanks to a New Deal project funding musicologists. Their defiance and faith that there could be a better America is reflected in the music of Woody Guthrie and Bessie Smith's *Nobody Knows when You're Down and Out* (1929). Authors too wrote of poverty in America – Richard Wright's *Notes of a Native Son* and John Steinbeck's *The Grapes of Wrath*. Many country singers after World War Two shared a history of poverty; Loretta Lynn's father was a coal miner and Dolly Parton and Johnny Cash were children of white sharecroppers.

World War Two

The attack on Pearl Harbor ensured the mobilisation of the whole nation regardless of race, gender or religion. The need for labour in northern factories required massive recruitment of black men and women workers and, despite resistance from many trade unions, saw the first large-scale organisation of African Americans within predominantly white unions. Their willingness to join unions, especially those organised by the Congress of Industrial Organizations (CIO), would help them find an ally in the future struggle for civil rights. This was particularly true in the case of the United Auto Workers (UAW) Union which provided funds for organisations such as the Southern Christian Leadership Conference (SCLC) and the Student Nonviolent Coordinating Committee (SNCC, pronounced 'snick').

They claimed that the wars in 1941 and 1918 were the same being a fight to save democracy, but the Nazis in Germany added a new element. The National Socialist state was built on the premise of racism which justified the extermination of so-called inferior races such as the Jews, Slavs, Romany and also the 'unfit', the disabled, homosexuals and political opponents. Every assault on Nazism by administration officials and the press was an attack on racism in the United States as far as African Americans were concerned. Ironically, fearing the power of southern Democrats, FDR was reluctant to integrate the military. In 1942 Randolph and others threatened a 'Double Victory' campaign which sought victory over the enemies of democracy overseas and in the United States. Five hundred thousand black troops fought in Europe and the Pacific in segregated regiments commanded by white officers – nothing had changed since the Civil War.

There were significant improvements such as allowing African Americans to have an air force squadron and black troops and under this pressure FDR issued Executive Order 8802 which established the Fair Employment Practices Commission to ensure all workers in defence industries would not suffer discrimination because of race, creed, colour or national origin. This was the first time the federal government introduced affirmative action, requiring companies to insert a clause in their defence contracts that they would not discriminate and the same applied to federal employment agencies. In response to criticisms, he issued Executive Order 9346 which gave the Commission independent status, field offices, staff and a $500,000 budget (Topping, 2008). Despite these shortcomings there were significant improvements such as the integration of the San Francisco shipyard, and the Orders provided the basis for post-war legislation.

But the most significant thing was the absence of segregation in Europe and the willingness of white women to freely socialise with African Americans – despite efforts in the United Kingdom to keep black and white soldiers in separate towns and villages. When the veterans returned from the war they found virtually nothing had changed and they were among the early leaders determined that things would change (Cobb Jr, 2014). However, many white veterans were equally determined they would not and played a prominent role in the massive resistance campaign North and South.

1

The Transformation of Politics: 1945–1960

The postwar migration of African Americans from the rural South contin-ued, forced out by virulent racism and poverty accentuated by the mech-anisation of cotton farming and the dangerous clouds of new fertilisers (Daniel, 2000). Many moved into the urbanising South but many more flocked into industrial cities of the North where they had full citizenship, forcing politicians, especially Democrats heavily dependent on the white working class in the North, to face the challenge of the 'New Negro'. The migrants outside the South in 1940 constituted 17 percent of the resi-dents of New York City and Detroit. Cleveland, Chicago, Philadelphia and Pittsburgh were home to 30 percent of African Americans living in the North and West (Issel, 1985). The unskilled located into growing urban ghettos, and some joined trade unions. But not all northern cities saw similar increases; for example, Milwaukee had few unskilled workers from the South but had a small number of long-term black residents, many of whom were middle class (Jones, 2009).

Wartime forced employers to hire black men and women but even pro-gressive unions such as the United Auto Workers (UAW) and the United Packing House Workers of America (UPHWA) resisted. Both insisted they would not discriminate but various branches did and the unions' efforts were weakened by disputes over housing: residential discrimina-tion was enforced by community groups and the federal government which ceded planning to local, state and city authorities (Halpern, 1997; Sugrue, 2008). Despite opposition from some union members, the Urban League and the National Association for the Advancement of Colored People (NAACP) urged blacks to join unions and reject employers' efforts to use them as strike-breakers. However, racism in hiring and employee resistance was exacerbated as plants moved to white-only suburbs (Sugrue, 2008).

But black people influenced elections by simply leaving the South and Franklin D. Roosevelt (FDR) won his fourth term in 1940 with a coalition of northern African Americans, the white working class and the segregated, Jim Crow, solid Democratic South. Also in 1940, black voters elected Adam Clayton Powell of New York as the second black congressman in the North. Twenty years later there would be six, all from the major industrial cities (two from Detroit and the others from New York, Philadelphia, Chicago and Los Angeles – the latter, like Milwaukee, having a small black electorate) (Jones, 2009). The black population in the North grew by 40 percent during the war and 80 percent voted for Truman and assured his election (Topping, 2008). The political manoeuvring after the war responded to these demographic changes.

A Truman biographer claims that the Missouri former shopkeeper 'moved to establish himself as a friend of the Negro' (Hamby, 1973). A recent study disputes this, arguing there was no personal conversion on Truman's part; rather, as an unpopular president, he needed every vote he could get in the upcoming 1948 election. But he also realised that to win he had to maintain America's postwar leadership (Iton, 2008). 'Both efforts were part of a large-scale postwar mobilisation for racial equality, one that built on the successes of the wartime movement' (Sugrue, 2008). The witch-hunt of the House Un-American Activities Committee (HUAC) blacklisted prewar radicals of both races. Singers Paul Robeson and Pete Seeger were attacked in the first anti-communist riot in the United States at Peekskill, New York in 1949 (Dunaway and Beer, 2010).

Although he favoured some legislative help for African Americans, Truman's support never matched his support for Jewish Americans and his reluctance was shared by many white liberals, both Democrats and Republicans (Fraser, 1994). 'Privately, he could still speak of "niggers", as if that were the way one naturally referred to blacks' (McCullough, 1992).

In the 1920s he had paid the $10 membership to the Ku Klux Klan (KKK) in what has been described as an act of 'amazing naiveté'. His sister, Mary, was confident that: 'Harry is no more for nigger equality than any of us' (McCullough, 1992). Truman, like the vast majority of white Americans, never understood the humiliation and fear imposed on African Americans. As Pauli Murray, a black feminist, lawyer and poet, wrote: 'the race problem was like a deadly snake coiled and ready to strike, and that one avoided its dangers only by never-ending watchfulness' (Murray, 1989).

Fair Employment

The end of World War Two saw mixed blessings for African Americans. Since 1944 there had been discussions in the Administration about the conversion of military to civilian working, and the Fair Employment Practices Commission (FEPC) was aware African Americans would be adversely affected as they had been after World War One. They were right. Although the seniority system helped some black men, black women were driven out of the auto industry in Detroit and other industries despite non-discriminatory policies of the UAW and the Congress of Industrial Organizations (CIO). It was mainly black women who lost well-paid work and returned to domestic and menial labour with no security, benefits or pensions (Sugrue, 2008). 'Black women were affected in a five-to-one ratio because discrimination forced them to be the last hired and trained' (Reed, 1991). These workers had been paid between 80 cents and $1.40 an hour. 'By November 1945, the exodus of minority workers from wartime jobs had turned into a virtual rout', and according to Alan Poston of the New York *Post*. White women were also encouraged to leave the factories. A Ford motor company short film urged them to buy a second car to shop and pick up children from school (Prelinger, 1992).

The FEPC feared layoffs would result in race riots. Riots did occur in Chicago when unskilled black workers were dismissed and often replaced by unskilled, illiterate white southern migrant labourers. However, in most northern cities there were few disturbances – unlike white riots in Texas and other states. Although widespread upheaval did not materialise, many black workers in the UAW and steelworkers did strike. In 1946 the Meatpackers of Chicago demanded higher wages and black workers resisted employers and police efforts to break the strike and remained loyal to the union. Eventually their victory came with support of local black churches (Halpern, 1997).

Truman's liberalism was tested in 1945 when the FEPC sought to end hiring discrimination by the Capitol Transit Company of Washington DC. The FEPC had successfully changed transport policies in 16 northern and western cities but DC had defied them for three years. The Commission sought the president's support. Three months passed. Finally, Truman's assistant told them the Administration could not act and a request to meet the president was refused. The chairman resigned. According to Truman, ordering the company to cease discriminatory practices violated congressional law.

His support for a permanent FEPC has been described as 'routine' (Hamby, 1973) and 'that as President he could no longer sit idly by and do nothing in the face of glaring injustice' (McCullough, 1992). Although he issued an Executive Order, it only enabled the FEPC to collect data and he accepted congressional defunding but the Committee had some long-term effect. 'In the new agencies, created by federal legislation in the 1960s, some of these FEPC veterans would help revive the struggle for fair employment practice' (McCullough, 1992). In the 1960s and 1970s John Hope Franklin II, a distinguished black historian, worked in the Office of Civil Rights and on the presidential Commission for Equal Employment Opportunity (CEEO). Marjorie Lawson served on the Task Force for Urban Renewal. Former FEPC workers were active at state and city level (Reed, 1991).

Some claim Truman's civil rights policy was merely smoke and mirrors. In a message to Congress he briefly advocated a permanent, funded FEPC but he did not stop a southern conservative from filibustering. But he spoke to a NAACP rally on 30 June 1946, the first president to do so, and appointed a civil rights special committee, chaired by the president of General Electric, Charles Wilson. Their report on 29 October 1947 recommended an anti-lynching law, abolition of poll taxes, protection of people during voting registration, integration of the armed forces, denial of federal funds to recipients who discriminated and an end to segregation in interstate transport (McCullough, 1992). (It would take more than 20 years before the majority of these recommendations were passed – if not enforced). However, some argue that the report, combined with action by the Justice Department, meant that 'by the end of 1947 … one could have no doubt that it was moving in a more liberal direction on Negro rights' (Hamby, 1973).

The reception given to many returning African American servicemen shocked Truman. The assault and blinding of a black soldier in South Carolina was one of 56 attacks on African Americans between June 1945 and September 1946 and these, combined with the bloody white police riot in Columbia, Tennessee, led to demands for a federal anti-lynching bill. As senator he had supported it but now he opposed it and social equality, but he did favour equality of opportunity (McCullough, 1992). Truman's stand on a federal lynching law was no different from FDR's in 1937.

But Truman realised he had to act partly because of the pressure from the African American community (Duberman, 1998). Concerned about KKK terrorism, Truman told the Committee on Civil Rights that he wanted the Bill of Rights 'implemented in fact. We have been trying to do this for 150 years.' On 29 June 1947 he told the NAACP annual general meeting that, 'If … freedom is to be more than a dream, each man must be guaranteed equality of opportunity. The only limit to an American's achievement should be his ability, his industry and his character' (Truman, 1956). This address 'was the strongest statement on civil rights heard in Washington since the time of Lincoln' (McCullough, 1992).

One of the groups pressuring the White House was the Congress of Racial Equality (CORE), set up in Chicago by James Farmer of Louisiana and Quaker members of the Fellowship of Reconciliation (FOR). Their goal was to 'eliminate racial discrimination' by 'inter-racial, nonviolent direct action.' In the 1940s, CORE members were involved in Chicago restaurant sit-ins and demanded integration of interstate transport (White, 1985).

Even in the most dangerous and racist states, African Americans were not prepared to wait for presidential action. With all-white primaries declared illegal by the Supreme Court in 1944, young black Mississippians tried to vote despite threats in newspapers such as the Jackson *Daily News* and from Senator Theodore Bilbo who was seeking re-election. The Reverend William Bender, the 60-year-old chaplain of Tugaloo College, defied the mob and was only stopped from voting by an armed deputy sheriff. Medgar Evers, a veteran later murdered by the Klan, was denied the right to vote in Decatur. Bilbo was re-elected but the Democrats had only allowed white votes in the primary and Bilbo was challenged by the NAACP and the Progressive Voters League in front of a Senate committee in Jackson. John Dittmer maintains 'the 1946 primary election and the subsequent challenge to Bilbo is a significant event in the history of the black struggle for freedom'. Openly challenging Bilbo in front of a Senate committee meant that 'in that crowded federal courtroom in Jackson the shock troops of the modern civil rights movement had fired their opening salvo' (Dittmer, 1995).

Democrats Transformed?

Despite Truman's limited accomplishments for African Americans they had one effect: '[T]he ostensible interest of Congressional Republicans in civil rights had been discredited' (McCoy, 1984). (This ignores the role played by liberal Republicans in the early 1960s.) But, the transformation of the Democratic Party into a predominantly northern liberal party was speeded up in the 1948 convention. Exhorted by Hubert Humphrey and liberals of the Americans for Democratic Action (ADA), the Democrats adopted 'the most sweeping civil rights plank ever written into a Democratic platform' (Hamby, 1973). Truman complained, recalling that as president his stand on civil rights was 'deliberately misconstrued to include or imply racial miscegenation and intermarriage. My only goal was equal opportunity and security under the law for all classes of Americans' (Truman, 1956). His anti-communism, with demands for loyalty oaths, drove many progressives out of unions and weakened opponents of discrimination (Sugrue, 2008; McAdam and Kloos, 2014). Although he had vetoed the anti-union Taft-Hartley Act it had been overridden. The CIO unions blamed Truman and did not endorse him but rather his Vice President Henry Wallace who was more radical. The black vote was crucial for Truman to win the election and also if he was to defeat the equally liberal Republican Thomas Dewey (Topping, 2008).

The 1948 Election

Historians agree that the 1948 election established civil rights as the major issue, endorsed by three out of four parties. Pundits were positive that Truman had no chance because the party was so divided. The right opposed the liberal platform and southerners, led by South Carolina Governor Strom Thurmond, walked out and set up the segregationist Dixiecrat Party with Thurmond as its presidential candidate (McAdam and Kloos, 2014). It has been argued that Democrats did not represent southern interests: 'It had become dominated by intellectuals, self-seeking labor leaders, and the most poignant of all for white southerners, insensitive Negroes.' Mississippi Senator James Eastland asserted that Walter White of the NAACP was 'a negro, who I am afraid to say, has more power in our government than all of the southern states combined' (Garson, 1974).

Henry Wallace, the former vice president, believed the Democratic Party was too conservative and he formed the Progressive Party and was its candidate. He went into the South and campaigned for civil rights. All his meetings were integrated. To defy segregation was brave but even braver were African Americans and whites who supported his campaign. In Virginia the meetings were orderly but in North Carolina there was serious violence. Memphis mayor 'Boss Crump' tried to stop Robeson from addressing a Progressive rally. The black community was not intimidated and the meeting was held at a meeting space offered by a black minister. In Columbus, Georgia, the KKK surrounded but failed to attack a Progressive rally because the politicians later discovered there were 100 armed black men protecting them, something that happened often in the 1960s when civil rights workers were in danger (Cobb, 2014). Robeson's biographer writes the Georgia meeting 'gave him hope for the future, regardless of how the '48 election itself came out – even as the outright murder of other blacks … continued to feed his anger'. Alabama mobs attacked Wallace but he held 'a dozen unsegregated meetings, and he set an example of courage and moral determination which even his bitterest liberal opponents found hard to denounce' (Duberman, 1998). Academic supporters in the South were often dismissed.

Some Republicans were alarmed at the loss of the African American vote, crucial in many northern states, and formed a National Council of Negro Republicans which saw the election of the first black US senator since Reconstruction, Edward Brooke of Massachusetts. Other Republican strategists noted that the limited civil rights programme proposed by Truman did not have popular white support. Adopting it would not benefit the party and the seed of the later southern strategy was planted (Topping, 2008).

It was easy for liberal critics to complain that Truman ignored his commissioned report on civil rights but a combination of southern Democrats and conservative Republicans made legislation impossible. But he did take executive action. He desegregated the Washington DC airport, his inauguration guests in 1949 were integrated and he appointed a black judge, William H. Hastie, to the federal courts (McCoy, 1984). The Justice Department supported cases against restrictive housing covenants and by the 1950s were ready to challenge 'separate but equal' upheld by the Supreme Court in *Plessy v. Ferguson* (1896). Truman 'often in spite of himself educated the nation ... [He] unleashed expectations he could not foresee desires he could not understand, and forces which future governments would not be able to restrain' (Bernstein, 1991).

Integrating the Military

Truman's major achievement was desegregating the military. He had tried in other ways to help minorities. Executive Order 9980 established the Fair Employment Board to ensure equal treatment of minorities in federal hiring. However, the lack of funding, civil service rules and the conservative nature of the Board limited its achievements. His next Executive Order 9981 stipulated that there should be 'equality of opportunity for all persons in the armed forces, without regard to race, color, or national origin' (White, 1985). It was opposed by the military, especially by Dwight

Eisenhower, formerly commander-in-chief of allied forces in Europe and then head of NATO. However, Truman ignored them partly due to the pressure from union leader Randolph, who threatened a boycott of the compulsory conscription into the armed services. Most historians believe Order 9981 had long-term benefits. There are those who strongly dissent (Pinkney, 1976). By 1952 the military was largely integrated but there were few minority officers and the Order had not been enforced in the National Guard or reserve services. 'The greatest battle had been won, however, thanks to the persistence of Truman and civil rights groups' (McCoy, 1984).

If presidents and congressmen were reluctant to act, the same cannot be said about African Americans. The NAACP Legal Defense Fund continued to challenge 'separate but equal' and CORE resorted to sit-ins and freedom rides – non-violent direct action. In 1947 CORE members took a 'Journey of Reconciliation' through the border states testing the enforcement of a Supreme Court ruling which stipulated that segregation in interstate travel was unconstitutional (Arsenault, 2006).

African Americans and Labour

African American fighters against inequality were subjected to harassment and accusations of communist sympathies, as was the labour movement, which during the postwar witch-hunts at the federal and state level purged radical union members (Sugrue, 2008). This was true for radicals in the South, like Memphis, Tennessee which had seen industrialisation and increased fear of unions (Daniel, 2000). The AFL and the 'cleansed' CIO unions when they were united in 1955 under the leadership of George Meany had only two black leaders on the executive council of the AFL-CIO – James Carney, former secretary-treasurer of the CIO and Randolph of the Brotherhood of Sleeping Car Porters Union (BSCPU). Participating unions were 'encouraged' to recruit without regard to race but the American Federation of Labor and Congress of Industrial Organizations (AFL-CIO) did not exclude racist unions although it used its power to expel communists. Liberals failed to change this (Marable, 1997). A 1970s study stresses the benefits of union organising in the southern black communities but concedes the moral force of the civil rights movement came from the black church. 'By abandoning the efforts to organize the unorganized the CIO ceased being a labor movement; and this, in turn, deprived civil rights activists of political and social space in which to operate' (Stoke and Halpern, 1994). This is only partially true. E. D. Nixon of the BSCPU was one of the main leaders in the Montgomery Improvement Association (MIA) and the bus boycott. He was also a member of the NAACP (Branch, 1989). And, in the North, despite resistance from some locals, not all unions were affiliated with the AFL-CIO and some acted to help African American workers (Halpern, 1997; Sugrue, 2008). Many writers claim the church was not a major force in the labour movement (Reed, 1986) but this underestimates the role of the black church in supporting union membership.

With limited access to the labour movement and virtually no political power, African Americans turned to the law and direct action. The latter has been described as provocation (Fairclough, 2001) but it was the only way they could win freedoms they were denied. The constraints on changing the status quo can be seen when the NAACP sought to amend federal aid to education ensuring it would not go to segregated schools. The civil rights champion at the 1948 Democratic convention, Hubert Humphrey, now a senator, opposed the amendment: 'As much as I detest segregation, I love education more' (McCoy, 1984). Rejected by politicians, the NAACP turned to the Supreme Court with increasing success.

A Restless Generation

Black and white teenagers had little to look forward to. In January 1945 *New York Times Magazine* published 'A Teenager Bill of Rights'. They wanted 'opportunities, in education and vocation ... regardless of sex, color or creed' (Savage, 2007). Parents who had experienced the deprivations of the Great Depression and suffered the dislocation from rural to urban living now enjoyed an age of consumption fuelled by high wages – partly fuelled by the growth of the military industrial complex. The so-called loss of China and Korea and the perceived threat from the Soviet Union meant unlimited Pentagon budgets and more corporations became dependent on this flow of money. Although youth culture worried elders in past generations with their flapper dresses and the zoot suits of Mexican and African Americans (Savage, 2007), postwar teens lived with the threat of nuclear annihilation. They ducked and dived under school desks to avoid fallout while their parents dug fallout shelters.

Many were disillusioned because they felt they had been betrayed and the fruits of postwar prosperity were not being constructively used. But teenagers acquired considerable spending power; never before had all classes of people between the ages of 13 and 19 had such disposable income. In the African American community during the 1940s and 1950s income increased fourfold even though it was barely over half that of whites. Young people spent more on entertainment, especially records revolutionised by the smaller and more durable 45 rpm, ideal for jukeboxes.

Despite initial conformity, this generation expressed itself in markedly different ways from their elders. They lost interest in Benny Goodman and Lionel Hampton, and black and white teenagers preferred crooners such as Frank Sinatra (Werner, 2000; Portis, 2002) and Johnny Ray – especially his blues-influenced tear-jerker *Cry*. Leroy Jones, later a black nationalist, loved Frankie Lane because he sang like a black man (Jones, 1984). In *Leader of the Pack* a good girl loves the leader of a biker gang from 'the wrong side of the tracks'. She leaves him because of parental pressure and weeps when he is killed.

Increasingly popular with black and white teenagers was the rhythm and blues played on black-owned radio stations. R & B has its origins in gospel, work songs and shouts common in the black community (Smith, 2004). The pre- and postwar R & B amplified the machismo of the blues – the strong man ruined by his woman's infidelity, nagging and demands for money e.g. Hogman Maxey, *Duckin' and Dodgin'* which was recorded while he was in Angola Prison. Delta blues men Charley Patton and Robert Johnson became heroes of white rockers in the 1960s.

Many have suggested that the African American community was matriarchal because slavery ensured men were helpless to protect female slaves, and this pathology persisted after the abolition of slavery. However, since the 1990s most scholars argue men played a significant role in the black community. But blues and R & B men reflect a sense of powerlessness and denigrate women. Black women singers objected and 'helped to shape a genuine debate over sex roles and domestic responsibilities in the black community'. Brian Ward argues that women like Dinah Washington and Big Momma Thornton 'gave as good as they got in the sex wars of the early 1940s and 1950s'. By inverting the roles male artists created and by portraying women's sexual powerfulness they 'shared much of the fatalism as their male counterparts when it came to the ideas of domestic happiness, peace and harmony' (Ward, 1998). In some Mississippi Delta blues the male singer complains about his woman and the female, in his presence, responds with an immediate challenge (Ferris, 1978). Black youngsters, such as the Kingston Trio, copied the older men, but changed and softened the sound and lyrics to appeal to white teenagers, especially girls. Later they included a harder beat and sexual innuendoes that encouraged rebellion against true womanhood, church constrictions and child-bearing. White teenagers escaped suburban boredom and entered a forbidden world created by segregation (Engelhardt, 1995). As a New Jersey native puts it: 'The adult world, that place of dishonesty, deceit, unkindness where people slaved, were hurt, compromised, beaten, defeated, where they died – thank you. Lord, but for now, I'll take a pass' (Springsteen, 2016).

Parents sensed this generational gap and schools showed short films to persuade white teenagers to follow middle-class mores. In one, popular with adults, a girl asks the boy if he is going to the school dance and he says he prefers a hotdog roast (Prelinger, 1992). James Dean is portrayed as a rebel without a cause, alienated by his father who is no longer head of the household. Teenagers empathised with the 'rebel', not why he rebelled. They bought records that John Freed, a Cleveland DJ, called rock and roll, black slang for sexual intercourse. Bill Haley's *Rock Around the Clock* (1955), first recorded by black singer Sunny Day, uses this euphemism. Johnny Cash captures the sense that life was cheap in this nuclear age in his *Folsom Prison Blues* where a man shoots another just to watch him die.

Some downplay the importance black music had on white singers such as Elvis Presley. But 'Southern musicians profoundly influenced musical development in the twentieth century, not because they embodied pure European or African traditions but because they dynamically exchanged and incorporated their vast musical knowledge … Black and white musicians were part of a vibrant cultural exchange that produced jazz, blues, country, gospel, rhythm and blues, rock 'n' roll, and soul music' (Daniel, 2000; Springsteen, 2016). Black and white performers were profoundly influenced by church music and saw no contradiction in playing the Devil's music in a bar on a Saturday and singing gospels on a Sunday (Smith, 2004). Little Richard attended a Pentecostal church.

Sam Phillips of Sun Studios in Memphis looked for talented former sharecroppers, 'rebellious high school students and young working-class musicians who were adventurous and hungry' (Daniel, 2000). A truck driver, Elvis Presley, hung around Beale Street bars and black clubs in Mississippi and Arkansas and dressed like young African Americans. At Sun Studios Elvis became a friend of the great blues man B. B. King (Guralnick, 1994). He also relied on black songwriter Otis Blackwell. Black teens were avid Elvis fans. Presley's thrusting hips copied Chuck Berry's, who sang *Maybellene* (1955) and *Johnny B. Goode* (1958). Elvis transferred Berry's riff from piano to guitar, which he held as if it was a penis. Liberated teenage girls loved their sexual gyrations. Presley's first hit, *That's All Right Mama,* was shaped by R & B rhythm and country music but 'he sang it in his own way' (Portis, 2002).

It may have been a 'lost revolution' in the South but this was the beginning of a rebellion shaped by southern black and white singers which gathered pace in the mid-1950s, exploded in the 1960s and persisted through the years of conservatism, led by Johnny Cash, Joan Baez, Aretha Franklin, Nina Simone, the Indigo Girls and Bruce Springsteen.

General Eisenhower Takes Charge

Dwight David Eisenhower (Ike) had never voted; no one knew his politics and Democrats and Republicans wooed him. Eisenhower chose the Republicans and the Democrats nominated Adlai Stevenson of Illinois and, to keep the South loyal, Georgia's Senator John Sparkman as his running mate. Civil rights was not mentioned in Stevenson's acceptance speech. The choice of a relatively liberal northerner and a conservative southerner became standard practice for both parties until 1992.

The Republicans emphasised communist subversion and opposed 'socialist' New Deal programmes. Eisenhower and Senator Richard Nixon of California swept into office. However, inadvertently, Ike strengthened the Supreme Court which would try to resolve the nation's conflict between its Creed and Deed. Certainly he was not prepared to defend the rights of African Americans. A sympathetic biographer admits: 'Essentially, Eisenhower passed on to his successors the problem of guaranteeing constitutional rights to Negro citizens' (Ambrose, 1984). Many southerners bolted the Democratic Party because of the race issue and voted overwhelming Republican, a party loathed since the Civil War and Reconstruction. Eisenhower carried Virginia, Tennessee, Florida and Texas and did well in other states and this was not lost on party strategists.

But Eisenhower had debts to powerful people who had ensured his nomination, and one was California governor Earl Warren, who delivered the state's delegates (Blum, 1991). He had chosen another Californian as his running mate and therefore rewarding Warren was essential. Bypassed for Attorney General, Warren was promised the first vacancy on the Supreme Court. It was an appointment Eisenhower deeply regretted (Ambrose, 1984). Chief Justice Warren was willing to meet the challenge of civil rights.

The *Brown* Decisions

Oliver Brown challenged segregation in the schools of Topeka, Kansas where state law said any city over 15,000 could segregate its grade schools which meant Brown was prevented from sending his daughter to the nearest school five blocks away and instead she travelled 20 to an all-black school. The NAACP had eroded *Plessy* in higher education and now challenged all school segregation, even though in 1951 and 1952 the Court referred a South Carolina case back to a three-judge panel who enjoined the authorities to ensure racially segregated schools should be equal.

Brown lost in 1951 when three federal judges ruled that the city's schools complied with *Plessy*. Cases were also brought against four states –

Kansas, South Carolina, Virginia and Delaware – as well as Washington DC. Brown was given leave to appeal to the Supreme Court. *Brown v. The Board of Education, Topeka, Kansas* was selected because it was a northern state with a flexible segregation law. The attack on *Plessy* was led by the African American lawyer Thurgood Marshall, director of the NAACP Legal Defense Fund. He relied on expert lawyers but also on sociologists and psychologists who argued that segregation was inherently unequal, was a denial of equal protection under the Fourteenth Amendment and damaged black schoolchildren, making them feel inferior.

A president can exert considerable pressure on the Court. Eisenhower invited Warren to the White House and insisted he sat next to John W. Davis, representing the segregationists. Eisenhower said that southerners 'are not bad people. All they are concerned about is to see that their sweet little girls are not required to sit in school alongside some big overgrown Negroes' (Ambrose, 1984). Eisenhower was not the first white man, nor the last, to exploit sexual fears of black men. In 1949 white Georgian southerner Lillian Smith warned in her book *Killers of the Dream*:

> In the name of *sacred womanhood*, of *purity*, of *preserving the home*, the lecherous old men, and young ones, reeking with impurities, who had violated the home since they were sixteen years old, whipped up lynchings, organized Klans ... aroused the poor and ignorant to wild excitement by an obscene, perverse imagery describing the 'menace' of Negro men hiding behind every cypress waiting to rape 'our women.'
>
> (Smith, 1994, italics in original)

Warren insisted on a unanimous ruling on *Brown* to prevent a later court from striking it down. On 17 May 1954 the Court's decision posed the question: 'Does segregation of children in public schools solely on the basis of race, even though the facilities are equal, deprive children of a minority of equal educational opportunity?' The answer was yes. They ruled that segregation was unconstitutional and a violation of due process (Miller, 1967). This was one of the most famous cases in US history.

Brown was a major victory for the NAACP and vindicated its policy to seek redress through the courts. The ruling has been called 'the single most important moment in the decade, the moment that separated the old order from the new and helped to create the tumultuous era just arriving' (Halberstam, 1993). Although school desegregation has not been a great success, *Brown* was the first major assault by the Court on racist laws. *Plessy* was overturned. But no acceptable standards for schools were set or a time scale for when desegregation should begin. The NAACP was invited to return to Court and indicate when they thought was appropriate.

Brown II unanimously ordered desegregation should be carried out 'with all deliberate speed'. There was no date for compliance (Miller, 1967; Blum, 1991). This was a serious error, based on Warren's belief that desegregation had started and school administrators needed time to adjust to the new ruling (Ely, 1976). 'Neither before or since has a constitutional right, that is personal and present been deferred and extended gradually to those who were entitled to exercise it by virtue of a constitutional amendment' (Miller, 1967).

The Court's hope for gradual compliance underestimated the resistance and ignored the violence consistently used to oppose any improvement in the conditions of black citizens – for example, the dynamiting and killing of so-called agitators in Alabama and Mississippi (Carter, 1995). However, some African Americans opposed desegregation. Harlem Renaissance author and conservative Republican Zora Neale Thurston said in 1955 that the ruling was insulting. She did not want 'someone to associate with me who does not wish to be near me' (Patterson, 1996). And it was an argument that would appeal to black conservatives and be shared by the vast majority of whites.

After *Brown I*, White Citizens Councils were formed to ensure a segregated society, starting in Indianola, Mississippi and backed by the KKK, state legislatures and the police. Resistance groups were set up across the Delta region, Texas, Louisiana and the border states. Within a year they had spread throughout the South and have been called 'the bourgeois Klan' (Carter, 1995). In Virginia there was a 'massive resistance' campaign against integration and some public schools were closed. In Prince Edward County the equal education struggle started at Moton High

School was led by Barbara Jones. Her uncle, Vernon Jones, had campaigned for civil rights in Montgomery, Alabama long before the bus boycott. Where the state elite passively resisted, the KKK led the opposition, particularly in North Carolina which had the largest Klan membership (Cunningham, 2013).

Harry Byrd's Virginia political machine concerned itself with registering white voters and exploiting the race issue. At first he called for passive resistance but quickly changed his approach and supported massive resistance (Lewis, 2006). One former governor recalled that during his term in office 'Negro influence was nil'. There was little support from the University of Virginia. The weak AFL-CIO state unions were the opposition's backbone. In Warren County schools were closed from 1959 until 1960 and the local textiles workers' union paid to keep a segregated school open. In 1958 they overwhelmingly voted for Byrd despite his anti-union record.

Some historians claim the fight to keep school segregation does not constitute 'massive resistance' (Lewis, 2006). However, the Virginia example fits the description they deny. James Kilpatrick, editor of the Richmond *News Leader*, recalled: 'There was talk then of blood flowing ankle deep in gutters. Men were saying "never" and they meant it' (Ely, 1976). It took military intervention to allow nine children into Little Rock High School (see the section 'Little Rock' below). John Kasper, a New Jersey racist, incited a riot in East Tennessee and in Nashville where he whipped up youths who stoned schools and he was involved in the bombing of the Hattie Cotton school (Egerton, 2006; Houston, 2012). The later riots in South Boston and Milwaukee cannot be described as demonstrations.

Virginians and the Citizens Councils used the Old South arguments that leaders of 'sovereign states' must interpose their authority between the federal government and the people and nullify federal laws and rulings of the Supreme Court they deemed unconstitutional. Senators Strom Thurmond and Richard Russell issued a 'Southern Manifesto' and most southern representatives, congressmen and senators signed, committing themselves to fight the *Brown* decision. There were three notable exceptions: Albert Gore Sr, Estes Kefauver of Tennessee and Lyndon Johnson of Texas. Johnson refused with the approval of southern senators who wanted him to run for the presidency. White southern liberals were overwhelmed and hopes for discussions on how to obey the Court never materialised (Daniel, 2000).

The Manifesto was designed to appeal to many in the North who were alarmed by the ruling. However, the Court only dealt with state-sanctioned intentional segregation. Although many school districts, as in urban Pennsylvania, obeyed the ruling, others relied on the argument for neighbourhood schools. 'In the North ... public officials claimed that segregation was just a fact of life, not mandated by law or controlled by the state' (Sugrue, 2008). And community groups, local governments and real estate agents collaborated to ensure the rapidly expanding suburbs stayed white ghettoes. Even if a black couple could afford to buy house insurance, companies would not sell protection. Northern schools remained as segregated as those in the South – if not more so (Jones, 2009).

Eisenhower insisted that school desegregation was a local matter. Despite riots in Clinton, Tennessee, and Mansfield, Texas, he said the federal government was powerless. And he angered NAACP members when he linked them to white segregationists. He told the press that the South 'was full of people of good will' and condemned 'the people ... so filled with prejudice that they can resort to violence; and the same way on the other side of the thing the people who want to have the whole matter settled today.' His biographer admits: '[H]e had gone to great lengths to divorce himself from the problem of race relations, and especially integration of schools' (Ambrose, 1984). He set the example for other presidents that courts would have to enforce *Brown*. In his memoirs Truman attacked Eisenhower because he failed to offer leadership. 'He didn't use the powers of the office of President to uphold the ruling of the Supreme Court of the United States, and I never did understand that' (Miller, 1974). Partly because of the NAACP's role in *Brown*, it has been suggested that the organisation was reluctant to support direct action. This is not true. For example, they supported the Detroit strikes and boycotts (Sugrue, 2005). Their challenges to segregation angered southerners and states passed repressive legislation to destroy the Association (Morris, 1984). Despite this, the NAACP supported families involved in the integration of schools and organised direct action campaigns. Their Legal Defense Fund represented people caught up in the mass arrests that were to come.

Little Rock

Politicians of both parties realised that attacking *Brown* and the Supreme Court decisions was an easy way to gain votes, encouraged by Eisenhower's lack of action. Two weeks before the first crisis in July 1957, he said: 'I can't imagine any set of circumstances that would ever induce me to send Federal troops into any area to enforce the orders of a Federal Court, because I believe that the common sense of America will never require it.' But Democrat Governor Orval Faubus of Arkansas proved him wrong.

Faubus was seeking re-election and faced stiff competition; his opponent had discovered that his father had been a socialist and that Faubus had attended the radical Commonwealth College and helped his father set up a socialist local group. To divert the focus of the electorate Faubus challenged the ruling of the Supreme Court (Daniel, 2000). Faubus was determined to keep the black children out and was certain the Administration would override his action. Little Rock had plans for compliance which would delay desegregation until 1963 (Miller, 1967). Nine volunteer African American students reported to Central High School in September 1957 but found it surrounded by Arkansas National Guard units. Faubus issued orders that the students should not enter because it was his duty to protect lives and property. Ignoring an injunction, he withdrew the troopers and Eisenhower was forced to send the 101st Airborne because the children were attacked by hysterical mobs (Beals, 1994). Writing under her married name, Melba Pattillo Beals, she depicts the treatment the students suffered. Melba Pattillo was assaulted and almost raped by a white man who yelled: 'I'll show you niggers the Supreme Court can't ruin my life' (Beals, 1994). Norman Rockwell, America's favourite artist, in a *Saturday Evening Post* cover portrays a young black girl in a white dress escorted by federal marshals. Although the NAACP supported the children, as did most church leaders, the battle led to divisions. Pattillo's father feared for her life and for his job.

Pattillo drew strength after meeting Thurgood Marshall: 'I looked at the man who seemed to have none of the fears and hesitation of my parents or the other adults around us. Instead he had a self-assured air about him as though he had seen the promised land and knew for certain we would get there' (Beals, 1994). She admits: 'I wonder what possessed my parents and adults of the NAACP to allow us to go to school in the face of such violence.' As she wrote in her diary: 'What will become of us if the NAACP is not strong? It feels as though the segregationists are attacking from all sides' (Beals, 1994). And Arkansas put the Association under increased pressure when State Attorney General Bruce Bennett demanded its records, including members' names, addresses, telephone numbers and details of contributors.

Pattillo survived the ordeal because of the unwavering support of her mother, grandmother and most black community members and the encouragement from a small group of whites. Despite the students' sacrifices, it was not until 1960 that Central was integrated, and by 1964 only 2.3 percent of all African American children in the United States attended desegregated schools (Blum, 1991; Sugrue, 2008).

But, as Beals observes: 'Once President Eisenhower made that commitment to uphold the law, there was no turning back. And even though later on he would waver and not whole-heartedly back up his powerful decision, he had stepped over the line that no other President had ever dared to cross' (Beals, 1994). Ironically, Eisenhower was forced to act as a result of pressure from the African American community (discussed in the next chapter), as well as the claim that the United States was the leader of the free world in the global struggle against atheistic communism. African Americans were well aware of the world movement for decolonisation in India and Africa and were determined not to be colonials in their own land. However, Eisenhower was reluctant to enforce *Brown* but the Supreme Court was not so unwilling. In 1958 in *Cooper v. Aaron* it made a sweeping ruling which made unconstitutional any law, 'ingenious or ingenuous', which sought to keep public schools segregated. Three new justices appointed by Eisenhower after 1954 reaffirmed *Brown* which had been made before their appointment (Ely, 1976).

Moton High School in Virginia was closed and a new one was built; by 2003 it was fully integrated with 47 percent black students and 43 percent white, and the Virginia legislature passed a resolution formally apologising for the massive resistance campaign. In other schools, North and South, it took much longer. Recent statistics demonstrate the resegregation of schools in the United States (Leadership Conference on Civil Rights Report, 2006). The rapid suburbanisation of the cities North and South drained the tax base and made inner city services and schools more unequal (Sugrue, 2008).

Republicans felt that their work on civil rights had not been appreciated by African Americans. They pointed out that despite the desegregation of all public facilities in DC, and the appointment to the White House of a former NAACP field secretary, Frederick Morrow, blacks continued to vote for Democrats. Republicans did not admit the failure of the president to condemn the murder of Emmett Till in Mississippi or his silence on the expulsion of the first black student from the University of Alabama, Autherine Lucy. She had successfully sued for admission but it was a Pyrrhic victory because the university authorities expelled her, accusing her of lying because she claimed that she had not been admitted initially because of her race. Eisenhower refused to offer any support to the Montgomery, Alabama bus boycott. He believed that the South was law-abiding and that it was impossible for the decisions of the Court to be entirely enforced (Ambrose, 1984).

The FBI and Black America

Eisenhower's biographer says his reluctance was partly based on reports from the Director of the Federal Bureau of Investigation (FBI), J. Edgar Hoover, that communists had infiltrated the civil rights movement. Hoover was the longest serving official in Washington's history and a fervent anti-communist since the 1917 Russian Revolution. But in 1953 he assured the HUAC that African Americans were not communist dupes. A 1954 Committee report, entitled 'The American Negro in the Communist Party', cited Hoover's assessment that of the 5395 leading communists 'only 411 were Negroes ... The fact that only 411 were found in this select group is strong evidence that the American Negro is not hoodwinked by these false messiahs.'

But Hoover's advice changed dramatically. He was always a racist and he was particularly alarmed by the *Brown* ruling and the Montgomery boycott. He warned Eisenhower in 1957 that the Communist Party had infiltrated the NAACP. Information was obtained through illegal burglaries and telephone taps. It was given to 'various opinion moulders within the government, [and] with portions leaked to "reliable and cooperative" newspaper reporters'. Hoover was certain African Americans exploited the murder of Chicagoan 14-year-old Emmett Till on 28 August 1955, while he was visiting his grandfather in Money, Mississippi. He was beaten to death for whistling at a white woman. His mother kept his coffin open which resulted in national and international horror, exacerbated by the murderers' acquittal. A year later they boasted to *Look* magazine that they were guilty. A memorial at the site of the murder has been vandalised and has now been taken down (*New York Times*, 24 October 2016). Some argue that Till's murder was the beginning of the civil rights movement. Hoover believed the NAACP, and men such as Randolph and Bayard Rustin, lied about their opposition to the Communist Party USA and Randolph was targeted as early as the 1930s after he contacted them about a black man's hand sent to him in the post by a Marcus Garvey supporter. Hoover added Randolph to his watch list (FBI Papers/ Randolph, Ulster University).

Subsequently, the FBI not only searched for communists but did everything possible to destroy the civil rights movement, the people who participated and its leadership (O'Reilly, 1994). The FBI would link lesbians, gays, bisexual and transgender (LGBT) people with communism, harass them and support excessive use of police violence against those deemed radicals and deviants. In World War Two the military did not harass gays because people, regardless of sexual preference, were essential. The same would be true during all subsequent wars (Faderman, 2015). In peacetime, Hoover had no problems persuading Eisenhower that LGBT people and other groups were subversive.

The 1957 Civil Rights Act

Melba Beals offers the best assessment of Eisenhower's attitude towards civil rights when she suspected that he was not a 'wholehearted' supporter and this is seen in his response to a bipartisan commission's proposal for a Civil Rights Bill recommending a Justice Department division to investigate civil rights abuses and ensure everyone their voting rights. But its supporters were opposed by the powerful Senate leader, Lyndon Baines Johnson (LBJ). For him the Bill meant a 'Senate fight over civil rights legislation [was] a losing proposition for the country, the Democrats, and himself'. But his presidential ambitions meant he needed support from all sections of his party and the country. And so, he sent it to the judiciary committee where it was buried (Caro, 2002; Woods, 2006). The Bill's revival was due to African American pressure and LBJ's ambition.

> It was clear to Lyndon that the pressure from southern blacks made change in the region inevitable ... If he could lead a major civil rights bill through the Senate, it would be the first Federal legislative advance in this field in eighty-two years ... A civil rights bill credited to Johnson would help to transform him from a southern or regional leader into a national spokesman.
>
> (Dallek, 1991)

His supporters, even Georgia Senator Richard Russell, understood legislation was needed if the Texan had any hope of getting into the White House. For the Republicans, Vice President Richard Nixon, who had championed civil rights legislation, was a supporter and was eager to make a gesture to ensure the rights of African Americans.

The Bill went to the House of Representatives in the winter of 1955 and at first Eisenhower gave public and private support but this changed when the Senate opposed it. He claimed he did not know what was in it, even though he had supported it for two years (Ambrose, 1984). Senator Richard Russell alleged it would empower the Justice Department and the federal government, including the armed forces, 'to force co-mingling of white and Negro children'. Hubert Humphrey said that Russell's 'tremendous ability was weakened and corroded by his unalterable opposition to the passage of any legislation that would alleviate the plight of the black man throughout the nation. He was a victim of his region, the victim of a heritage of the past, unable to break out of the bonds of his own slavery' (Dallek, 1991).

Russell did not completely oppose the Bill but sought to weaken the Justice Department's powers and was particularly keen to retain jury trials for breaches of civil rights because only southern white voters were eligible for jury duty. Eisenhower was willing to sign a Bill that was 'more symbol than substance' (Ambrose, 1984). However, it was a radical break with tradition and it was inevitable that more effective legislation would be needed. An analysis of the House and Senate voting shows that the Democrats were deeply divided. 'Quite simply, this important piece of breakthrough legislation was primarily the work of the Republican, not Democratic, lawmakers' (McAdam and Kloos, 2014).

Strom Thurmond, formerly head of the short-lived Dixiecrat Party, attempted to kill it with a 24-hour filibuster but a much weakened Civil Rights Act was passed, the first since Reconstruction, and only then thanks to LBJ's masterly arm-twisting of the Senate (Woods, 2006). For many African Americans struggling to survive and pull down the walls of segregation, it was a sham. Ralph Bunche, a Howard University professor, a critic of the NAACP and a member of the National Negro Congress, and A. Philip Randolph believed that it would have been better to have had no Act. However, Bayard Rustin argued that it was 'very important because it was evidence that Congress was prepared to act' (D'Emilio, 2003).

The Cold War and Civil Rights

Apart from pressure from the African Americans for change, it was also America's role in world affairs after 1945 that had a significant impact on the US civil rights struggle. Truman and Eisenhower were engaged in a Cold War with the Soviet Union. Truman's eagerness to be the leader of the free world and support democracy in Western Europe with the Marshall Plan contrasted sharply with his approach to democracy in the United States. No American president ever showed this commitment to freedom and economic progress for African Americans in Mississippi, Alabama, Illinois or Ohio (Gilmore, 2008; McAdam and Kloos, 2014). Instead Truman capitulated to his European allies and supported France's return in their colony in Indochina.

The Truman Doctrine was essential to stop communist totalitarianism: 'The free people of the world look to us for maintaining their freedoms. If we falter in our leadership, we may endanger the peace of the world – and we shall endanger the welfare of the nation.' But the South was totalitarian and:

> Like other colonial people, Southerners were restless, impatient with the oppression of the past, and uneasy about the direction of the future. National political leaders realized that the racial system of the South presented a diplomatic problem, for to attract countries emerging from colonialism the U.S. could not afford the embarrassment of segregation and disenfranchisement.
>
> (Daniel, 1986)

African Americans were troubled by Truman's policies. Paul Robeson denounced the support given to Western Europe, especially Britain, who oppressed colonial populations of Africa and Asia, while at home black Americans would have to fight for democracy. NAACP leaders did not want to alienate potential allies and refused to support Robeson's anti-Cold War crusade and even his demands for a federal anti-lynching law. Three thousand black and white delegates met in DC and Truman agreed to meet a delegation led by Robeson. Truman told them this was not the right time for an anti-lynching bill, ignoring the 70-year struggle to pass one. Reminded that the Nuremberg trials were in progress, he retorted that Britain and the United States represented 'the last refuge of freedom in the world'.

Robeson declared that the British were 'one of the greatest enslavers of human beings'. African American attitudes were changing and if the government did not protect its black citizens they would protect themselves. 'In Robeson's mind, the domestic civil liberties issue was inescapably linked to the international question of peace' (Duberman, 1998). Bayard Rustin was convinced that a people whose ancestors fought a revolutionary war would be sympathetic to the freedom struggles in West Africa. After visiting there, he toured northern cities, including Milwaukee, and was well received (D'Emilio, 2003).

W. E. B. Du Bois, for many years editor of the NAACP magazine *Crisis,* published *Color and Democracy* in 1945. Du Bois linked civil rights, African nationalism and socialism. In 1947 he authored an appeal to the United Nations and, like Robeson, attacked American intervention in Korea (White, 1985). Robeson told delegates at the 1951 National Labor Conference on Negro Rights that the threat of communism was a diversion and the enemies 'are the lynchers, the profiteers, ... the atom bomb maniacs and the war makers'. The black elite and others opposed Robeson's plan that black African Americans should take their fight for freedom abroad and refuse to fight for America (Iton, 2008).

Congress passed the Internal Security Act, known as the McCarran Act, to set up detention camps for so-called subversives in times of emergency. It passed over Truman's veto. Robeson and Du Bois were persecuted. They sought to charge Robeson with contempt of Congress and he was denied a passport (Duberman, 1998). Disillusioned, Du Bois went to live in Ghana. Most liberal white intellectuals preferred to join the anti-communist ADA and the Congress of Cultural Freedom. Although they attacked the excesses of the HUAC, they policed 'the intellectual community for signs of weakening in the anti-Communism struggle' (Matusow, 1986).

Apart from pulling troops out of Korea, with a two-state solution that future presidents would attempt in numerous crises, Eisenhower embraced the Truman Doctrine but was totally indifferent to the oppression of African Americans. His Secretary of State, John Foster Dulles, promised to free Eastern Europe from Soviet oppression – without intending to do so. But Hungarian students and workers believed him. In 1956 they tried to overthrow the communist government and were crushed by Soviet and Warsaw Pact tanks. Many fled to Austria and Vice President Richard Nixon was sent to report on the situation. He concluded that the first priority was caring for refugees but 'we must not lose sight of the historical significance of this mass migration of people from an area of slavery to an area of freedom' (Lasky, 1957). Abolitionists had said the same about escaping slaves. But Nixon, like others, did not show a similar concern for African Americans fleeing southern violence and oppression.

Robeson attended the Soviet reception in DC to celebrate the 39th anniversary of its revolution and his reaction to events in Eastern Europe was shared by the wider black community. Black newspapers from Pennsylvania to California agreed with him about the Hungarian freedom fighters. The San Francisco *Sun Reporter* asked rhetorically:

'How can America in good faith blow such loud horns about the freedom of Hungarians, when such a large portion of her own population is deprived of freedom guaranteed by the Constitution of the United States' (Duberman, 1998).

The Administration opposed the 1956 British, French and Israeli invasion of Egypt, and it is suggested that this proves 'American policy, in general, was to support colonial peoples attempting to win national independence' (Ambrose, 1984). Eisenhower's opposition to the Suez invasion was to stop the new nations from following the Soviet model. African American doubts about his anti-colonialism were justified because of Eisenhower's support for French colonial rule in Indochina. Just as he left the civil rights issues to the next presidents, he would delegate Vietnam to future presidents. And it was a price that led to disproportionate suffering for African Americans who contrasted his stand over Egypt with his refusal to challenge southern governors and politicians who defied the Supreme Court. The more Mississippi Senator James Eastland and fellow southerners denounced the Soviet denial of democracy in Eastern Europe and its 'enslaving the people', the more they highlighted their resistance to bringing democracy to the South (Asch, 2008).

Truman and Eisenhower gave lavish monetary support to the doomed French effort in Vietnam and Eisenhower even contemplated sending troops. To persuade the American people that action in Southeast Asia was vital, unlike intervention in Alabama, Eisenhower outlined why it was essential to act. He stressed the advantages of raw materials vital to the economy but like the vast majority of Americans he was oblivious to the crisis facing industry in cities such as Detroit. Thomas Sugrue points out the Rust Belt of northern cities 'began unheralded in the 1950s' (Sugrue, 2005).

Ignoring the racial crisis Eisenhower said people must not live 'under a dictatorship that is inimical to the free world'. Ignoring the growing racial crisis, he warned: 'You have the broader consideration that might follow you would call the "falling domino" principle. You have got a row of dominoes set up, you knock over the first one and what will happen to the last one is the certainty that it will go over very quickly' (Ambrose, 1984). This domino theory dragged the United States into the Vietnam war which resulted in the killing of millions of Vietnamese and over

50,000 Americans, a disproportionate number of whom were African Americans. Truman and Eisenhower's commitment to this French colonial war would bind Eisenhower's successors and undermine efforts to overcome the massive resistance to end segregation and overcome poverty.

Perhaps it was merely coincidence that in the year of the Hungarian invasion a civil rights bill was introduced into Congress and passed a year later. The British had conceded independence to its colony Ghana (Weidner, 1962), and this most likely had the same influence on the passage of the bill. Just as reports of an Ethiopian emperor had a powerful impact on pre-war black people in the North, the same was true with the rapid British and French decolonisation of Africa. Ironically, new African presidents would not suffer the humiliation of Jim Crow legislation when they travelled in the southern states. (However, as late as 1966, this author was asked if he minded staying on the floor of a hotel reserved for Africans visiting the Tennessee Valley Authority.)

For black nationalists the link between their status and colonialism was obvious. 'Afro-Americans have always been responded to as a colonised people, not unlike the overseas victims of European colonialism, and relegated to a system of birth-ascribed stratification, similar to that of India's untouchable caste' (Pinkney, 1976). It was not only black nationalists who cooperated with Africans seeking freedom. Thurgood Marshall of the NAACP acted as legal advisor to Kenyan nationalists in their talks with the British government in 1960 (Weidner, 1962) even though NAACP leaders had previously sought to avoid involvement in African politics. 'The contradiction of a "free" America and their "unfree" descendants in the US was an immediate and important parallel which was reiterated by many civil rights advocates' (Marable, 1997). Later, civil rights workers in the Free South Africa Movement (FSAM) would fight apartheid.

African American leaders were not the only ones inspired by the demise of the British Empire. India, led by Gandhi, escaped British rule in 1947 using non-violent resistance and greatly influenced African independence movements; Gandhi was a hero to those who formed the front line in the battle against the southern way of life. At the height of the harassment from white students at Central High, Melba Pattillo's grandmother told her to read and understand what Gandhi had accomplished without violence. The girl wrote in her diary: 'I knew about Gandhi, about his courage even in the face of people beating up on him and calling him ugly names. I didn't think I was that strong and pure' (Beals, 1994).

But Pattillo had heroes closer to home than the nationalist leaders of India and Africa. On 1 December 1955 she read in the local newspaper about the arrest of Rosa Parks in Montgomery, Alabama, who had refused to give up her seat on a bus to a white man. 'Our people were stretching out to knock down the fences of segregation … I felt such a surge of pride when I thought about how my people had banded together to force a change. It gave me the hope that maybe things in Little Rock could change' (Beals, 1994). It was that hope that motivated hundreds of thousands of African Americans, North and South, to take up the struggle to tear down the walls of segregation.

2

Grass-Roots Struggle in the South: 1954–1959

It was on Thursday, 1 December 1955 that the 42-year-old Mrs Rosa Parks, who inspired the young Melba Pattillo, was arrested. Returning home from her day's work as tailor's assistant in a Montgomery, Alabama department store, she took her seat on the bus and a white man was left standing. The driver ordered her to move because a city ordinance did not allow a black person to sit parallel with a white passenger. Mrs Parks refused. Three times she was ordered to move and she said 'No'. Warned that she would be arrested, she told him to go ahead. He called the police and she was taken to jail. These events sparked the Montgomery bus boycott (Garrow, 1988) and no one involved realised that this was the first step in the massive struggle of African Americans to overthrow the so-called 'southern way of life'.

Mrs Parks has often been portrayed as a woman who acted because of her tiredness and sore feet but as Angela Davis observes: 'Now of course, this particular way in which history is remembered represents the woman as passive participant – as someone without agency' (Davis, 1994). Rosa Parks has pointed out that at 42 she did not think she was old and although tired her refusal to move was because she was tired of giving in.

African Americans were tired of giving in and were determined to destroy Jim Crow. The national parties were forced to act because of pressure from people who were denied the vote and the right to hold political office. Segregation ensured black southerners taught in their own schools and separate colleges and worshipped in their own churches. The most segregated moment in the United States was, and is, the Sunday morning church service. Out of these institutions African Americans forged the weapons to war against their daily humiliation. Marxists regard religion as an opiate for the masses but it was the Christian faith which inspired the civil rights movement. The Bible stories of Egyptians enslaving Jews and the flight to the promised land inspired enslaved African Americans and this longing for justice and belief in redemption also inspired the freedom struggle.

Many black church leaders and their congregations, often the poorest sharecroppers, as well as students and later their teachers would find themselves at the front line in the assault on segregation because southern racists violently resisted the *Brown* decision which challenged their way of life. When states banned or restricted the National Association for the Advancement of Colored People (NAACP), African Americans responded by turning to community leaders and formed groups such as the Montgomery Improvement Association (MIA), the Alabama United Christian Movement for Human Rights and the United Christian Movement Inc. of Louisiana. Later students organised the Student Nonviolent Coordinating Committee (SNCC). These were just a few of many southern groups. Many leaders were NAACP members. Ella Baker served as the national field secretary in 1941 and 1942 and in 1943 was director of branches. She toured the South covering 27,000 miles, attended 519 meetings and was president of the New York branch after the War, but her efforts working for the NAACP did not ensure good relations with the organisation's chairman, Roy Wilkins. She left and became associate director of the Southern Christian Leadership Conference (SCLC) (Morris, 1984). Male domination of SCLC leadership led to her resignation and she then worked with students to set up the SNCC. Most white southerners were surprised that African Americans wanted to desegregate schools and were unaware of the mounting dissatisfaction of black southerners with their status as second-class citizens. The whites did not remember the streetcar boycotts that had occurred between 1900 and 1906 (Meier and Rudwick, 1970) or the 'wave of rebellion that engulfed most of the leading black colleges in the 1920s [which] was one of the significant aspects of the new Negro movement' (Wolters, 1975). Ignorance was not only a southern problem; most northern politicians, when not ignorant, were indifferent about the African American community. Truman and Eisenhower, like presidents after Radical Reconstruction, were not prepared to challenge Jim Crow.

Louisiana Protest

Black people in the South were prepared to act and their first bus protest occurred in Louisiana. In March 1953, more than a year before the Supreme Court's ruling in *Brown,* African Americans in Baton Rouge successfully petitioned the city council to allow seating on a first-come, first-served basis. Although passengers were mostly black, the drivers were white and refused to obey the ordinance. After a four-day strike, the Attorney General supported the drivers and declared the ordinance violated segregation laws.

In June the black community began a mass boycott of the transport system. T. J. Jemison of the Mount Zion First Baptist Church, a relative newcomer to the city, led the boycott. He had been president of the NAACP local branch and was highly regarded in the community. His radio appeal for support was successful. His church was the centre for meetings and when enthusiastic supporters proved too numerous they moved to the segregated school. Bars were closed in the evenings, a community police force was organised and thousands of cars ensured free rides because charging would result in prosecutions for operating an unlicensed taxi service.

Jemison was not the only black preacher to challenge Jim Crow. All the black preachers in Baton Rouge actively participated and through their United Defense League urged congregations to stay off the buses. Sermons were used to exhort the faithful and raise money to keep the boycott going. Although their action ended with Jemison accepting a compromise solution, it was the first direct action led by southern church leaders. Other preachers were quickly informed about the boycott and the Reverend C. K. Steele of Tallahassee, Florida and the Reverend

A. L. Davis of New Orleans both knew about Jemison and they led similar actions in their cities. Martin Luther King Jr and Ralph Abernathy in Montgomery, Alabama continued the battle started by Jemison (Morris, 1984).

Mrs Rosa Parks

The first boycott was in Baton Rouge but Montgomery included all the elements that characterised the civil rights movement. Leading black preachers and their congregations were joined by NAACP activists who in turn combined with college lecturers and students and union organisers. Mrs Parks was not a tired seamstress but rather an active member of the NAACP since 1943, had served as the Montgomery branch secretary for the previous decade and worked closely with the young members of the Association's Youth Council. A council member, Claudette Colvin, had been arrested in March 1955 because she had refused to give up her seat to a white passenger. Mrs Parks had discussed with E. D. Nixon, a fellow member of the NAACP and president of the Alabama branch of the Brotherhood of Sleeping Car Porters Union (BSCPU), about Colvin's arrest and to use it to challenge the Montgomery bus ordinance. No action was taken because Colvin was charged with assault as well as breaking the ordinance. It was felt the support needed would not materialise because she was an unmarried teenager and they believed she was pregnant.

Mrs Parks not only knew Nixon, an organiser in the city since the 1920s, but also worked with him on NAACP voter registration drives. Nixon introduced her to Clifford and Virginia Durr who were considered to be white southern radicals. Friend of Lyndon Johnson and Hugo Black, the Supreme Court justice from Alabama, Clifford Durr had resigned from the Federal Communications Commission in protest over Truman's Loyalty Programme. It was the Durrs and Nixon who went to the jail on hearing of Mrs Parks' arrest, who posted the bail bond and who agreed that her case would ensure a successful boycott. Mrs Parks, despite her husband's reservations, was urged by her friends to be the test case (Garrow, 1988; Branch, 1989).

She was easily persuaded and aware of the consequences. She had attended the Highlander Folk School in Knoxville, Tennessee, headed by Myles Horton, a friend of the Durrs who had sponsored her visit. Mrs Parks wrote to the Highlander six months after her arrest saying she was 'hoping to make a contribution to the fulfilment of complete freedom for all people' (Garrow, 1988). Highlander has been described as a 'modern American movement halfway house'. According to Aldon Morris these houses are distinctive because of 'their relative isolation from the larger society and absence of a mass base'. The schools were not designed to have a mass base (Morris, 1988). The organisers, such as Myles Horton and Ella Baker, trained activists, developed media contacts, held workshops and imbued attendees with knowledge of past struggles and a vision of a multi-racial democracy. The pupils would form the mass base. Certainly, Mrs Parks' belief in such a democracy was re-enforced by her stay in Tennessee. When she refused to obey the bus driver she was acting, not merely reacting.

In this respect, Mrs Parks was no different from other women in the civil rights movement (Olson, 2002). Once African Americans, women and men, refused to accept their inferior status, her impact was widespread and felt by all sectors of American society. However, in the Movement, women were often treated as second-class and black men saw themselves as the leaders and white politicians and the press focused on the role of these men, such as Martin Luther King Jr, Ralph Abernathy, John Lewis and James Farmer.

When they first became involved black women were not gender conscious but rather concerned with the struggle for justice and liberty for both genders, but they came to understand that black men's liberty was the first priority. Women and men put their bodies on the line (literally) when they challenged Jim Crow. When activists, such as Diane Nash, called for 'jail no bail' they did not suggest that this applied to men only. Cynthia Fleming argues black women grew impatient with white women in the Movement who complained that they were only doing menial tasks. Black SNCC worker Cynthia Washington told Fleming that Casey Hayden's grumbling did not make sense to her. 'What Casey and other white women seemed to want was an opportunity that they could do something other than office work. I assumed that if they could do something else they'd probably be doing that' (Fleming, 1994).

Although black women accepted black male leadership it would become a source of difficulty. But at first they were accused by white women coworkers of deferring to the black ministers and even if they criticised male activists, they still accepted male leadership. Anne Stanley's explanation for this behaviour is that black women 'did not consider themselves oppressed by black men either in or out of the movement, and in some respects considered that black men are worse off than black women' (Crawford et al., 1993). It was their experience that made them much more conscious of gender issues.

Mrs Parks was concerned about freedom – not simply her rights as a woman. Following her arrest, she was not only helped by E. D. Nixon but also by some faculty and students at Alabama State College in Montgomery, an institution for black students only. Mrs Jo Anne Robinson had joined the English faculty in 1949 and was a keen community activist. Robinson was president of the Women's Political Council (WPC) and she had been active in the NAACP. As a state employee her membership endangered her position at the College and to continue her work she and others had set up the WPC. She and the members had worked throughout the early 1950s attacking the poor treatment of African Americans on the buses. She, Nixon and Rufus Lewis, head of the Citizens Steering Committee, pressured city commissioners to modify the segregation ordinance. As early as 1954, Robinson had written to Mayor W. A. Gayle warning him that the WPC was considering a bus boycott. When Mrs Parks was arrested, Mrs Robinson called Nixon and they agreed that the WPC should issue a leaflet calling on the black community to stay off the buses the day of the trial. Student volunteers helped run off thousands of copies and distributed them. In the leaflet she appealed to everyone, including children, to stay off the buses. About Mrs Parks she wrote: 'This has to stop. Negroes have rights too, for if the Negroes did not ride the buses, they could not operate. Three-fourths of the riders are Negroes, yet we are arrested, or have to stand over empty seats. If we do not do something to stop these arrests they will continue. The next time it may be you or your daughter, or mother' (Garrow, 1988).

With the decision made, it was vital to win the support of the wider community who were not members of the NAACP or the WPC.

The people who could mobilise the necessary mass support were the ministers of the segregated churches. Nixon realised that he needed the commitment of black preachers such as Abernathy, secretary of the Baptist Ministers' Alliance, and it was Abernathy who told Nixon to call the young minster at the Dexter Avenue Baptist Church, Martin Luther King Jr.

King and the Boycott

The boycott was in advanced planning when King was called and even then he hesitated. He had already declined a request to lead the local NAACP branch because of other commitments but eventually he acquiesced to a meeting at his church which was attended by 70 black leaders. It did not augur well for the success of the boycott because it was disorganised and confused but Abernathy, supported by Jo Anne Robinson, took over and those who were still present voted to support the boycott. They decided they should call a mass meeting on the Monday night and afterwards King and Abernathy issued new leaflets urging people to attend and prepare for the boycott. Over 200 volunteers distributed the leaflets and black taxi drivers agreed to carry passengers on the day of the boycott at a standard charge of ten cents.

E. D. Nixon told Montgomery *Advertiser* reporter Joe Azbell about the planned protest and urged him to get a leaflet and interview people in the community because it was a good story for the Sunday paper, always a quiet day for news. And as Nixon hoped, it was the featured story which was picked up by the local television station. The City Police Commissioner Clyde Sellers in the television interview asserted that the boycott was going to be enforced by black 'goon squads' and that he was confident that their community would not be intimidated and it would fail. The white-owned newspapers and television ensured any African American who had not read the leaflet or heard about it at sermons would know because they would have either seen the newspaper headline or heard Sellers on television. It was not the first time, and certainly not the last, when white folks unwittingly supported the struggle (Garrow, 1988).

On the Monday morning, 5 December 1955, the boycott was more successful than the leaders had hoped and later, in an unprecedented display of solidarity, several hundred blacks went to the court house to witness the trial of Rosa Parks. It took five minutes and she was fined ten dollars. Following the trial the boycott organisers proposed that the bus company should allow seating on a first-come, first-served basis with blacks filling the bus from the back and whites from the front. The system would ensure that no one gave up their seat or was forced to stand over an empty one and rude drivers or those who assaulted a black passenger should be disciplined or fired. Abernathy wanted black drivers hired because African Americans made up 75 percent of the passengers. If these modest demands had been met there would have been no boycott and Montgomery would not have become known as the Walking City. But the white council's determination to resist ensured that it continued. The authorities, having selected the path of resistance rather than accept minor modifications of the ordinance, transformed a one-day boycott into a year-long struggle for total bus desegregation.

The leaders were aware that existing groups could not coordinate the campaign and a new organisation was needed. The NAACP did not have the mass membership and the WPC could not openly organise because most were state employees and would be dismissed. The head of the Interdenominational Ministerial Alliance was unsuitable because Reverend L. Roy Bennett lacked leadership abilities. As in any protest there were divisions about who would be the best leader of the newly formed MIA. But all factions agreed that the ideal person would be the newcomer Martin Luther King Jr head of the most prestigious black church and who had a Boston University doctorate (Garrow, 1988). But as J. Mills Thornton has pointed out there is a danger that King's role 'may be overstated. In Tallahassee, Tuskegee and Greensboro, it is only his example we are dealing with ... In Albany, Birmingham, St. Augustine and Selma, he and his organization went into the city in response to the invitation of local black leaders to assist them in effecting local goals of local importance, whatever may have been the national implications of their decision to do so.' Thornton stresses: 'In Montgomery ... King's role was even more completely than elsewhere a function of local circumstance. He played no significant part in creating the Boycott'

(Thornton, 1989). However, a recent study demonstrates that King was not so reluctant to take a leadership role because he understood that it was not simply about a Chicago bus company enforcing southern segregation but the beginning of a much wider assault on capitalism which underpinned a racist society and inequality for all poor people (Jackson, 2007).

The all-black MIA joined forces with the white Alabama Christian Movement for Human Rights (ACMHR) which was holding a meeting in Montgomery. A member of the ACMHR board, Thomas Thrasher a Montgomery minister, set up talks between the MIA and the city commissioners. The talks failed. The Chicago company National City Lines, which owned the Montgomery bus service, refused to send an arbitrator as requested by MIA. And the resistance of the white community grew, with threats against the alternative transportation service the African American residents had established. King called his friend Jemison in Baton Rouge who told him about the free ride service they had organised in their protest and King followed his advice and made the necessary arrangements.

White Resistance

The commissioners' refusal to compromise encouraged the more extreme segregationists in the city. Obscene and threatening phone calls were received by MIA leaders. City police commissioner Clyde Sellers along with Mayor W. A. 'Tacky' Gayle and commissioner Frank Parks joined the White Citizens Council (WCC), a South-wide organisation first established in Mississippi to defend Jim Crow. It was estimated by the local newspapers that Council membership had grown from 6000 at the beginning of February 1956 to 12,000 by the end of the month (Thornton, 1989). This growing resistance led to widespread harassment and the first arrest of King on 26 January 1956 for speeding at 30 in a 25 mile per hour zone. Four days later his house was bombed and his father and father-in-law pleaded with him and his wife to leave the city.

To many it seemed that the segregationists were united. They were not. The boycott 'revealed conclusively that segregationists at the grassroots and municipal levels were … unsure of their tactics' (Lewis, 2006).

In 1958, three years after the boycott, George Corley Wallace ran for the governorship and, although he believed in rigid segregation, he stressed better education, reduced unemployment and improved health services for all Alabamians. In a 1987 interview he claimed he knew nothing about the boycott except for what he had read in the newspapers (Washington State University, Digital Library). This was an attempt to rewrite history. Montgomery contributed to his decision to abandon his moderate segregationist politics. The Golden Gloves boxing champion was thrashed by John Patterson who was a virulent racist. Having lost to a race-baiter, Wallace swore he would 'never be out niggered again'. He became the leader that grass-roots segregationists were looking for. His decision and lust for power would have a profound effect on the nation and its political debates into the 21st century.

King later recalled the vehemence with which most southern whites sought to defend segregation and the abuse against the black walkers. He was so fearful of the hatred that surrounded him that he almost quit the leadership but his faith meant he overcame his qualms.

> And it seemed to me at that moment that I could hear an inner voice saying to me: 'Martin Luther, stand up for righteousness. Stand up for justice. Stand up for truth. And lo I will be with you, even until the end of the world.' I heard the voice saying still fight on. He promised never to leave me alone. No never alone. No never alone.
>
> (Garrow, 1988)

The bombing of his home made him more determined to continue the struggle and not merely to make segregation more pleasant for African Americans but to end the Jim Crow system itself. Alabama had an anti-boycott law and in February 1956 the city fathers were determined to use it and 100 members of the MIA were charged by the grand jury whose members asserted that: 'We are committed to segregation by custom and law and we intend to maintain it.' Their intransigence strengthened the determination of the community and those indicted were not intimidated. As King told a mass rally: 'There are those who would try to make this a hate campaign. This is not a war between the white and the Negro but a conflict between justice and injustice. This is bigger than the Negro race revolting against the white. We are not just trying to improve the Negro of Montgomery but the whole of Montgomery' (Garrow, 1988).

The genius of King was his ability to articulate the African American struggle in terms that were immediately understood by millions of Americans, white and black. Later in his determination to follow the example of Gandhi, who had inspired Melba Pattillo and her grandmother in Little Rock, he would contribute to the transformation of municipal struggles over segregated buses, or later student protests against segregated lunch counters, into a great crusade for democracy in America. He would face black and white Americans, northerners and southerners, to challenge a system that had rarely been questioned. The white resisters of Montgomery and other southerners who simply said 'segregation now segregation forever' only made King, other leaders and grass-root activists more determined to triumph. The tragedy was that most Americans ignored or refused to listen to King's appeal for economic as well as legal justice because the message was too radical (Jackson, 2007).

The fierce opposition from the white South in the form of mass indictments for the first time stirred an indifferent northern public and to some extent the media. Despite Gene Roberts' and Hank Klibanoff's defence of the press, it would take violence and murders, mostly of white civil rights workers, to result in major coverage (Riches, 2017). But the mass indictments resulted in the collection of $12,000 in the North. The *New York Times* and the New York *Herald Tribune* carried front page stories in 1956 of the events in Montgomery and King's address to a mass rally was his first to get national coverage. On network television, which limited news to 15 minutes, ABC compared the Alabama protesters to Gandhi and the city officials to the British trying to shore up their empire. It was a theme King took up in the first of his many speeches in the North about the boycott. Addressing an audience of 2500 people at Brooklyn's Concord Baptist Church, he reminded them that Gandhi had brought down British rule with passive resistance. But the Montgomery marchers found the major source of inspiration from Christianity. As King told a reporter: 'I have been a keen student of Gandhi for many years. However, this business of passive resistance and nonviolence is the gospel of Jesus. I went to Gandhi through Jesus' (Garrow, 1988).

'Not a One Man Show'

This was not just a protest led by a charismatic leader but rather, as Jo Anne Robinson correctly described it to a black reporter at the time: 'The amazing thing about our movement is that it is a protest of the people. It is not a one man show. It is not the preacher's show. It's the people. The masses of this town who are tired of being trampled on, are responsible. The leaders could not stop them if they wanted to' (Garrow, 1988).

Although Robinson's assessment was correct, King's leadership was increasingly emphasised, especially by sympathetic outsiders such as the African Methodist Episcopal (AME) Church, the National Council of Churches and the Fellowship of Reconciliation (FOR). Bayard Rustin, the African American pacifist and civil and labour rights fighter, and the Reverend Glen Smiley, a white officer of FOR, came to Montgomery to speak with King and other community leaders. Smiley, a Texan and fellow southerner, was profoundly influenced by the non-violent direct action teachings of Gandhi but found that, although King admired the Indian's leadership, King admitted that he did not know very much about him. Smiley wrote: 'King can be a great Negro Gandhi, or he can be made into an unfortunate demagogue destined to swing from a lynch mob's tree' (Garrow, 1988). King would choose to follow Gandhi and not the demagogue – a role white political opponents tried to impose on him.

King had to face the court and not the lynch mob. He was the first indicted boycott leader who was tried, found guilty and fined $500 with another $500 in court costs or 368 days in jail. His conviction was appealed and the cases against others were held over until the appeal court ruled. Meanwhile a suit challenging the constitutionality of the city's bus segregation ordinance was filed on 1 February 1956 and on 5 June the federal district court ruled in *Browder v. Gayle* that it was unconstitutional. The city commissioners were not willing to accept the ruling and they decided on two further steps: first they appealed to the federal Supreme Court, and second, on the 13 November, they filed for an injunction to end the car pool. But it was too late. On the same day the Supreme Court upheld the lower court. It was agreed at a mass meeting on 14 November that the boycott should be called off as soon as the desegregated buses started to move. After over a year, on 21 December, the first African American to climb aboard and sit in the front of a Montgomery bus was Martin Luther King Jr.

The victory at Montgomery was based on a well-organised protest by the black community that practiced non-violent direct action combined with the NAACP strategy of using the courts to overthrow the Jim Crow system. As the first tentative steps to challenge segregation met resistance from the white community, the goal of black Americans changed from amelioration of the system to its overthrow. When black people showed they were determined to fight for justice, white resisters turned to violence and threats of violence. On 17 January 1957 two homes, including Ralph Abernathy's, and four black Baptist churches were bombed. Later that month a bomb made of 12 sticks of dynamite was found on King's porch and defused.

White Sympathisers

One of the homes bombed that 10 January was that of the Reverend Robert Graetz, a minister at the black Lutheran Church in Montgomery who was the only white minister to openly support the boycott. The deeds and words of a few white people played a part in its success. It was all very well for King and Abernathy to talk about a multi-racial democracy; in the segregated world of Montgomery, there were very few blacks who had any reason to believe that there were whites who shared their dream. Robert Graetz and his wife by their daily actions were living proof that such people existed. And they were not alone. Texan Glen Smiley of FOR did much to persuade King that Gandhi provided the role model he was searching for. Clifford and Virginia Durr contributed much to its success. And it was not only people who had long been associated with the struggle for civil rights who gave encouragement to black protest leaders. Although they probably did not want sweeping change, there were white citizens of Montgomery brave enough to write to the *Advertiser* supporting black complaints about the bus system. In this rigidly segregated society, Mrs I. Rutledge wrote that she did not know one white person who thought it was 'right that a Negro may be made to stand that a white person may sit down'. Her letter must have reassured boycott participants. Miss Juliette Morgan compared the boycott to Gandhi's salt march. She was absolutely convinced that: 'Passive resistance combined with freedom from hate is a power to be reckoned with' (Garrow, 1988).

Even in the darkest moments there were other white folks who supported the struggle for justice. Two years later in Little Rock, Arkansas, the 15-year-old Melba Pattillo and nine other African American teenagers faced the bayonets of the National Guard and the fury of white racists as they attempted to desegregate Central High School. She drew strength from women like Rosa Parks and the calm self-assurance of Thurgood Marshall. The extent of her and other young black people's ignorance of white people can be seen in the beliefs of her friend Marsha: 'She said white people didn't perspire, so I had to be certain that I didn't let them see me perspire. I was petrified on that first morning I was going to school.' Her fear was increased by a hysterical mob and their attempts to attack her friend Elizabeth Eckford. The next Sunday the newspaper had an advertisement showing the white mob with their 'twisted, scowling faces with their open mouths jeering'. The ad had been paid for by a white man from a small Arkansas town and it read: 'If you live in Arkansas and study this picture know shame. When hate is unleashed and bigotry finds a voice, then God help us all.' As she recalled: 'I felt a kind of joy and hope that one white man was willing to use his own money to call attention to the injustice we faced.' And during her time at Central High, she was helped to survive the threats and abuse by a young student named Link who took great risks and managed to prevent her from being seriously attacked. Her mother and grandmother were worried. 'Although I too, was undecided about trusting Link, I continued to defend Link as both of them came up with a dozen reasons why I shouldn't trust this white boy' (Beals, 1994). Her relatives' doubts must have been shared by many black people in Montgomery.

It was not only individual acts of courage and statements of support that made African Americans aware that there were white folks who shared their dream. White southerners played a leading role in the Southern Conference Education Fund (SCEF), a long-established organisation which had fought for civil rights and equality during the 1940s and 1950s when segregation was never questioned. All those active in SCEF realised that people of goodwill, black and white, needed encouragement. Their semi-annual meetings and workshops involved the wider community, and one in 1958 was held at the all-black Fisk University in Nashville, Tennessee and was addressed by Aubrey Williams. Fisk students, energised by what they had been taught, were major leaders in the 1960s struggle. The Fund 'became the nerve center of inter and intra-racial communication in the South' (Fosl, 2002).

Aubrey Williams, president of the SCEF, came from an old established Birmingham, Alabama family and had graduated from Maryville College, Tennessee. After a short time as a minister he did social work, joined FDR and his New Deal programmes and became aware of the racism in the Works Progress Administration. He fought hard to stop it and became a close friend of A. Philip Randolph and Mrs Roosevelt (Branch, 1998). Forced out of his job in 1943, he returned to Alabama, worked with the National Farmers Union, edited a farm journal and built homes for black families. Throughout the postwar period Williams also worked with poor white families of the South because he believed they 'were the likeliest material in the country from the lumpen proletariat, that would form the mass base of a racist, fascist movement'. Because of the Depression millions of them had moved North and taken their virus with them. The poor white is 'a very dangerous man, and he must be cured, and during the process of cure he must be guarded from destroying others' (Klibaner, 1989).

Williams, despite his isolation from the majority of white southerners, influenced people such as James Dombrowski, a Tampa, Florida native who graduated from Emory in 1923. At a northern graduate school he did his PhD on labour history and Christian socialism. A founder member of the Highlander School in 1932, he was staff director until 1942 when he joined SCEF where he worked for 30 years advocating non-violent change in the South and persuaded many black clergymen to support Highlander (Klibaner, 1989). Other southerners had strong connections to the region and its left-wing radicalism. Myles Horton from West Tennessee founded the Highlander Center and his wife, Zilphia Horton from Arkansas, was its cultural director. His father had been a member of the Workers Alliance. A photo of King at Highlander was plastered on billboards across the South as proof that he was a communist.

Williams persuaded Carl and Anne Braden to stay in the South and offered them jobs as SCEF field secretaries. Carl, a Kentucky native whose father was a railroad worker, was a socialist but was influenced by his mother's Catholicism (Braden Papers, University of Tennessee, Knoxville (UTK). He attended seminary but turned to journalism and worked at the Louisville *Courier Journal.* Unlike Carl, Anne came from an upper middle-class family and was brought up in Mississippi and Alabama. She attended private schools and graduated from an exclusive college and then worked as a journalist in Birmingham and Louisville. 'For Anne Carl's world was a shattering, albeit liberating experience. The emotional and intellectual walls that segregation and years of indoctrination in white superiority had built around her crumbled under the impact of sharing social, political, and simple human experiences on an equal basis with black people' (Fosl, 2002). In 1954 they agreed to help a black friend, Andrew Wade, who wanted a better home but it was in an all-white neighbourhood and so they bought it and sold it to him. The racial tension was inflamed by the belief that Braden was a communist. Found guilty of conspiracy, he served eight months of a 15-year sentence until the Supreme Court ruled the state law was unconstitutional (Fosl, 2002).

King made frequent visits to the North which led to friendships with other whites who sympathised with the Montgomery boycott. Bayard Rustin introduced King to Harris Wofford, the first white man to graduate from Howard University, Washington DC law school, the premier black university in the United States. Wafford was a friend of E. D. Nixon. He also introduced King to Stanley Levison, a New York lawyer, who worked with Ella Barker to raise funds for the MIA. Levison became a close advisor to King. They agreed they needed a regional group that would end segregation everywhere in the South. As bombs were being planted in Montgomery on 10 January, Rustin drew up plans to challenge bus segregation but he also knew they had to challenge 'the entire social, political and economic order that kept us second class citizens ... Those who oppose us understand this.' The two weapons chosen to win the war were voting power and mass direct action. The Southern

Leadership Conference, later called the Southern Christian Leadership Conference (SCLC) by King, was born in 1957. Although Medgar Evers of the NAACP was on the committee, he resigned because Roy Wilkins, NAACP chairman and its board members, distrusted the new organisation – even though they were prepared to work with it.

Although suspicious of one another, the leaders of these groups presented a united front in negotiations with any Administration. King, Randolph and Lester B. Granger of the National Urban League, an organisation representing black business, met with President Eisenhower to stress the black minority's concerns. The four men agreed that Randolph would give the opening statement and the others would address three points each. When they met Eisenhower he defended his Administration and refused to promise any further action. And the pressure at the local level seemed even less successful with the city of Montgomery refusing to respond to further demands for the desegregation of schools and parks. The city commissioners felt no urgency and the MIA was divided by factional disputes.

After a short visit to India, King took part in a second march on Washington on 18 May 1959 to demand school desegregation. Along with Roy Wilkins and Tom Mboya of Kenya, King was one of the main speakers. An estimated 26,000 took part and one consequence of the rally was a meeting with Vice President Richard Nixon. King was very impressed with Nixon's support for the civil rights campaign but the Montgomery minister qualified his opinion: 'If Richard Nixon is not sincere he is the most dangerous man in America' (Garrow, 1988).

Despite their efforts, Rustin, King and Levison had not created an effective national lobbying organisation. With the increasing acrimony between King and E. D. Nixon, the MIA had become moribund and King left the city and moved to another church in Atlanta. However, the boycott showed how grass-roots activism could be effective. It directly influenced the passage of the civil rights acts of 1958 and 1960. On the other hand, it strengthened the determination of white southerners to resist the burgeoning movement of African Americans who were prepared to struggle for justice.

Ironically, much of white resistance was sustained by their religious faith that found its deepest expression in their hymns and the same was true for those in the struggle who were inspired by spirituals, gospel and shouts. Although conventional hymns like *Onward Christian Soldiers*, or gospel songs such as *This Little Light of Mine*, strengthened the determination of the folks in Montgomery, they were sung in chapels and churches and not while folks walked to work. Perhaps King had no idea what an important part music, religious and secular, would play in the years ahead – how singing created anthems for the Movement that would galvanise millions in the United States and around the world. It may be that he overcame his gloomiest moments by recalling his visit to the Highlander Folk School in 1957 where he heard Zilphia Horton, Pete Seeger and Guy Carawan sing an old spiritual that had become a union song: *We Shall Overcome*. As King said to Anne Braden at the time, 'There's something about that song that haunts you' (Garrow, 1988).

3

The Struggle Intensifies: JFK and a New Frontier? 1960–1963

Despite the sit-ins and boycotts of the late 1950s, which sought to capitalise on the success of the Montgomery boycott, it was not clear as the new decade began whether the African American community would be singing *We Shall Overcome* at the end of the decade. Martin Luther King Jr had joined his strong-willed father in Atlanta. As King started his new career, southern Democrats were pleased that a young senator from Massachusetts, whom they had promoted for the vice presidency in 1956 because he had opposed the Civil Rights Act, was organising his campaign for the presidency. While John Fitzgerald Kennedy (JFK) was readying his assault for the White House, King dreamed of winning control over the National Baptist Convention and it seemed that the desegregation of Montgomery's buses was the end of the struggle and the Southern Christian Leadership Conference (SCLC). Apparently JFK was not interested and it seemed King did not want to continue the fight. But whatever reluctance Kennedy showed for civil rights in his desire to keep southern Democrats on side, the younger generation of African Americans were not prepared to walk away.

The Greensboro Sit-in

Four black students in Greensboro, North Carolina, entered the Woolworth's store on the afternoon of 1 February 1960 and sat at the whites-only counter; when they were not served they promised to return the next day. This was not the first sit-in protest; many had occurred in the 1920s and especially after World War Two. Between 1956 and 1959 similar demonstrations had occurred in at least 16 other cities, 'but few of them made the news, all faded quickly from public notice and none had the slightest catalytic effect anywhere else. By contrast, Greensboro helped define the new decade' (Branch, 1989). Two of the students were former officers of the National Association for the Advancement of Colored People (NAACP) Youth Council and the NAACP provided bail money and its lawyers represented 1300 students who were arrested (Cunningham, 2013).

The Southern Regional Council, an interracial group of moderates, issued a report a few months after the Greensboro sit-in. 'Almost from the beginning the sit-ins have been referred to as a "Movement" ... No one ever speaks of the "school desegregation movement." One accomplishment then of the sit-in was to achieve, almost from the start, this recognition' (Laue, 1989). This is not strictly correct. Jo Ann Robinson had called the Boycott a 'mass movement'.

During the summer of 1960, 79 sit-in demonstrations were led by students – 78 in the South, with North Carolina (18), Florida (12) and Virginia (10) having the most. The students said they participated not only out of personal frustration but also out of their commitment and belief in justice. 'Your relationship with the movement is just like a love affair', one student said. 'You can't explain it. All you know is it's something you *have* to do' (Laue, 1989).

Perhaps the 1960s protests came to be called the 'Movement' because the students from North Carolina State Agricultural and Technical College captured the spirit of the moment. It is difficult to explain the heady sense of optimism that the younger generation felt – that nothing was impossible and no problem need go unsolved. The ageing General Eisenhower was known by the youth largely for his love of golf and his heart attacks, and he and their elders had made so many mistakes it was time for the young to solve the world's problems. They would not repeat the fearmongering of the older generations' warnings of imminent atomic attack, which had made their children fear a nuclear holocaust. Teenagers in school loyally pledged allegiance to the flag and in every school they were told of the unique promise of the United States. Many wanted to fulfil the dream that they believed their parents had forgotten. It was this idealism that motivated southern black students and their white supporters. Regardless of what they actually achieved, King and JFK captured the hopes and dreams of these baby boomers.

The older generation, caught up in mass consumption, reminded their children that they were fortunate to live in the richest democracy on earth while they ignored the injustices faced by the poor and minorities, especially in the South, where whites-only schools and churches taught that the natural order was white supremacy which dangerous radicals and liberal dupes wanted to destroy. The young began to doubt. As Paul Goodman observes in *Growing Up Absurd* in 1960: 'Now the law and religion side against them, the Southerners are manic with wounded conceit and sexual fear; their behavior on integration should not be referred to the Attorney General but to the Public Health Service.' He adds: 'All this has come banging down on the children as the battleground. Yet, paradoxically, among all the young people it is perhaps just the young people of the South, whites and Negroes both, who must find life worth living these days, because something real is happening' (Howard, 1982).

After three days of sit-ins over 80 students were involved and reports reached Reverend James Lawson in Nashville of others across North Carolina; by the following Thursday, a long-time fighter against segregation, Reverend Fred Shuttlesworth from Birmingham, Alabama, came to preach in Greensboro. He understood their significance and telephoned Ella Baker: 'You must tell Martin that we must get into this.' He was certain the sit-ins would 'shake the world' and North Carolina NAACP leaders warned that the Association must work with the young (Cunningham, 2013). King had not started the sit-ins but he was among the first to support them when black newspapers treated them as pranks and the white media ignored them. Three weeks after they started, King addressed a Durham rally: 'Men are tired of being trampled over by the iron feet of oppression… What is new in your fight is the fact that it was initiated, led, and sustained by students. What is new is that American students have come of age. You now take your honored places in the world-wide struggle for freedom' (Branch, 1989). He did not acknowledge their actions had saved the day after the Montgomery tensions.

The Nashville Sit-in

James Lawson was overwhelmed by volunteers who wanted to take part. Approximately 500 students from Nashville's black colleges – Fisk, Tennessee State, Meharry Medical and the Baptist seminary – insisted on immediate action. Lawson tried to dissuade them and explained only 75 had finished non-violence training and there was no bail money if they were arrested. They did not care and so he gave them a crash course on non-violence. 'The Nashville students destined to establish themselves as the largest, most disciplined, and most persistent of the nonviolent action groups in the South – extended the sit-in movement into its third state. Their success helped form the model of the student group – recruited from the campuses, quartered in the churches, and advised by preachers' (Branch, 1989). A Fisk student, Marion Barry Jr was elected chairman of the new organisation, the Student Nonviolent Coordinating Committee (SNCC) set up on 17 April 1960 at Shaw University, in Raleigh, North Carolina (*The Student Voice*, June 1960).

Twelve days after the first protest, Nashville students sat in at dime-store lunch counters. Led by Chicagoan Diane Nash, they swept the city. They were viciously attacked and in the following weeks more than 150 were arrested. Nash told the judge she wanted 'jail no bail' because to pay fines meant accepting 'the injustice and immoral practices that have been performed in the arrest and conviction of the defendants' (Houston, 2012). Sixty chose 'jail no bail', which became a slogan of the Movement. Downtown, stores were integrated and African Americans were hired in non-menial positions for the first time. On 7 March in Knoxville, Tennessee, the Knoxville College black students, led by Bob Booker and white students from the University of Tennessee, Knoxville (UTK), held a sit-in and eventually all the counters were integrated (Proudfoot, 1990). In Chattanooga white shoppers rioted (*The Student Voice*, August 1960).

At Atlanta University, for an SNCC meeting of 13–14 May, Reverend James Lawson wrote a statement of purpose:

> Through nonviolence, courage displaces fear, love transforms hate. Acceptance dissipates prejudice; hope ends despair. Peace dominates war, faith reconciles doubt. Mutual regard cancels enmity. Justice for all overthrows injustice. The redemptive community supersedes systems of gross social immorality.
>
> (*The Student Voice*, June 1960)

Accepting non-violence was not easy – nearly every southern black household owned a gun or rifle. Mrs Annie Rankin of Mississippi chose passive resistance when she sat in at a Natchez store and remained non-violent throughout her years in the struggle. But a black man murdered for voting for a black man in Jefferson County in 1967 tested her and she wrote to friends that 500 were waiting for the white killer and 'if he shows up he is a dead duck' (Rankin Papers, Mississippi Digital Library, Tugaloo College). But non-violence was the road to redemption. It was a choice supported by representatives of SCLC, the Atlanta Congregational Churches, the American Friends Service Committee (AFSC) and CORE. SNCC formed subcommittees for coordination, communication and finance, had an Atlanta office, and held regular monthly meetings. They raised funds and sought close cooperation with the NAACP but, on Ella Baker's advice, they refused to be a subordinate organisation of SCLC.

Recognising the importance of good communication, they published a newsletter to be distributed to every group, covering the struggle and resistance throughout the South. They produced pamphlets and statements for the press. They stressed the need for a 'system of flash news to alert the nation of emergencies and serious developments' (*The Student Voice*, June 1960). Professional journalists Carl and Anne Braden helped them. This was needed in the face of the increasing resistance shown by the 35 percent growth in the North Carolina KKK (Cunningham, 2013) and the South-wide membership of White Citizens Councils. They hoped the mainstream media would carry some of their news. *The Student Voice* played an important role in creating a mass movement to overcome segregation and white opposition. In October 1960 its headline read: 'PARKER STILL JAILED.' Richard Parker of Florida State

University was in jail with a broken jaw. He had participated in the Jacksonville sit-in on 25–26 August, and was inside for 90 days and lost 25 pounds in weight (*The Student Voice*, October 1960).

For students, the first day of the Greensboro sit-in, 1 February 1960, was Freedom Day. In *The Student Voice* editorial in August 1960 they complained: 'The political ramifications of the student protest movement are often underestimated and glossed over.' But, as the Movement gained strength, the students widened the battle: '[I]t's imperative that we look into the possibility of engaging in political activity on all levels, local, state and federal and forcefully inform politicians of their views.' It was they who had made the parties include in their platforms the strongest civil rights planks ever written. They needed to dramatise 'the most blatant denial of civil rights that exists in this country today – the denial of the right to vote to millions of citizens in the South.' To achieve this African Americans had to overcome fraud, intimidation and violence. On top of this there was the further barrier of state laws that denied the vote in federal elections to those who did not pay a poll tax, or who failed to pay taxes that was not ruled unconstitutional until the Twenty-Fourth Amendment (1964). And literacy tests enforced by white registrars overwhelmingly disenfranchised black people and were used as late as 1966 in Virginia. The *Voice* urged students, from North and South, to hold protest rallies and pickets on election day. 'As citizens working for the betterment not only for our communities, but of the country and the world we … are willing to do that which is often unpopular to see that neither we nor our fellow-citizens are forced to endure second-class citizenship' (*The Student Voice*, August 1960).

King Meets Kennedy

The SNCC was following a policy originally set out by King and the union leader A. Philip Randolph. On 9 June the picketing of the Democratic and Republican conventions was to underline their belief that the 1960 Civil Rights Act was inadequate. Harlem Congressman Adam Clayton Powell defended the Act and denounced King and those who criticised it as a 'captive of socialist interests' – the very claim made by southern resisters and the FBI. Powell forced Bayard Rustin's resignation at the SCLC New York office because Rustin feared his homosexuality would hurt the Movement and discredit King.

However, King met privately with JFK. King distrusted him because southern delegates had supported him for the vice presidency in 1956 and because he was a friend of the segregationist Alabama Governor John Patterson. King and JFK agreed that executive leadership and legislative action were urgently required to ensure voting rights and end housing discrimination. Afterwards King told the press: 'I was very impressed by the forthright and honest manner in which he discussed the civil rights question. I have no doubt that he would do the right thing on this issue if he were elected' (Bryant, 2006). Despite Harris Wofford's support for JFK, King refused to endorse him. Senator Lyndon Baines Johnson (LBJ) of Texas, who challenged JFK for the Democratic nomination, was confident that he could win the black vote and was encouraged when African American leaders organised a campaign – the 'Nonpartisan Crusade to Register One Million New Negro Voters' – which was really an attempt to register only Democrats.

But King had more immediate problems. Students at the five black colleges in Atlanta wanted to take part in the Movement and they were infuriated by store owners who refused to desegregate, especially Richard H. Rich. On 19 October, 75 students went into action and within 30 minutes the first arrests were made in Rich's store. King joined the students and was arrested. Like them, he refused to post bond and spent his first night in jail (*The Student Voice*, October 1960). He had forgotten he had broken his Alabama probation order when he had been found guilty on trumped-up charges of tax evasion. He was not released with the others but transferred to DeKalb County jail handcuffed and guarded by a police dog (Garrow, 1988).

Vice President Richard Nixon was campaigning; he was told what had happened but ignored Atlanta black Republican John C. Calhoun's advice to telegraph Mrs King. Nixon wanted to capitalise on Eisenhower's breakthrough in the solid Democratic South. King's wife, Coretta, called Wofford and he urged JFK to telephone her, which he did (Dallek, 2003). Robert Kennedy was furious: 'You bomb throwers probably lost the election. You've probably lost three states ... the civil rights section is not going to do another damn thing in this election.' He was also angry with the judge who had jailed King and said it was a constitutional right for a defendant to post a bond. King was released. Although JFK denied the call was a deliberate attempt to win the African American vote, Democrats circulated a flyer in black-only precincts: 'No Comment: Nixon versus a Candidate with a Heart, Senator Kennedy: The Case of Martin Luther King.' King thanked JFK for his 'moral courage' and Daddy King, a Republican, said, with much exaggeration, 'I'll take a Catholic or the Devil himself if he'll wipe the tears from my daughter's eyes. I've got a suitcase full of votes – my whole church for ... Senator Kennedy' (Schlesinger, 1979). More effective was Chicago mayor Richard Daley whose black precinct captains turned out the vote (Grimshaw, 1992).

Executive Action

JFK's election was largely owing to the surprising acceptance of the vice presidency by LBJ and African American votes, but appointing his brother Robert as Attorney General did not augur well for those in the Movement. Robert was an undistinguished graduate of Harvard and Virginia Law School, and had served as a counsel to McCarthy's 'communist' and homosexual 1950s witch-hunt. Robert knew action on civil rights was necessary but he preferred to protect his brother rather than civil rights workers. 'He had not known many black people, knew little about segregation, and had not thought about the federal role in promoting desegregation' (Arsenault, 2006). Wofford persuaded the Justice Department to support SNCC's voter registration, supported by the SCLC and the NAACP. He advised JFK to use executive orders to advance civil rights rather than rely on a conservative-dominated Congress. The president's civil rights credentials are contested: he was either a bystander (Bryant, 2006) or someone who kept his promises (Bernstein, 1991). Both characterisations fit his years in office.

The Civil Rights Commission and the Civil Rights Act were renewed in 1960 and the commission's reports forced federal agencies to hire more African Americans. JFK avoided segregated meetings (Sugrue, 2008). Irving Bernstein points out: 'The Kennedy policy on civil rights in 1961

called for a minimum of legislation and a maximum of executive action'
(Bernstein, 1991; Arsenault, 2006). But JFK discovered that presidential powers raised hopes which could not be met. When NAACP leader
Roy Wilkins proposed swift executive action, he was brusquely dismissed
with a 'no' (Bryant, 2006) and Wilkins complained especially about
JFK's failing to keep a campaign promise to desegregate federally funded
housing with 'one stroke of the pen'. As the days passed, thousands of
pens arrived at the White House emblazoned with the famous phrase
but he would not act because housing desegregation had the potential
for great violence nationwide. 'Any governmental intrusion of race into
housing was certain to arouse deep emotions' (Bernstein, 1991; Jones,
2009). Eventually, in November 1962, after the mid-term elections, JFK
signed an executive order without effective enforcement powers. The pen
had no ink in it.

In federal employment, JFK ensured the integration of the Coast
Guard Academy and issued Executive Order 10952, setting up the
President's Commission on Equal Employment Opportunity (CEEO) –
the first Order to have enforcement sanctions. Based on FDR's FEPC, it
applied to federal employment and government contractor agencies. LBJ
was chairman but he believed affirmative action was necessary to ensure
equal opportunity. Although sanctions were rarely used, the NAACP
and the Urban League used CEEO data to sue companies and unions;
they wanted the Commission strengthened but realised that it was still a
major step forward. Companies in Illinois and Indiana promoted black
workers,and shipyard unions and a company in San Pedro, California
were required 'to eradicate separate seniority lines for black and white
workers' (Sugrue, 2008). There were notable successes in the South when
Lockheed in Marietta, Georgia, heavily dependent on defence contracts,
integrated its workforce and hired and promoted African Americans,
which influenced the practices of other southern companies.

Employers complained, and with some justification, that they were
complying with demands from their workers for segregated facilities.
The steelworkers and the United Auto Workers (UAW) union both had
a good record when it came to civil rights, despite some opposition in
union branches (Sugrue, 2005, 2008). Union leader Randolph had campaigned for years against the racist practices of American unions and, in

November 1962, Johnson met with George Meany, head of the AFL-CIO, and officials of 116 unions who agreed to end any discrimination on the basis of race, creed, colour or national origin in hiring, apprenticeship training and promotion opportunities. 'While gains were made in this program, some unions did not sign on and a few, particularly in the building trades, did not affix their signatures' (Bernstein, 1991).

As John and Robert Kennedy sought gradual change, largely through executive action, they were under constant pressure and JFK tried to head off criticism with his reassuring style. The NAACP's leadership believed he shared their ideal to improve the conditions for the poor in the United States and especially overseas with the Peace Corps. But he refused any attempt at legislative action at home, certain that it would be futile with a conservative Congress.

Whatever the Kennedy administration's intent, the students in the SNCC and CORE were not prepared to accept gestures, and throughout 1960–61 they organised protests and voter registration drives. Lane College students worked in Fayette and Haywood counties, Tennessee, and 861 African Americans in Haywood County voted for the first time in the 1960 election. The wealthy white landowners evicted their tenants; the homeless were aided by the SNCC and housed in a Freedom City (*The Student Voice,* November 1960). Students were also involved in church kneel-ins, theatre stand-ins and beach wade-ins.

The Freedom Rides

It was the Freedom Rides, organised by CORE's James Farmer, that created a crisis which gained international news coverage and, as he explained later: 'We were counting on the bigots of the South to do our work for us. We figured that the government would have to respond if we created a situation that was headline news all over the world, and affecting the nation's image abroad' (Bernstein, 1991).

Edward B. King, of SNCC, telegrammed JFK: 'At this time in the history of our great nation when we are telling the people of Asia, Africa, Latin America and the free world in general that we desire to be their friends, Negro Americans continue to be assaulted by Southern reactionaries' (Bernstein, 1991). King and the NAACP refused to participate but Farmer and CORE decided to force JFK to act. In 1946 the Supreme Court in *Morgan v. Virginia* ruled that interstate transport segregation laws burdened interstate commerce and were unconstitutional. In 1960 in *Boynton v. Virginia* the Court ruled against segregated bus depots. Just as the students in Greensboro challenged lunch-counter segregation, CORE chose to test the enforcement of these decisions. The first riders, six white and six black – later 450 would take part – left DC on 4 May 1961, to ensure the law's effectiveness and 'bring nonviolent direct action to the forefront of racial justice' (Arsenault, 2006).

On 14 May, after several minor incidents, the Greyhound bus pulled into the Anniston, Alabama depot, 60 miles from Birmingham. JFK's friend, the racist Governor Patterson, who had endorsed Kennedy, refused to provide protection for those he later called 'damned fools' (Public Broadcasting System Freedom Riders, 11 July 2011). The KKK was there. They attacked the riders and followed the bus out of town, and when it stopped because of a puncture the mob set it on fire. The students were lucky to survive but were undeterred; they continued on another bus to Birmingham where police chief Eugene 'Bull' Connor gave his men the day off because it was Mother's Day. A mob pounded them with baseball bats, lead pipes and bicycle chains, leaving a rider permanently paralysed. One of the attackers, Gary Thomas Rowe, an FBI informer, had pre-warned Hoover about the planned attack. Nothing was done.

Some refused to accept defeat and, led by Diane Nash, insisted on completing the journey. The 21 riders, three white, were told they would not get protection, and they were badly beaten in Montgomery, Alabama and Jackson, Mississippi. This was carried on national and international news (Houston, 2012) when JFK was preparing to meet Soviet leader Nikita Khrushchev shortly after the Cuban Missile Crisis. JFK defended his actions against Cuba and claimed he was acting for the free world. This claim, which followed the bombing and assault on the Freedom bus in Birmingham, meant he had to act (Houston, 2012). But, 'as part of its political strategy, the Administration deflected attention away from the President onto the Justice Department' (Bryant, 2006).

Farmer knew Justice Department lawyers could no longer ignore southern massive resistance and, in September 1961, Interstate Commerce

Commission regulations ordered desegregation on interstate transport. However, African Americans knew it was one thing to issue orders and another for them to be enforced. When this author arrived at a bus depot in Selma, Alabama in 1966 at 3 a.m., there were no 'whites only' signs but the station was rigidly segregated. It is not correct that: 'By the end of 1962 James Farmer's Freedom Riders and Robert Kennedy's lawyers had abolished Jim Crow on interstate transport' (Bernstein, 1991).

The Integration of 'Ole Miss'

The confrontation JFK wanted to avoid was brewing in Mississippi. It would make Little Rock seem quiet by comparison. A Mississippi share-cropper's son and an Air Force veteran, James Howard Meredith, applied to the main state university at Oxford ('Ole Miss'). The Democratic rulers of the state were a mix of moderate racists such as John Coleman and virulent segregationists such as Governor Ross Barnett. State judges refused Meredith's admission. Judge Sidney Mize concluded the university was not racially segregated even though no African Americans had studied or taught there. After a series of appeals, Supreme Court Justice Hugo Black, a native of Alabama, ordered Meredith's enrolment. Barnett went on television. The people of Mississippi had a choice: either they submitted to the tyranny of the federal government or they acted like men and resisted. He called on the pro-slavery arguments of his ances-tors: 'Mississippi, as a Sovereign State, has the right under the federal Constitution to determine for itself what the federal Constitution has reserved to it.' He would interpose the authority of the state between the people of Mississippi and federal government tyranny. Attempts to enrol Meredith peacefully were futile.

The University Board of Trustees surrendered to Barnett. On several occasions his deputy acted out interposition on the university steps – arguments and actions that George Wallace when Governor of Alabama would later use with greater impact. Barnett attended a football game and addressed the cheering crowd saying he would never allow desegre-gation, and as the days dragged on the Ole Miss students became more agitated. The governor, John Patterson, who was a friend of Kennedy and had supported his vice presidential bid, refused to take JFK's call, saying he had gone fishing (Patterson interview, PBS, Freedom Riders, 2011).

Kennedy was forced to act and the Cabinet agreed to keep the army in reserve and use federal marshals and prison staff to minimise the risk of violence. The extreme right-wing General Edwin Walker called for volunteers to protect 'Ole Miss'. While Barnett postured at the stadium, he failed to realise the changing situation in Washington. Not wanting a repeat of Little Rock, Robert Kennedy used the crisis for political advantage and told his assistant, Nicholas Katzenbach: 'If things get rough, don't worry about yourself; the President needs a moral issue.' Robert realised that civil rights would play a prominent part in the 1964 presidential election and JFK needed to keep the northern black vote. A frustrated and angry Robert accused LBJ of not doing enough at the CEEO to secure more jobs for black people (Dallek, 2003).

On 30 September Meredith was smuggled into the university, accompanied by 170 federal marshals, and registered as a student; the mob remained unware. But when the state highway patrol was withdrawn there was major violence and students and outsiders hurled bricks and started fires. Tear gas made matters worse. The students were too busy rioting to listen to JFK's appeal for peace in which he flattered the state for its battlefield honours and the university's gridiron prowess. The first fatality occurred at nine o'clock that evening. Paul Guilhard, an Agence France-Presse reporter, was shot in the back and later an Oxford resident was killed while others were wounded by rocks and gunshots. Order was not restored until almost 7 a.m. Ross Barnett and 'Ole Miss' gave Robert the moral issue he wanted and gave his brother the tactics he was sure would beat George Wallace.

Internal Divisions and External Pressures

The Kennedys had not made any commitments on civil rights and it was the Movement's direct action tactics, which King supported, that proved successful. Despite reservations the NAACP did too, although many leading members resented figures such as King and stopped the SCLC from introducing individual membership because it was competing with the NAACP. This hurt the SCLC but the damage was limited by using direct mailing and personal solicitation to raise hundreds of thousands of dollars. King's speaking fees ensured an equal amount. One of the biggest fundraisers was Harry Belafonte who, ironically, had been promoted by record companies and parents for his innocuous calypso singing.

Stanley Levison, a New York businessman, and 'Jack' O'Dell, a long-time union man and civil rights activist, supported and advised King and raised funds for the SCLC. The FBI claimed they had had connections with the Communist Party USA, and that Levison was a senior Soviet spy assigned to control O'Dell. Hoover persuaded Robert Kennedy that the Movement was run by communists (O'Reilly, 1994). Although Hoover knew Levison and O'Dell were no longer communists, he got Robert to agree they should be wiretapped. This was the beginning of a plan to destroy King and the Movement and to wipe out all radical groups in a Counter Intelligence Program (COINTELPRO). For the Movement, charges of communism were a great threat and they had to distance themselves from former party members. Levison told King that he and O'Dell had been members of the Communist Party. Hoover sent a copy of this wiretap to Robert Kennedy and to weaken the struggle further he leaked documents about O'Dell to the *New York Times* and the New York *Herald Tribune*. King lied, claiming that Levison and O'Dell had resigned from SCLC. The FBI knew that that they had not (Brandt, 2006). Hoover's paranoia extended to gays who were starting to leave the closet and who copied the organising methods and tactics used by civil rights leaders. For example, the church in San Francisco and its black minister backed Hispanic and black gays who were fighting for their civil rights (Faderman, 2015). While searching for communists and homosexuals, Hoover did nothing to investigate the massive white resistance campaign. A 1960 Mississippi circular denounced white 'fence-sitters' and urged people to 'BE A HATER' (MDL, accessed January, 2016).

The FBI continued to cause serious problems but they were not the only ones. Students and SNCC members were increasingly restive about their lack of funds and believed, rightly, that money from worldwide sympathisers of their direct action was being used to promote SCLC. King and the SCLC were given celebrity status in New York while the SNCC, led by men and women such as Robert Moses and Ella Baker, struggled to create a mass base for the Movement with voter registration and the education of African Americans in Freedom Schools. Ella Baker's resignation from the SCLC and the appointment of Wyatt Walker had not eased relations between the groups. King was also viewed as an upstart by the leadership of the Black Baptist Convention. The autocratic convention president had openly criticised the sit-ins. King was too young to challenge for the leadership but persuaded a friend to stand. The old guard elected the autocrat; King lost his position as vice president and convention members refused to support the SCLC (Garrow, 1989).

The Albany Movement

The divisions in the Movement help to explain what many consider to be the failure of the Albany, Georgia campaign. Charles Sherrod, who had worked with Robert Moses in Mississippi, decided to tackle the repressive regime in Southwest Georgia and organised young African Americans in the city, especially students at Albany State College. He bypassed the older leadership who were NAACP members. Alarmed college administrators tried unsuccessfully to remove SNCC organisers from the campus. The college president supported police chief Laurie Pritchett who made numerous claims that he knew about Gandhi and non-violence. The press reported and praised Pritchett for defeating non-violent direct action with non-violence and admired his men's courtesy when making arrests. Local and national pressmen not only accepted his boasts but passed on information about planned demonstrations and targets. Even two journalists who have written admiringly about the press coverage confess that one reporter was 'a fink' (Roberts and Klibanoff, 2006).

Distrust of journalists covering Albany meant activists tried to shape news coverage. The students knew that the reporters had not visited county jails because, if they had, they would have seen and might have reported the beatings meted out by local sheriffs and their deputies and witnessed Georgia's old-fashioned brutality and violence (Riches, 2016).

Their failure reinforced demands to ban journalists from meetings and to create an alternative newspaper system (radicals of the late 1960s and 1970s shared the same distrust and established the 'underground press'). Pritchett, when not exploiting the press, relied on older community people as spies and paid others as informers. But the city fathers were concerned that the arrests of King, Abernathy and 500 protestors had affected business and they insisted that King should be released. Albany confirmed Movement members' belief that: 'the national public had taken little offense at Albany's establishment of what one observer termed "an efficient police state."' And, 'so long as the Laurie Pritchetts of the South succeeded in maintaining segregation … that eschewed public violence and brutality, it seemed that the Kennedy brothers would be content to leave civil rights on the back burner' (Garrow, 1988).

But it was not left there. Robert Kennedy was persuaded not to intervene when Albany protesters were prosecuted for obstruction of justice, perjury and illegal picketing. Cases involving white folks' brutality and murder attempts were not investigated by the FBI because Hoover claimed they had no jurisdiction and it was a state matter even though 150 FBI agents supported Pritchett. The police and FBI agents did not investigate the case of Camilla King, wife of one of the Albany Nine, who lost her child after a police beating. One scholar suggests the Administration wanted to secure prosecutions to deter violence at the forthcoming March on Washington. They were concerned about communists they believed had infiltrated the Movement; the trials would save the Civil Rights Bill and encourage black moderates rather than King and Randolph (Bryant, 2006).

Fortunately for King, the Movement and the United States, few Pritchetts enforced southern white supremacy, but rather it was police chiefs such as Eugene 'Bull' Connor in Birmingham, Alabama. When white racists bombed Bethel Baptist Church there, King insisted that the president should act. African American leaders were united, and went to the White House to demand a stronger stance on civil rights at home and improved relations with Africa's newly independent nations. JFK said he could do nothing because of Congressional opposition and it would take one more struggle, resisted by white violence, to force him to act.

King and Birmingham, Alabama

King went to New York and informed Harry Belafonte of their plans for a march; he agreed to raise money for those who would be jailed and gave substantial sums himself. Meanwhile in Birmingham things did not start well, with few participating. Newspapers and television relied on beatings to capture reader and viewer interest. At first Connor disappointed them when he showed restraint. He was helped also by the internal divisions in the Movement, especially between SCLC's Wyatt Walker and James Bevel. Despite the tensions, King cautioned that they needed to work with black preachers and to urge businessmen to negotiate.

Connor's patience snapped. On 8 April 1963 a small group of marchers led by A. D. King were stopped by snarling German shepherd dogs and the attack on one demonstrator was captured by a news photographer. The picture featured in media around the world. After this, King decided to march on Good Friday, despite a court injunction. His arrest, along with that of Abernathy, meant that the Administration could no longer duck the challenge of the Movement.

With King in solitary confinement, the president called Coretta King to reassure her that everything would be done to protect her husband. At the same time Birmingham white Christian clergymen and Jewish rabbis issued a statement published in the Birmingham *News,* asserting that the demonstrations were unwise – they were organised by outsiders – and praising the police for their restraint. A copy of the paper was smuggled into King's cell, along with a pen. Using toilet paper, he wrote an eight-page rebuttal: 'Letter from Birmingham City Jail'. He bluntly answered the charge that he was an Atlanta outside agitator: 'Injustice anywhere is a threat to justice everywhere.' Business and local politicians refused to negotiate and the African American community had every right to act non-violently and it was not 'untimely' because they had waited '340 years for our constitutional and God-given rights'. The time for waiting was over. A creative tension 'in society ... will help [people] rise from the dark depths of prejudice and racism to the majestic heights of understanding and brotherhood'. Defying unjust laws was not a criminal act: 'One has not only a legal but a moral responsibility to obey just laws. Conversely, one has a moral responsibility to disobey unjust laws.' Instead of supporting those fighting segregation, southern white religious leaders had remained silent behind the 'anaesthetized security of stained glass windows'. Although King accused, he also reassured. It was the Movement's non-violence that would redeem America and his reaction to their 'silence' and 'laxity' were 'tears of love. There can be no deep disappointment where there is not deep love' (Washington, 1994).

The American Friends Service Committee published King's letter as a pamphlet; it was reprinted in journals 'with almost a million copies circulating in churches and [finding] their way to Robert Kennedy, Burke Marshall and others in Washington ... The 'Letter' became a classic of protest literature, the most eloquent and learned expression of the philosophy and goals of the nonviolent movement ever written' (Oates, 1994).

King's absence while in jail gave James Bevel, who had married coworker Diane Nash, the opportunity to take control of the Birmingham protest. He realised the Movement had never filled the jails and that the students of Miles College were not willing to be jail bait. He was well aware that high school students were eager to join the protests but they had been held back by adults. Bevel had no doubts. Ignoring their teachers and parents, thousands of high school students took to the streets. The police were fooled by several diversionary marches organised by him, Andrew Young and other volunteers armed with walkie-talkies (Young, 1996). On 3 March the police used dogs and fire hoses – so powerful that they stripped bark off trees – on the teenagers and 250 were arrested, a number which increased by another 1000 three days later. By 7 May the jails were filled with 2500 students. Many older people joined in and Birmingham became the site of a great mass movement.

JFK and Robert's eagerness to compromise only 'demonstrated again that in the short run, at least, they preferred order to justice' (Dittmer, 1995). The Administration had to find a settlement. 'The success of Birmingham should not be judged by its impact on Congress: the initiative for the civil rights bill came from the Administration, not the legislature. And the evidence strongly suggests that the SCLC demonstrations played a decisive role in persuading the Kennedy administration in introducing legislation' (Fairclough, 2001).

The Attorney General had tried to defuse black protest for two years but now the Kennedy brothers were alarmed at the prospect of a race war. Their fears were not without foundation. A Milwaukee sit-in protest, for example, against the Birmingham police riots led to arrests and death threats from local KKK and Nazi Party members (Jones, 2009). Robert Kennedy was left in no doubt of the seriousness of the situations after a meeting in New York with novelist James Baldwin, sociologist Kenneth Clarke, and singers Lena Horne and Harry Belafonte. CORE activist Jerome Smith was present, waiting for medical treatment following one of many beatings he suffered. Smith and Baldwin were furious with Kennedy's indifference. Smith told him about the abuse he had received in the South and warned him: 'When I pull the trigger, kiss it good-bye.' When asked by Baldwin if he would fight for the United States, Smith shouted: 'Never! Never! Never!' Kennedy was angry but as his friend and biographer writes: 'He began, I believe, to grasp as from the inside the nature of black anguish. He resented the experience, but it pierced him all the same. His tormentors made no sense; but in a way they made all sense. It was another stage in his education' (Schlesinger Jr, 1979).

The March on Washington

Another aspect of Robert Kennedy's education was formed by the desperate efforts of the SNCC, CORE and SCLC to register voters in areas such as Gadsden (Alabama), Danville (Virginia) and Plaquemine (Louisiana) throughout the summer of 1963. The attempts ended in failure. The resistance underlined how easy it was to maintain white supremacy. It was obvious that the courage of civil rights workers alone would never bring democracy to America but King did not want these failures to destroy their faith, which had made the challenge possible in the first place. Taking up the idea first proposed by Randolph, King decided that a march of 100,000 on Washington would prove there was mass demand for jobs and social justice. Bayard Rustin was a major organiser of the march. Before the event in DC, King and Walter Reuther, president of the UAW, led almost 200,000, mostly black, residents on a Detroit March for Freedom (Sugrue, 2008).

Fairclough argues that the Washington march had minimal impact on the legislative process. He underestimates the amazing scene of at least 250,000 black and white demonstrators in front of the great American icon, the Lincoln Memorial. It was a familiar speech to many who had heard King before but it was a revelation to millions of Americans (Olson, 2002). For the first time leading representatives of most of the major religions and denominations were united behind the civil rights cause. Tens of millions of North Americans watched on television and heard King articulate the Movement's goals in terms of the American Dream which they all shared. Patricia Hedgeman, the only woman on the March Committee, understood that his attacks were also on the economic system that perpetuated racism, poverty and unemployment. For King, Randolph and Rustin the march was for '*Jobs* and Freedom' – civil rights and economic change were inextricably joined (Jackson, 2007). However, most preferred, and still do, to see the march as seeking civil rights for black people only.

Black Americans had been promised progress but all too often the Dream became a nightmare (Coates, 2015). Postwar unemployment rose inexorably with the emergence of the Rust Belt, which had its origins in the late 1940s. Detroit, for example, lost 147,000 manufacturing jobs between 1947 and 1963; and the consequences of rising poverty were shorter life spans for African Americans and considerably higher infant mortality rates (Sugrue, 2008; Jones, 2009). The flight of whites to suburbia lowered tax revenues, resulting in poor services, schools, lower educational funding and bad policing. The white exodus ensured segregated housing which was encouraged by developers as in the case of Levittown, Philadelphia. From the 1940s housing segregation, reinforced by legal and illegal means, meant that Detroit and Milwaukee were as segregated as Selma and Birmingham. The 16th Street Bridge in Milwaukee was called the 'longest bridge in the world' because it joined Africa and America – it connected one of the most rigidly segregated cities in the United States (Jones, 2009). Milwaukee has been described as 'the most polarized part of the most polarized state in a polarized nation' (Mayer, 2016).

African Americans who took part in the Washington march were well aware of what was happening and that is why the demand for jobs was so important to them. When Angela Davis spoke of King 'reconceptualizing' the Movement when he went to Memphis to support the sanitation workers' strike in 1968 (PBS Frontline, 1997; Honey, 2007) she failed to credit his understanding from the start of the civil rights movement of the link between poverty and oppression.

Marching to the Music

Music continued to separate young people from their parents. The witch-hunt against popular music was led by fundamentalist preachers and politicians. Senator Estes Kefauver's 1954 subcommittee hearings on the danger of drugs and horror comics reported they were major contributors to degeneracy among the young. If adults worried in the 1950s, they had no idea the vital role the record world would play in uniting protest movements and in creating the 'Generation Gap'. The innocuous recording by The Kingsmen, *Louie Louie*, caused a moral panic over alleged obscenity and it was banned by radio stations. After a two-year FBI investigation agents concluded it was obscene. But it was their report that was pornographic.

Yet by 1960 the Hollywood movie *The Apartment* satirised the American Dream: the best way to achieve its material benefits was to rent your apartment to philandering superiors. Parental failure to live by their professed morals was not lost on teenagers who listened to sexually explicit rock songs on black-owned radio stations. Little Richard's father was a minister but that did not stop him recording *Tutti Futti, Good Golly Miss Molly* and *Long Tall Sally*. His crossover popularity was such that John Lennon recorded the latter in 1964. Sam Cooke, son of another minister, recorded romantic songs but adapted his style, introducing a greater gospel sound and his message; *A Change is Gonna Come* was a bestseller. However, most of his stronger political songs were not released until after his death (Ward, 1999).

Blues and jazz appalled some in the black religious community: pop, R & B and rock and roll were an anathema to many black ministers – especially ministers of the Sanctified Church. However, the assumption that all black churches saw the blues and its later developments as evil is an oversimplification (Smith, 2004). Despite the opposition from conservative black religious leaders, it was spirituals and gospel songs that fuelled the ecstasy and gripped worshippers and which also profoundly influenced young and old in the Movement. The combination of spirituals and 1940s labour songs were to become anthems. But the binding force of protest music did not start during the Montgomery boycott, with its gospel and spirituals performed by the Montgomery Gospel Trio. The shift came with the Nashville sit-ins that revised gospel songs such as *Get On Board* and *Got Up This Morning My Mind Set On Freedom*. The Freedom Riders also turned to the old union songs they learnt from James Foreman of the Congress of Racial Equality (CORE) and other labour organisers – for example, *We Ain't Gonna Let Nobody Turn Us Around* (Dunaway and Beer, 2010). John Lewis said that it was music that kept Movement workers bonded and singing from cells, reassuring colleagues that they were well (Lewis interview, PBS, Freedom Rides).

In Albany, Georgia, Guy Carawan introduced young protesters to what would become the national anthem of the Movement. When the students were worried about the flagging spirits of activists, Carawan told them about an old union song which may have originated as a late 19th-century spiritual, *If In My Heart, I Do Not Yield, / I Will Overcome Some Day,* which was changed to 'we' either during a 1909 strike of mine workers or by the Food and Tobacco Workers Union in South Carolina in 1947. Picketers from the 1947 strike taught it to Zilphia Horton at Highlander Folk School and later she taught Carawan. It has been argued that outside the Movement it was hardly known, but it was sung at every march or protest and heard by many thousands on television, especially the millions who viewed the 250,000 black and white people holding hands and singing it at the March on Washington. In fact, *We Shall Overcome* proved that music was a powerful force that united and strengthened the Movement in a way no one had expected. The queen of gospel, Mahalia Jackson, recorded it. It later inspired many other people struggling for a just world in countries such as South Africa, France, Japan, Northern Ireland and China.

Bernice Reagon, an SNCC worker, accepted Carawan and Pete Seeger's proposal to form a group to spread the word to the wider American community and raise funds for the Movement. The Freedom Singers were born but the spiritual–labour songs they sang underwent changes and, like gospel, lines could be added by anyone in the demonstration or march. In Birmingham a young boy added the lines: 'We are not afraid / We are not afraid today / Deep in our hearts / We are not afraid today.' Later Reagon was approached by five black women who established Sweet Honey In The Rock, who still perform concerts promoting civil rights and who stress feminism and black consciousness. The bonding created by music was instinctively understood by Fanny Lou Hamer whose gospel singing thrilled the often dispirited, troubled and endangered activists. Mrs Hamer would stand and sing and re-ignite their determination. Her favourite was *This Little Light of Mine*. But her inspirational leadership really started in 1964 during the Freedom Summer.

And despite what some music critics say, the Movement's music was crossing over to the new generation of white urban folk singers. For example, Bob Dylan's first recording reflected the younger generation's opposition to nuclear weapons. He soon picked up the racial injustice in the United States. *A Pawn in the Game* was performed at a Greenwood, Mississippi voter registration drive and is about the murder of NAACP worker Medgar Evers. The poor white man, the 'pawn' who pulled the trigger, is a product of the racism of America. Although it was released in 1964, he recorded it in 1963 and it was very popular with both black and white record buyers.

Murders and Mounting Resistance

Some argue that the Freedom Riders' success in challenging the conscience of many Americans and the introduction of a weak Civil Rights Bill proved that Robert Kennedy had a good appreciation of African American grievances. But there were concessions to appease segregationists that failed and the racist violence continued. On 15 September, three weeks after the March on Washington, four young black girls were murdered when the Sixteenth Street Baptist Church in Birmingham was bombed. This was the deadliest attack of seven bombings in the city in the previous six months, or the previous 17 from 1956. Phil Ochs, the civil rights and anti-war protest singer, drew on country-style music and captured the mood after the bombing with his *Here's to the Land of Mississippi*, repeating the line 'Mississippi find yourself another land to be part of'. The barbarity of the murder of little girls preparing for Sunday school disgusted the nation and pressured the Administration to arrest the people involved. Few were bothered that two young black men had been shot and killed moments after the bombing.

The FBI knew from KKK informants who was responsible but Hoover argued they could do nothing because they did not have the authority to investigate; in reality he did not want to upset local police (O'Reilly, 1994). It was not until 1977, after the *New York Times* and Los Angeles *Times* went to the Justice Department threatening to publicise FBI non-cooperation, that the truth was discovered. The documents released proved that Robert Chambliss, a notorious bomber, had planted the bomb. He was convicted for the murders. The Bureau did not release their tape recordings of Klan meetings and it was almost 38 years after the killings that Thomas Blanton was sentenced on four counts of murder. As *Newsweek* reported, it was belated inadequate justice, and 'broader accountability [was] non-existent. But the Blanton conviction is not reconciliation, but relief that he was not set free and weary resignation' (14 May 2001). This 'weary resignation' was reflected in the remarks of Birmingham mayor Bernard Kincaid, after the trial of Blanton's accomplice and fellow Klansman, Bobby Frank Cherry, who was also found guilty of murder and sentenced to life in prison in May 2002. Kincaid hoped the city would 'put the infamous chapter behind us and turn our attention to the future' (nbc.news.org, 22 May 2002). The 86-year-old Blanton asked for parole because he wanted 'to die a free man' and it took the state parole board 86 seconds to deny him his request (CNN.com, 3 August 2016). By 2002 many Americans shared Kincaid's longing to forget the past and the deaths of four black girls and their killers Chambliss, Blanton and Cherry.

Even at the time of the bombings, southern politicians were content to remind white southerners of the Civil War and the pro-slavery appeal to interposition and nullification. Governors re-enacted the drama at schools and universities but its most effective exponent was Governor George Wallace of Alabama who stood in the doorway of the state university and fuelled the violence because he had vowed to keep in place 'segregation now, segregation forever'. Wallace saw his opportunity: 'the very notion of couching the confrontation as a constitutional issue was precisely in keeping with Wallace's strategy: an abstract struggle between "states rights" and the "central government"' (Carter, 1995).

The Mississippi Sovereignty Commission (MSC), like other southern committees, spied not only on southerners but also on northerners they considered dangerous to their way of life. The great black photographer of the Movement, Ernest Withers from Memphis, Tennessee, was an MSC and FBI informer. The Commission, who were entirely committed to maintaining segregation, 'even inspected a 2-month-old baby to determine if it was part black' (Chicago *Tribune*, 7 June 1998). Even though the president knew nothing of this spying, JFK did not want a repeat of the violence at Ole Miss and this enabled Wallace to use his pro-slavery argument to stoke fear and bigotry in the North (Sugrue, 2004; Jones, 2009). He persuaded many that Movement opponents were not racists but defenders of the Constitution. In the short term, however, his intransigence meant that JFK accepted the need for legislation and gave a powerful television address in which he promised to send a Civil Rights Bill to Congress (Dallek, 2003). Seconds after he had finished speaking a shot rang out in the humid Mississippi night in Jackson and Mrs Medgar Evers found her husband, the head of the state NAACP, dying on the front porch (Garrow, 1988). His killing drove many black people to despair and anger, captured by Nina Simone in her *Mississippi Goddam*, which was a return to the Delta Blues. She sang: 'Lord have mercy on this land of mine / We all gonna get it in due time.' The southern radio stations destroyed the record, preferring not to acknowledge their growing isolation.

The violence that southern politicians had encouraged, and which the FBI had done nothing to stop, was aided by the general indifference of northern newspapers and network television. It was in this climate of fear and hatred that JFK went to Dallas, Texas. The assassination of the young president plunged the nation into mourning and into a period of great uncertainty. And African Americans and their liberal white allies grew increasingly worried about the obvious popularity of the conservative Republican Barry Goldwater of Arizona and Alabamian George Wallace. There were dire predictions that if the supporters of these two joined forces, the United States was on the brink of becoming a fascist state.

4

Triumphs and Tragedies: LBJ, the Great Society and the Limits of Liberalism 1963–1968

As Lyndon Baines Johnson (LBJ) took the oath of office on Air Force One shortly after the announcement of the president's death, Jacqueline Kennedy stood near him in her pink bloodstained suit. The Texan had fought her husband for the 1960 Democratic nomination and had stunned political pundits when he agreed to be the vice-presidential candidate. The scene of a grieving wife whose husband had been assassinated was something that Movement people knew well, like the death of Medgar Evers whose killer, Byron De La Beck, was convicted only in 1994. His would not be the last death of those in the Movement. There are parallels with 1945 following FDR's death. Truman was little known and distrusted. Although his achievements for African Americans were limited, he was the first president to openly attack the evils of discrimination. Many remembered the uncertainty after FDR's death. Now they must cope not with the sudden death of the president but with a president's assassination. The next five years would see important triumphs and tragedies but at that moment African Americans worried about the accidental president. Would he be true to his region or their supporter?

For some in the Movement the 1963 union of black activists with white liberalism had its dangers. 'The central dilemma of the first stage of the black freedom movement emerged: the existence and sustenance of the civil rights movement neither needed nor required white aid and allies, yet its success required white liberal support in the Democratic Party, Congress and the White House' (West, 1993). Another sees JFK, a traditional conservative politician, unwittingly 'aroused among millions a dormant desire to perfect America' thus becoming the 'reluctant champion of Martin Luther King ... Only later, during Lyndon Johnson's term as President would the limits of liberal goodwill become apparent and the flaws of liberal reform be exposed' (Matusow, 1986). Revisionists gloss over the doubts that liberal goodwill existed in 1963 and others deny that young black protesters wanted white liberal support. Others fail to acknowledge the activists' sacrifices and courage forced presidents and many others to believe that the American Dream was not an illusion. The current majority opinion is that 1960s liberalism not only failed to achieve its limited goals but also harmed the United States and the people it sought to help. For revisionists government does not have social responsibility – the poor are poor because they lack the will to succeed.

As vice president, LBJ championed ultra-conservative judicial appointments, increasing his critics' fears (Navasky, 1971), but JFK had done the same. However, his assassination and his 1963 Civil Rights Bill encouraged many to consider him a liberal. The legislation would grant Justice Department powers to file desegregation suits to overcome resistance to school desegregation in the South and North. Discrimination in public places was to be illegal. JFK also wanted to cut federal funds to discriminatory state programmes. A narrow majority of Americans supported his stand but a 1963 Harris poll showed that of the 6.5 million who voted for him in 1960, 4.5 million would not have done so in 1964 because of civil rights (Bernstein, 1991). Many of the disillusioned were urban white working class such as in Detroit (Sugrue, 2005) and Milwaukee. As in many northern cities, politicians exploited local fears (Jones, 2009).

The Civil Rights Act 1964

The proposal was resisted because many Americans believed it would destroy their way of life (Sugrue, 2005; Jones, 2009). But Johnson initially overcame the doubters' fears and the Civil Rights Act has rightly been 'heralded as one of the greatest achievements of LBJ's administration'. Segregation was banned in all public facilities. It also 'raised the issue of "public" versus "private"'. And 'the Administration supported the view that any privately-owned enterprise that accepted tax-payer's funds or business was "public"' (Anderson, 1995). Private companies that discriminated could be denied federal funds. LBJ's strategic role had always been to reassure civil rights leaders, and the NAACP and the Urban League trusted him to get it passed (Wood, 2006; Sugrue, 2008). The same was true for union leaders, especially Walter Reuther of the United Auto Workers (UAW) union (Beschloss, 1997). Johnson had supported the bill as vice president and had given speeches in favour, knowing many bitterly opposed it – an opposition increased by civil rights supporters' demonstrations.

Robert Kennedy, for some, played an important role in persuading Senate Republican leader Everett Dirksen to win votes (Graham, 1994), but LBJ, a master Senate manipulator, would not have asked for Robert's advice. Johnson said the Ivy Leaguers 'don't know any more about Capitol Hill than an old maid does about fuckin'' (Woods, 2006). His plan to win bipartisan support was outlined to Assistant Attorney General Norbert Schlei in June 1963 before JFK's death (Woods, 2006). LBJ 'did a masterful job of using the publicity powers of the presidency to press for a Civil Rights Bill' and he knew the danger posed by demagogues like George Wallace (Graham, 1994), and used the governor's resistance to win over the doubters. He appealed to black leaders to avoid protests because they would undermine his efforts to build a majority. But mainly he wanted northern political support: 'He would have to run for re-election in 1964, and he had less than a year to convince northern and western liberals that a southerner was an acceptable leader of the national Democratic party' (Caro, 2012). This assumption that all liberals existed in the North and that they supported the legislation is an overstatement (Sugrue, 2005). Critics ignore the fact that LBJ's legislation was much stronger than Kennedy's proposal. Johnson won an historic first when he created a two-thirds vote to stop a filibuster.

In his 1964 State of the Union address he said: 'As far as the writ of federal law will run, we must abolish not some but all racial discrimination. For this is not merely an economic question – or a social, political or international issue. It is a moral issue and must be met.' He linked civil rights to his battle against international communism. 'Today Americans of all races stand side by side in Berlin and Vietnam. They died side by side in Korea. Surely they can work and eat and travel side by side in their own country' (PBS, National Experience archive). Johnson shared some of his fellow southerners' prejudices, but he was motivated by a genuine desire for social justice. 'With the single exception of Lincoln, he was the greatest champion with a white skin that they had in the history of the Republic. He was to become the lawmaker for the poor and downtrodden and oppressed' (Caro, 2012).

But most civil rights leaders declared the Act inadequate because it did not tackle the core problem of poverty. They ignored his address to Georgetown University graduates and seemed to have missed his State of the Union address: 'Unfortunately, many Americans live on the outskirts of hope – some because of their poverty, and some because of their color, and all too many because of both. Our task is to help replace their despair with opportunity … This administration today, here and now, declares unconditional war on poverty in America' (PBS, archive). This was what King, Randolph and Rustin were fighting for (Carter, 2009).

A consensus would become increasingly difficult and LBJ's ambition to complete the New Deal with his Great Society was defeated by the increasing opposition to him from King and young SNCC leaders as much as the war in Vietnam, a legacy of previous presidents. For someone who worried about national unity, he was dismayed that a few days after signing the Act, Harlem and Brooklyn in New York City, Rochester, New York and Jersey City, Paterson and Elizabeth, New Jersey were torn by riots (Johnson, 1971). And no one foresaw the rebellion against paternalism, for free speech and assembly at the University of California, Berkeley led by former CORE and SNCC activists. While conservatives and many liberals cheered his foreign policy, the former were determined to destroy his dream of completing the New Deal.

The Mississippi Freedom Democratic Party

For many civil rights supporters, such as UAW's Reuther, the overriding aim in 1964 was a Democratic Party victory under LBJ (Beschloss, 1997). The growing popularity of the Alabama governor in the North was worrying. In March 1964 'George Wallace's presidential campaign blew through Wisconsin like a tornado, churning up white reaction and sharpening racial tension across the state'. Some newspapers, business-men and especially blue-collar workers supported his denunciation of the Civil Rights Act. He told a cheering crowd in Milwaukee, 'if he ever had to leave Alabama, "I'd want to live on the South Side of Milwaukee"' (Jones, 2009). He did well in primaries in Indiana and Maryland which later prompted him to run as an independent in 1968. An equally out-spoken opponent of the Act was Arizona Senator Barry Goldwater who was seeking the Republican nomination.

SNCC struggled to register voters in Mississippi. Mrs Fanny Lou Hamer, the youngest of 20 children of black sharecroppers in Sunflower County, had never known she had the right to vote (Asch, 2008). She attended a meeting and volunteered to register. She said: 'The only thing they could do to me was kill me and it seemed to me like they had been trying to do that a little bit at a time ever since I could remember.' She and her husband were dismissed from Senator James Eastland's plan-tation but, with her husband's support, she persisted in her efforts to register despite a brutal beating that left her permanently injured (Asch, 2008). She joined SNCC in 1963 and went for training with SCLC in Charleston, South Carolina (Mills, 2007). SNCC and Hamer fought to bring democracy to the most undemocratic state in the Union and their arch enemy, Eastland, fought them using their language of freedom but combined with the dangers of race-mixing and black men raping white women (Asch, 2008). Mrs Hamer knew about 'mongeralization'; her grandmother had been raped by many white men and most of her children were born because of these assaults (Lee, 2000).

Undaunted by Eastland's demagoguery, men and women, black and white, participated in the South Carolina Voter Education Project headed by Septima Clark. In 1964, Wendy Samstein, a white student volunteer, observed: 'There was no relief from [the daily and brutal confrontation] there was no outrage ... when Negroes were beaten and killed. Nobody seems to care about that, nobody seemed to give a damn' (Ransbury, 2003). Margaret Madrid, in California, congratulated the editor of the San Francisco *Chronicle* for publishing an article using her daughter's letters, written from her jail cell for teaching at Greenwood Freedom

School. She tells the editor he has left out (or censored) two key paragraphs she was positive her daughter wanted published. 'Sunday night a local Negro was killed in Quitman County about 200 miles north of Greenwood, but I haven't seen anything about it in the press. Also last Saturday a Negro was found with his head cut off in Monticello, down in Lawrence County.' There was no investigation, no FBI agents, and no arrests (San Francisco *Chronicle*, 18 July 1964). Rabbi Ben-Ami was dismissed by Temple B'nai Israel for supporting the Movement and Anne Braden offered to send him a copy of the *Southern Patriot* in a plain envelope because her name and address 'might hurt you in some way' (University of Southern Mississippi, digital library (USMDL), 15 October 1964).

The Movement in Mississippi formed an umbrella organisation called the Council of Federated Organizations (COFO) to overcome organisational disputes. Robert Moses, a New York student, was elected director of voter registration and NAACP's Aaron Henry president. They concentrated on the highest areas of black population and White Citizens Council (WCC) resistance (Hamer interview, USMDL). Julian Bond recalled that: 'The biggest change in SNCC came in '63–'64 when we decided to build political organizations as well as just try to get people to register to vote' (Stoper, 1989). Although he did not oppose SNCC's efforts, Stokely Carmichael, a recent graduate of Howard University, was not very enthusiastic and later demanded it should change (Joseph, 2014).

The Freedom Summer registered voters and intended to send delegates to represent Mississippi at the Democratic Convention by establishing the interracial Mississippi Freedom Democratic Party (MFDP) at a rally in Jackson at which Charles Cobb suggested recruiting white northern students (Carson, 1981). MFDP would force LBJ and the nation to make a moral choice. On 13 June the first volunteers started training at Western College for Women in Ohio. Oxford, Ohio was a paradise compared with Oxford, Mississippi. David Denis, Moses' assistant, recalled ten years later: 'We knew that if we brought a thousand blacks, the country would have watched them slaughtered without doing anything about it. Bring in a thousand whites and the country is going to react.' As Denis admitted it was SNCC's 'sorta cold' assessment that a white college student's death would focus 'more attention to what was going on than for a black student getting it' (Raines, 1977).

Eight days later two whites did 'get it'. Three COFO workers left Meridian, Mississippi to investigate the burning of a black church. They disappeared. James Chaney a black organiser, and Michael Schwerner, a CORE member, along with Alan Goodman, one of the first Ohio volunteers, were reported missing to the Justice Department (Mills, 2007). The FBI response was typical. SNCC staffer Bob Zellner, a white student from Alabama, recalled agents' behaviour in McComb, Mississippi when rioters tried to gouge his eyes out. The Bureau took pictures and one assured Zellner that he had not been alone; the agent had taken notes. 'I realized they were a bunch of gutless automatons ... This guy thought it would *comfort* me to let me know that he was out there recording my death' (Morrison and Morison, 1983).

Prior to the disappearance of Chaney, Schwerner and Goodman, there had been over 150 cases of violence and intimidation against Movement workers and local black residents who supported them. The federal authorities failed to act on any of them. The young California woman's letter from the Mississippi jail summed it up: 'But if those dead men were white as are the boys missing in Nashoba County something would be done.' Americans only cared about the white volunteers, and when they left she wondered if national concern about conditions in the South would end. 'This summer will not only show Mississippi in its true colors to the people of the nation, but this summer will show the colors of this nation to the world' (San Francisco *Chronicle*, 18 July 1964).

She was right. The men's disappearance 'immediately focused national attention on the Summer Project' (Carson, 1981). But the national authorities did not act despite appeals from the parents of Goodman and Schwerner to Robert Kennedy. Twenty-four incidents occurred between 21 and 26 June after FBI agents arrived in Mississippi, and a further 39 including bombings and shootings between 26 June and 10 July (*The Student Voice*, 3 June and 15 July 1964). Dr Israel Zwerling wrote to Kennedy about his son's brutal treatment (Zwerling to Kennedy, 13 July 1964, UMDL). There was no response. The first bodies found were of Charles Moore, a student and Henry Ezekiah Dee both murdered by the Klan. It took the Canadian Broadcasting Company and Moore's brother to solve the murder in 2005 and not until 2007 was one of the killers, James Ford Seale, convicted (CBC, 'Mississippi Cold Case', documentary, 11 February 2007).

It was later alleged that a black man who spied for the Mississippi Sovereignty Commission had accompanied the men from Ohio and gave the Commission their car details and licence plate number. The files, full of his spying on people, meetings and planned actions, were passed to WCC and the KKK. He was never arrested or questioned. A British television documentary, 'Murder in Mississippi', investigated the identity of Agent X, and claimed that he was J. R. Bolden from Canton, the state vice president of the NAACP (Secret History, Channel 4, 1991).

The federal government eventually searched for the missing men and drafted in 200 naval personnel, Justice Department officials and 150 FBI men. They found the bodies of nine murdered black men and none were investigated. After paying informers, the civil rights workers' bodies were found on 4 August in an earth-filled dam near the town of Philadelphia (Carson, 1981). Ella Baker told MFDP delegates: 'The symbol of Mississippi politics lies in these three bodies that were dug from the earth this week' (Mills, 2007). Twenty men, including the sheriff of Nashoba County, were arrested and charged for the murders by the state. This was gesture politics. It took three years to convict and imprison seven for depriving the victims of their civil rights. But although bitter and angry, CORE leaders in 1964 did not want to do anything that might help Goldwater or Wallace, and James Farmer assured administration officials there would be no trouble at Johnson's meeting in Syracuse, New York.

Englishman Alan Parker directed a travesty of the events in a film called *Mississippi Burning* (1988) which treats the events as southerners imagined the course of post-Civil War Reconstruction. A northern Justice Department official (Carpetbagger) drives a southern FBI man (Redeemer) to investigate the murders. The Yankee bungles everything and alienates the white locals. The FBI man and his fellow southerners understand the South and will ensure justice. A black agent, when none were in the FBI, threatens to castrate the mayor and make him swallow his own testicles (the KKK had done that to a black man). The case solved, the Redeemer drives the Scallywag out of the South. All black people are ignored. The only powerful image is a broken headstone on James Chaney's grave, smashed by locals because the film was made.

The killings increased. SNCC challenged regular state delegates, confident the MFDP interracial, pro-LBJ slate would replace the old order (*The Student Voice*, 5–19 August, 1964). Ella Baker later said she had never been optimistic but was hopeful because LBJ needed black support. SNCC and their allies lobbied hard. Initially, King, Randolph, the UAW, the ADA and the NAACP supported the MFDP (Ransbury, 2003). But that faded. Andrew Young admits he considered the Mississippi project as 'unnecessarily dangerous' because Movement workers had no protection, rural people were too practical to support such a scheme and northern radicals abused the students' idealism and manipulated local black leaders. He admits the MFDP 'did transform politics in Mississippi, by planting the seeds that would be harvested later' (Young, 1996). Stokely Carmichael was also sceptical (Joseph, 2014). At the convention MFDP's allies deserted them, even Reuther of the UAW (Beschloss, 1998). Hubert Humphrey pressured MFDP to accept two delegates – Aaron Henry of the NAACP and Reverend Ed King, white chaplain of Tougaloo College. LBJ knew the hazards of being too closely identified with King (Miller Centre, University of Virginia, tape recording LBJ to George Reedy, 4 July 1964).

LBJ 'pretended to negotiate' with the MFDP (Young, 1996) but listened to southern Democrats. Texan John Connolly warned: 'If those baboons walk onto the convention floor we walk out.' Moses' biographer points out: 'The Administration and the party at this juncture lay bare their inability to understand not only the moral premise on which the creation of the MFDP rested but also the very real dangerous and physical battle the delegates had fought to get there' (Burner, 1994). Humphrey's appeasement proved costly in his presidential bid. Johnson does not refer to the MFDP in his autobiography, only the cheering delegates (Johnson, 1971).

The SCLC, NAACP and Urban League urged the MFDP to accept Humphrey's compromise; only a coalition with unions and liberals would ensure significant reforms and force conservatives to leave the Party. The conservatives did and supported Goldwater (Jackson, 2007). But SNCC members felt betrayed and Alabama activist, John Lewis, told Andrew Young: 'Andy we have shed too much blood in Mississippi to accept a compromise … People were murdered in Philadelphia, and there is no punishment. When we try to register to vote, we get sent to jail, we are beaten, we are threatened. We can't back down, we've come too far' (Young, 1996). A SNCC member recalled Bob Moses saying: 'We are not here to bring politics into our morality but to bring morality into our politics.' Later Moses said it was not solely about race but rather the Democratic party was 'organized around the middle class … but we were challenging them on the existence of a whole group of people who are the underclass of this country, white and black, who are not represented' (Burner, 1994). But many of the white working class had a new hero and Wallace's appeal in the primaries made him a national figure and reflected the growing backlash against the Movement. For example, in Wisconsin he got 24.5 percent of the vote and in Milwaukee 31.3 percent (Jones, 2009).

The 1964 Campaign

Fortunately for Johnson and Humphrey, the Republicans were deeply divided. Barry Goldwater had opposed the Civil Rights Act and supported states rights. And his hawkish foreign policy ensured a Democratic landslide. Significantly the Democratic Party base in the South was crumbling. Three southern states – Arkansas, Florida and Tennessee – voted Republican, and LBJ won Virginia solely because of the African American vote. Only in his home state of Texas did the majority of whites support Johnson.

> The rejection of Negroes from the traditionally integrated Republican party, the lack of support the Democratic ticket received from local and state Democratic figures in the deep South, and the clear delineation of Senator Barry Goldwater's position favoring states rights and 'local option' of segregation all contributed toward a Democratic victory.
>
> (*The Student Voice*, 25 November 1964)

After the election, the MFDP challenged the seating of five congressmen. Those who testified were all women (Mills, 2007). Hamer's speech to the congressional committee was dramatic and widely reported but others were not, including the testimony of Mrs Annie Rankin who had worked with Mrs Hamer, and like her had been imprisoned and intimidated (Rankin USMDL, Tugaloo College). Their challenge failed and civil rights legislation depended on the remaining liberal Republicans (McAdam and Kloos, 2014). But liberal California governor Pat Brown lost to Ronald Reagan whose cry for 'law and order', following the 1965 Watts riot, ensured that racial politics would dominate the Republican Party. Goldwater's southern successes convinced many in the Party that supporting progressive reform was pointless. Liberal Republicans and Democrats were decimated in the 1966 elections. The Young Americans for Freedom urged their Party to keep faith in Goldwater and the southern resisters (*New Guard*, July 1965).

Selma

Once in the White House, LBJ was reluctant to seek more legislation preferring gradual southern compliance with the Civil Rights Act (Johnson, 1971). But after their brutal experiences, SNCC and SCLC volunteers were determined to force the issue. They decided on a showdown in Selma, Alabama. The nation would witness again the 'genteel South' rioting to perpetuate white supremacy – a region where, despite the efforts of Robert Moses and many others, only 6.4 percent of Mississippi African Americans were registered voters.

The situation was just as dire in Alabama. Selma had a 29,000 African American majority, but made up only 3 percent of the registered electorate. The sheriff of Dallas County, including Selma, was Jim Clark, a racist demagogue, who had attacked blacks often and especially during the registration efforts in 1963. Assisted by judges and indifferent federal officials, Clark emasculated the voting rights drive. SCLC's James Bevel wanted dramatic action and called on King to respond. He did not. Bevel and 15 black groups were determined to confront Clark and his paramilitary forces (nevri.com, accessed 4 February 2016) and defy the ban on marches and meetings to force the federal government to act.

Selma whites were divided. There were 'stupid racists' who backed Clark and 'smart segregationists' who supported Wilson Baker the Director of Public Safety. According to one: 'The trouble is too many of our people fear the white man more than they do the Negro and won't speak up against Clark' (*The Student Voice*, 26 March 1965). The 'smart' man, Baker, arrested American Nazi Party Leader, Lincoln Rockwell, but the 'stupid racist', Clark, arrested 67 blacks seeking to register. Six days later on February 4 startled whites saw a black woman knock him down twice after he hit her. Three deputies dragged Annie Lee Cooper to the ground; Clark sat on her stomach and clubbed her senseless. 'The sound of the clubbing could be heard through the crowd that had gathered in the street. By the next day the political echoes of the beating had resounded around the country' (Weisbrot, 1991). Clark continued to defy federal court rulings. Johnson instructed the new Attorney General, Nicholas Katzenbach, to draft legislation providing federal protection to those registering. With hundreds in jail, Clark imprisoned the men he believed were communist agitators: King and Abernathy. From his prison cell King wrote a letter addressed to the nation demanding federal voter registration protection.

'Bloody Sunday' and the March on Montgomery

Nearby towns held marches supporting the Selma campaign. On 18 February in Marion, state troopers shot and wounded Jimmie Lee Jackson who was protecting his mother and grandfather from the local police. He died six days later after being refused treatment at the whites-only Selma hospital. His death was just one of many not prosecuted, including a black Baltimore postman William Moore walking to Alabama to support the Selma activists. The 15 September 1963 bombing of the black 16th Street Baptist Church when four girls were blown to bits had caused outrage; but a day later the murders of 13-year-old Virgil Ware and 16-year-old Johnny Brown Robinson there were not investigated (*The Student Voice*, 26 March 1965). All these murders, and others, went unpunished, despite the black community's pleas for justice.

This sort of indifference makes 'Bloody Sunday' of 7 March 1965 inevitable. King planned a march from Selma to Montgomery to build mass support for LBJ's Voting Rights Act, that was endorsed by Republican Everett Dirksen. With King in Georgia, Hosea Williams of SCLC and John Lewis of SNCC led 600 from Selma's AME church towards the Edmund Pettus Bridge and were met by state troopers wearing Confederate battle flags, sheriff's deputies and mounted police armed with clubs and cattle prods. Clark said they had two minutes to return to the church – the troopers charged after one. John Lewis refused to retreat. They fractured his skull. Five women were also among the first to be beaten, including Amelia Boynton who was clubbed and tear-gassed. Clark unleashed his mounted forces who later joined a mob attacking people in the city's black section.

ABC television interrupted the film *Judgement at Nuremberg* to show the police riot to 49 million viewers. Most Americans were horrified but in Harlem and Philadelphia the response was different. Harlem youth called for Malcolm X to end non-violence and in Philadelphia, Pennsylvania white politicians exploited growing white resentment (Sugrue, 2009). But liberal senators, such as Republican Jacob Javits of New York, denounced the terror. LBJ recalled: 'The Alabama state troopers took matters into their own hands. With night-sticks, bullwhips and billy clubs, they scattered the ranks of the marchers ... The march was over. But the struggle had just begun' (Johnson, 1971); and for others, like Father Groppi in Milwaukee, it was a 'conversion experience' (Jones, 2009). But if some Americans were not outraged, it was a crucial turning point for the Movement with many younger members of SNCC eager to retaliate. As Julian Bond recalled, the problem with non-violence was that many African Americans in the Deep South 'carried guns for self-defense as a matter of custom' (Cobb, 2014). Non-violent activists realised they could only keep faith in their methods because they knew armed black people protected them.

King was alarmed and flew in from Atlanta and the divisions between him and most SNCC leaders were exposed. King chose to lead a symbolic march to the bridge and, as they approached, Clark's police and state troopers on the other side seemed to leave the road open (Carter, 1995). Cleveland Sellers and James Forman wanted King to advance. Abernathy recalled that SNCC workers 'felt betrayed' because King lacked courage: 'It was the first time that such an accusation would be made, though not the last. Soon, very soon, the advocates of violence would be saying that Martin was too timid to lead the movement, and then that he was too cowardly' (Abernathy, 1989). But King refused to defy a federal court injunction or to walk into Clark's trap and led the marchers back to the church.

Forman said the only reason they had not been attacked was because white folks were participating. Sellers, Forman and Stokely Carmichael were increasingly sceptical about non-violence, and bitter that violence against African Americans was virtually ignored whereas the slightest injury to white people was widely reported. It took an attack on four white Unitarian ministers to galvanise LBJ. The Reverend James Reeb of Boston, a 38-year-old father of four, was savagely beaten and died two days later in hospital (*The Student Voice*, 26 March 1965). Johnson immediately telephoned Mrs Reeb to express his sympathy. But Carmichael had sworn, after his arrest on the march to Montgomery, he would never be arrested again. At a meeting of cheering supporters he told them to stop begging for government help and rely on Black Power. 'Like a preacher standing before a flock of hungry parishioners, Carmichael began a rhythmic call and response. "We want Black Power!" he repeated five times in rapid succession' (Johnson, 2014).

But LBJ exacerbated the mounting divisions in the Movement by failing to send troops and, instead, he appealed to moderate leaders for peace to ensure passage of the Voting Rights Act (Caro, 2012). He appointed Bufford Ellington, former Tennessee governor and a member of his Administration, to contact George Wallace. He warned Ellington, 'you are dealing with a very treacherous guy' and 'he is a no-good son of a bitch' (Miller Center tape, LBJ to Ellington, 3 March 1965). At the White House meeting with Wallace, Johnson told him to stop living in 1865 and as Wallace tried to brazen it out LBJ demanded: 'Why are you fucking over your President?' (Woods, 2006). Wallace insisted he lacked the funds to protect the march authorised by federal Judge Frank Johnson. LBJ took Wallace into the Rose Garden and assured the press that the governor would protect American citizens. He returned to the Oval Office, federalised the state troopers and sent Ramsey Clark, the new Attorney General, to take charge. LBJ later rejected accusations that he had not done enough, and made a typical southern complaint: 'Once again my Southern heritage was thrown in my face. I was hurt, deeply hurt. But I was determined not to be shoved into hasty action' (Johnson, 1971).

When the marchers reached Montgomery, King assured them 'segregation is on its deathbed in Alabama' and concluded, perhaps answering his young critics, when it would happen:

> How long? Not long, because no lie can live forever.
> How long? Not long, because you still reap what you sow.
> How long? Not long, because the arm of the moral universe is long but bends towards justice.
>
> (Branch, 2007)

He closed his speech including lines from the Battle Hymn of the Republic: 'He hath loosed his fateful lightning / of his terrible swift sword.' The fateful lightning struck the next day when Mrs Viola Liuzzo was ferrying marchers back to Selma. A white woman driving with a black man, Leroy Moton, was breaking the most sacred belief of the southern code of 'honour'. She had been attacked several times that day and now a car sped past and three shots were fired. Mrs Liuzzo was killed. Moton stopped the car and tried to revive her. Her blood saved his life because when the assassins came to the car they assumed he was dead (Branch, 2007). FBI chief Hoover ordered agents to investigate her background, eager to find anything damaging. They found nothing. However, he told LBJ that Mrs Liuzzo was a drug addict and there were needle marks on her arms and informed Nicholas Katzenbach that 'she was sitting very, very close to the Negro in the car ... It had the appearance of a necking party' (Woods, 2006). Magazines *Time* and *Newsweek* published similar FBI slanders. Despite Hoover's lies, unlike most murders in Alabama, this one was solved because FBI informer Garry Rowe was riding with the killers.

While the consensus among SNCC, SCLC and CORE was breaking down, LBJ struggled to maintain unity with liberal Republicans and Democrats to meet the crisis. Initially reluctant to take precipitate action, he agreed with the congressional leaders to address a joint session on 15 March. It lifted him above a great tactical politician because he knew his promise would virtually destroy his beloved Democratic Party in the South (Cohen, 2016). However, he gained the status of a statesman. He linked the violence at Selma with the opening skirmishes of the American Revolution and the end of the Civil War. And then, 'in a Texas version of the southern Baptist rhythm and tenor Martin Luther King had mastered' (Woods, 2006), Johnson stated: 'There is no issue of state rights or national rights. There is only the struggle for human rights … Their cause must be our cause too. Because it is not just Negroes, but it is all of us who must overcome the crippling legacy of bigotry and injustice.' He closed with the Movement anthem: 'And … we … shall … overcome' (Johnson, 1971).

The 1965 Voting Rights Act

Four months later, on 6 August 1965, Johnson signed the Voting Rights Act. It was the vindication of a struggle that had seen so much violence, death and brutality. But the strain between the civil rights leaders and the man from Texas was evident at this ceremony. It was not King's earlier anti-war speech but rather James Forman of CORE whom LBJ virtually snubbed at the signing ceremony perhaps because of CORE's central role in the confrontation. Julian Bond said in 1968: 'The '64 and '65 Civil Rights Acts took the pressure off the country. People weren't concerned about civil rights because they figured they'd done what they should do for it' (Stoper, 1989). LBJ confirms this: 'With the passage of the Civil Rights Acts of 1964 and 1965 the barriers to freedom began tumbling down. At long last the legal rights of American citizens – the right to vote, to hold a job, to enter a public place, to go to school – were given protection' (Johnson, 1971). These arguments meant it was difficult to enforce desegregation. Mississippi Senator John Stennis called for countrywide desegregation hoping 'it would spark a broader, national backlash … that would provide relief for white southerners' (Crespino, 2007). But even though school desegregation was initially successful in the South, little was achieved in most northern cities. Milwaukee and Detroit remained largely segregated partly because of suburbanisation and claims that schools should be for neighbourhood children only (Jones, 2009; Sugrue, 2009). Many still view the struggle as solely against segregation and for voting rights.

However, strong federal oversight of voter registration and the abolition of the poll tax and literacy tests ensured major change in the South. For example, in Mississippi the percentage of black voters rose from 6 to 59. Southern black voter numbers tripled and for the first time African Americans were elected sheriffs and education board members and eventually state representatives. LBJ hoped that once African Americans had the vote all parties would need their support (Woods, 2006; Crespino, 2007). He told John Lewis to register black voters. 'You've got to go back and get those boys by the balls' if he wanted to overcome massive resistance (Berman, 2015).

Like Randolph, Rustin and King, LBJ knew it was more than voting or hotel accommodation – the root problem was economic. He addressed Howard University students and declared: 'You do not take a person who, for years, has been hobbled by chains and liberate him, bring him to the start line of a race, and then say you are free to compete with others.' It was 'not just equality as a right and a theory but equality as a fact and equality as a result' (Carter, 2009). He sought to emulate his hero FDR but go further and wipe out poverty that affected more whites than blacks. He pushed through Medicare for older people and Medicaid for those below the poverty line. To help end hunger he introduced a food stamp programme, provided for training schemes and increased the federal government's role in affirmative action and education. Initially many social schemes were run by local activists but state politicians worried that they were losing patronage and forced out the volunteers (Woods, 2006). The billions appropriated provided considerable help for all the poor, despite later cuts. Liberal and radical activists wrongly critiqued the Great Society as the Great Sham. As the conservative backlash mounted, encouraged by politicians, especially George Wallace, the word 'welfare' became a euphemism for lazy black people, even though it overwhelmingly benefited the white population and the elderly (Cohen, 2016).

Politicians and scholars have often tended to deride the liberal response to the Movement challenge. This continuing assault on 1960s reforms and its counterculture ignores 'the deep roots in the simmering politics of race and neighborhood in the North well before the 1960s' (Sugrue, 2005). Although LBJ and the Movement's actions exacerbated these long-term prejudices, the stridency of these attacks on the central government's role, the persistent attempts to weaken or kill the Voting Rights Act (now aided by the Supreme Court) and the determination to dismantle the Great Society programmes that benefited the poor and vulnerable (Mayer, 2016) suggest that the liberals of the 1960s were more successful than their detractors acknowledge. Despite setbacks, segregation and denial of the vote, especially in the South, was eroded. In 11 southern states more than 430,000 blacks were registered voters in 1966. 'It was', one South Carolinian observed, 'an expression of the will to citizenship and responsibility of the mass of Negro Southerners – the underlying strength of the people that had given rise to the movement' (Watters, 1971).

In 1965 a white woman was murdered because a black man was a passenger in her car but 30 years later an African American wrote a book to explain to his children that before the Civil Rights Act they would not have been allowed to stay in the same hotel as their mother (Gates, 1995). He says nothing about their parents' interracial marriage which was unlawful in many states despite the Supreme Court ruling in *Loving v. Virginia* (1967). The southern honour code was too powerful. Alabama waited until 2000 to repeal its ban.

Civil Rights and the Anti-Vietnam War Movement

Despite long-term gains, US intervention in Vietnam increased tensions with LBJ and within the Movement. Howard Zinn, SNCC member and history professor, criticised NAACP's Roy Wilkins, CORE's James Farmer and SNCC's members for their silence. 'Movement people are perhaps in the best position to know just how immoral are this nation's actions in Vietnam … They understand just how much hypocrisy is wrapped up in our claim to stand for the "free world" … SNCC always prided itself on a special honesty, on not playing it "safe" … Shouldn't it now say, at this crucial moment, that FREEDOM NOW must be international' (*The Student Voice*, 30 August 1965).

After Zinn posed the question 'Should civil rights workers take a stand on Vietnam?', King urged LBJ to stop the bombing and seek negotiations. King was concerned that the Great Society programmes would be underfunded, especially because Johnson refused to increase taxes to pay for the war. But LBJ had used a lot of political capital winning his reforms. He wanted to be the first president to achieve true justice, equality and end poverty but he was equally determined not to be the first president to lose a war. His tenacity undermined his authority. It has been claimed such a balancing act was impossible and was the major cause of the collapse of liberalism (Cohen, 2016).

King privately urged Johnson to change his Vietnam policy but did not want to lead anti-war protests and left that to the Students for a Democratic Society (SDS). The SDS included sit-ins and teach-ins that they had learnt from the Movement. King was silent on the war because he wanted action to solve the dire problems of the inner cities. However, by 1967 he realised that LBJ would fight on. It was King, not Johnson, who broke off relations and King refused invitations to the White House, forcing the president to rely on the advice of NAACP's Roy Wilkins. LBJ saw King's speeches as unfair criticism of his Great Society that had particularly helped African Americans.

King Goes to Chicago

At Northwestern University, SCLC's James Bevel, two weeks after Selma, said they intended to 'close down' Chicago in 1966. Five months later King and Andrew Young worked with the city's Coordinating Council of Community Organizations. Most historians judge their efforts a humiliating defeat. '[W]hite exclusiveness was an unshakeable reality, [and] to confront it head-on, from a position of political isolation was self-defeating.' It resulted in white liberals questioning 'the viability of nonviolent tactics' (Fairclough, 2001). It was also poor timing after major disturbances in Cleveland, Atlanta and San Francisco.

Certainly, challenging Chicago Mayor Richard Daley meant SCLC was fighting one of the most powerful men in the Democratic Party and threatened the liberal desire for consensus. Johnson needed Irish

Americans' support and Daley had black precinct workers who opposed the civil rights establishment. The fight against Chicago's housing discrimination added to the racist backlash. There was a similar, if less violent, response to Father Groppi and the Young Commandos' efforts in Milwaukee (Jones, 2009).

As King led the marchers through Gage Park white residents, infuriated by attempts to integrate their neighbourhood, screamed they were 'cannibals', 'savages' and 'niggers'. One sign read: 'The only way to stop niggers is to exterminate them.' Daley told King to go back to Georgia. The veteran of many southern struggles told the press that he had never seen as much hatred and hostility on the part of so many people (Oates, 1994.) The city's long history of racism meant the scenes were reminiscent of the riots of 1919. A *New York Times* reporter said: 'I think the people from Mississippi ought to come to Chicago to learn hate' (Roberts and Kilbanoff, 2006). Daley resorted to police violence used by southerners but combined force with gestures. He proposed a poverty programme for Chicago that enlarged his patronage in the black community and this kept their votes.

King's challenge fuelled massive resistance, something that Chicago liberals and his close advisors, Rustin and Levison, feared. Part of the political fallout was that Senator Paul Douglas, an open housing supporter, was defeated by Republican Charles Percy in that year's US senate election. George Wallace gained more popularity in Milwaukee and Wisconsin. The Chicago Catholic church was deeply divided with the archbishop not liking King and a white supremacist priest elected city alderman.

The Chicago Freedom Movement did make very small gains. SCLC received $4 million from Housing and Urban Development which helped rehabilitate some housing. Community groups were aided and worked effectively for many years, including Jesse Jackson's Operation Breadbasket. The Office of Education awarded $100,000 grant to improve the skills of Lawndale residents. But the violence of the Daley machine and the poor federal response convinced most African Americans and liberals that reforming the city was impossible. But the Movement had a long-term effect. In 1983 black voters and their liberal supporters of 1966 elected African American Harold Washington as mayor (Ralph, 1993).

The FBI and Martin Luther King

The SCLC in Chicago, and in cities such as Milwaukee, Detroit and Cleveland, faced institutional racism which confirmed King's views that the roots of racism were economic. Chicago radicalised him and he stressed the need for Christian Socialism (Jackson, 2007). Nationally, African Americans and poor whites fought each other for scraps from the table. Ella Baker did not appreciate fully how much they shared the same economic vision (Olson, 2003). King's socialism took him further from the liberals and confirmed to Hoover that civil rights workers, campus activists and anti-war protestors were communists.

Hoover organised a massive counter-intelligence programme (COINTELPRO) to infiltrate all groups he considered unpatriotic. This involved unauthorised wiretaps, break-ins into offices, homes and doctors' clinics (known as 'black-bag jobs'), and infiltration and payment of informers. Other methods included sending letters to Black Panthers and other radicals claiming someone was a police spy or their partners were having sex with an associate. Hoover had protected KKK terrorists, such as the bombers of the 16th Street Baptist Church, but he was eager to discredit civil rights organisations and back nationalists. He revealed to the press that Bayard Rustin was a convicted homosexual and asserted he was formerly a communist labour leader with continuing 'Red' associates (D'Emilio, 2003). Ironically, one FBI target, A. Philip Randolph, contacted them in the 1930s because a Garveyite had sent him a black man's hand through the post. The FBI did reply but added Randolph to their spying (FBI reports, microfilm, Ulster University).

Black congressman Adam Clayton Powell supported Hoover, claiming that King and Rustin were sexual partners, and forced Rustin's resignation from the SCLC (D'Emilio, 2003). But King continued to work with Rustin and considered him a friend despite pressure from supporters who were concerned that the media would use these charges to destroy him (Garrow, 1988). Roy Wilkins fed Hoover's paranoia about King, SCLC and CORE members. When FBI documents were released years later, Wilkins angrily denied he had collaborated in Hoover's plans to smear King.

Hoover described King as a 'notorious liar' shortly after it was announced in 1964 that King had been awarded the Nobel Peace Prize. William Sullivan, assistant director of the Bureau, wrote and sent an unsigned letter in which he called King 'a dissolute, abnormal, moral imbecile' who was guilty of 'incredible evilness'. King was urged to commit suicide: 'You are done. There is but one way out for you. You better take it before your filthy, abnormal fraudulent self is bared to the nation' (Garrow, 1988). The FBI reports of King's infidelity were true but it is claimed many have glossed this over (Chappell, 2014) but that is incorrect. But with so many threats it is hardly surprising that African Americans had little faith in the FBI or an administration that seemed to have forgotten their shared concern about poverty. Instead, they were accused of fomenting trouble and LBJ was unaware of the pending violence. Presidential assistants visited major cities in the North and West and were oblivious of the dangers. After staying in Detroit in May 1967 they failed to discover any evidence that the situation was dire. A massive riot occurred two months after they left. They knew nothing about armed Black Panthers in Oakland, California or the Panthers' efforts to help people in Watts.

Malcolm X, Black Power and the Black Panther Party

The Nation of Islam and Malcolm X

Many younger black people believed southern white resistance was succeeding and non-violence was pointless but did not understand that self-defence had always had an important role. The Louisiana Deacons for Defence and Freedom provided armed support after James Meredith was assassinated on his march from Memphis to Montgomery (Fairclough, 1999; Cobb, 2014). The Deacons and other armed groups protected Movement workers who faced beatings and death, and imprisonment in jails such as the notorious Parchment, Mississippi and Angola, Louisiana. And the most charismatic man to challenge the SCLC's faith in non-violence was Malcolm Little.

Malcolm's parents, Earl and Louise Little, were members of Marcus Garvey's 1920s black nationalist movement. They were driven out of Omaha, Nebraska in 1929, and from Lansing, Michigan when whites torched their home. Malcolm's claim that his father was lynched cannot be substantiated or that Garveyism influenced Malcolm. He was involved in petty crime, then robbery and graduated into drug abuse and pimping. In prison he met a member of the Nation of Islam (NOI), widely known as Black Muslims, was converted and changed his 'slave name', Little, to Malcolm X (Marable, 2011).

The NOI was founded in 1930 in Chicago by Wallace Fard and was investigated by the FBI in the early 1940s. That continues. Despite surveillance and misinformation, the Nation in the 1950s grew in the northern cities. Their religious views were based mainly on Elijah Muhammad's teachings that Allah made people black and an evil chemist and his followers' experiments created the white devil race. Allah swore that the devils would enslave blacks but at judgement time whites would be destroyed (Essien-Udom, 1964). It has been suggested that Malcolm X used 'vituperative language against whites [but] that did not mean he hated whites or he was trying to make blacks hate them. Rather his purpose was to wake up blacks that they needed to love each other' (Cone, 1993).

Whatever his intentions, his demands for segregation angered not only many white liberals but also the majority in the Movement. He said their tactics and goals were a waste of time and their hope for justice from a white man's government was folly. As early as 1960 he debated with Bayard Rustin on radio station WBAI New York and distanced the NOI from black nationalists. His insisted he and Rustin shared the same aim but wanted to achieve it differently. 'We say the only way is the religious approach; this is why we stress the importance of moral regeneration.' Rustin easily proved that the vast majority of blacks wanted to be equals within American society and that political participation would ensure the national and state governments would legislate to ensure equality. The NOI had and would never achieve anything (Marable, 2011). But the radio debate did not feature anti-Jewish attacks that Jews were 'Christ-killers' – central to Black Muslims' beliefs and shared by other black and cultural nationalists such as Ron Karenga and LeRoi Jones and fundamentalist Christians (Amiri Baraka). Later these opinions severely damaged Jewish support for the Movement. Segregation or integration? The Muslims' call for total segregation was espoused by the members of the Republic of New Africa who demanded that five states of the South should be handed over to black people (SMDL, Tugaloo, 2009).

Malcolm X's popularity and charisma worried Elijah Muhammad who tried to dissuade him from visiting Mecca but Malcolm insisted and discovered that Muslims came in every colour. It has been argued that Malcolm was reluctant to leave the NOI (Cone, 1993), but when he returned he set up his own Sunni mosque and accepted he had put himself in great danger. He insisted black and white should struggle together to overcome racist oppression. He compared African Americans to Jews: 'The biggest difference between the Jew and the Negro is that the Jew never lost his pride. He knew he had made significant contributions to the world, and his sense of his own value gave him the courage to fight back. It enabled him to act and think independently, unlike our people and our leaders' (Dyson, 1995). Eventually Malcolm apologised for his assaults on King. Malcolm's assassination by NOI members means that we will never know what this dramatically changed man would have achieved: 'He gave millions of younger African Americans newfound confidence. These expressions [of black pride and self-respect] were at the foundation of what in 1966 became Black Power, and Malcolm was its fountainhead' (Marable, 2011). Malcolm X remains a martyr. The man who later took over the leadership of the NOI was Louis Farrakan, who has been accused of plotting Malcolm's murder.

Black Power

It started with Carmichael. For many critics, such as Rustin and King, it was an empty slogan that damaged the Movement (King, 1967; D'Emilio, 2003). It may have done but it had widely differing meanings. Amiri Baraka admits: 'We had no stated ideology except black' (Baraka, 1984). It has been suggested that Carmichael's speeches helped make euphemistic racism respectable and persuaded northerners that those who lived south of the Mason–Dixon Line had been right all along. This ignores the long-term racism of northerners. Father Groppi tried to explain Black Power in Milwaukee but failed (Jones, 2009).

However, Black Power had different meanings and was not only held by young people. For Mrs Annie Rankin, Black Power was political representation and ending the Vietnam war. She wrote: 'Now about Mr Carmichael he is a great leader and has open a lot of people's eyes.' He had shown many young men the truth about the war. 'I am a Black Power fighter and will be until white power fall to the ground.' With county elections coming 'these Southern Honkies are really getting nasty but I get nasty with them.' She insisted she would be non-violent but would 'get them off me' (Rankin to Stewarts, 25 April 1967, USMDL, Tugaloo). When this author listened to Carmichael at an all-black college he never mentioned white people and instead attacked the students for their obsessive consumerism, not knowing their history, ignoring the local black poor and wanting to be white by straightening their hair and dyeing it blond.

But the expulsion of white members from the SNCC in December 1966 disillusioned many supporters, including many black Movement people (Dittmer, 1995). Members of the Southern Student Organizing Committee (SSOC) proposed a whites-only programme among the Appalachian poor. They were vigorously opposed by Anne Braden, who explained why they should rethink their Mountain Project. In a memo to them in June 1966, she warned: 'I can see why Negroes want to build organizations of black people and build their [black] consciousness as a people.' But: 'The last thing in the world we need is a "white consciousness." … we already have a "white consciousness," with all the evil and destruction that indicates. What we need to do is tear it down.' The problem was not just a waste of their time: 'I think you may be creating a Frankenstein. I think you may well find that you have organized groups and organizations that become a real danger – to the South and to all you stand for' (www.crm.org/docs/SSOC-Braden). Few established groups backed Black Power espoused by the purged SNCC, although it is claimed Rosa Parks was a supporter (Theoharis, 2013). Carmichael and King remained friends, but Emmie Schrader Adams of SNCC recalled many black and white students followed Braden's advice and kept working together (Holsaert et al., 2012).

After the division in the SNNC it would be easy to assume that white musicians who had done so much for the Movement would be ignored by young African Americans and that black singers would seek exclusively black audiences. This was not always the case. Nina Simone, who had written and recorded numerous songs for the Movement, notably *Mississippi Goddam*, had an enormous crossover appeal, especially among white intellectuals and northern college students, and the same is true for Aretha Franklin and her hit *Revolution* and James Brown with his funk number *Say it Loud – I'm Black and Proud* (1968) which included church call and response. But the growing disillusionment is reflected in Franklin's *Respect* (1967). Although white artists such as Joan Baez, Pete Seeger and Bob Dylan still had black followers, it is notable that a Simone concert raised almost twice as much as one by Joan Baez. And by the late 1960s, Janis Joplin from Texas 'had put on the mask of musical blackness' and generally had little 'appeal to black audiences [who] found little they recognized and nothing they wanted … in her music. She did not understand racial stereotypes and only helped to perpetuate them' (Ward, 1996). Joplin remarked that 'she combined white and black choir voices inspired by Bessie Smith' (Wilson and Russell, 1996). But many black artists went out of their way (a very long way according to Harry Belafonte) to turn their backs on gospel, jazz and R & B that had inspired members of the Movement. Young people preferred John Coltrane – not knowing that Du Bois in *The Souls of Black Folk* (1903) urged black people to be proud of their sorrow songs, gospel and blues.

White singers, like Elvis Presley, became enthusiastic Wallace backers to keep their white audience and commercial appeal (Ward, 1998). Only with the emergence of rap do we see some artists supporting a separate black state. But such a black nation was illusory and the Black Power conviction that city riots were harbingers of revolution was absurd and led them down the road to the black separatism of the 1890s, the self-help ideology of Booker T. Washington, combined with a warped interpretation of Marxism and romantic notions of African history and culture.

Some sympathise with the nationalists' motivations, but argue it was not only FBI intimidation and police violence that explains their failure; rather they did not understand the role of class and the new black elite. '[T]he narrow nationalists preferred to damn material reality, and embrace sterile cultural mutterings and blind dogmas of death. The Old Guard simply watched their critics bludgeon themselves into political oblivion' (Marable, 1991). However, some argue that Black Power had wide support in cities such as Philadelphia and its advocates provided an effective reform programme to replace the ineffective liberal reforms (Countryman, 2006). Black Power had a major impact on young Native Americans who formed the American Indian Movement and in South Africa where Steve Biko led a Black Power movement.

The Black Panthers

Although every group involved in the Movement wanted power for African American people, the Black Power slogan has almost universally been associated with Stokely Carmichael (Theoharis, 2013; Peniel, 2014) but its origin was in Lowndes County, Alabama where John Hulett and others organised voter registration. They changed their original name to the Lowndes County Freedom Organization (LCFO), with Hulett as the first chairman. Alabama law required political parties to have symbols and the LCFO chose the black panther. Hulett warned that if they were 'pushed into the corner we will come out fighting for freedom or death' (John Hulett Speech, May 1966, veterans of the civil rights movement. org). Self-defence was widespread throughout the black community long before the Movement began (Cobb, 2014).

The Black Panther Party was formed in Oakland, California, led by Huey Newton and Bobby Seale and took its name and logo from the Lowndes County group. The BPP uniform of black leather jackets, black berets and guns appealed to the machismo of many black men but it terrified many whites and intensified the so-called 'white Backlash', an assessment vigorously argued by Bayard Rustin (D'Emilio, 2003). At first the Panthers claimed the old leadership ignored the urban ghettos and the poverty, unemployment and police violence that plagued urban neighbourhoods everywhere. Initially they set up food services, established schools (like the Movement's Freedom Schools in the South), voter registration and free clinics for their communities. These efforts resulted in wide support in black sections. Ironically, the National Rifle Association later praised the Panthers' determination to have assault weapons (NRA Media.org).

Initially they were willing to work with white radicals and dismissed black cultural nationalism, but their recruitment of pimps, drug pushers and gang members encouraged the cult of violence and gangsterism in their ranks. Their apprehension of informers led to paranoia which resulted in expulsions and even killings. Fearing infiltrators they were reluctant to recruit. Seale admits that their members 'do all kinds of crazy things like intimidating people, romping and running in the streets, acting like fools. They give the Party a bad name' (Seale, 1991). He glosses over serious crimes or that Huey Newton was an autocratic and violent leader whose behaviour saw the collapse of the group (Fairclough, 2001). What is rarely noted is that these tendencies were there from the beginning. The Panthers' minister of information, Eldridge Cleaver, in *Soul On Ice* (1968), boasted that he had practised raping black girls and women to prepare himself to carry out 'insurrectionary rapes' of white women.

They failed to produce a plausible political programme with their espousal of Maoism, content to sell or wave Mao's *Little Red Book*. With no viable plans they ensured their defeat (Fairclough, 1991; Jones, 2009). They descended into feuding factions – enthusiastically assisted by the FBI. Police killing of Panthers, as in the case of Fred Hampton in Chicago, gravely weakened them and ensured a quick demise. And others suffered. In Louisiana three Panthers were found guilty of killing a policeman and sentenced to life without parole. Kept in solitary confinement, combined they served more than 113 years in the notorious Angola prison: Robert King for 29; Herman Wallace for 41 and only freed because of his terminal cancer (*Independent,* 9 June 2015). Albert Woodfox, in solitary for nearly 50 years, was not released until February 2016 after pleading no contest to a murder he did not commit (Los Angeles *Times,* 19 February 2016). The continued poverty and persistent racism and segregation have meant that rap artists have revived and revised the role of the Panthers.

Black Nationalism and Black Women

Black nationalists emphasised women's second-class status. Many academics claim that enslaved men were denied their patriarchal role because slave marriage was forbidden and power rested solely with the owner and the resultant matriarchy still shapes the black family. Many African Americans were offended by this view. Daniel Patrick Moynihan's 1965 report 'The Negro Family' claims that – 'in essence the Negro community has been forced into a matriarchal structure, which because it is out of line with the rest of American society, seriously retards the group as a whole and imposes a crushing burden on the Negro male and, in consequence, on a great many Negro women as well'. Paula Giddings comments: 'The Moynihan Report was not so much racist as it was sexist' (Giddings, 1984). Most white sociologists supported Moynihan, but so did members of the SNCC after whites were expelled. Angela Davis, while working on an SNCC rally in Los Angeles, was criticised for 'playing such a leading role in the organization, [and] some of them insisted we were aiding and abetting the enemy who wanted to see Black men weak and unable to hold their own'. Ron Karenga, the cultural black nationalist, told her that: 'A woman was supposed to "inspire" her man and educate his children' (Davis, 1994).

Pauli Murray sympathised with many of their goals but was alienated by the 'coercive power' of young militants. She recognised 'my barely disguised hostility toward the Black Revolution was in reality my feminist resentment of the crude sexism that I perceived in the leaders' (Murray, 1989). Baraka insisted women should be submissive to 'wiser' black men: 'It was but a short step from this sort of thinking to advocate that women remain politically barefoot and literally pregnant' (Giddings, 1984; Iton, 2008). Sexism always existed in the SCLC and the NAACP and a King coworker stated: 'Martin ... was absolutely a male chauvinist' (Oates, 1994); it was one reason why Ella Baker resigned from the SCLC (Ransbury, 2003).

Male resentment was partly due to the tradition that black women were encouraged to get a good education because parents often believed that daughters suffered less discrimination in getting employment. And the women's rights movement failed to understand that black women were *relatively* successful when faced with the double discrimination of being black and women. '[T]he failure to effectively challenge Moynihan's solution (black patriarchy), with all its implications retarded both movements' (Giddings, 1984). Black women would later revolt against the efforts of black men to dominate them.

President Johnson and Black Power

Johnson's response to Black Power was to say he was 'not interested in black power or white power'. In retirement he acknowledged: 'Black power had a different meaning to the black man, who until recently had had to seek the white world's approval and for whom success had come largely on white people's terms. To such a man black power meant a great deal more in areas that mattered the most – dignity, pride, and self-awareness' (Johnson, 1971). It is a pity that he did not understand this as president but this was when ghettos across the country were in flames and misguided radicals proclaimed the 'revolution' would be spearheaded by the Panthers and their white allies, the Weathermen (later the Weather People). His views of the Black Muslims and Black Panthers are not given in his memoirs but Johnson could not take criticism from those who did not share his liberal beliefs and values (Woods, 2006).

To better understand the city riots he set up a National Advisory Commission on Civil Disorders headed by liberals Otto Kerner and Richard Brooke, the latter a black Republican senator from Massachusetts. Their report blamed the riots on white racism and recommended $30 billion in additional expenditure. Johnson knew this was not feasible. 'Setting such an unattainable goal could easily have produced a negative reaction that in turn might have endangered funds for the many valuable programs we had fought so long to establish and were trying so hard to strengthen and expand' (Johnson, 1971). At the Riverside Baptist Church in New York in 1967 King joined the president's critics but also fought the backlash from black nationalists and white conservatives. He said: 'A few years ago there was a shining moment in that struggle. It seemed that there was a real promise for the poor – black and white – through the Poverty Program. These were new experiments, new beginnings.' It was not riots but the Vietnam War that had virtually destroyed these efforts. With America committed to violence abroad he would not criticise violence in America's ghettos (Oates, 1994).

Politicians and the affluent middle class had to be made to understand that the great majority of the disadvantaged were whites, Hispanics and Native Americans and the Great Society reforms, with all their strengths and weaknesses, were not designed to benefit African Americans only. King planned a Poor People's Campaign – a rainbow coalition of the disadvantaged would converge on Washington DC and live in Resurrection City until legislators acted. He ignored concerns of others, such as Rustin, who said: 'I knew Martin very well ... but he did not have the ability to organize vampires to go to a bloodbath' (D'Emilio, 2003).

Murder in Memphis

King never led the march. His friend James Lawson was helping black Memphis sanitation workers who were in a bitter strike against an intransigent mayor and council who were indifferent to the appalling working conditions that had led to deaths of colleagues. The men marched with placards declaring 'I AM A MAN' but that was not how the power structure in Memphis saw them. As the resistance mounted and union recognition was denied, Lawson contacted King and urged him to support the strikers. He did and then returned to work on the march. With no progress in Memphis, Lawson said King should return and fight alongside the workers (Honey, 2007; Jackson, 2007). The SCLC's lack of formal structure gave him flexibility and ensured he could go to Memphis despite his hectic, exhausting schedule but it also meant that too often he was reacting to events rather than shaping them. But King believed that the strike was a step towards radical change in the economic system. But when he came he had to concede that a self-proclaimed nationalist group, the Invaders, could take part in the protest. They did. Far from helping, they rioted and stole money from the strike funds.

King was determined to overcome the militants. On 3 April 1968 at a church rally he recalled how in 1959 he had been stabbed in New York. He said a young white girl wrote: 'I read in the paper of your misfortune and suffering. And I read that if you sneezed you would die. And I'm simply writing you to say that I'm so happy you did not sneeze.' And he was glad he had not because he would not have seen the advances made and despite the difficulties, the triumphs that lay ahead. He concluded: 'Like any body I would like to live a long life; longevity has its place but I am not concerned about that now. I only want to do God's will. And He's allowed me to go to the mountain top. And I've looked over. And I've seen the promised land. I'm not worried about anything. I'm not fearing any man. Mine eyes have seen the the glory of the coming of the Lord' (Washington, 1991).

The next morning, standing on the Lorraine Motel balcony, he was assassinated. Just like murdered Movement workers his killing was not effectively investigated and it was not until 1978 that the lone-killer story was discredited. America had lost the greatest black spokesman of the century, a man who explained with calm passion the meaning of the civil rights struggle in speeches that would transform the lives of many of them. He had spoken with the emotional fervour of an Old Testament prophet that galvanised young and old, black and white to follow the non-violent road to justice. Everyone who heard that sermon was certain, that like Moses, he had been to the mountain top and seen the promised land.

Despite appeals for calm, riots swept the country. For a week 100 towns and cities saw rioting with 46 killed, 3000 injured and 27,000 arrested. It took 21,000 federal troops and 34,000 National Guardsmen to restore order after the destruction of $45 million's worth of property. Congress, which earlier had defeated a minor budget measure for rat control in slums (sneeringly dubbed a 'civil-rats' bill) did pass a fair housing bill following King's assassination. Although discrimination in rent and selling houses was made illegal it was left to individuals to prove they were victims. Passage of the bill was ensured with a clause to appease whites which made incitement to riot a serious federal offence. It was a far cry from the early years of the Administration when 60 educational acts, including the Head Start programme, and Medicaid and Medicare achieved so much for the education and health of some of the poorest people in America. And Johnson's support for the Movement has been described rightly: 'No president, not even Abraham Lincoln, had so forthrightly identified himself with the Constitution, and with the values of the country with the cause for equal rights for African Americans' (Woods, 2006). Johnson never shed all his prejudices but he understood the plight of African Americans during his life in Texas and, even more so, the effects of poverty when as a young man he had taught Mexican

American children. He made significant gains in the fight against poverty and discrimination but radicals on the left and right agreed that liberalism had failed.

The first to challenge LBJ was Democratic Senator Eugene McCarthy, who promised to withdraw from Vietnam. Many young white liberals supported him. Others hoped Johnson's arch enemy, Robert Kennedy, would enter the race. As the New York senator's friend writes melodramatically: 'He [Johnson] had always known that, as in the classic Hollywood western, there would be the inevitable walk down through the long silent street at high noon, and Robert Kennedy would be waiting for him' (Schlesinger, 1979). And Kennedy believed he could heal the rift between black and white based on his conviction that his brother was a civil rights martyr and his contempt for LBJ that dated back to his ferocious battle to win JFK's nomination and LBJ's refusal to offer him the vice presidency in 1964 (Woods, 2006). There was no shoot-out because Johnson announced on television, to an astonished audience, that he would not seek re-election.

It seemed certain that Kennedy would be nominated and elected. And many, especially the poor, working class and minorities believed he understood their plight and wanted to make the American Dream a reality. When he broke the news of King's assassination in an Indianapolis ghetto while cities burned across the nation, he said that he understood that some would hate white people but reminded them that it was a white man who had killed his brother. In the dark cold night he spoke from a flatbed truck and told them that his favourite poet was Aeschylus and quoted him: 'Even in our sleep, pain which cannot forget falls drop by drop upon the heart until, in our own despair, against our will, comes wisdom through the awful grace of God.' Then he took his campaign to California and after winning the primary he told his cheering supporters in Los Angles: 'We are a great country, an unselfish country and a compassionate country. I intend to make that my basis for running' (Schlesinger Jr, 1979). The cheering soon stopped. Hysterical weeping replaced it. Kennedy had been assassinated. For many African Americans this was the murder of the last white politician they could trust.

On 12 December 1972, shortly before his death, Johnson told a meeting: '[T]o be black in a white society is not to stand on level and equal ground. While the races may stand side by side, whites stand on history's mountain and blacks stand in history's hollow. We must overcome unequal history before we overcome unequal opportunity' (Woods, 2006). Johnson's quiet revolution had had dramatic effects, especially on his beloved South, despite his deepest fears that his war on racism and poverty might result in a resurgent ultra-conservatism.

5

The New Right and Civil Rights: 1968–1989

For those caught up in the Movement, 1968 seemed to be the year that the old elite's rule was ending. In Northern Ireland, France, Germany and Japan students believed they were the vanguard of a revolution that would sweep away both liberal and conservative establishments. Had they not forced LBJ not to run for re-election? And they were determined to fight LBJ's chosen candidate, a long-time supporter of civil rights, Vice President Hubert Humphrey. He had betrayed them at the 1964 Atlantic City Convention and supported the war in Vietnam. Humphrey relied on Johnson and Chicago boss Daley. Eugene McCarthy, an anti-war Democrat, continued his campaign and his popularity rose but he failed to win over Kennedy supporters. He behaved like a spectator rather than someone trying to expound clear policies and many anti-war delegates supported Senator George McGovern of South Dakota.

Chicago 1968

At the Chicago Democratic Party convention, millions of TV viewers saw ruthless attacks by Daley's lieutenants on anti-war delegates and the media in the convention hall. CBC news anchorman Walter Cronkite deplored what he called 'fascist' tactics. Democrat Senator Ribicoff said

Daley's tactics reminded him of the Gestapo. The police riot continued outside. Daley claimed he was upholding law and order against violent hippies and the majority agreed with LBJ who, using his favourite phrase, said he wanted 'to get them by the balls'.

George Wallace of Alabama appealed to the growing numbers alienated by the civil rights and anti-war Movement. Northern blue-collar workers and ethnic voters, especially Irish and Polish, gave him a rapturous welcome in cities such as Milwaukee and Detroit (Sugrue, 2005; Jones, 2009). He and his advisors, mainly southerners, including his speech writer KKK member Asa Carter, decided Wallace should run as an American Party candidate. He knew he could not win but he was convinced he could capture enough Electoral College votes to throw the election into the House of Representatives (Carter, 1995). He hardly disguised his racism campaigning in the South, but in the North he focused on loss of the union seniority system, big government limiting freedom to sell houses, and children bussed from inner city schools into white neighbourhood schools. This was combined with a populist assault on banks, Wall Street and federal government bureaucrats. But he made one mistake. He chose retired General Curtis LeMay as his running mate. LeMay wanted to 'bomb Vietnam into the Stone Age' but supported civil rights, citing the US military as the ideal integrated society. Disillusioned supporters drifted back either to the Democrats or overwhelmingly to the Republicans and the man who had risen from the politically dead: Richard Nixon, the voice of new conservatism – who was widely known as 'Tricky Dick' because of scandals during his vice presidency.

Politically dead? He had been defeated by the narrowest of margins by JFK and he hated the Kennedys and liberal easterners (Kutler, 1998). In 1962 he lost his bid to be governor of California and told the press: 'You won't have Richard Nixon to kick around anymore' (Ambrose, 1989). Journalists wrote his political obituary. Fellow Republicans had dropped him and chose Goldwater in 1964. But they had ignored Nixon's travels around the 'rubber chicken and green pea' circuit talking to American Legion groups and suburbanites who were angry and scared by civil rights marches, city riots and anti-war demonstrations. He reassured them that they were 'the silent majority' and civil rights workers and radicals would not be allowed to flout the law. Nixon embraced racism (McAdam and Kloos, 2014).

Nixon writes that King 'worked to resist extremists in the movement, those who wished to resort to violence to reach their goals'. But radicals 'sometimes caused him [King] to be more extreme in his public views than he otherwise would have been'. He believed 'King's death left black Americans without a nationally recognized leader who combined responsibility with charisma' and like most Americans he believed that African Americans, 'the other', needed their own leader and although some might be 'reasonably effective ... none could match his [King's] mystique and his ability to inspire people – white as well as black – and to move them' (Nixon, 1978). However, he did not condemn the southern states for failing to uphold their constitutional duties to protect the lives of their black citizens. According to a diary entry after a meeting with Nixon in 1969, his closest advisor, Bob Haldeman, wrote: '*Went through his whole thesis re: blacks and their genetic inferiority.*' (Perlstein, 2008, italics added).

Nixon's Southern Strategy

Nixon knew that opinion polls, excluding Wallace supporters, showed the vast majority backed him. The strategy was not to attack Wallace but to maintain that a vote for him was a wasted vote. Nixon calculated that he might lose the Deep South but he was determined to carry the border states of Tennessee, Kentucky and Virginia, as well as the Carolinas and Florida (Nixon, 1978). He chose Maryland Governor Spiro Agnew as his running mate to strengthen this plan. Agnew was perfect for Nixon. After the 1968 Baltimore riots, Agnew forced Black Panthers to publicly strip and denounced the black leadership as 'Hanoi-visiting ... caterwhauling, riot-inciting, burn-America-down type of leaders'. When told about this Nixon responded: 'That guy Agnew is really an impressive fellow. He's got guts. He's got a good attitude' (Ambrose, 1989).

Nixon encouraged Agnew to play 'dirty politics', attacking Humphrey as 'soft on communism' and crime while he, Nixon, could stand above the fray. He wrapped himself in the American flag and told crowds suffering wounded nationalism that he would restore the nation's greatness. In Springfield, Ohio he proclaimed: 'We must gain respect for America in the world.' The Woodstock Festival crowds cheered Jimi Hendrix's brilliant tortured rendition of the national anthem but it was another weapon in Nixon's armoury. 'A burned American library, a desecrated flag ... these are the events which in effect squeeze the trigger which fires the rifle which kills young Americans.' LBJ's 'war on poverty was not a war on crime', according to Nixon, 'and it was no substitute for a war on crime' (Nixon, 1978). Most blue-collar Democrats agreed.

Nixon knew his audience. In 1968 after the black athletes protested at the Mexico Olympics and after riots in New York, Los Angeles, Detroit and Newark, black people's efforts to highlight their problems were portrayed as attacks on America and law and order. In a national radio address, Nixon warned: '[W]e face the prospect of war in the making on our society. We have seen the gathering hate, we have heard the threats to burn and bomb and destroy.' The riots were the beginning of an 'insurrection' and force should be met with force. The nation understood the 'resentments' and 'grievances long suppressed but the lesson has been learned. Further disturbances could engulf, not only our cities, but all the racial progress made in these troubled years.' He exploited whites' deepest fear: the violent black male. The carefully crafted speech was for a white nation that had generously completed the task of giving black citizens their rights. White rioting in the South, Chicago and Boston, and the Klan with its bombing and murders, were not mentioned. In this coming race war Nixon had 'cast himself as the white's field marshall' (Perlstein, 2008). The apparent triumph of this southern strategy saw later Republicans and party managers Lee Atwater and Carl Rove use less coded ways to link race with law and order and welfare.

Like Wallace, Nixon denounced the Supreme Court – a major part of the New Right strategy. In *Miranda v. Arizona* (1966) the Supreme Court ruled suspects must be told their constitutional rights upon arrest and have access to a lawyer. To Nixon 'there appeared to be more concern for the rights of the accused than for protection of the innocent' (Nixon, 1978). The Court should follow a strict construction of the Constitution, an argument that southerners had used against *Brown*. A study of massive resistance concludes:

> [T]he facade of a unified southern resistance crumbled into its constituent parts, leaving only those that were sufficiently subtle in their approach, or that had chosen encoded overtly racist appeal in such a way to make them palatable to a broader, non-sectional audience to continue their work and to move imperceptibly into a steadily evolving landscape.
>
> (Lewis, 2006)

This is an excellent description of Nixon's campaign.

It was not only the New Right's opposition to civil rights, LBJ's poverty programme, inner city rioting and black power that explains Nixon's success and his successors' appeal to the 'silent majority' but also 'urban anti-liberalism [which] had deep roots … From the 1940s through the 1960s Detroit fashioned a language of discontent directed against public officials, blacks and liberal reformers who supported public housing and open housing' (Sugrue, 2005). A black candidate for mayor in 1969 was defeated solely because of white opposition. Ethnic inner city and sub-urban voters supported the police who were notorious for their brutality against African Americans.

Opposition escalated after *Milliken v. Bradley* (1974) which ordered inter-district bussing to ensure metropolitan-wide integration of edu-cation. The desegregated boundaries of the city frayed; whites fled and moved to suburbs built with municipal and private funding. Ghetto pop-ulation density was re-enforced when federal public housing funds were only used for inner city housing. By the 1980s Detroit was predomi-nantly black. The few African Americans who moved to suburbia were subjected to violence and arson. A 1960s effort by the Department of Housing and Urban Welfare to mandate construction of suburban inte-grated low-income housing increased opposition and the scheme failed (Sugrue, 2005).

The 1968 election reflected the marked rightward shift by northern blue-collar workers who rejected the legacy of FDR – although some AFL-CIO leaders tried to keep them loyal. But despite Humphrey's fight, Nixon was elected. Nixon received 43.4 percent of the popular vote,

Humphrey 42.7 and George Wallace 13.5. However, most Wallace voters would have supported the Republicans. It was not as close as it appears.

Nixon, an isolated figure, held passionate hatreds for intellectuals, dissenters and critics, especially press and television journalists. Barry Goldwater said Nixon was the most dishonest person he had ever known and that Nixon would readily lie to his wife, family, the Republican Party, the American people and even the world. And Nixon's attitude towards African Americans, despite revisionist views, was not promising. In his 1960 campaign he had complained he had to speak about 'all that welfare crap'. In 1967 he wrote in the *Reader's Digest* that 'far from being a great society, ours [America] is becoming a lawless society'. Rustin argued that Black Power rhetoric contributed to Nixon's election: 'Passionate self-assertion can be a mask for accommodation' (D'Emilio, 2003).

Charleston Hospital Workers' Strike

Nixon's southern strategy was tested when Charleston, South Carolina officials refused to increase wages of hospital workers to $1.30 an hour. The workers struck. African Americans had made some electoral gains largely due to Septima Clark, a black educator and NAACP member, and her voter registration work. However, city officials were obdurate.

Strikers were coordinated at the Morris Brown United Methodist Church. Clark was on the aid committee. A boycott of downtown business contributed to the loss of $15 million in tourist income alone. With no local unions, the workers relied on support from national unions, such as the New York branch of the Retail, Wholesale and Department Store Workers (AFL-CIO). When the Medical College found out they fired 12 union recruiters and 450 workers walked out. Financial assistance came from other northern unions such as the United Auto Workers (UAW) union. Local textile companies favoured a quick settlement, fearing unionisation would spread to their employees. The pressure paid off. On 26 June 1969 the union was recognised, employers introduced a check-off system and the dismissed workers were re-instated. Like the 1968 Memphis sanitation workers' strike, the unity of church, Movement and union leaders ensured success. But for long-term civil rights worker Andrew Young the strike was:

> the last major campaign waged by the SCLC. We had hoped that Charleston would be the beginning of something new; but it turned out to be the end of the direct-action phase of the movement for us, and of the application of direct-action techniques developed in the sixties.
>
> (Young, 1996)

Although this might be true for the SCLC and the civil rights movement as defined by the 1960s, African Americans played a leading role in the anti-war demonstrations and sit-ins. Black and white civil rights workers knew only too well that it was the poor and black who suffered the highest casualties in the American army. The killing of students at Kent State University by the Ohio National Guard and at Jackson State University by Mississippi state troopers led to a nation-wide strike by university students. Mass protest did not die in 1969.

Nixon and Abernathy

Nixon's first meeting with the new head of the SCLC, Ralph Abernathy, was not auspicious. Abernathy sought a White House meeting when he was in South Carolina helping the Charleston hospital workers. Nixon declined. Abernathy organised demonstrations to heighten awareness of the strike and there were arrests. Eventually, on 13 May 1970, Abernathy and his aides flew to Washington to meet Nixon. It was disastrous.

Nixon ascribes the failure to Abernathy and his associates and he calls it a 'shambles' because the SCLC leader was 'either unprepared or unwilling, or both, to have a serious discussion. Instead he postured and made speeches. He began by reading a list of demands and spent the rest of the times restating them in more colorful ways. Nevertheless he seemed pleased that we had made the effort and in the end he thanked me profusely for taking the time to meet with them' (Nixon, 1978). But he had sent a note to his advisors, John Ehrlichman and Bob Haldeman: 'This shows that my judgement about *not* seeing such people is right. No more of this!' (Ambrose, 1989). Nixon was not amused when Abernathy told the waiting press that it was one of the most 'fruitless' meetings he had ever attended. Later, Abernathy claimed that Nixon was 'full of earnest resolve and high blown rhetoric'. But he was not fooled. 'They had been so certain that their economic double talk had mesmerized all of us' (Abernathy, 1989).

Abernathy may have been an inadequate leader, but undoubtedly Nixon's racism influenced his recollection of this meeting. In a White House tape Nixon states: 'With blacks you can usually settle for an incompetent because there are not just enough competent ones. And so you put incompetents in and get along with them, because symbolism is vitally important. You have to show you care' (Summers, 2000). Perhaps it was this symbolism that later persuaded him to appoint an admiral as the first black Assistant Secretary of the Navy and another as chairman of the Federal Communications Commission.

According to Nixon he reassured his advisor Daniel Patrick Moynihan that actions, not words would demonstrate his sincerity. Moynihan replied: 'The time may have come when the issue of race could benefit from a period of "benign neglect." The subject has been too much talked about.' For Moynihan the debate was controlled by 'hysterics, paranoia, and boodlers on all sides. We need a period in which Negro progress continues and racial rhetoric fades' (Ambrose, 1989). Nixon said 'benign neglect' was taken out of context by congressional and media critics. He defends himself, proud of his affirmative action programme.

Affirmative Action

Although opposed to quotas in job hiring, Nixon was determined that federal contractors would employ more minority workers, and contractors had to set a goal for affirmative action. Federally funded construction projects in Philadelphia had to increase minority workers from 4 to 26 percent. Conservatives argued Title VI of the Civil Rights Act prohibited affirmative action and stipulated that no one could be denied the benefit of federal financial assistance based on race, colour or national origin. Nixon writes that he was attacked by congressional conservatives and that

Everett Dirksen had told him: 'As your leader in the Senate of the United States, it is my bounden duty to tell you this thing is about as popular as a crab in a whorehouse.' The proposal would split the Republican Party and he could not support it (Nixon, 1978).

Nixon ignored his advice. Ironically, he acted on the policy first argued by LBJ when the latter was vice president. Affirmative action was introduced in October 1969 at a federally funded hospital project and extended to building trades unions in New York, Pittsburgh, Seattle, Los Angeles, St Louis, San Francisco, Boston, Chicago and Detroit. Nixon fought off congressional and AFL-CIO union opposition. By 1972 the plan covered 300,000 firms, many not involved in the construction industry. Nixon recalls how disappointed he was with the 'luke warm support from most of national black leaders who tended to minimize the results we had achieved, or to complain that we had not gone far enough'. He wondered if they were 'more interested in dramatic tokenism than the hard fight for actual progress' (Nixon, 1978). And it has been considered that it 'represented a major step forward in enforcing the Civil Rights Act by extending equal employment opportunity' (Fairclough, 2001).

But why would a conservative and, as the Watergate tapes reveal, a vitriolic racist expand LBJ's liberal Executive Order of 1965? It is not as paradoxical as it appears. 'Faced with growing urban violence, government officials wanted programs with quick and visible payoffs to fend off social chaos.' If Nixon did temporarily ignore 'benign neglect' there were other reasons for this apparent switch. He wanted to punish organised labour which led the opposition to his Supreme Court nominees and to break up the coalition of unions and civil rights groups. Nixon was aware white union members would fight to keep the seniority system and control over labour contracts whereas civil rights groups would support any effort to break down institutional racism. He knew blue-collar Democrats saw affirmative action as quotas which endangered 'white jobs'. The goal was to destroy union support for the Democrats that originated with the New Deal and had kept them as the major party (McAdam and Kloos, 2014).

And he used his new-found working-class friends for another purpose. He was deeply worried about the ongoing demonstrations against the war, especially after the Kent and Jackson State killings. He sought

Haldeman's advice about a protest march in New York City planned for 8 May 1970. Haldeman suggested that they recruit the Teamsters Union, which was not in the AFL-CIO, because it had 'regular strike-breaker types ... they're gonna beat the shit out of some of these people'. They did. Construction, glazier and plasterer unions eagerly joined the 'Hard hats' riot against an anti-war rally. Their union leaders, who had ties to the Mafia, were feted by Nixon at the White House as patriots and defenders of the 'silent majority'. He appointed the mob-linked head of the building workers' unions, who had organised the violence, as his Secretary of Labor (Summers, 2000).

Supreme Court Nominations

Nixon used Supreme Court appointments as part of his southern strategy, not merely because they were conservative. He spoke of liberal judges with what he described as 'colorful language' and particularly disliked Thurgood Marshall who was appointed by LBJ. He believed: 'Marshall was just there because he was black and three others were "real boobs"' (Kutler, 1998). His first nomination in 1969 was Clement Haynesworth of South Carolina who was opposed by labour and civil rights groups. Nixon did not fight for him because defeat was inevitable. He was determined to profit from the debacle and decided 'to settle for an incompetent' and, defying the American Bar Association's advice, he named Judge G. Harold Carswell for the vacancy. A life-long segregationist, Carswell's rulings on the Florida circuit court reflected his racism and the Supreme Court had frequently overruled him. Even a sympathetic biographer of Nixon admits Carswell's qualifications were simply 'non-existent' (Ambrose, 1989; McAdam and Kloos, 2014). Senator Roman Ruska of Nebraska defended Carswell, declaring that many Americans were mediocre and they should be represented on the Court.

Nixon denied Carswell was a racist and despite warnings from his Party persisted and in April 1970 submitted the nomination for Senate approval knowing it would be rejected. It was. Nixon called a press conference and lashed out at senators who defeated Haynesworth and Carswell. 'When you strip away all the hypocrisy the real reason for their rejection was their legal philosophy … and also the accident of their birth, the fact that they were born in the South.' He would never nominate another southerner; they should not be subjected to 'character assassination'. He concluded: 'I understand the bitter feelings of millions of Americans who live in the South about the act of regional discrimination that took place in the Senate yesterday.' Later, Nixon defended Carswell's support of segregation as 'youthful indiscretions' and that he 'would have past muster by the standards of other times' (Nixon, 1978). But many in the South were insulted by Carswell's nomination as if this fourth-rate judge was the best the South could offer. Senator Albert Gore Sr of Tennessee voted against Carswell as 'an insult on the integrity of the Senate' (Ambrose, 1989). Consequently, Gore was one of the first casualties of the southern strategy. Nixon illegally funnelled huge sums of money to Gore's opponent who exploited Gore's vote against Carswell, his record on civil rights and opposition to the Vietnam war.

These nominations plus his opposition to make King's birthday a national holiday (on the latter he wrote over a memo, 'No! Never!') were to capture more southern white votes. Nixon was prepared to use the politics of symbolism. But 'the South wanted more than symbolic defiance' (Ambrose, 1989). And he was given the chance to do that and to continue to discredit the Supreme Court.

School Desegregation

His first attempt to deliver the southern conservatives' programme failed. The Secretary of Health, Education and Welfare (HEW), Robert Finch, approved a plan to force Mississippi schools to desegregate or lose federal funding. Senator John Stennis demanded Finch reverse it and Nixon ordered Finch to ask the Court for a delay. The Supreme Court in *Alexander v. Holmes County Board of Education* ruled that the 'all deliberate speed' of *Brown II* no longer applied and ordered the immediate end of the dual school system. John Mitchell, the Attorney General, advised: 'Do only what the law requires, not one thing more' (Ambrose, 1989). He told Nixon: 'Leave the issue to the courts because seeking injunctions and bringing lawsuits was not only a slower, more careful procedure but would place the onus of enforcement on the courts and not the White House' (Greene, 1992).

Adam Fairclough claims 'that under Nixon the dismantling of Jim Crow proceeded apace' and points to the rapid integration of southern schools but admits the federal courts were responsible, not the Administration. The new Chief Justice, Warren Burger, nominated by Nixon, turned out be almost as liberal as his predecessor Earl Warren. In *Swann v. Mecklenburg* (1971) the Court insisted on city-wide bussing to overcome state legislated 'parent choice' and 'neighbourhood' schools. Educational reforms after World War Two had closed small and inadequate rural schools, children were bussed outside their neighbourhood and parents had no choice. Bussing was welcomed countrywide because it meant better schools. In the South it was also popular because it was used to segregate schools. But now the slogan was 'No forced bussing' and 25 staff at HEW resigned because of Nixon's policy. He reassured southern senators he opposed it. Later he admitted: 'I felt obliged to uphold the law; but I did not feel obliged to do any more than the minimum the law required, while hoping the Court would eventually see how its well-intentioned ruling was both legally and socially counterproductive.' The *Brown* 'philosophy' that desegregation would improve the education of blacks and whites was wrong, African American children would harm the education of white children and 'excessive transportation of students was definitely inferior.'

At a White House meeting Nixon said black children were not equal with white children and black teachers were not as good as whites (Miller Center.org Nixon tape, 14 March 1972). He fails to write about his moratorium on bussing or his attempts to fund segregated academies that had sprung up across the South as wealthier whites withdrew from the public education system. Despite this Nixon declares he was an 'ultra-liberal' on racial issues and his opposition to 'forced integration of education and housing' was correct (Nixon, 1978).

While Nixon was fighting for his political life after Watergate a federal judge ordered the desegregation of Boston's inferior all-black schools, and students from the Roxbury ghetto were to be bussed into the Democratic South Boston, an Irish working-class ghetto. The consequent white riots cheered southern segregationists. In Detroit the courts tried to deal with the effects of suburbanisation which resulted in bitter battles led by Michigan Governor Roy Milliken and ensured Wallace's victory in the 1972 Michigan primary. 'So long as schools remained part of the metropolitan system that distributed tax dollars and social benefits unevenly, the impact of multi-cultural education and diversity would be minimal' (Sugrue, 2008). This conclusion is underlined in a recent government report (*Guardian*, 19 May 2016).

Shirley Chisholm: A Black Woman Seeks The Presidency

The occasional disputes between black and white women working in the SNCC during Freedom Summer were minor compared with male chauvinism and the failure of white feminists that affected the election campaign of Shirley Chisholm in 1972. The first black New York Congresswoman symbolised the new politics of the 1970s and as an early member of the National Organization of Women (NOW) and the National Women's Political Caucus (NWPC), it seemed these organisations would support her. Although her failure was largely due to lack of finances, poor organisation and preparation, it also 'revealed the shortcomings of the Black and feminist movements, shortcomings that would fundamentally damage both.' Eventually, NOW supported her. 'But the belated support for Chisholm was too slight to have any impact. The lesson that could be learned was that Black women also figured lightly in the priorities of the women's movement' (Wilson and Russell, 1996).

Emmie Schrader Adams claims that historians have exaggerated the role of male chauvinism (Holsaert et al., 2012) but it is a fact that prominent black men, such as Julian Bond, Jesse Jackson and mayors Richard Hatcher of Gary, Indiana and Clarence Mitchell of Atlanta vigorously opposed her. They held a meeting with others, such as black nationalist Amiri Baraka, where they considered three options; run 'favourite son' candidates in several states, support George McGovern, or select a male black candidate. Her defence of Angela Davis, imprisoned for murder, kidnapping and conspiracy, did not help her. The male-dominated Black Panther Party was the only group to endorse her and they were politically powerless. 'She concluded that the failure of her campaign was due more to sexism than racism, and the realisation was demoralising' (Giddings, 1984). In 1983 she did not seek re-election for Congress.

Many black women believed white feminists failed Chisholm because their paramount concern was the right to own their own bodies and control reproduction by abortion. Although she did not raise it during her campaign, African American women had good reason to be concerned. Eugenicists in the medical and scientific professions were motivated by racism and advocated sterilisation. Without criticising Chisholm, Angela Davis maintains the abortion campaigners should have included 'a vigorous condemnation of sterilization abuse that had become more widespread than ever'. Evidence she obtained from the Director of Population Affairs estimated that the federal government had funded between 100,000 and 200,000 sterilisations alone (Davis, 1984). Doctors and hospitals frequently aborted and sterilised black, ethnic and poor white women because they endangered the gene stock. White feminists saw *Roe v. Wade* (1973), which legalised abortion, as a victory and ignored the experience of many African American and poor women. They did not appreciate fully how conservatives would make abortion an issue to undermine many hard-won civil rights gains.

Black, lesbian feminist Cherl Clarke argued for a female coalition of black and white. 'What drew me to politics was my love of women, the agony I felt observing the straight jackets of poverty and repression I saw my own family in.' Early feminists were 'exclusive and reactionary' but all feminists had to unite because heterosexual men 'colonized' women's bodies and lesbians denied men power. 'Lesbian feminists can be compared to the ... civil rights activist of the 1960s who was out there on the streets for freedom, while many of us viewed the action on television' (Moraga and Anzaluda, 1983). But it was especially difficult for black lesbians. A daughter told her mother she was a lesbian and had a white partner. After the initial tirade, she was told if she had to be a lesbian she should choose a black woman (Wilson and Russell, 1996). African American women looked increasingly to white women for support and Fanny Lou Hamer became 'a revered figure in the women's movement' (Dittmer, 1995). Meanwhile, black men continued their search for a new leader.

The Politics of Euphemism

Bussing, law and order, and abortion were the politics of euphemism as practised by Nixon and the New Right. Opposition to 'forced' bussing was the coded reassurance that he would ignore the aims of even moderate civil rights groups. His persistent calls for law and order targeted the alleged danger of violent dissenters either civil rights activists, anti-war demonstrators, environmentalists or consumer groups. It is claimed his 'war on drugs' announced in 1968 was based on his belief that he 'had two enemies: the anti-war left and black people.' John Ehrlichman is quoted as saying, 'by getting the public to associate hippies with marijuana and blacks with heroin … we could arrest their leaders, disrupt their meetings' and every night television would reinforce their message (*Harper's Weekly*, archive 21 August 2016). Nixon's New Federalism transferred welfare programmes to the states and was another concession to resisters who argued liberals undermined state sovereignty. His denunciation of federal civil servants was in reality an attack on the Great Society and welfare and designed to reinforce the myth of lazy black people.

LBJ watched from his Texas ranch as his 'beautiful woman', the Great Society, was taken apart. 'It's a terrible thing for me to sit by and watch someone starve the Great Society to death … Soon she'll be so ugly that the American people will refuse to look at her; they'll stick her in a closet to hide her away and there she'll die' (Kearns, 1976). While federal and state politicians either bled or exploited the welfare programmes of the Great Society, people like Fanny Lou Hamer fought at a local level to expose the corruption in Medicaid and poverty schemes in Mississippi (Dittmer, 1995). Recent scholarship has been more sympathetic to Nixon but concedes that his goals often weakened his more progressive policies (McAdam and Kloos, 2014).

Black Capitalism

Nixon's opposition to Great Society programmes was shared by a number of Democrats who had voted for them and by some African Americans who campaigned against liberalism (Iton, 2008). For them Johnson's efforts were inadequate and did not meet the dire needs of the poor or help ghetto dwellers; they made things worse. Black capitalism was the answer. At the August 1968 convention in Miami Nixon declared:

> Black Americans – no more than white Americans – do not want more government programs which perpetuate dependency. They don't want to be a colony in a nation. They want the pride and the self-respect and the dignity that only comes if they have an equal chance to own their homes, to have their own businesses, to be managers and executives as well as workers, to have a piece of the action in the exciting venture of free enterprise.
>
> (www.presidency.ucsb.edu)

The speech was widely praised. Nixon writes that prior to his election black business got only $8 million of federal government contracts but by 1972 it was $242 million and during his presidency 'government grants, loans and guarantees directed to helping minority business enterprises had jumped from $200 million to $472 million' and the 'receipts of black-owned companies jumped from $4.5 billion in 1968 to 7.2 billion in 1972' (Nixon, 1978). The programmes to aid black capitalists combined with disillusionment with liberal reforms brought Nixon unexpected allies. Former black nationalist Roy Innis became an advisor. During the 1972 campaign Nixon lauded 'black militants [whose] talk these days is ... the doctrines of free enterprise than [of] the welfarist'. Nixon won the ultra-conservatives' goal – the poor were responsible for their poverty; government made things worse.

However, he had other motives than to support black free enterprise. 'Nixon's adoption of internal colonialism and his use of it to denounce the welfare state was nothing short of political genius. Nixon gave the appearance of progressivism that required little government expenditure' (Sugrue, 2008). Black Republicans even praised life-long racist Strom Thurmond. And Black Power's attacks on liberals 'defanged' white America's greatest fears (Ogbar, 2005). And after his re-election he followed Erlichman's advice that the Office of Minority Business would 'put the Administration in a good light without carrying a severe negative impact on the majority community' (Sugrue, 2008; Chappell, 2014).

Although his statistics about black business are impressive, they do not include important measures by Democratic congressmen. But Nixon rightly claims there was significant expenditure between 1968 and 1972. Once the plan was established, both parties endorsed black capitalism and subsequent presidents, Reagan and George H. W. Bush, approved set-aside programmes – although they opposed quotas (Graham, 1994). An African American Democratic congressman proposed an amendment to the $4 billion Public Works Employment Act to stimulate the economy. It required a 10 percent set-aside for minority business. It was approved with virtually no debate. The original act designed to aid disadvantaged businesses now included set-asides for racial minorities – another grievance for the white majority.

If Nixon wanted an African American middle-class Republican voting bloc he failed. In 1972 blacks remained loyal Democrats and Nixon's plan to funnel money to black candidates, in particular Jesse Jackson, was not approved (Summers, 2000). As it turned out it was not needed. An attempted assassination left Wallace partially paralysed and out of the race. Nixon swept the Deep South but Democrats kept control of Congress. Nixon's China visit, his promise to end the war in Vietnam helped him but he did not campaign for Republican candidates. 'Nixon completely wrote off all local races, telling Erlichman that the Republicans had raised the "worst crop of candidates in history"' (Greene, 1992). Nixon's paranoia mounted as the opposition mounted. Attempting to destroy his enemies led to Watergate, a massive abuse of power, followed by frantic attempts to cover it up. Black Congresswoman Barbara Jordan, from Texas, calmly outlined his crimes at the televised House hearings and her defence of the Constitution made her a national heroine (Rogers, 1998).

Protest and Separatism in Music

Nixon's admiration of Merl Haggard's *I'm an Okie from Muskogee* that attacked the counter culture and Ron Karenga's insistence that only African culture mattered did not stop young whites and blacks buying radical records. 'Although there was no longer much crossing of the racial divide from the other direction in 1971 around a third of Top Forty hits were by black artists' (Ward, 1998). For example, Gil Scott Heron in *Comment #1* (1970) declaimed: 'When the paleface SDS motherfucker dares / Look hurt when I tell I tell him to go and find his own revolution.' But most black artists faced a dilemma – how to appeal to a crossover audience for commercial success and at the same time promote black pride. James Brown's *Say It Loud I'm Black and Proud* (1968) was popular with white audiences as were many soul and funk recordings.

Stevie Wonder recorded Dylan's *Blowing in the Wind* which topped the black charts. But the blatant, violent sexism of male singers, reflected in old blues, angered women of all races. Black women eventually went on the attack but in doing so they unintentionally reinforced stereotypes of black males by portraying them as unfaithful, often lazy and violent – playing 'macho' to hide their weakness. Black women were strong and independent. But these shifts in black music appealed to some white teenagers and even more so in the 1980s and 1990s when politicians and the general public interest in minorities waned. Christian conservatives tried to fight back with their own rock songs such as *In America*. However, their limited success was damaged when several lead singers came out as gay (*Guardian US,* 8 June 2016).

Assessing Nixon

Bill Clinton generously assessed Nixon's contribution to civil rights as significant compared with Republican presidents who came after him (Clinton, 2004). This is partly true but ignores Nixon's motivation – his racist appeal to white voters North and South. Nixon converted a few of the black bourgeoise but did not care that the vast majority of African Americans would never vote for him. He was happy to exploit white fears to neutralise his opponents. It was the blunt talking, brutal law officers that Nixon admired, like Philadelphia police chief Frank Rizzo who boasted he would make 'Attila the Hun look like a faggot' (*The Nation,* 24 October 1977). Nixon did not have 'a compelling commitment to decency in race relations in all areas'. Unlike LBJ, he failed to give presidential leadership to tackle poverty and discrimination. 'Richard Nixon did not want to be the nation's leader. He only wished the problem would go away.' As for the racial crisis: '[H]e passed on his best opportunity for greatness' (Ambrose, 1989).

But before his resignation in disgrace he had ensured his right-wing views would live on with his appointments of four conservatives to the Supreme Court. The allies of the Movement understood the long-term consequences for those who had relied on the courts in their struggle for justice. Ralph Abernathy, recalled: 'The civil rights movement was no longer as fashionable as it once had been.' Future battles would be smaller and more complicated and would not get media attention. 'Watergate had been a better show than anything we had managed to stage' (Abernathy, 1989). He was not surprised when in 1976 he was asked to resign the leadership of the SCLC.

Civil Rights and Gerald Ford

Ford has been described as an old-fashioned, establishment centrist Republican (McAdam and Kloos, 2014). A former Speaker of the House, he had been a Nixon loyalist and became vice president when Spiro Agnew pleaded no contest to bribery charges. This accidental president was, according LBJ, a man who could not 'chew gum and walk at the same time.' A Nixon critic concludes: 'Clearly, Nixon thought that by promoting Ford, generally seen as a genial but limited Republican journeyman, was also good impeachment insurance' (Emery, 1994). Ford's loyalty was reflected in the pardon he awarded Nixon after Watergate. In a rare proclamation, he pardoned Nixon for 'all offences against the United States which he, Richard Nixon, has committed, or may have committed' (Emery, 1994). The Senate investigation into Nixon's term in office and the White House tape recordings revealed his sanctioning felonies (too many to enumerate here) and his vehement anti-Jewish bigotry and racism.

Ford's pardon was not his only distinction; he had the worst civil rights record since 1945. Ford 'paid less attention and less support to civil rights in [his] public statements' than previous presidents (Shull, 1993). Following the violent attacks on the Selma-Montgomery march, Ford supported legislation to allow use of 'maximum power to the federal government to prevent further violence and to protect the constitutional rights in Selma, Alabama' (Carter, 1995). He voted for the 1964 Civil

Rights Act and the Voting Rights Act of 1965 but when Nixon sought to weaken the voting rights legislation he had Ford's enthusiastic support. When Ford became president he never urged Congress to consider any civil rights legislation and issued no executive orders to advance the cause. And his dislike of liberal justices was well known. He had worked enthusiastically on Nixon's behalf to impeach Supreme Court Justice William O. Douglas who was considered too liberal. Nixon appointees at the Justice Department gave Ford information that they were certain would result in Douglas's impeachment and when Ford failed they complained: 'Ford took the material we gave him and he screwed it up' (Carter, 1995). And many conservatives were angered when John Paul Stevens, Ford's only appointment to the Supreme Court, authored a majority ruling that the Communications Decency Act (1996), censuring internet pornography, was unconstitutional.

However, he did not 'blow it' for the New Right when it came to appointments to federal appellate and district courts. In the district courts, 90 percent of his appointments were white and 98 percent were male. None of these judges were deemed qualified by the American Bar Association. He was more consistent with the appellate courts – 100 percent were white males; however, the ABA considered 17 percent as well qualified (Shull, 1993). Some argue that Ford was too moderate because he supported the Equal Rights Amendment and failed to strongly oppose abortion. They suggest he deliberately sidelined conservatives and did not hide his contempt for California's governor, Ronald Reagan. From this perspective Ford's 'anachronistic view of the new reality' meant that 'it would be the penultimate hurrah the moderate Republican establishment would enjoy' (McAdam and Kloos, 2014).

Despite his neglect, Ford tried half-heartedly to win African American votes in his 1976 campaign against the governor and peanut farmer from Georgia, Jimmy Carter. He thought black voters would not support a white southerner and they would help him win the urbanising border states. But increasingly the Republican Party was for whites only, especially men, and Ford chose the path of his mentor – Nixon. 'Gerald Ford's version of the Southern strategy delivered nearly two-thirds of the white vote to the Republicans' (Werner, 2002). He exploited fears of 'forced' bussing which would destroy neighbourhood schools. In the election campaign Nelson Rockefeller, former liberal and Ford's appointee as vice president, kept the South loyal when he claimed that the president was like George Wallace.

However, ultra-right conservatives such as Patrick Buchanan, who had led the massive resistance to the Movement in Virginia and was an early Nixon supporter, believed that Nixon and Ford had failed by their actions and inactions to reverse the liberal gains of the 1960s. In a seven-page memorandum to Nixon, Buchanan claimed he had surrounded himself with liberal advisors and conservatives were 'the niggers' of his administration (Ambrose, 1989). And nothing in the Ford Administration persuaded him that things had changed and he supported Ronald Reagan as the leader of the 'silent majority' who would sweep liberals out of Washington. However, most conservatives stuck by Ford but his hope of retaining the South failed. Carter carried the southern states and kept the African American vote. It seemed that the Republican strategy was totally misconceived. It was not. Both parties learnt that to win the presidency they needed someone who was ultra-right (Reagan) or candidates like Carter who was from the South.

Jimmy Carter's achievements were highly praised in a Civil Rights Commission report in 2001. Appointments of African Americans and women to prominent positions helped forge coalitions that have been the strength of the Democratic Party (see Chapter 6). But Carter's ability to do more was limited by his one-term presidency – defeated by a former minor Hollywood actor, former sports commentator who avoided service in World War Two, the first divorced candidate who lauded family values and who was an infrequent church-goer.

Ronald Reagan had been a New Deal liberal but after the war became, like Robert Kennedy, an enthusiastic supporter of the witch-hunt against communists and other homosexual 'deviants' (Faderman, 2015). Reagan became an FBI informer. His assault on liberalism ensured his election as governor of California. However, the first television debate against Carter proved Reagan's incompetence and his staff resorted to the 'black bag' operations (break-ins) and stole Carter's notes before the second debate which Reagan won.

Reagan, Racism and the New Right

An ardent supporter of Barry Goldwater in 1964, Reagan had spent years attacking liberals even in his own party. Nelson Rockefeller was a traitor. When Reagan ran for governor of California he refused to repudiate the extreme right-wing John Birch Society knowing Nixon's doing so had hurt him in 1962. Reagan campaigned for a Birch candidate as governor, although in a statement he criticised the organisation's leader. When he asked why he had not supported the 1964 Civil Rights Act, he shouted: 'I resent the implication that there is any bigotry in my nature. Don't anyone ever say that' (Dallek, 1984).

It was not true. Reagan was the first and only president to start his campaign in Mississippi where he attended the all-white Neshoba County Fair near Philadelphia, close to the site where the bodies of the three civil rights workers were found in an earthen dam. He was cheered by the Confederate flag-waving crowd. African American commentator Bob Herbert noted that Reagan 'knew exactly what he was doing when he told that crowd: "I believe in states rights."' Reagan's defenders have tried to 'put his appearance into a racially benign context.' However, perhaps a better assessment has been: 'Reagan ... was elbow deep in the same old fashioned race-baiting Southern strategy of Goldwater and Nixon' (*New York Times*, 13 November 2007). He embraced the Lost Cause but needed to widen his appeal and exploit national patriotism. He asked to use Bruce Springsteen's *Born in the USA* as the theme song for his campaign seemingly oblivious of lines such as: 'So they put a rifle in my hand / sent me to a foreign land / to go and kill the yellow man.' Springsteen refused. Just as Woody Guthrie 1930s' radical socialist *This Land Is Our Land* is often sung at American Legion meetings, Springsteen's *USA* was adopted by many conservatives as a second anthem. Reagan shared this naivety.

He was not naive when it came to exploiting right-wing views. Indifferent to the needs of millions of Americans, not solely African Americans, he supported the American Medical Association's fight against Medicare and Medicaid and argued that: 'Medical care for the aged is a foot in the door for government takeover of all medicine.' Income tax was 'a progressive system spawned by Karl Marx and declared by him to be the prime essential of a socialist state.' Reagan was convinced that the threat to America came not only from liberals but from the 'socialism' of the Democratic Party that destroyed individual initiative (Boyarsky, 1981). He followed Nixon's example and linked welfare and crime to African Americans. He constantly repeated the story of a black Chicago woman, Linda Taylor, a so-called 'welfare queen' who exploited the welfare system paid for by hardworking white folks. '[S]he has eighty names, thirty addresses, twelve Social Security cards and is collecting veteran's benefits on non-existent husbands … Her tax-free cash income is over $150,000.' In fact, Taylor was convicted in 1977 for 'welfare fraud using two, not 80 names which she used to collect 23 welfare cheques worth $8000 not $150,000' (McAdam and Kloos, 2014). The *New York Times* reported his racial slur in front of a southern crowd when he complained about a 'young buck' receiving food stamps. The stream of attacks on welfare reinforced the belief only black people benefited and that it bred crime among them.

Reagan's defenders deny he was a virulent racist like Strom Thurmond but he happily allowed Lee Atwater, a protégé of Thurmond, to run his campaign and it was Atwater who organised Reagan's Mississippi campaign opener. He joined the White House staff. In an interview in 1981, Atwater spelt out the southern strategy: 'You start out in 1954 by saying "Nigger, Nigger." By 1968 you can't say nigger – that hurts you, backfires. So you say stuff like, uh, forced busing, states' rights and all that stuff, and now you're getting abstract.' He added: 'Now you talk about taxes, and all these things you are talking about are totally economic things and a byproduct of them is, blacks get hurt worse than whites … this stuff, is much more abstract than even the busing thing, uh, and a hell of a lot more abstract than "Nigger, Nigger."' (*The Nation*, 13 November 2012).

It is difficult to believe that Reagan was unaware of these views because that was exactly what he did in the campaign and as president. But Reagan talked about his years at college favouring an integrated football team and as a sports commentator wanting major league baseball to hire black players. But these were early years. Later he denounced the Civil Rights Act and Voting Rights Act, and opposed laws on fair housing and school bussing. As California governor his constant themes were 'morality, law and order, strong leadership and family values. Reagan was particularly skilled in relaying his message in a non-threatening way.' He combined resistance to civil rights legislation with 'opposition to anything that smacks of bigotry and discrimination. We must make those who walk with prejudice walk alone' (McAdam and Kloos, 2014). But his campaigning exploited the 1960s Movement. Television advertisements consisted of graphic images of race riots and anti-war protesters which fed the majority's sense of isolation, especially among northern blue-collar workers, middle-class suburbanites and the rural North (Mark, 2007). Reagan, whose 'family values' were questionable, won the evangelical vote that had backed Jimmy Carter, a southern Baptist.

Unlike Ford, he met 1960s civil rights leaders after his election and promised job training for inner city youth and to end the so-called 'dependency culture' caused by a welfare state. Abernathy agreed and blamed Democrats who saw 'welfare as a benign thing rather than a millstone around the neck of the black population' (Abernathy, 1989). Concerned that the Republicans were winning over white voters, Abernathy criticised African Americans for their loyalty to the Democrats. In 1980, Charles Evers and Hosea Williams endorsed Reagan, perhaps hoping they would influence the Administration. Despite their support: 'Ronald Reagan received the lowest percentage of the black vote of any Republican presidential candidate in history' (Shull, 1993).

Abernathy was soon disabused. At the inauguration party he was an 'honoured guest' and treated as an important person but Reagan ignored him and his companions and there was no meeting with Reagan or his senior officials and he 'didn't get past a third-echelon staff member ... No one, it seems, knew or cared about the president's promises' (Abernathy, 1989). Abernathy and the old guard were naive. 'What he failed to appreciate was that Reagan was a different type of activist. Instead of extending civil rights, he sought to reduce the government's role' (Shull, 1993). As Atwood said in the interview, the talk would be about the economy and tax cuts because 'a byproduct of them is blacks get hurt worse than whites.'

Reagan admitted this later. In his first year he refused an invitation to the NAACP annual meeting because of a prior engagement – a riding holiday. He attended in July 1981 and angered delegates when he claimed the plight of many African Americans was the result of liberal

Democratic programmes. 'Many in Washington over the years have been more dedicated to making the needy people government dependent, rather than independent. They've created a new type of bondage.' He followed this up with: 'The Emancipation Proclamation freed black people 118 years ago, today we need to declare an economic emancipation' (Dallek, 1984). His slogan was 'government is not the solution, government is the problem'. As a critic points out: 'By contrast, civil rights leaders had long seen big government as the key to solving persistent inequality.' It was a long way from the 1960s. 'White youths embraced hip hop culture [but] few seemed interested in the problems of the ghetto.' 'Indeed, images of aggressively jewellery-laden black men hardly made the case for state funding for the deserving poor.' Rap singers added a new divisiveness and membership of the NAACP went into steep decline (Tuck, 2008). But this did not mean the old issues involving inequality were not a focus of protest but rather it was a struggle to maintain past victories, especially by Black Caucus groups at federal and state level and city representatives who united progressives by community action which ensured the struggle continued.

The New Right Budget

Reagan's first budget, based on so-called supply-side economics, was intended to be the start of a revolution that would sweep away years of accumulated 'state dependency'. Budget director David Stockman in a 1987 *Atlantic Monthly* interview pronounced: 'The Reagan Revolution, as I had defined it required a full frontal assault on the American welfare state. Forty years worth of promises, subventions, entitlements, and safety nets issued by the federal government would be scrapped or drastically modified.' This 'minimalist government' would offer 'even-handed justice and no more'. Free market economics would liberate the nation, and deregulation would 'increase capitalist wealth and the expansion of private welfare that attends it'. The cuts to Aid to Families with Dependent Children meant that 400,000 were refused assistance and 279,000 had their benefits reduced. With the Food Stamp programme reduced, 1 million lost benefits worth 6 billion dollars over three years and 'the size and unprecedented nature of the first year cuts had both an immediate and substantive impact on the poor and, more important, a longer term corrosive effect on the policy norms and expectations' (McAdam and Kloos, 2014). Reagan asked for a 30 percent cut in taxes for the highest earners and got 23 percent. The marginal rate of tax for top earners fell from 70 percent to 50 and corporate tax from 13 cents to 8 per dollar and estate taxes by $150 billion over five years (Dallek, 1984). Between 1977 and 1987 family income of the richest grew from $94,476 to $129,962 while the poorest 10 percent had earnings cut by 10.5 percent (Shull, 1993). This seriously eroded New Deal and the Great Society reforms (McAdam and Kloos, 2014). Combined with a massive increase in military appropriations, one moderate Republican said: 'Pray God it works. If this economic plan doesn't jell, where are we going to get the money from?' The result was the 1982 recession. He cut $35 billion from social programmes, and added nothing to Carter's scheme for inner city training and education. He shifted welfare from the federal government to the states and then slashed state support from 12 to 3 percent at a time when they were suffering from recession, high rates of poverty, homelessness and a crisis in health care (Sugrue, 2008). Benjamin Hooks of the Urban League denounced the budget as bringing 'hardship, havoc, despair, pain and suffering on blacks and other minorities' (Shull, 1993).

He continued Nixon's 'War on Drugs' but emphasised the dangers of marijuana to white suburban kids. Whereas three previous presidents had focused on hard drugs Reagan cut federal research into the effects of these by 15 percent and the money went as block grants to the states. His so-called 'Drug Tsar', Dr. Carlton Turner, had no knowledge of drug abuse and ignored scientific reports commissioned by Nixon and Carter. He was ridiculed when he declared that smoking marijuana resulted in homosexuality. There was no strategy except Nancy Reagan's solution – 'Just Say No.' Nobody cared that drug abuse had fallen to its lowest level ever.

It was African Americans who were the greatest victims of drug laws as Nixon is alleged to have planned. Between 1985 and 1987, 99 percent of all drug trafficking defendants were African Americans; the percentage imprisoned topped 50 percent although blacks were only 12 percent of the population. A war started against marijuana used by white suburbanites was extended to crack cocaine, treated solely as a black problem in the inner city. A 1986 law stipulated possession of five grams of crack would result in a mandatory five-year sentence but the same sentence would be imposed only after 500 grams for powdered cocaine used largely by affluent white Americans (ACLU Report, 21 May 2002). Turner's successor ignored treatment and social problems. There was massive evidence that he was achieving nothing but the arrest rates reassured the Silent Majority that he was winning and 'that imprisonment of ten of thousands of young African Americans made the country safer' (Tuck, 2008). Despite spending trillions of dollars, drug use in all communities has spiralled and the spending continues to rise with a request in 2016 for $25 billion to fund one programme.

Did Reagan's economic revolution fail? According to Stockman it did. He claimed Reagan did not cut welfare programmes which are 'family destroyers'. In his *Atlantic Monthly* interview he admitted that it was difficult to sell 'trickle down', that is, cutting taxes on the rich which might benefit the poor and middle class. The budget did not work and Reagan raised taxes that only hurt the middle class and poor – regardless of race. Many black and white women worked two or three jobs for many hours below the minimum wage and had to pay for their own travel. If they had children there was no day care. They were among the millions with no health care and inadequate education (Ehrenreich, 2001). When Reagan retired to California his conservatism was overwhelmingly popular despite the gross income, educational and health inequality. He left a deficit of trillions of dollars, more than the combined national debts of all previous presidents. Although George H. W. Bush, his challenger in the 1980 primaries, had called it 'voodoo economics' the anti-tax rhetoric would not be disavowed by future presidents (McAdam and Kloos, 2014).

Ironically, Abernathy and some older Movement leaders had derided LBJ and his Great Society but not all African Americans and white liberals shared their Reaganite views. Jesse Jackson did not. In his presidential campaigns in 1984 and 1988, especially the latter, he called for a Rainbow Coalition – a title used by King in his Poor People's Campaign – and gained the endorsement from many liberals, if not all of the old Movement leadership. He won 13 primaries and caucuses.

Jackson has been dismissed 'as someone who belongs to the interminable list of protest politicians who legitimize themselves by projecting images of association with King and the civil rights movement' (Reed, 1986). The contention is Jackson's challenges had no influence on poor black voters. This ignores the fact that Jackson proved for the first time an African American could be a viable presidential candidate. A historian of the post-King period writes, 'national memory has been unkind to Jackson. But it also failed to grasp the real achievement of the 1980s in the struggle for black rights and black political power' (Chappell, 2014).

The Commission on Civil Rights and the IRS

Reagan not only cut welfare but he severely weakened the United States Commission on Civil Rights (USCCR) following Nixon, who had dismissed the head of the Commission because he supported bussing to desegregate schools. But Nixon's appointment of Republican Arthur Fleming as its new head had backfired because he became an outspoken critic of Nixon. Fired, he called a news conference and announced that his dismissal signalled a retreat on affirmative action. A NAACP spokeswoman commented: 'What the [Nixon] administration is trying to do is not just put civil rights on the back burner, but take it off the stove completely.' Reagan, however, sought to disarm his opponents when he chose one of the new breed of black conservatives, Clarence Pendleton of the San Diego Urban League, to ensure the weakening of the USCCR. He was Reagan in black-face. Pendleton was a staunch believer in self-help and free markets, and opposed affirmative action and bussing. The president was not concerned that: 'The increased politicization of the commission perpetuated [his] image as an opponent of civil rights.' Reagan defeated the liberals and transformed USCCR so that it accepted the New Right's opinions on civil rights (Shull, 1993).

Reagan's defenders claim he 'was so cut off from the counsel of black Americans that he did not even realize he was offending them' (Cannon, 1991). But he was responsible. A president who could not recognise his only black Cabinet officer was not someone who would seek advice. In 1982 he supported the Baptist Bob Jones University in South Carolina and the Goldsboro Christian Schools in North Carolina when they challenged the Internal Revenue Service (IRS) because it denied tax exemptions to segregated schools. The IRS policy was confined to schools that refused to desegregate – a policy that Nixon, Ford and Carter had supported. Although a very few minority students were eventually admitted to Bob Jones, the university prohibited interracial dating and marriage. Both complainants insisted their policy was lawful because of the constitutional separation of church and state. Later Reagan said: 'All I wanted was that these tax collectors stop threatening schools that were obeying the law' (Cannon, 1991).

In the resulting storm of protest he was told African Americans viewed him as a traitor. He said his proposed legislation was to stop IRS bureaucrats from making social policy. He promised that segregated schools would not have tax-exempt status. This was the politics of symbolism. 'Black Americans were supposed to accept the picture of a compassionate President opposed to discrimination, while conservatives were supposed to see his action as a victory over arbitrary bureaucrats and for the rule of law.' The Administration only backed down when it worried about losing moral authority but continued to reassure conservatives that the Party had 'lined up with white suburbanites in opposition to government insistence on equal rights for minorities' (Dallek, 1984). Increasingly Republicans courted the racist vote and exploited Reagan's opposition to strong central government. 'The success of Reagan in the 1980s owes much to the forms of argument provided by conservative intellectuals in the previous two decades' (Aughey et al., 1992).

Renewal of the Voting Rights Act

New Right conservatives, especially the growing number of southern Republicans in Congress, were not content with budgetary measures but wanted to repeal the Voting Rights Act (1965) that Nixon and Ford had renewed. They expected Reagan to fight liberal Democrats and the dwindling number of liberal Republicans who were determined to keep it. The Act allowed that where an unstated percentage of voters in a district were not registered, federal registrars would be sent in to ensure they were thus transforming southern politics. In Mississippi, African American enrolled voters had increased from 6.7 percent to 59.8 percent in three years. Reagan did not want the Act renewed and, no longer needing to court liberal Republicans, he vetoed it in 1988 (Berman, 2015). He opposed the 1988 Civil Rights Restoration Act (CRRA) designed to reverse a Supreme Court ruling in *Grove City v. Bell* (1984) that directed, for example, that a university department practising discrimination would lose federal funding but the university permitting it would not. This dramatically limited the scope of four civil rights acts. The CRRA stipulated that organisations and institutions had to be in compliance with civil rights legislation if they were to receive federal funding.

He warned that the Act 'dramatically expands the scope of the federal jurisdiction over state and local governments and the private sector, from churches and synagogues to farmers, grocery stores, and businesses of all sizes'. It diminished individual citizens. His critics responded that they were simply restoring a situation that had existed before the Court ruling. The vociferous support of evangelical leader Jerry Falwell and his Moral Majority harmed Reagan's cause. Falwell argued that churches would be forced to hire homosexuals, drug addicts with AIDS as teachers and youth workers. Even many conservatives thought this was nonsense and although Congressional Republicans were divided, 21 senators and 52 representatives voted with the Democrats to override Reagan's veto (Shull, 1993). But in the long-term he won. Reagan's major achievement, which had (and has) long-term consequences, was his four appointments to the Supreme Court. Chief Justice William Rehnquist had opposed the Civil Rights Act, Antonin Scalia and Sandra O'Conner were opposed to minorities' rights and Anthony Kennedy was conservative on many issues. The Supreme Court had shifted dramatically to the right. And Reagan was helped by a number of conservative academics who mounted attacks on the Voting and Civil Rights Acts (Berman, 2015).

Not even Reagan's most ardent apologists would suggest he had the slightest interest in affirmative action. Johnson's Executive Order 11246 which made federal contractors hire African Americans and other minorities was anathema to Reagan. A consent agreement negotiated by Birmingham, Alabama's first black mayor, Richard Arrington, encouraged Reagan to back court cases that opposed affirmative action. But his opponents prevented him. Failing in this he starved enforcement agencies of resources. Like Nixon he believed there were no competent African Americans and chose poorly qualified conservative black people. Clarence Thomas at Education slowed school desegregation and was promoted to head the Equal Employment Opportunities Commission. This was 'the most controversial appointee of all. Thomas knew that if he wished to get ahead with these conservatives he would have to oppose affirmative action' (Hudson and Davies, 2008). Thomas did.

Reagan, Gays and Aids

Reagan exploited the gay and lesbian movement for equality. After the 1969 Stonewall Riot, following a police raid on a New York gay bar, the Gay Liberation Movement was organised. Gays had not been considered a serious threat to society because they were in the closet and powerless. (By 2016 the Stonewall gay bar would become a national monument (bbc.news.us/stonewall, 26 June 2016).) Asked in 1982 if AIDs was now considered an epidemic an Administration press officer asked: 'What is AIDS?' Told that people were dying every day he replied: 'I don't have it, do you?' (Faderman, 2015). But the so-called 'gay plague' heightened public belief that 1960s liberalism had undermined the nation's moral fabric. Evangelicals proclaimed the disease was God's retribution.

Pat Buchanan declared gays were a public health menace and that 70 percent of the Democratic Convention delegates were 'queer'. An African American delegate confronted Buchanan's fear-mongering: 'I know what it means to be called a "nigger" and I know what it means to be called a "faggot" … And I understand the difference in my bones. I can sum up that difference in one word: *none*.' (Faderman, 2015). However, many black gay men and lesbians remained closeted, ridiculed by rappers and rejected by their own community (Wilson and Russell, 1996). Black film producer Spike Lee proved the persistence of anti-gay attitudes in his dreadful movie, *She Hate Me* (2004), ridiculing black lesbians.

Even after his actor friend Rock Hudson had AIDS, Reagan refused to help and ensured cuts in health research funding. The Administration did nothing even when informed heterosexuals were infected. The US did not join the UN campaign to prevent millions of deaths, or 51 countries using television advertisements advising on AIDs prevention. This inaction encouraged homophobia. His Surgeon General, a Christian fundamentalist, ignored medical advice, but eventually released a report admitting AIDS was an epidemic requiring urgent action, especially sex education. But Reagan said it would not be a priority in health programmes (Shilts, 1987). When warned about its seriousness his answer was 'Thank you for supporting me.' In fact, Reagan made it an additional weapon when he linked AIDs to the decline in family values, the abuse of 'welfare queens', and law and order (*Guardian US*, 11 March 2016).

Music as Social Protest

The black anger with Reagan was shared by many white protest singers. Harry Chapin and Bruce Springsteen are typical. Chapin in *There Is Only One Choice* sang about: 'Your old folk eating dog food / and your children eating paint.' And Springsteen and the E Street Band combined folk, R & B and rock to lament the decay of American industry and urban neighbourhoods in *Factory*, and in *Taxi* where individualism is in reality crushing isolation. Chuck Berry and other African American artists had a large crossover audience. Berry appealed to sexual freedom in his *My Ding-a-Ling* (1972), black slang for penis. The politicians continued to denounce black music and Nixon wanted Curtis Mayfield's *Pusherman* banned.

There is no consensus about the difference between hip-hop and gangsta rap (*Ebony*, September, 2013), and the terms are used interchangeably by Stephen Tuck (Hudson and Davis, 2008). It is easier to separate political rap and gangsta rap (Caldwell, 2008). The former looks inward to the ghetto with a sense of defeat, a fear born of neglect and official violence that individuals cannot control. Grandmaster Flash in 1982 issued a recording including the lines: 'cose they got me on the run / I feel like an outlaw.' Gangsta rap is assertive and shows they are not cowed by police oppression or the racism of the white society that dominates them. Niggaz With Attitude in 1988 issued *Straight Outta Compton* that emphasises the importance of gang membership. 'When I'm called off / I got a sawed off / Squeeze the trigger and bodies are hauled off.' And some gangsta is crudely and violently sexist. The *Compton* recording has the following lines: 'So what about the bitch that got shot? Fuck her / You think I gave a damn about the bitch? / I ain't a sucker.'

Many of the rappers claimed it was music designed for a black audience that white people could not understand. But it was white companies that promoted gangsta rap. It was a former president of the Disney Corporation who invested large sums in this music and Time Warner controlled the distribution of the black-owned Death Row records contracting artists such as Tupac. Time Warner was run by white executives and signed mainly white artists (Barnet and Burris, 2001). These entrepreneurs recognised that rap appealed to young white men because it 'tells "white" consumers how "cool" they are, or at the very least how cool gangsta African Americans are and therefore how cool they *can* be' (Caldwell, 2008, italics in original). And the young whites assimilated the 'culture' of rap, the clothing, braids and heavy jewellery, but cared little about the plight of the ghettos. By 1997 white males were rappers, the first being Eminem. Whether inward looking or in-your-face assertive, rap added to the perception that many black young people, whose predecessors had faced danger and death in the Movement, were exploiting their own community.

Reagan's Legacy

Just as LBJ caught the liberal mood of the nation in 1964 to pass sweeping victories for the Movement and to try to end poverty with his Great Society, so Ronald Reagan exploited the fears of a nation and undermined civil rights and welfare legislation. But some see the Reagan Revolution as something he would not recognise – that he was a consensus politician who failed in his stated aim of overturning the welfare state. His achievements were minimal. At the same time the authors argue that he 'aggressively courted the religious right' who adopted extreme positions on social issues which effectively drove out the moderates; that he completed Nixon's southern strategy which meant 'Republicans dominated Congress and that ensured young ultra-conservatives would finally kill off the moderate wing of the party' (McAdam and Kloos, 2014). They do not mention the role of the new conservative black middle class, the beneficiaries of liberalism, whose achievements were a direct result of affirmative action. During Reagan's eight years he appointed 78 federal appeals court judges and 280 in the district courts – 94 percent white, 95 percent male and Republican 'who reflected the ideology and makeup of the Reagan administration' (Berman, 2015). Scandals and senility prevented him from wiping out more liberal gains. It was his successors who almost accomplished that. Reagan may not have completed his revolution but his opinions have shaped the ideas of many Democrats as well as Republicans (McAdam and Kloos, 2014).

Under Reagan, young people were increasingly disillusioned. And older Movement men were quick to blame young black men. Ralph Abernathy complains they do not appreciate those who fought for justice: 'Had it not been for the character and courage of these simple people, we would not have raised a generation of leaders and nothing would have changed. We would still be looking from afar at the high walls of an impregnable city.' He grieves for Movement people who died and 'my heart also aches for those anonymous generations who never saw the Promised Land' (Abernathy, 1989).

It was not forgetting that made liberals and Movement veterans despondent. With the New Right ascendancy they were certain that all the Movement's gains would be lost and the country would return to the 1950s. Historian Charles Payne returned to Greenwood, Mississippi in the late 1980s and observed, 'the style of contemporary Black leadership struck me as rigorously top-down.' He correctly points out that 'this was against the history of the Black struggle and growth in the Delta … it seemed to have special poignancy' (Payne, 1996).

African Americans were mainly forced into preserving gains, and they were often successful. For example, Movement people formed the Free South Africa Movement (FSAM), forcing Reagan to abandon his support for the apartheid regime. And FSAM was well organised and built a wide coalition. Moreover 'the campaign was not just against Reagan's foreign policy, but a chance to express anger against the Reagan presidency in general' (Tuck, 2008).

He made the 'city' more impregnable than at any time since the 1957 Civil Rights Act and the struggle would be more difficult and strategies more complex but the fight would continue and a charismatic leader was not needed. Many people's lives had been changed forever by the Movement. They were determined to continue the struggle (Holsaert, 2012). And this included the South.

6

Transformation: A New South?

LBJ had always wanted consensus politics but by 1967 he faced massive opposition from the left who wanted the Vietnam war ended and from black power advocates who wanted nothing more to do with liberalism and who dismissed the Great Society as a sham. The Vietnam War meant disproportionate deaths of black men (*Nitty Gritty,* 1 September vol. 2, no. 2, Civil Rights, MDL). Conservatives claimed LBJ was not doing enough to win the war and wasting money on unpatriotic welfare scroungers. He admitted: 'There were deep divisions in the country, perhaps deeper than we had experienced since the Civil War. They were divisions that could destroy us if they were not attended to and ultimately healed.' On his return to Texas he walked beside the Pedernales River and reflected that as president: 'I had given it everything that was in me' (Johnson, 1971).

However, LBJ had shattered the broad alliance which had brought him so many legislative successes. Knowing that the Voting Rights Act would destroy the solid Democratic South it was essential that the Supreme Court protected his Great Society. When Earl Warren said he would retire, LBJ chose liberal Tennessean Abe Fortas to replace him. Fortas would have been the first Jewish head of the Court. Illinois Senator Dirksen (Republican) and Mississippi Senator James Eastland (Democrat) blocked the appointment by two votes. Dirksen feared he would lose his position as minority leader of the Senate and Eastland was furious that Fortas had urged Jews to support the Movement that, according to Johnson, Eastland interpreted as a conspiracy of Jews and African Americans to take over the country (Johnson, 1971). Eastland personified the old South.

What the Eastlands did not appreciate was that the civil rights struggle and the anti-war movement not only profoundly influenced African American lives; they transformed the lives of many white southerners as well as northerners. And despite later Republican gains at the federal and governorship level (Crespino, 2007), things were different at the city, town and county level. The characterisation of the South as home to only violent, racist, insular Bible-thumping rednecks who forever relive the battles of the Civil War is an oversimplification.

Southerners have been accused of shackling themselves to a 'false image', but that image is as much an invention of northerners and Hollywood as of unreconstructed southerners. There has always been another South. Many liberal southerners did fail to meet the challenge posed by the civil rights movement, but there were many who, in the finest sense, upheld the southern tradition of honour. Certainly some judges refused to enforce *Brown*, and Mississippian William Cox, appointed by JFK to a federal court, called African Americans 'niggers' and accused some of them of behaving like a 'bunch of chimpanzees'.

But others acted differently. Judge Frank Johnson became a federal judge of the Alabama District Court thanks to Eisenhower, and was promoted to the 5th Circuit Court of Appeal by Carter who respected his support for the civil rights struggle. Johnson frequently confronted his old law school associate, George Wallace, and won. Although southern liberals and radicals have their critics, they played a valuable role during the repressive years of the 1940s and 1950s when the plight of African Americans was ignored by most of the nation. These people, like Lillian Smith, Carl and Anne Braden, Ella Baker and Septima Clark kept alive the dream of a just South – a just nation. They continued their fight into the 1960s and beyond. They would be joined by a significant number of southern students who fought for civil rights, anti-poverty campaigns, the anti-war movement, feminism and LGBT rights.

Black southerners proved their courage when they accepted they would be beaten, jailed or even murdered in their fight against the likes of Eugene 'Bull' Connor and Sheriff Jim Clark. Foremost in the struggle were southern African American men and women of all ages – it was their battle and they were determined to be victorious. Their refusal to accept second-class citizenship, their fight for justice and the overthrow of Jim Crow forced many southerners to question the received wisdom of their political, religious and educational leaders.

However, it is also important to remember that liberal white governors such as Winthrop Rockefeller and his successor Dale Bumpers of Arkansas defied reactionaries. Senator Albert Gore Sr had the courage to face the challenge of civil rights and the anti-war movements. The stands taken by these men and others were also made possible because the Movement's activities encouraged them to break down the silence of the South. But there was another revolution in southern voting that persists to this day. Since the Civil War, the vast majority of white southerners had voted Democrat. Only in isolated areas such as East Tennessee or northern Alabama was it possible for Republicans to be elected. However, the Republican southern strategy changed and the Party turned its back on judges like Frank Johnson. Only thanks to the Voting Rights Act can Democrats, especially black Democrats, win at the state level or as congressmen. From the election of Nixon to George W. Bush, with the exception of little-known governors such as Carter and Clinton (both of whom were elected either because of the Watergate scandal or because of an economic depression), the South has been solid Republican. But demographic changes meant Virginia, North Carolina and Florida contributed to the election of the first African American president.

The Senator

Albert Gore Sr of Tennessee grew up on a farm during the Depression and struggled to get an education. He taught in a small school and lived with a coal miner and his family whose poverty made a profound impression on him. In 1938, at age 29, he was elected as a pro-New Deal congressman, and in 1952 he was elected to the US Senate where he served until 1970. He called himself a 'maverick' because he said most Tennesseans were mavericks.

Gore describes himself as a populist – a movement at the turn of the 20th century which he considers 'an outstandingly liberal movement' and a lost opportunity in which African Americans and poor whites could have united against the reactionary forces. He was certain that the New Deal, Fair Deal, the Great Society and the platform of George McGovern in 1972 would see the eventual triumph of populism. Although critical of some aspects of the New Deal, he became a self-confessed 'extravagant admirer' of FDR. He supported Truman's liberalism and opposed Strom Thurmond's Dixiecrat movement. 'Fortunately, not enough Southerners were willing any longer to follow blindly this advance to the rear.' Politically the 'significance of the Dixiecrats was the willingness of the Bourbon leaders to desert the Democratic Party *in order to maintain white supremacy*' (Gore, 1972, italics in original).

When the Supreme Court ruled that 'separate but equal' schooling was unconstitutional and ordered desegregation, Gore was not one of the 'political heroes'. He had never exploited race-baiting but he was not 'a torchbearer for racial equality in my first campaign for the Senate in 1952' (Gore, 1972). But he solicited black and poor white votes on economic and social issues by confronting Memphis 'Boss' Ed Crump who had controlled the city's African American vote for many years. Gore believed the Crump machine would be destroyed if African Americans had an independent vote.

After *Brown,* he described himself as a moderate and defended the ruling. Many southerners contended: 'Moderation means gradualism and gradualism means race mixing.' In Tennessee anti-desegregation groups, such as the White Citizens Council, spread across the state. Gore knew that 'moderation' for most southerners meant nothing short of communism because, even before *Brown*, politicians in Georgia and Mississippi had anticipated school desegregation and Georgia had tried to convert the public school system into a private one (Gore, 1972).

East Tennessee saw the worst violence. The small town of Clinton had too few black schoolchildren to justify a separate high school and they were bused to a segregated one in Knoxville; efforts to prepare people for desegregation failed. The white Baptist pastor Paul Turner was beaten for offering to walk the children to school and his example did not prevent it being bombed in 1958. However, segregationist candidates were defeated in the next town elections. There were brave citizens who wanted to obey the law (Greene, 1982).

Gore admired Governor Frank Clement sending the National Guard to Clinton, but southern opposition was growing and Citizen Councils were set up in every state. For Gore the Councils were 'formed to intimidate the Negro and keep the whites in line'. He was one of three southern senators who refused to sign the 1956 'Southern Manifesto' after the Court upheld *Brown* in its *Cooper v. Aaron* decision. Later Gore describes it as a 'bit of low doggerel' and that: 'I regarded the manifesto (what an irritating and pretentious name!) as the most unvarnished piece of demagoguery I had ever encountered.' He knew 'that nothing but tragedy and sorrow could come of this open defiance of the law, this cheap appeal to racism' (Gore, 1972).

He voted for the 1957 Civil Rights Act because 'it did place Congress on the side of social justice and ... the mere passage of civil-rights legislation was itself worthy of note'. But why did he support segregationist Buford Ellington's run for the governorship? Gore was a Party loyalist. More importantly, he had presidential ambitions and he needed Ellington's support in the 1960 convention. This act of political expediency went unrewarded. Ellington backed LBJ.

Gore worked with JFK even though many southern voters distrusted anyone from the North, especially from Massachusetts, and because JFK was a Catholic. After the election Gore backed JFK's civil rights policy, especially the desegregation of 'Ole Miss' which he hailed as the end of the interposition argument. But he would not support Kennedy's tax-cutting policies which he believed, correctly, favoured the rich and would prevent social and economic reform to help the poor.

He had much in common with LBJ but there were important differences. 'One was that I had grown stronger in populist leanings and had become an inveterate enemy of special privilege, while Johnson had become a bedfellow of big money, oil and the military brass.' LBJ was aware of Gore's feelings. In a secretly taped conversation with Georgia Senator Richard Russell about a 1964 tax-cutting bill, LBJ complained that the senator was 'not being very wise in your southern strategy' and that he, Harry Byrd and Gore 'ought to let that damned tax bill come on out' (Beschloss, 1997). Gore believed: 'It had always seemed perfectly logical to me that government should play an active role in the nation's business affairs, and I had never lost faith in the government's ability to guarantee economic justice to all its people' (Gore, 1972).

It was Gore's populism as much as his mounting opposition to the Vietnam War, which he considered a rich man's war and a poor man's fight, that led to disputes with Johnson. Despite these tensions both fought for Medicare assistance for the elderly and Medicaid for the poor. Additionally, they pushed through federal aid to elementary and secondary state education. Gore voted for the Voting Rights Act of 1965 and its 1970 renewal, and the Fair Housing Act of 1968 (Gore, 1972). The housing act's importance has not been sufficiently recognised according to a recent study (Chappell, 2014).

There is no indication what he thought about the Movement sit-ins. When asked about the Freedom Rides he sent a letter to someone in Chattanooga (name redacted) that he deplored the violence in Alabama, hoped the Administration would be reasonable and 'avoid provocation' and it was a matter for the courts and 'not ... mob rule' (Tennessee Electronic Library, Volunteer Voices.org). This was a cautious reply and it is uncertain if he is referring to whites as well as blacks.

He considered the 1968 presidential campaign 'a travesty on democracy' because all the candidates supported the Vietnam War. He campaigned for Hubert Humphrey as the man to extricate the United States from the conflict. He recalled it was a time 'when the label patriotism was prevalent ... when frustration, bigotry, recrimination, fear, and littleness of spirit and mind spread across the land like waters from a flash flood'. He knew Richard Nixon would target liberal Democrats and he would be 'in the eye of the storm'. Gore believed Nixon's southern strategy was 'based on the concept that people will have enough prejudice, provincialism, intolerance and ignorance that if the national leadership will make an appeal to it, it will win' (Perlstein, 2008). What he did not know was that Nixon was illegally funding his opponent. The easy thing for Gore would have been to trim. He did not. He continued his assault on the war in Congress and in speeches across the country.

When Nixon nominated two conservatives, Clement Haynesworth and Harold Carswell, for the Supreme Court, Gore considered them unfit and their nominations a deliberate provocation. 'It had become the litmus test of loyalty or disloyalty to the South, of white supremacy and civil rights for blacks with no room left for moderation or reason. When my name was called I voted a firm "No", and I felt good inside' (Gore, 1972). His anti-war, civil rights and the judicial nominee votes won him support from the growing number of radical students at the University of Tennessee, Knoxville (UTK), and other campuses across the state and with black voters (*Libra*, 22 October 1970).

But his progressivism has one blemish. Like Humphrey, he had not voted for the 1964 Civil Rights Bill. He claims it allowed 'middle rank' functionaries in the Department of Health, Education and Welfare (HEW) 'unspecified powers ... to withhold funding to a school system because one school refused to follow its guidelines on integration' (Gore, 1970). This was an arbitrary use of power: cutting funding for a system because one refused. However genuine his belief about arbitrary powers might have been, he must have known it was not a question of merely one school failing to follow HEW guidelines but rather a complete system – as in the case of the massive resistance to school desegregation in Virginia.

The President

Jimmy Carter of Plains, Georgia was fond of recalling his populist background and his mother, Lillian, claimed her father was close friends with black and white populist leaders. A biographer writes: 'Lillian has painted her father with a golden brush' (Kaufman, 1993). Whatever Lillian said, there is no evidence that Carter was a populist in the 1950s and 1960s. He has been described as a racial paternalist who did not question segregation – but this was the case for nearly all southerners. Carter writes about his childhood black friends but admits he had none as he grew older (Carter, 2015).

From 1959 to 1961 he served on the Americus and Sumter County Hospital Board and was on the Sumter County Education Board, and accepted segregated schooling. He claims he 'wanted to equalize educational opportunities as much as possible' and that armed services desegregation affected him when he was in the navy. The *Brown* decision made him 'support in a relatively unobtrusive way the evolutionary process of ending the more oppressive elements of racial distinction in our community' (Carter, 2015). The evidence for this is thin. As chairman of the Education Board he did not initiate changes in the school system and opposed the construction of a school in the black community. He admits he was guilty of naive unawareness (Glad, 1980) but he glosses over these failures in his most recent memoir (Carter, 2015).

Also he did not help an inter-racial Christian community known as Koininia. A neighbour who had lived in the commune was threatened by nightriders and expelled from the local Baptist church which he attended. But he helped ease a boycott of a store owner who supplied the community (Glad, 1980). This is not necessarily racism and whatever his shortcomings it was not necessarily expediency either. If it was, he would not have refused to join the Citizens Council which resulted in the locals painting on his office door: 'COONS AND CARTERS GO TOGETHER' (Carter, 2015).

As a state senator from 1963 to 1966, he attacked special interest groups' influence over the state legislature and stressed care for the poor, the underprivileged and the unrepresented in government. 'This experience in the legislature spurred him to seek the governorship but there were strategies that Carter and his campaign managers would later regret. Carter opposed bussing to achieve racial integration, and he visited a segregated private school' (Kaufman, 1993).

Other aspects of his campaign are not so negative and his later moderation as a governor is not so surprising. Undoubtedly, Carter wanted to win the Wallace vote but he also knew the biggest grievance in Georgia was the inequity of the tax system. He used the populist language of opportunity, equal treatment, removal of tax inequalities, obedience to school desegregation orders and state government reform. A sceptical view is that: 'It was more an attempt to articulate the deeper feelings and frustrations of the small people – their suspicions of the urban centers, the rich, the big interests – than a fundamental challenge to the established centers of power' (Glad, 1980). It is true that after his election as governor he did not trim the power of the banks and big business but he declared at his inauguration that the days of segregation were over. The number of black state employees rose from 4850 to 6648, services for the learning disabled were improved and over 100 health centres opened. He understood that change was important if the state was to attract northern investment. His governorship was successful. His crusade for honesty in government had wide appeal, and he was persuaded to seek the Democratic nomination.

It was ludicrous that a one-term governor of a southern state would even try. Obviously, Nixon's resignation following the Watergate scandal and Ford's pardon greatly helped someone campaigning for honest government. The main reason that Carter, and later Reagan, were nominated was because of primary reform intended to ensure a better process of selecting candidates and most states chose primaries and participatory conventions. Democrats favoured them after Humphrey was foisted onto the Party by backroom boys. 'The reforms ... have had a more enduring and consequential impact on the nominating process and the political influence wielded by movement groups' (McAdam and Kloos, 2014). The diminished power of the elites in both parties ensured that it was possible for someone without Washington experience to win the nomination.

Rank outsider Carter won not only the presidency but also the majority of black votes, even in Massachusetts, despite northern rivals saying African Americans would never vote for a white southerner. His victory proved Gore's argument – a southerner who had popular appeal on economic issues and was liberal on racial matters could be elected president. According to opinion polls it was not African Americans outside Congress that worried about the Georgian, but the Congressional Black Caucus and Senator Ted Kennedy – who fought his health care plan and whose opposition 'proved fatal' (Carter, 2015). The Caucus were determined to fight Carter's anti-inflation goal as something that would result in cutbacks in programmes designed to help the disadvantaged – that he was following the New Right agenda. However, these problems were made worse by his inexperience of Washington.

Two black women were appointed to his Cabinet: Juanita Kreps, Vice President of Duke University, was his Commerce Secretary; and Patricia Howard, Dean of Howard University Law School, was Secretary of Housing and Urban Development. Andrew Young, Atlanta Congressman and former Movement leader, was the first African

American to serve as US ambassador to the United Nations. This was not the symbolic politics of Nixon and Bush. It is not absolutely certain that Carter knew that Midge Constanza, head of his Office of Public Liaison, was a lesbian or that she had taken her partner, Jean O'Leary, a well-known activist, and three gay men to the White House in 1977 (Faderman, 2015). But it is very likely he did because Constanza had had FBI background checks.

He fulfilled his promise to increase the number of minorities in the judiciary. Carter appointed more African Americans and Hispanics as federal judges than any president before him. Unlike Reagan, and later Bush, he gave additional powers to the Justice Department to enforce the Voting Rights Act and strengthened the Equal Opportunities Commission to fight job discrimination. Minority businesses had their fair share of federal contracts and for the first time some federal funds were deposited in black-owned banks.

The first challenge to affirmative action came from a former white marine named Allan Bakke who sued after he had been refused entry to the University of California Davis medical school because the university operated an affirmative action policy so that African Americans and other minorities with lower entrance scores gained places. The university was correcting its previous discrimination. Bakke won his case in the Supreme Court of California and the Regents appealed to the US Supreme Court. Whatever position Carter took on *Regents of the University of California v. Bakke* was bound to cause him trouble. The Jewish community, who had also suffered discrimination, especially by universities, supported affirmative action which set targets, but not quotas. Labour unions, many still traditionally Democrat, opposed affirmative action whereas the black community that had voted 89 percent for Carter naturally supported affirmative action and quotas. At first the Attorney General gave no advice but after consulting with Carter, the Administration submitted a brief that strongly endorsed the university's controversial policy. The Court in a 5–4 decision ruled that affirmative action was constitutional but quotas, as used by the university, were not. It was widely acknowledged in the African American community that the Justice Department brief was 'one of the major contributions to the cause of civil rights' (Kaufman, 1993).

But that did not stop the criticism that he had not spent enough on inner city social programmes. Most African Americans believed the government's role was central and Carter did increase their employment and raised income because so many obtained jobs in the government sector (Sugrue, 2008). A coalition of moderate and former civil rights leaders, led by Coretta King, fought for a full employment act. Carter had problems. '[Since] the 1960s, partly because of the civil rights struggle, certain liberals were coming to see unions and government as part of the problem' (Chappell, 2014). Carter signed the legislation but Republicans pushed through a balanced budget measure that severely weakened it. This failure was included in the US Civil Rights Commission Report (1978) but overall it praised Carter's determination to protect the gains of the Movement.

As president, Carter was the first to understand the growing power of the feminist movement and appointed a commission that travelled through the states and asked women what they wanted. Congresswomen Shirley Chisholm and Bella Abzug had won funds from Congress for a National Women's Conference in Houston. Chisholm and Abzug supported Gloria Steinem, a leading white feminist, in organising it. Steinem later asserted: 'This conference may take the prize as the most important event that nobody knows about' (*New Yorker*, 19 October 2015). There were 2000 delegates and 18,000 observers in a racially mixed audience that demanded equality for women and lesbians and the right to abortion. Among the main speakers were Carter's wife, Rosalind, Maya Angelou, Chisholm and former First Lady Betty Ford. All supported the platform as well as the so-called Minority Women's Plank.

However, many black women in the Movement and black feminists, who formed the Cohambee River Collective in 1974, insisted that feminists were white middle-class women who were often racist. They were annoyed by many white feminists who compared their status to 'slavery' and black women resented the criticism that they put fight against racism suffered by black men first. But white women were profoundly influenced by the civil rights struggle. Steinem claimed that anyone who had suffered discrimination meant 'you're sensitive ... on every level. I learned feminism largely from black women. Women of color basically invented feminism' (*New Yorker*, 19 October, 2015).

Although Carter exaggerates his integrationist sympathies as governor, they cannot be questioned during his presidency. He obeyed court rulings and enforced them, he helped the poor and minorities, especially the black and Hispanic communities, and fought to preserve the gains made by the Movement as in the *Bakke* case. Despite all his efforts, some prominent civil rights leaders supported Republican Ronald Reagan. But the divide of the black elite and most black voters was not as surprising as the decision of evangelicals, especially southern Baptists, to support a candidate who rarely attended church, a divorced man who talked about family values despite his dysfunctional family, and a man who had signed a liberal abortion act as governor of California.

Jimmy Carter is wrongly blamed for encouraging conservative evangelicals which empowered them to lobby against minorities, women and the LGBT community. Allegedly his faith strengthened the Moral Majority and the New Right (McAdam and Kloos, 2014). Carter admits his friendship with the evangelist Billy Graham. He met Jerry Falwell, the Moral Majority leader, who exploited the issues of prayer in schools and tax-exempt status for religious schools, but they did not change Carter's belief in the constitutional separation of church and state. He refused Falwell's demand for an amendment allowing prayer in schools. Carter supported abortion in cases of incest, rape and endangerment of the mother's health. It was this principled stand and Reagan's eagerness to adopt Falwell's agenda that ensured Reagan's victory in 1980. Carter is correct: 'The melding of the religious right with the Republican Party has been permanent since then' (Carter, 2015).

African Americans in Congress, as Governors and Mayors

The South has seen a major transformation of its politics and one that some are determined to reverse. The Movement brought democracy to vast areas of the region of one-party Democratic rule that had been propped up by flagrant anti-democratic devices, violence and intimidation that denied African Americans the franchise. After the 1965 Voting Rights Act, Republican Governor Linwood Holton was elected governor of Virginia, a state that had adopted massive resistance to stop school desegregation. He was the first Republican governor since 1874. But in 1970 he said: 'As Virginia has been the model in America's past, let us now endeavor to make today's Virginia a model in race relations. Let us, as Lincoln said, insist upon an open society "with malice toward none and charity for all".'

In the 11 states of the former Confederacy, the black registered voters had increased from 1.7 million voters to 2.7 million between 1960 and 1966 – a result that had cost many in the Movement their lives. With the enforcement of the Voting Rights Act and the courage of local people it was 4.3 million by 1980. The effect was most profound at the local level. By 1980 Dixie had elected 2600 black women and men as officials and mayors. The latter included the cities of Tuskegee and Birmingham, Alabama and Atlanta, Georgia. In 1983 Harold Washington was elected mayor of Chicago with black and white votes. He was popular. He beat the Daley machine but died shortly after his re-election. Charlotte, North Carolina had resisted school desegregation and the Supreme Court over-ruled their bussing plan, but later it elected a black mayor, Harvey Gantt, where the black population was only 25 percent. He was a widely respected architect, and beneficiary of the sacrifices of the lowly in the Movement. The Movement made these successes possible aided by Supreme Court rulings in *Gomillion v. Lightfoot* (1960), *Baker v. Carr* (1962) and *Gray v. Sanders* (1963) that overturned gerrymandering devices designed to deny black representation.

Gantt ran for the US Senate and seemed certain to win – the first black man from the South who would have been elected since the 1860s. He challenged Jesse Helms, a racist who had never won by large margins. Helms used television advertisements showing white hands crumpling a piece of paper and a voice-over saying, 'you needed that job and you were best qualified. But they gave it to a minority because of a racial quota.' It has been suggested the advertisement had little effect on Helms's victory (Mark, 2007). To put it mildly that is very debatable.

No African American had been governor of a state and the highest post had been Lieutenant Governor in Louisiana after the Civil War. The first elected black governor was in Virginia in 1989 when L. Douglas Wilder defeated a conservative Republican. Wilder defended abortion but modified his position on the death penalty. His victory largely depended on black votes. Some argue 'that the South's recently acquired two-party politics may become one party for blacks and one party for whites, a disquieting reminder of the past' (Cooper and Terrill, 1991). This ignores the fact that white votes made these victories possible. The election of a black mayor in the town of Philadelphia, Mississippi, near where the three civil rights workers were murdered in 1964, depended on white voters. However, a 2013 Supreme Court ruling has virtually destroyed the Voting Rights Act – the greatest achievement of the Movement.

In the larger northern cities racial polarisation made it almost impossible for African Americans to be elected where white people were in the majority (Sugrue, 2005). And when they won office many problems were beyond their control. Coleman Young, the first black mayor of Detroit in 1974, according to his critics, was responsible for the decline of the city. Despite his demands for improvements in employment, education and housing for ghetto people, he spent much of his time with the wealthy white elite. But 'by the time Young was inaugurated the forces of economic decay and racial animosity were far too powerful for a single elected official to stem' (Sugrue, 2005). Black mayor Wilson Goode of Philadelphia faced angry complaints from black residents about an armed black separatist group, MOVE, barricaded in a house in their street. The police advised Goode that their siege had failed and recommended an alternative. It worked. The house was destroyed and the only survivors were a woman and child. However, other homes were destroyed and Goode has the distinction of being the only mayor to bomb his own city.

Maynard Jackson appeased white business leaders and won the Olympic Games for the city, claiming Atlanta was 'too busy to hate' despite the large presence of white extremists. Fellow African Americans gained almost nothing from his election. The same complaint was made against Charles Evers, former Movement leader active in sit-ins and self-appointed head of the National Association for the Advancement of Colored People (NAACP) in Mississippi (Annie Rankin to Caroline and Bill Stewart, 8 January 1970, SMDL). Student Nonviolent Coordinating Committee (SNCC) founder Marion Barry became mayor of Washington DC and was arrested by the FBI and found guilty of taking cocaine and enjoying sex parties (*The Washington Post*, 19 January 1990). He served time in prison. A short time after his release he was elected to the city's governing body.

Women, many active in the Movement, had a much better record but were generally only successful as mayors of the smaller towns. However, over 50 African American and Hispanic women have been elected to the House of Representatives since 1964; only two were Republican. Women have won congressional seats in the Southern states of Texas, Florida, Georgia, Alabama, North Carolina and Virginia. Carol Moseley Braun (Illinois) was elected to the US Senate in 1992 (historyhouse.gov) and fought for civil rights and women's issues. The most outstanding Congresswoman was Barbara Jordan. Elected to the Texas legislature in 1966, she was instrumental in establishing the Texas Fair Employment Commission and the introduction of a state minimum wage. She was the first woman elected to Congress from a Deep South state and in 1972 won national attention after her speech at the 1976 Democratic convention. But it was her straight and forceful examination of people involved in the Watergate scandal that played a major part in the House impeachment of Nixon (Rogers, 1999).

In addition to these high-profile successes for African Americans in the South there were also crucial changes – there are now black state troopers, city police officers, sheriffs and deputies. Many of the white officers responsible for riots and murders were ousted. The constant humiliation imposed on people of colour has eased. In Alabama the integration of the police force was the result of a remarkable judge whose support for the law brought no reward from presidents who followed the southern strategy.

The Judge

Frank Johnson, born in Winston County, northern Alabama, was a devout Baptist and a life-long Republican. The hill country had opposed slavery and the Civil War and this ensured that many became Republicans. Although never poor, the Johnson family knew about poverty because they lived in a coal mining, not cotton, area where most miners worked in appalling conditions, had low pay and were short-lived. His under-standing and sympathy was reinforced when he married an impoverished miner's daughter, Ruth Jenkins.

At law school at the University of Alabama a fellow student was George Wallace and they accepted segregation as normal. Johnson explained 'I wasn't confronted with it like I would have been had I grown up down in the Black Delta, in Lowndes County or Macon County or someplace like that.' However, Johnson never accepted the belief in white superiority. His wife openly challenged the system when she was the first white woman to graduate from the 'predominantly' black Alabama State College. She said, as a youth 'I was known as a "nigger lover".' (Yarborough, 1981).

In 1955 President Eisenhower appointed him to the Alabama Middle District Court and the Johnsons moved to Montgomery. Later, while on the 5th Circuit Court of Appeal, he heard cases from across the Deep South and surprised many with his rulings on civil rights. During the Montgomery boycott, Fred Garner, one of the two black lawyers in the city, filed a case for Aurelia Browder and 11 other women who challenged city segregation ordinances. Johnson and Richard Rives attacked *Plessy v. Ferguson* (1896) and argued 'that the separate but equal doctrine can no longer be followed as a correct statement of law'. Montgomery did not appreciate Johnson's liberal views. 'Behind his back and in the press, his rulings were subject to vitriolic abuse; relations with certain employ-ees cooled noticeably; and at times even his friends and employees were made to feel community resentment' (Yarborough, 1981).

Although appointed, he was confronted by politicians who knew that the way to get votes was to defy the courts. It was not only Wallace who solicited the racist vote but also Governor John Patterson who bit-terly attacked court decisions as undermining law and order. Johnson overruled them. Patterson and Wallace tried to impede the Civil Rights Commission investigation of voter discrimination and they refused access to the records. Johnson ordered them to comply and officials to testify and when Wallace ignored the court, Johnson cited him for con-tempt and threatened to jail him. Wallace was tried and found not guilty. Johnson said: 'this court refuses to allow its authority and dignity to be bent or swayed by such politically generated whirlwinds' (Yarborough, 1981). When Wallace was a state judge he had frequently and publicly boasted he would defy the federal government and courts, but secretly he obeyed the government and court and helped the Commission (Carter, 1995).

Johnson insisted African Americans had the right to vote and attend integrated schools. In 1963 Wallace, as governor, was determined to keep schools segregated and sent state troopers to Huntsville to surround the school. Many parents condemned his 'grandstanding' and the Montgomery *Advertiser* editorialised: 'Alabama is not a banana republic.' Johnson ordered desegregation of the university and considered Wallace's stand in the door with contempt. He ensured Wallace complied with the Supreme Court. In November, Auburn University had to admit an African American graduate student, Harold Franklin.

Johnson's battle with Wallace continued. In 1963 the Movement saw the Freedom March from Selma to Montgomery as another opportunity to demand the vote. Segregationists were determined to resist. Sheriff Clark's beatings caused outrage and Johnson issued an order to stop further marches because he did not want more people injured. Wallace and King agreed on a symbolic march after the NAACP negotiated with the judge (Yarborough, 1981). The Movement wanted voting rights and Johnson argued a constitutional 'theory of proportionality'. The march would cause public inconvenience and the right to protest 'should be commensurate with the enormity of the wrongs that are being protested and petitioned against ... In this case the wrongs are enormous. The extent of the right to demonstrate against these wrongs should be determined accordingly' (Walker, 2012). Johnson approved a route and required Wallace to provide protection. Wallace denounced the ruling and accused his old law school associate of prostituting 'our law in favor of that mob rule while hypocritically wearing the robes and clothed in the respect built by great and honest men' (Carter, 1995).

Johnson was concerned about the wider implications of civil disobedience, especially the Freedom Rides. He maintained: 'The philosophy that a person may – if his cause is labelled "civil rights" or "states rights" – determine for himself what court decisions are morally right or wrong and either obey or refuse them according to his own determination, is a philosophy that is foreign to our "rule-of-law" theory of government' (Yarborough, 1981).

In 1972 he made a sweeping attack on the care in state mental institutions which he declared were 'human warehouses' and ordered Wallace to comply with strict standards of care and to establish human rights committees for every hospital with wide-ranging powers to ensure the protection of patients. In the same year, in *Newman v. Alabama*, he ordered that the appalling neglect of state prisoners' health care should cease and set up a human rights commission to see his order was fulfilled. Wallace told the press that Johnson needed a 'good barbed wire enema' (Walker, 2012).

Jimmy Carter admired Johnson and following the FBI's involvement in the Watergate scandal wanted Johnson to clean up the Bureau. However, because of poor health Johnson asked him to withdraw his name which Carter did reluctantly. After Johnson recovered, Carter appointed him to the 5th Circuit Court of Appeal in 1979. When Governor John Patterson, who had opposed Johnson, praised his civil rights role and inducted him into the Alabama Academy of Honor (Yarborough, 1981). Patterson thought the Movement was over. If so he was wrong. In *Bowers v. Hardwick* Johnson supported gay liberation, striking down Georgia's sodomy law (Faderman, 2015). In 1995 Bill Clinton awarded him the Presidential Medal of Freedom for his courageous stand on civil rights (Walker, 2012).

White Students

It was African American women and men and students, especially from schools and colleges, who led the struggle for justice, and they were the ones who faced the greatest danger. But their struggle inspired many white students, not just in the North and West but also in the South. They faced a greater dilemma than most northerners because they challenged the myths their parents, schools and preachers had elaborately woven to ensure white supremacy. And their response to events was as complicated as their elders. Just as Frank Johnson and the Movement tried to bring the South into the 20th century, his son, Johnny, led the University of Alabama campaign for Eugene McCarthy. When George Wallace and his Klan friends and state officials plotted against the

Democratic Party, the Tuscaloosa students passed a resolution that state officials should return to work but Wallace could stay away from the state for as long as he wished.

Johnny Johnson had the experience and support of his parents but others did not. Those who stood with the Movement were part of a longer tradition of southern radicals from the 1890s (Fannin, 2003) and continued to do so in the repressive years of the 1940s and 1950s. But one study assumes that apart from 'islands' such as Austin, Texas, New Orleans, Louisiana and Atlanta, Georgia, southern students were not merely untouched but positively antagonistic to anti-war protesters, the free speech movement, women's rights and LGBT rights. 'In 1968 two movies were popular. *The Graduate* was a hit in large liberal cities, while *The Green Berets* played to crowds in small-town America. Few southern universities witnessed demonstrations' (Anderson, 1995). This assertion is absurd. Many southern white students were active in the civil rights, free speech, anti-war, women's rights and LGBT movements and *The Graduate* was not radical. The hero is a man without a cause who seeks marital bliss and the movie only once briefly refers to Berkeley dissenters.

The southern student activist was no different from his northern counterpart – both faced repression from national and state governments. They established groups and used the Movement's methods. Like northerners they were a minority. The southern students' alignment with civil rights was as complicated as their elders'. The South was not solid. It never had been. Students at the University of North Carolina, Chapel Hill (typical small-town America!) were active in the Movement and Ralph Allan was a leader in the SNCC.

In 1960 UT Knoxville students petitioned the trustees to end segregation and the board complied. Students from the all-black Knoxville College organised sit-ins and were joined by white students at UTK. Perhaps most historians do not acknowledge these actions because typically local papers reported the city's Movement, if at all, on the back pages next to the obituaries (Proudfoot, 1990). A year later, in Louisville, Kentucky white students at the Presbyterian and Baptist seminaries were arrested for participating in sit-ins. White and black students in Nashville who joined the sit-ins were jailed (*The Student Voice*, April and May 1961). Students activism was so widespread that Miles Horton of the Highlander Folk School, Monteagle, Tennessee organised a workshop on 'The Role of the Student in the Changing South'. The workshop held on 11–13 November 1960 was attended by 80 students from black and white universities throughout the South.

Bob Zellner was involved. Son of a Methodist minister, he was raised in Alabama and went to Huntington College in Montgomery. He recalled his youth in a segregated South: 'It was just the way things were. You didn't think about it. Sometimes when you are inside the system, you can't see it very well. But children are not born racist. They are taught to have racial attitudes' (Morrison and Morrison, 1987). This was the experience of Judge Frank Johnson and Carter. Unlike them, Zellner witnessed something that quickly changed his views. The KKK burnt crosses on the campus lawns and despite pressure he refused to leave the college. He became an outspoken critic of those who resisted change. After graduation, he joined the SNCC, went to McComb, Mississippi and was jailed for registering voters. He had been reluctant to take part in a protest march after a black civil rights worker was murdered because he believed it was black people who were leading the struggle. He was persuaded to join and became another victim of police violence. Zellner participated in the Selma to Montgomery march: 'My parents supported me, but it was very alarming for my mother. She was always pleading with me to be careful.' She had good reason – his grandfather and uncle were KKK members and had threatened to kill him. When he was at a demonstration in Danville, Virginia in 1963 hundreds were hospitalised, and when he and others were attacked the FBI reassured him they were taking notes.

But as more and more southern white students rejected Jim Crow and sided with the Movement, younger black southerners became suspicious of their motives. This culminated during the Freedom Summer and after an angry meeting it was decided the SNCC would be an all-black organisation but Zellner was considered 'just one of the niggers'. As a charter member who had been beaten and imprisoned he was told he could stay as a staff member and attend meetings, but he could not vote. Zellner refused. 'It was playing into the hands of the enemy to have a formal exclusion of whites from SNCC.' Despite his disappointment he refused to be bitter (Morrison and Morrison, 1987).

He joined the Southern Student Organizing Committee (SSOC) but followed Anne Braden's advice and worked with integrated groups. Although SNNC and CORE became all-black movements, southern students remained profoundly influenced by their experiences. Zellner worked with Anne and Carl Braden and the SCEF, and also with white and black pulpwood cutters who formed the Gulf Coast Pulpwood Association in 1967 (Mississippi Freedom Democratic Party Newsletter, 27 November 1967 USMDL). Many pulpwood workers earned less than $3000 a year. On 23 September 1971, in Laurel, Mississippi, Zellner persuaded African American Charles Evers, the mayor of Fayette and independent candidate for governor, to address the workers who had been in a four-year-long strike against the Masonite Corporation (undated report to SCEF, USMDC). The Association's white president was James Simmons of Forest Home, Alabama. Evers told them: 'I've always known that the poor black and the poor white would some day get together. Thank God, it's beginning here in Jones County.' Union member Justin Pullman agreed. 'People are beginning to see that rich people are out for just one thing – more money. The only way to stop them is for all the poor people to get together, no matter what the color of their skin is. Black and whites is brothers' (*New York Times,* 24 September 1971). The strike was broken and the union destroyed (Dorothy Zellner to SCEF, USMDL).

Music – Unity and Divergence

Although the Black Panthers were strictly segregated the leadership appreciated the power of music in the struggle and its importance in the Movement – an understanding not shared by its street gang members. They dismissed cultural nationalists' rejection of protest music and attacked their obsession with African music (Ogbar, 2005; Iton, 2008).

For black and white people, music and singing ensured they could reach across the gulf that separated them as they linked arms in churches, Freedom Schools, halls, the homes of rural poor black people and on marches. When incarcerated in segregated prisons they sang and created a unity that infuriated their guards. White students had been taught that they should have no social relationship or friendship with their inferiors.

In the Movement they could touch and sing with young and old, men and women who were the 'invisible' people. Ella Baker and Fanny Lou Hamer understood music's power. Even resisters did. However, the all-black SNNC weakened that bond. Black macho views such as 'Bitch stop fucking. Put the dick down. Get a job' (Iton, 2008) had no appeal to those who had struggled for equality.

Initially, some black women put up with this type of assault and considered 'white' music a 'death march'. 'White adaptations of black music has succumbed to the great white death urge, going from bland rock to suicidal punk and homicidal heavy metal in less than twenty years ... We must pull back from white America, because it is now a great rush of lemmings towards the sea' (Lattany in Early ed., 1993). Movement white women and men did not view music this way. Music festivals kept many ties between students as did shared memories of past sacrifices. The three- and six-string dulcimer and mandolin, popular among Appalachian folk singers, brought protest songs from Kentucky to Tennessee, North Carolina and across many states in the South. White women sang a cappella with country/blues songs. West Virginian Hazel Dickens toured the halls and universities throughout the South singing the radical miners' songs and recorded many on LPs such as *Come All You Good Miners* and *Coal Mining Woman*. Her *Black Lung* hauntingly protested the miners' working conditions. An elderly mountain man at the Eno Musical Festival in North Carolina noted wistfully: 'Too many of them educated folks never understand that folk, gospel, lining, white and black blues, they always have muddled with each other' (interview with the author). Sparky Rucker, a gay black blues man from Memphis, acknowledged the influence of mountain folk on his compositions and singing.

More than the Vote

Many white activists who had worked in the Deep South and border states were involved in marches against the Vietnam War, fought for open housing, protected poor residents from eviction, employed lawyers and law school staff to prevent police violence against minorities, and established cooperatives and free integrated schools. Students such as David Bowen from Memphis, Tennessee in 1965 helped integrate the city's swimming pools and Tom Wilson from Mississippi defended the right of African Americans to desegregate state universities. These were not insignificant acts and it took great courage to break the southern code as did Jimmy Jackson of Winston Salem, North Carolina who defied his KKK father.

The southern underground press fought for free speech and defence of LGBTs. UTK's *Paperbag, Up-Country Revival, Libra, Bad News, Rhapsody* and the *Knoxville Gazette* publicised the work of poor communities, fought city planners and land developers, ran cooperatives, advertised low-cost food and insisted on keeping interracial unity. Many other southern university towns and cities had a lively underground press, such as *The Great Speckled Bird* in Atlanta, all reporting on women's rights, gay liberation and war resistance. In Jackson, Mississippi the editors and staff of *Kudzu* were threatened by gun-toting FBI men. The Bureau and city and state police intimidated printers and advertisers, tactics which eventually destroyed the counter-culture media.

The Free Speech Movement and mounting radicalism alarmed trustees of Berkeley, California and they were joined by university administrators across the nation. Students at Auburn University, Alabama invited anti-war activist William Sloane Coffin to address them and the university president banned him. At UTK, the Administration did the same to African American comedian and civil rights activist Dick Gregory and drug guru Timothy Leary. The students sued and the Court struck down speaker policies as a denial of free speech guaranteed under the Constitution. This willingness to challenge university's *in loco parentis* policies happened across the region. They wanted a better, just and equal society and better education, a more informed understanding of their multi-cultural society and demanded African American studies programmes, better appreciation of the sciences and arts and cuts in bloated sports and business programmes. They were to be the next leaders and they were not being properly prepared. Dan Pomeroy, chairman of the history graduates' union at UTK, wrote to the trustees that students wanted to improve the university's standing. Activists 'resent the fact that not only are the students denied an effective voice in working for that change, but that change in general is now suspect on this campus' (Riches, 1987). He forecast the swing of higher education to conservatism.

The history of southern students who opposed the war in Vietnam has been virtually ignored. Some southern students, like those from the East and North, adopted non-violent disobedience when they rallied against the war. Their attendance at national anti-war rallies has barely been researched. In 1966 when Lieutenant General Lewis Hershey, director of Selective Service, came to UTK, 500 students opposed his visit. They demanded reform of the draft system because it 'placed the burden on the poor, the disadvantaged and the black man' (*Libra*, September 1966). John Z. C. Thomas, a graduate student from Montgomery, Alabama, started the Vietnam Education Group, most of whom were southerners. Anti-war organisations existed on virtually every southern campus and all took part in national as well as local protests.

After Nixon's invasion of Cambodia in 1970 the opposition was nationwide. When four students were killed on 4 May at Kent State University, Ohio students almost everywhere went on strike. At UTK Jimmie Baxter, the first black student president of an overwhelmingly white university, headed the action which also protested the National Guard shooting to death six black people in Augusta, Georgia and the killing of two black students at Jackson State, Mississippi. The strike was 70 percent effective. And at least 31 southern colleges and universities were involved. Unarmed National Guardsmen cleared the University of South Carolina campus; a 100-man police riot squad quelled rioting at the University of Alabama, Tuscaloosa and classes were cancelled in three universities in Florida to head off trouble. Violence broke out at Durham University and University of North Carolina, Chapel Hill. The strike at the University of Virginia was reported as '80 percent effective' (*Libra*, 1970).

Nixon was badly shaken and desperately wanted to visit a university. Billy Graham helped him. Despite student and faculty protests, the evangelist used the UTK football stadium in May for a revival. To help the beleaguered President, Graham called one day 'A Youth Rally'. The 'youth' were overwhelmingly elderly and 1500 anti-war students carried signs with the commandment 'Thou Shalt Not Kill'. A student from Sweetwater, Tennessee recalled: 'On that particular day, I saw a lot of people that came to the Billy Graham Crusade with hate in their eyes.' (*Esquire*, September 1970). On the following Tuesday, 27 people were arrested and one student fled to Europe. The national media did not report it but underground newspapers did.

There was one thing the resisters could not crush and that was the lasting power of the personal transformation of those who had struggled together in an attempt to make the American Dream a reality. An SNCC worker summed up her experience and that of many others: 'It was one of the most significant periods in my life and certainly the most far-reaching one. It is a foundation upon which I continue to build my current life's work, service to the community, and personal and family relations' (Doris Derby in Holsaert et al., 2012).

David Duke and the Old South

The majority of southerners, like northerners, did not share these sentiments and were determined to resist change. Opponents clung to the myths and bigotry of the old South. There were those like Mississippi Governor Haley Babour who wanted to rewrite history, claiming Citizens Councils fought the KKK to ensure school desegregation (*Huffington Post*, 1 November 2011). Others wanted to increase tourism. James Hood said: 'Mississippi was ground zero for civil rights. We can turn what we long tried to hide into a great asset' (Meridian *Star*, 8 June 2011).

'For those who insist that southern whites have undergone a fundamental change in their racial views since the 1960s, it should give pause that Duke received roughly the same share of the vote that a white supremacist would probably have received thirty years earlier in Louisiana' (Klinkner and Smith, 1999). The role of David Duke in that state's politics tells us more about the condition of the Republican Party in the South. When Duke was a candidate for the Nazi Party and the KKK, he made absolutely no progress in state politics. As the authors admit, it was only when he joined the Republican Party that opposed affirmative action and demanded welfare cuts and law and order that he won election to the state legislature in 1989 as a Republican. He followed the script Lee Atwater gave to Reagan – you cannot say 'nigger' anymore, just say bussing or tax cuts – they hurt blacks more. During the century of black disenfranchisement, he would have won virtually 100 percent of the vote. In January 2003 Duke pleaded guilty to charges of stealing money from supporters, partly to pay off his gambling debts. He was jailed (*Time*, 20 January 2003). In 2016 he endorsed the Republican nominee Donald Trump to the disgust of many in the Party but only won 3 percent of the vote when seeking re-election to the Louisiana legislature. Duke failed the Atwater test of coded racism. The white backlash was not confined to the South, however, as is evidenced by the militia movement, racist police killings and the 'alt-right' of the internet.

LBJ empowered African American voters but this was largely due to the courage and sacrifices of African Americans, especially the forgotten. But few credit the change in many white people's attitudes, men and women like Constance Curry and Johnny Johnson, as well as the better-known politicians such as Al Gore Sr or Jimmy Carter. It was carpetbagger, George H. W. Bush and his son who exploited the fear and anger of white folks who saw themselves as the dispossessed.

7

Willie Horton and the Southern Strategy: George H. W. Bush 1989–1993

Angry, white blue-collar voters flocked into groups such as Restore Our Alienated Rights (ROAR) and the Republicans were eager to win them over from the Democratic Party. The goal was to unravel the gains made by disadvantaged people including women since FDR's New Deal and LBJ's Great Society. Although some Christian Coalition supporters might have been politically pragmatic (Watson, 1999), most fundamentalists in the Moral Majority and the Catholic Church wanted abortion abolished. They linked their opposition to abortion to other issues such as feminism, affirmative action, prohibition of prayers in schools, any form of desegregation and the growing demand of the LGBT community for their human and civil rights. The Ultras believed there was a communist plot to destroy America. Fuelling this backlash was the growing awareness and dread that white people were gradually becoming the minority: this was exploited during the presidential campaigns in 2008, 2012 and 2016. A civil rights and anti-war activist historian contends that this national mood had begun in 1980 by the calculated use of bussing black children into working-class and poor white neighbourhoods (Zinn, 1980). Bussing was exploited earlier, but it is correct that George H. W. Bush, a former congressman, head of the CIA and Reagan's vice president, heightened polarisation along racial lines.

But Bush Sr had problems as a would-be president. He was born in New England, one of the most hated regions in the Union because allegedly it harboured Democratic, liberal un-Americans. How was he to continue the southern strategy as a New Englander and exploit the New Right's distrust of government when he had spent most of his life in politics and Washington DC? He decided to claim he was from Texas, wear the obligatory Stetson and cowboy boots, and to live on a ranch. He convinced the Ultras that his vice presidency proved he had adopted their positions. Some see him as a centrist who did not realise how far the Party had moved to the right (McAdam and Kloos, 2014). But this overlooks his eight years under Reagan and it is difficult to accept he was unaware of what was happening in the Party.

Before his conversion he had tried to win the Party's nomination and derided Reagan's 'voodoo economics'. Once beaten, he quickly adopted the theories of unfettered free markets and this partly explains why he won the presidential nomination. But he had to explain away other 'deficiencies' before his vice-presidential nomination, such as his vote for the Equal Rights Amendment, abortion and federally funded contraceptive services. He repudiated these stands. He had supported Reagan's efforts to amend the Constitution to allow states to require some form of religious observance in schools even though the Supreme Court said that the Constitution insisted on separation of church and state. Like all candidates, he exploited patriotism and during his campaign and presidency he argued Congress should outlaw the burning or desecration of the flag (Lowi and Ginsburg, 2008).

Willie Horton and the 1988 Campaign

Lee Atwater in 1990 said it was impossible to use the word 'nigger' but only 'welfare' or 'tax cuts' to embrace racism. Bush did not use the 'N' word but the oldest racist stereotype – the black male who raped white women. Atwater had controlled Reagan's campaign and, as noted above, had chosen to open it in Mississippi's most racist county. He knew Bush had to keep that vote. After all, Strom Thurmond, a vehement racist who fathered a black child, and Jesse Helms were powerful senators who still spoke for the old South (Crespino, 2007). This southern base was essential but not enough and it was up to Atwater to save his employer from almost certain defeat. A May Gallup Poll showed that Bush had a lowly 38 percent and was trailing his Democrat opponent Massachusetts Governor Michael Dukakis by 16 percent. 'Three Democratic losers, George McGovern, Jimmy Carter, and Walter Mondale, had had negative ratings of 27, 28 and 29 percent respectively in their unsuccessful campaigns of 1972, 1980 and 1984. Bush's negatives topped all of theirs' (Johnson, 1991). The Atwater campaign wanted to portray Dukakis as an ultra-liberal and thereby increase the governor's negatives in the eyes of the electorate.

Thirty New Jersey voters who had supported Reagan in 1984 and who were thinking of returning to their traditional Democratic allegiance were selected by a marketing firm. Participants were asked a series of questions put by Bush campaign officials which emphasised the dangerous platform of Dukakis. They were unaware that the survey was organised by the Republican Party. The questioners stressed that Dukakis, as governor of Massachusetts in 1977, had vetoed a bill requiring schools to give the pledge of allegiance. In addition, they were told that he belonged to the American Civil Liberties Union (ACLU) with no explanation that the ACLU not only defended left-wing radicals but also the KKK and other extremist groups.

Exploiting law and order concerns, they told them that as governor Michael Dukakis had vetoed mandatory sentences for drug dealers and the death penalty. Dukakis had approved the furlough programme for Massachusetts prisoners. His revolving door policy gave weekend furloughs to first-degree murderers not eligible for parole. While out, they suggested, many committed other crimes, such as kidnapping and rape, and many were still at large. The survey emphasised the case of Willie Horton who had raped and murdered a white woman in Maryland when he was on furlough. The case had been widely reported and there was no need to give his name – these were crimes associated with black men. 'Now Michael Dukakis says he wants to do for America what he's done for Massachusetts. Americans cannot afford that risk' (www.pbs.org/frontline/atwater/script). Once again there were significant omissions such as that the previous governor, a Republican, had supported the furlough measure. Half of these voters surveyed switched their allegiance to Bush.

Despite denials, Lee Atwater continued to exploit racism, re-enforcing the link between race, law and order and the growing alarm about social change. The goal was to heighten fear, especially in the North (Sugrue, 2005; Jones, 2009). Whereas George Wallace had relied on 'the age-old southern cry of "Nigger, Nigger"', he substituted the equivalents of apple pie and motherhood: the rights of private property, community control, neighborhood schools, union seniority' (Carter, 1995). But Wallace was a third-party candidate in 1968 and 1972, who only influenced the course of those elections – he could not win the presidency. However, even a Republican, born in Massachusetts with a Harvard education who claimed to be a Texan, had a chance.

Willie Horton gave Bush a crime that enabled him to exploit the Wallace strategy that pushed the Party further to the right. 'Richard Nixon initiated the use of thinly coded race words that hinted at violence. Ronald Reagan imitated the practice in 1980, and George Bush took it to a cynical level in 1988 with his Willie Horton advertisements' (Nightingale, 1993). One ad involved a revolving door with prisoners entering and leaving and viewers were told that hundreds were still on the loose. Another, paid for by a Bush support group, named Willie Horton whose face filled the screen and the crimes he committed were detailed. Bush never repudiated it although he was asked to many times. The insatiable sexual black man has a long history. Richard Wright's novel *Native Son* (1940) set off a moral panic because he portrays Bigger Thomas's fears he will be accused of rape after accidentally killing a white girl. Dismembering and burning her body and burning it in a furnace, without remorse, frees him existentially. He is no longer the victim. For whites such stories fed their oldest nightmares (Riches, 1980).

Ironically, national television's response to the Horton advertisements was the only time all three major networks criticised the Bush campaign, but by continually repeating it in news bulletins they gave him free advertising and stoked national racism. Political commentators who argue that negative campaigning is counter-productive have been proved wrong because it has featured in every presidential election from 1800 to the present. Bush denied that he was responsible but he knew his election strategist, Lee Atwater, was behind it. 'In depicting Willie Horton as a symbol of Dukakis' alleged softness on crime, the Bush campaign fomented racial fears for political purposes and appealed to the worst elements of the American character' (Johnson, 1991). This is underlined succinctly: 'Race is poison, but it's poison for their side' (Eric Altman, pbs.org/frontline). Atwater's deathbed apology meant nothing to the African American community and the consequence of the Bush campaign was that black voters supported Democrats at record levels. Former Movement leaders such as Ralph Abernathy withdrew their support for the Republicans.

Patriotic speeches were combined with visits to flag manufacturers and all-white American Legion meetings where audiences were constantly warned that Dukakis was an unpatriotic, ultra-liberal whose weakness over law and order threatened America. At no time did Bush admit that rising crime and poverty were linked to the 'voodoo economics' he had derided in 1980 and then fervently supported. As Michael Males argues: 'The higher rates of unwed childbearing among blacks and Latinos relative to whites reflect the greater poverty of non-white populations. Where statistics on income are available we find low-income whites also experience disproportionately high levels of these problems' (Males, 1996).

Dukakis tried to fight the southern strategy by choosing moderate Texas Senator Lloyd Bentsen as his vice-presidential partner. Dukakis was lampooned when he rode in a tank to overcome charges of lack of patriotism. But Willie Horton haunted his dream of becoming president. In November Bush won the election with 53.4 percent of the popular vote as opposed to Dukakis's 45.6 percent. Apart from the overwhelmingly black district of Washington, the ten states the governor won were all in the North whereas Bush carried all the former Confederate states. His margin of victory in the South was even greater than his national figures – 58.3 percent compared to 40.9 percent.

One analyst has conceded racism was part of the Republican strategy but asserts that it was not 'the factor'. He suggests that the regional disparity in white support for the Democratic Party 'would have been lessened significantly had the public's attention in the campaign been focused on economic issues and not on highly charged social issues' (Lamis, 1990). But that was the Republican plan – Bush dismissing economics with sound bites and the Democrats failing to capture voter interest in the economy. As Atwater and Bush knew well, exploiting controversial social issues such as civil rights for African Americans and other minorities, the supposed permissive violent 1960s, law and order and abortion ensured political gain. It is always difficult to persuade voters with discussions of national debts, industrial disinvestment and capital flight overseas. Republicans had diverted attention from economic difficulties that an increasing number of Americans struggled to overcome and which were exacerbated when Bush followed Reagan's economics (Sugrue, 2005). A poor Democratic campaign made it easier for Bush.

'A Kinder, Gentler America'

At his inauguration Bush called for 'a kinder, gentler America' which 'we must hope to give them [our children] a sense of what it means to be a loyal friend, a loving parent, a citizen who leaves his home, his neighborhood better than he found it.' He continued that in this society shaped by public generosity the community would care for 'the homeless, lost and roaming' (www.presidency.ucsb.edu). That so many were in such a parlous state after eight years of Republican government proved their economic mismanagement.

Although Bush was using the romanticised ideal of American individualism, many of his critics, black and white, saw it as coded racism. And it was not the rural and urban poor who benefited under Bush after the $8 billion Savings and Loan Companies debacle. Many of the homeless had been the victims of the corruption in the Department of Housing and Urban Development. Central to the scandal that unfolded in the first days of the Bush Administration was the Reagan political appointees who had funnelled tens of millions of dollars to government employed political consultants. Presiding over this corruption was Samuel R. Pierce, a Wall Street lawyer who was Reagan's only black Cabinet member. The beneficiaries were Republicans such as the Watergate-disgraced John

Mitchell, Nixon's Attorney General, and Carla Hills, Bush's special trade representative (Johnson, 1991).

His laissez-faire economic polices encouraged corporations to entice staff from rivals by paying millions of dollars in 'golden parachutes' and generous stock options. When they left their jobs, even if they failed, their contracts rewarded them with more millions and stock options. The number of African Americans, Hispanics and other minority men who benefited from this were miniscule (Piketty, 2014). The situation for black women was hardly better – both sexes were overwhelmingly in traditional jobs such as cleaners, janitors and junior secretarial posts. The growing demand for high-tech skills closed doors for upward mobility because inner city schools were poorly equipped. Funding for these schools was sharply reduced because politicians were happy to comply with white suburbanites' demands for lower taxes. Anti-poverty and development schemes were underfunded because of the shrinking tax base caused by business and white flight. All these problems were compounded by the continued decline in heavy manufacturing (McAdam and Kloos, 2014).

When the motor industry moved plants from Detroit and Flint, Michigan many skilled and well-paid jobs for African American men disappeared because housing discrimination barred them from moving to the plants in the suburbs. The land was left barren and turned into parks. The city's 'largest area of job growth since the 1980s has been part-time, contingent work'. According to one urban historian, the only hope for Detroit and other cities 'comes from the continued efforts of city residents to resist the debilitating effects of poverty, racial tension, and industrial decline' (Sugrue, 2005).

Despite their limitations the New Deal and Great Society had brought a marked improvement in equality. The minimum wage in 1969 was $1.60, the equivalent of $10.10 in 2013, taking into account inflation and the lower than 4 percent unemployment. But when Reagan and Bush froze the minimum wage to $3.65 it resulted in a drastic cut in the purchasing power for the working class and the poor. The policy was particularly harsh on African Americans and other inner city minorities: 'The United States of the twentieth century is not synonymous with a great leap forward in social justice. Indeed, inequality of wealth is greater today than it was at the beginning of the nineteenth century.' The consequence? 'Hence the lost US paradise is associated with the country's beginnings: there is a nostalgia for the era of the Boston Tea Party ... not for a heyday of state intervention to curb the excesses of capitalism' (Piketty, 2014). Bush was an enthusiastic non-interventionist and for him the answer was 'a thousand points of light' which he defined as federal support for voluntary organisations and he vetoed a plan for inner city enterprise zones because the Congressional proposal included tax increases and increased government intervention in the economy.

Rodney King and Police Violence

What is unusual about the Rodney King case is not what happened but rather that it received so much national and even international attention. It is not an exaggeration to claim that throughout their history in America – North and South – African Americans have been beaten, murdered, lynched and oppressed. Irish, German or Norwegian arrivals could use their 'whiteness' to Americanise themselves and thus overcome American nativism. For example, the rioting against Irish Catholics before the Civil War diminished when they gave up their language and waved the American flag. Their contribution to the Union cause is vaunted but the greater contribution of free and enslaved black people was entirely ignored until the late 1950s (Blight, 2001). The willingness of Irish and other immigrants, such as the Polish, to assault African Americans in cities such as Detroit, Milwaukee, Chicago, New York and Philadelphia helped them to become true Americans. Racism created the 'two-ness' that W. E. B. Du Bois wrote about in 1898 – 'two souls, two thoughts, two unreconciled strivings, two warring ideals in one dark body, whose dogged strength alone keeps it from being torn asunder'. They were, they are, forced into a battle between their colour and trying to be Americans.

In 1990, 56 percent of whites believed African Americans were prone to violence and Bush harped on this persistent fear even though only 6 percent of murders and 9 percent of rapes were committed by black men attacking white victims. And in prison they were subjected to the violence of guards and racist prisoners, especially by members of the Aryan

Nations. But because one-third of muggings in America's cities were by African Americans against whites, the link between violence and race was re-enforced and increased the long-term racism in the North. The incarceration rates of black youth and men were far higher than whites, and blacks were jailed in cases where whites were only fined. Rural and small town crime is overwhelmingly white whereas black crime is largely confined to the cities and was, and is, black-on-black. Incarceration rates, especially of black men, increased rapidly as state prisons were handed over to private companies.

The Rodney King case was known because five police officers were filmed beating a black man on an empty stretch of highway. New technology captured them and it would continue to do so in increasing numbers but the result would almost always be the same: innocent police and threatening black males. The white community had always sanctioned police brutality against black men – from using live ammunition in riot control by Frank Rizzo in Philadelphia in 1964 to the killing of 27 Black Panther Party members in 1969. The police were protecting society, that is white privilege, and themselves. 'The 1991 videotape of Rodney King's beating on a California motorway showed the connection between racism and state repression in America' (Nightingale, 1993). The authorities had to prosecute because of the film. The jury's not guilty decision re-enforced African Americans' belief that they would never get justice, that the judicial system benefited white people and it was part of the system of control over the black community. Many argue that no white person can understand African Americans' 'fear [of] the destruction of the body … which is heightened by the "illusion" of the American Dream' (Coates, 2015; Mayer, 2016). They responded in the only way they thought they could with riots which served to re-enforce the stereotypes of them as violent. And rioting only damaged their community because they were locked in the ghetto.

Increasingly the problems of the poor were equated with inherent laziness, sexual promiscuity and contempt for authority by African American, Hispanic and other minorities in the ghettos. Individual faults explained the rise in crime and poverty, one-parent childbirths, marriage breakdown and neglect of parental responsibility (D'Souza, 2014). But these problems were common to white and other ethnic communities.

Bush and Civil Rights

Bush faced not only problems of mounting budget deficits but also a partisan Congress. Reagan had vetoed the 1988 Civil Rights Restoration Act (CRRA) designed to reverse the limitations imposed on civil rights laws by four decisions of the Supreme Court which made it very difficult for a complainant to prove job discrimination. The CRRA was a major step to end federally funded civil rights legislation as well as to extend civil rights legislation to women, the elderly and the disabled. Reagan did everything he could to kill it but Democrats, supported by some Republicans, overrode his veto.

In *Wards Cove Packing Company Limited v. Antonio* (1989) the Court ruled against Asian American women that their employer was guilty of discrimination. The Court majority dismissed their case, arguing it was a matter of different employment practices which led to different effects on different people. A company was free to set working patterns as it saw fit. It shifted the burden of proof from the employer to the employee. Congress proposed legislation to allow jury trials in cases where the complainants brought charges of discrimination by employers. It shifted the burden of proof back to the employer. The Civil Rights and Women's Equity Bill was submitted to the Senate sponsored by Ted Kennedy of Massachusetts and Albert Gore Jr of Tennessee. It would not just apply to African Americans but was extended to include gender, disability, religion and national origin, reducing the issues of race and quotas. However, Senator Bob Dole, the Republican minority leader, complained that the legislation went too far.

At first Bush was not involved but as the resistance mounted, the Administration, led by Vice President Dan Quayle, realised the president's opinion was crucial. He vetoed it. 'The veto represented the first defeat of a major civil rights bill in the last quarter of a century.' He exploited white fears that it gave unfair advantages to African Americans at the expense of white people. He defended his veto: '[H]e used the word *quotas* seven times in five paragraphs' (Klinkner and Smith, 1999). In the same year he vetoed a 'quota bill' designed to aid Native Americans, claiming that 'it is so seriously flawed that it would create more problems than it would solve'.

He was caving in to the right wing of his Party. Although his aides sought to limit the damage by claiming they supported some legislation for African Americans, such assurances were not accepted by the black community and the veto angered not only them but also many other minorities. The Senate was forced to compromise. Damages paid by an employer guilty of discrimination were limited and it defined the legal defences that employers could use. They added a clause that extended civil rights protection to employees in the executive and legislative branches of the federal government. Bush had to sign it but complained it amounted to 'racial quotas'. To protect himself from the conservatives, a leaked directive proposed the abolition of federal government affirmative action programmes that had existed since LBJ's 1965 executive order. An administration spokesman denied Bush knew about it. As Shull has claimed: 'The controversial directive was to be appended to the bill, but the White House issued a new statement in the president's name eliminating the directive. Presumably President Bush tried to do by administrative means what he had failed to do legislatively' (Shull, 1993).

The veto of the civil rights bill and the controversy over the directive confirmed for most African Americans that the Bush Administration was content to lead the resistance to black equality. The Justice Department's Civil Rights Division had supported the struggle during LBJ's term in office, but Bush followed his master. Reagan had appointed William Bradford Reynolds to head the Division – a man who opposed court-ordered busing and affirmative action, and who complained about 'unlawfully' imposed quotas. He consistently sought to narrow the meaning and enforcement of civil rights laws. When he left, Bush nominated William Lucas, a conservative black Republican, a tactic he often resorted to.

Lucas had enthusiastic supporters among conservatives because he attacked racial quotas, supported tax exempt status for racially segregated private schools and denied that recent Supreme Court decisions impeded equal opportunity. Faced with such views, African American Representative John Conyers from Michigan, withdrew his endorsement of Lucas. Jesse Jackson and the mayor of Detroit, Coleman Young, did also. Liberal groups that had initially approved of him backed away and only the SCLC continued to support him. Faced with mounting opposition, Bush was determined to have Lucas in the Justice

Department and appointed him to a position that did not require Senate confirmation. Lucas had a dubious distinction: he was 'the first black candidate for federal office rejected by the Senate after being formally nominated'. Further evidence of President Bush's opposition was reflected in his refusal to appoint members to the Civil Rights Commission, ensuring there were only four members instead of the eight required. It collapsed (Shull, 1993).

Appointing a Judge

Following Reagan's example, Bush nominated judges who supported the conservative agenda. Thurgood Marshall, the lead lawyer for the NAACP in *Brown*, retired in 1991 and George Bush nominated a poorly qualified African American, Clarence Thomas, who has been described as 'the most controversial Supreme Court nomination in U.S. history' (Shull, 1993). Initially Thomas had the overwhelming support of the black community but this diminished as accusations against him mounted (Dye and Zeigler, 2002). And for one African American political commentator: 'Thomas has emerged as the high court's most aggressive advocate of rolling back the gains Marshall fought so hard for' (*Time*, 2 June 1995).

The president knew that Thomas was a devout believer in the conservative agenda, so much so that fellow conservatives on the Court often wrote dissenting opinions on cases that favoured curtailing government and limiting civil rights (Coyle, 2013). Thomas also opposed class action suits which enabled large numbers of people to seek justice. Like Booker T. Washington at the turn of the 20th century he is a firm believer in self-help. His opposition to affirmative action was well known although he had benefited from it because, despite an average academic background, he was admitted to Yale University law school. Ironically, it was at Yale that he regretted his earlier support for civil rights and opposition to the Vietnam war (*Atlantic Monthly*, 14 July 2015). In his memoirs he claims that he flirted with black nationalism but he did not say at his confirmation that he had held the same views as the Nation of Islam and religious fundamentalists, or admit that they were shaped by his early membership of the Catholic Church and training to be a priest.

After working in the Monsanto company law department, he assisted a Republican senator before his appointment to the federal court in Washington DC. He continued to benefit from the quota system when Bush nominated him as the token black for the Supreme Court. However, during the Senate hearings, a law professor and fellow black conservative at Oklahoma University, Anita Hill, accused him of sexual harassment when she had worked with him while he was head of the Equal Employment Opportunities Commission (EEOC) (Mayer and Abramson, 1994; Wilson and Russell, 1996). He said he would not play the race card but Thomas accused liberals and women's groups of a 'high tech lynching of uppity blacks' (Thomas, 2005). It was a cynical abuse of the horrors of lynching but very effective. He lied at the committee hearings when he insisted he would respect legal precedents and the separation of powers of the Court and Congress. There was an unprecedented campaign waged by the Administration as opposition mounted. Members of Congress were subject to veiled threats and Bush even bussed all the black people from Thomas's birthplace of Pin Point, Georgia to demonstrate for the nominee outside the Senate Building (Mayer and Abramson, 1994).

He was narrowly confirmed by 52 votes to 48 because liberals and African Americans were divided. Liberal Joe Biden closed the hearings before all the evidence against Thomas was presented (Mayer and Abramson, 1994). The vote in favour by Orin Hatch (Utah) was no surprise but Biden joined Hatch in the attacks on Hill's integrity. Paula Giddings observes that: 'Black women have been stereotyped as immoral, insatiable, perverse: the initiators in all sexual contacts – abusive or otherwise' (Giddings in Ruiz and DuBois, 1994). It may have been 'politically brilliant' for Bush to appoint a black conservative (Klinkner and Smith, 1999) but it cost him the support of even more African Americans and especially women who constitute the largest voting bloc. Most women remain consistent Democrats and cost the Republicans four presidential elections.

On the Court he followed the ultra-conservative views of Scalia who favoured extending the death penalty to children aged 15 and above (Males, 1996), and supported him in the first eight cases he heard. The Court's ruling in *Freeman v. Pitts* (1992) weakened school desegregation and was later backed by Thomas who criticised the plans, claiming they denigrated black school teachers and black children who did not need integrated schools. Wade Henderson, NAACP Washington director, said that: 'If Thomas had been on the court at the time, he would have opposed the decision in *Brown v The Board of Education*.' Henderson was right when Thomas concurred in the opinion *Missouri v. Jenkins* in June 1995. In 1989 the Court ruled in *Webster v. Reproductive Health Services* that states had the right to limit abortions. At his confirmation hearings in 1991, Thomas agreed with the Court. He even opposed the Bush Administration when it favoured 'broadly interpreting the Voting Rights Act' (Shull, 1993). Bush appointed social conservatives to lower federal courts which had a long-lasting effect on civil rights.

In addition to changing the nature of the courts, Bush weakened gains made by the Movement by radically reducing federal government financial support and staff for civil rights and anti-poverty programmes. There was a dramatic drop in the number of cases brought by the Justice Department to enforce school desegregation, fight discrimination in housing sales or to pursue employers accused of discrimination. Although the Court had limited affirmative action, they did not rule it out as unconstitutional. In a 5–4 finding in *United States v. Paradise*, Alabama was required to hire African Americans in the Department of Safety and as state troopers 'to correct the effects of past discrimination' (caselaw.findlaw.com). But they made it difficult for individuals to seek redress. Bush was pleased that this made cases harder. The significance of the judicial appointments made by Reagan and Bush was evident in a 1989 Court's ruling. In *Richmond v. Crosen* the majority voted that the city's set-aside programme, which required that '30 percent of construction contracts should go to minorities, including African Americans, was unconstitutional because it violated equal protection guaranteed under the Fourteenth Amendment' (Dye and Zeigler, 2000). It re-instated the 1873 *Slaughter Houses* ruling which had given corporations protections designed for individuals, thus weakening the protection of formerly enslaved people.

But Bush and the Republicans thought that some gestures to African Americans might help them win control of the House of Representatives or some state legislatures. Unlike Reagan, who had met black leaders once every year, George H. W. Bush met them more than 40 times in his first two years. Reagan had vetoed legislation imposing sanctions on South Africa; Bush favoured strengthening them and called for the release of Nelson Mandela. Much of this was symbolic politics because the meetings produced no results and he could do nothing about South Africa anyway. It was easier for him to support black people thousands of miles away rather than those in his own backyard. Even though he increased the EEOC budget, very little was accomplished. Significantly, his major achievement strengthened segregation when he won funding for 'historically black colleges' that was well received by middle-class African Americans. The administrators of these all-black institutions and black academics praised him just as they did when he denounced the murder of a civil rights lawyer in Atlanta and a federal judge in Alabama. He appointed a liberal Republican as head of the Civil Rights Commission. The African American historian Manning Marable claims: 'The net impact of Bush's verbal and political overtures to black America reaped impressive political gains' (Marable, 1991). However, 'overtures' were not actions and it is difficult to see where he made 'impressive political gains'.

African Americans in Mississippi

Although the civil rights movement suffered reversals at the federal level during Bush's term in office, African Americans increased their power at the local level. This was true even in the Deep South where resistance to civil rights for blacks was the fiercest. LBJ knew when he signed the Voting Rights Act of 1965 that he had destroyed the coalition crafted by FDR that had made the Democrats the majority party in Congress after 1932. The Republican Party moved increasingly to the right and wooed segregationist Democrats. But as the Democrats lost votes for national posts in Congress and for the presidency, they reluctantly came to accept that if they were to have any influence at state level they would have to compromise with and seek the support of black voters. And they found this difficult.

Their first reaction had been massive resistance and violence. After the Voting Rights Act the Mississippi legislature redrew state districts to ensure only one black representative would be elected out of 122 house members and two senators. Hinds County, which included the capital of Jackson with 40 percent black population, did not have a single black representative from the ten districts. But compliance with the Voting Rights Act was forced on the state after African Americans sued 14 times and went to the Supreme Court nine times. In 1979 the Mississippi legislature voted there would be only one member per district and 15 black Mississippians were elected to the house and two to the senate. In all subsequent elections their representation increased.

The inadequate support of the federal government did not stop this progress. By 1988 black representatives in the state house increased to 21 and to four in the senate, and after 1992 black representation in the house jumped to 31 and in the senate to ten. African Americans held significant power on state committees, especially on those responsible for education, and they built a biracial alliance which ensured the states' Education Reform Act (Shaffer and Menifield, 2002). When the Bush Administration was cutting federal aid to education, such as the very successful Head Start programme for young children, in 1989 black and white Mississippi Democrats passed the School Equity Funding Act giving state funds to poorer school districts and requiring all districts to have property taxes that would support public elementary and high schools. Obviously, the latter benefited richer areas most but the funds and tax did improve black education. And the coalition would produce further successes in the 1990s, and not just in education.

However, African Americans in Mississippi were no different from many white people in the United States and were deeply divided on abortion after the Supreme Court in *Roe v. Wade* (1973) had declared abortion constitutional. *Roe* was particularly complex for black women who used abortion when they were raped by white or black men – even though they shared the religious belief that abortion was a sin. Another fear was not without some foundation. It was widely believed by black women and ethnic minorities across the country that abortion was part of a wider conspiracy to wipe out the 'race'. Certainly, sterilisation without consent was long practised to limit reproduction of all poor women, upheld by the Supreme Court in *Buck v. Bell* (1927), continued well into the 1970s – and still happens. However, the pregnant white middle class had no worries because it was relatively easy for them to arrange an illegal termination. In 1986 the black senators in Mississippi and 25 percent of the representatives favoured legislation that required minors to have parental consent before an abortion. Governor Ray Mabus, elected by a coalition of blacks, poor white and liberal white Mississippians, vetoed it and consequently more black legislators joined anti-abortionists to override the veto (Shaffer and Menifield, 2002). When Bush Sr and Bill Clinton exploited the law and order issue in the 1992 presidential election campaign, black members of the Mississippi legislature were deserted by their white Democratic colleagues. The demand for tougher action against juvenile crime meant that black representatives feared they would be seen as 'soft on crime' which most Americans believed was the product of 1960s permissiveness and the civil rights movement's defiance of the law.

Many people of colour recognised that black-on-black crime did not bother the authorities and rioting could be confined to ghettos. But budget cuts and inflation under Bush reduced money for policing and the FBI. They needed more money to hire more staff to fulfil the political and the white public's demands for action. One answer was the creation of the 'serial killer' in the 1980s. A man who killed more than once was no longer a mass murderer, but rather a single degenerate individual who carefully selected his victims. '[T]hese killers attack the presumed security of society.' The killer was white, the crime was sexual and the victim was white. 'The panic surrounding the serial sex murder was particularly aimed at suburban families who shopped in malls, whose young children played in their neighborhoods, who relied on the security of their homes for the preservation of their nuclear families, and who sent their children to college' (Milligen, 2006). These upper- and middle-class white Americans were now under attack from white deviants, a theme exploited in movies such as *Silence of the Lambs* (1991). The form of racism that permeates these movies is not that the killer is black but rather depraved (usually 'white trash') who are no better than 'niggers'. White officers are the expert operatives – except in the film *7* in which the black actor Morgan Freeman is the lead investigator.

Responding to the increased national fear and racial tension, black members in the Mississippi legislature followed the course taken by blacks at the federal level and other states. To increase their influence they set up a Black Caucus. The caucus system added to black political experience making it easier to be elected at the federal level. Black women were helped especially. Corrine Brown was elected to the Florida 1st District in 1993 after serving ten years in the state legislature and Cynthia McKinney in Georgia after serving at state level from 1988. And it was not confined to southern black women as more African Americans registered to vote. Julia Carson from Indianapolis, after representing her district for 18 years, was the first black woman to be elected to the House of Representatives from Indiana. Barbara Lee in Oakland California became leader of the House of Representatives' Black Caucus and she had served at local level from 1990 to 1996. These political successes were visible expressions of black power and destroyed the myth that black people were unfit to hold office.

Women of Colour and the New Conservatism

Clarence Thomas opposed civil rights not only for African Americans but also for women, gays and lesbians. More black women began to defend abortion and feminism and argued the Movement had made them see the need to resist gender and LGBT discrimination. Male chauvinism in the Movement encouraged them to join their white sisters (Wilson and Russell, 1996; Brandt, 1999). And the 1980s New Conservatism meant women had to struggle, despite their differences, to hold on to the gains they had made. Ultra-conservatives, such as Pat Buchanan, attacked Bush for not being tougher on the feminist movement. But Bush campaigned against abortion, and dramatised the number of single mothers (that is black) who endangered so-called white family values. Many black men supported patriarchy and angered an increasing number of black women. Angela Davis explained: 'women of color included white women' (Davis, 1998). Carol Moseley-Braun, the first and only black woman elected as a senator in 1992 for Illinois, was asked what was worse – racism or sexism: '[If] someone has their foot on the back of your neck it doesn't really matter why it's there' (*The Washington Post*, 12 February 2014).

Pauli Murray had shared this view and joined with white feminists to set up the National Organization for Women (NOW). In the 1960s Movement black women had considered race more important than gender and had been reluctant to join white women's rights groups or feminists who seemed to neglect the fight against racism. Paula Giddings challenged this. Black women should join their white sisters to fight male oppression. Sexism in the wider community often meant African American men preferred light-skinned women but men resented the apparent ease these women had getting college education and jobs. Black men ignored the difficulties of darker women in finding work (Wilson and Russell, 1996). Women were often, especially in rap, portrayed as promiscuous 'bitches' and 'whores' (Darieck Scott in Brandt, 1999). It was not only rappers. Prince's lyrics for *My Sugar Walls* were sexist, crude and pathetic and his album *Purple Rain* includes a number, *Darling Nikki*, which opens with a man watching a woman masturbate in a hotel lobby.

This objectification made many women of colour change their minds. Increasingly women called for a wider alliance not only because of sexism in the wider community and popular culture but also because of the threat from the courts and the Bush Administration. Equal opportunity laws for women in education and employment were weakened by the courts but it did not end the widespread male fear that their dominance was under attack. Bush exploited this to reassure and win men's votes. The Small Business Administration reduced funding to women's enterprises; did not undertake mandated job evaluation schemes, despite their vital role for equal pay; and day centres had funding cuts, as did shelters for battered women and legal aid centres (Kerber and De Hart, 1991).

Bush's only concession was a re-election campaign promise of a small tax concession for the poorest families to help with day care costs. He could not keep it because he lost the election. Black and Hispanic women, especially, were often the only family providers, usually in very low-paid jobs. Working partners were also in pitifully paid work. This so-called 'under class' suffered disproportionately because state and federal government did not provide child support or improve an inadequate transport system and they did not benefit from fair and equal labour laws because they were non-unionised workers (Ehrenreich, 2001).

After his election in 1988 Bush boasted he had 'kicked a little ass'. The 'ass' involved was Democrat Geraldine Ferraro, the first woman vice-presidential candidate. She said: 'There are rumours about me being involved in lesbianism, about my having affairs, about me having an abortion' (Faludi, 1992). Despite all the evidence, she was convinced, wrongly, that her gender had ensured the Democrats' defeat. One short-term effect was to reduce the number of women candidates but this was reversed in 1992 when black and white women candidates, overwhelming Democrats, increased and many were successful. Dubbed 'the year of the woman' by the popular press, there was much talk of a Political Action Committee (PAC) to increase the number of Democratic pro-choice women congressional candidates, the so-called EMILY'S List. Some worried Republican women set up their own PAC to fund pro-choice women for the Senate and House (WISH List). Bush's vetoing civil rights legislation because it included gender equality and his talk of 'kicking a little ass' played a major role in his losing re-election. The switch of so many women to the Democratic Party was aided by Hillary Clinton who was an accomplished lawyer and unafraid to give her opinions. The fact that she was pro-choice also appealed to many.

George H. W. Bush and the Gay Community

Most African Americans had fought to overcome state laws against inter-racial marriage. The prime reason was to stop the lynching of black men believed to be obsessed with white women, something highlighted in the 1915 film *Birth of a Nation* (Allen, et. al., 2000). Black men were murdered even if the relationship was consensual. Despite their support for heterosexual marriage, most African Americans shared society's horror when it came to same-sex relationships whether they were intraracial or interracial. This loathing was highlighted by Mapplethore's explicit photographs of black and white gay men exhibited by the National Endowment of the Arts in Cincinnati, Ohio. A judge denied demands it should be shut down (*New York Times*, 8 October 1990). The major-ity believed the courts were undermining American values by support-ing gays. In 1992 Madonna published her book *Sex*. Photos showed her 'performing' with black and white lesbians, having sex with stereotypical black men and S&M with white and black women. She claimed she was a liberated woman but LGBT people saw it as cheap exploitation.

Gays and lesbians of all races had suffered discrimination in the armed services. General Colin Powell, the first African American head of the Joint Chiefs of Staff, opposed their serving in the military, claiming gay men would be unreliable in combat and they and lesbians would not be accepted by straight personnel. It was the same argument used by Eisenhower when Truman ordered the desegregation of the military. Ironically, in World War Two, Eisenhower had ordered that all homosexuals should be discharged and his assistant offered to resign because she was a lesbian. He rescinded the order (Faderman, 1992). The demand for personnel meant questions about sexual preferences had been perfunctory (Faderman, 2015). In effect, he operated a 'Don't Ask, Don't Tell' policy that would later be introduced by Clinton. Senator Barry Goldwater, the 1964 presidential Republican nominee, argued that lesbians and gays had fought in all America's wars.

However, gays and lesbians challenged their discharges despite the financial and publicity risks and took their cases to civilian courts. For example, Leonard Matlovich as a young man had joined the John Birch Society and was a racist. Serving with black troops changed him. He admitted his homosexuality and reminded his black commander that: 'It means *Brown v Board of Education*.' The civilian court judge lashed the military but supported their regulations. Navy Ensign Vernon Berg was told by a black officer: '[H]omosexuals are not accepted by their comrades. They're outcasts.' Miriam Ben-Shalom was court-martialled and appealed to a civilian court. The judge reminded the military that their arguments were those used to racially segregate the military. The Secretary of the Army ignored the court order and Reagan and Bush appointees refused to overturn the army board's decision. The Supreme Court would not consider the case (Faderman, 2015).

Bush encouraged the backlash against homosexuality, attacked gay rights and encouraged homophobes like Anita Bryant. Although he had given occasional assurances to African Americans and women, if not action, he did not for gays and lesbians. According to him, homosexuals were not 'normal' and at the Republican National Convention in 1992, they were the subject of fierce attacks in the name of family values. The racist journalist, Pat Buchanan, who had fought Bush for the nomination, gave a vitriolic speech at the convention on homosexuality. Bush's response was to declare a 'religious war' against gays and he worked closely with anti-gay extremists such as Reverend Donald Wilson of Tupelo, Mississippi and Californian Reverend Louis Sheldon (Signorile, 1993). After the GOP convention *Time* magazine wondered, 'After Willie Horton Are Gays and Lesbians Next' (Miller, 1995).

However, Bush left it to Vice President Dan Quayle to rally anti-gay groups and encouraged them to initiate action in the states. In Oregon the electorate were asked to vote on Ballot Measure 9 intended to amend the state constitution declaring homosexuality as 'abnormal, wrong, unnatural, and perverse' and on a par with bestiality. The referendum proposed by Christian fundamentalist groups was backed by the evangelist Republican Pat Robertson, leader of the Christian Coalition (Watson, 1999). The campaign was marked by neo-Nazi attacks and some homosexuals were murdered. Although defeated, 42 percent supported positive discrimination.

In Colorado gay discrimination was narrowly approved and violence against the LGBT community rose by 300 percent (Signorile, 1993). On 20 May 1995 the Supreme Court struck it down as a violation of the Constitution. The decision did not stop the military's witch-hunt. Between 1982 and 1992 over 13,000 gays and lesbians were dismissed. Bush also continued Reagan's neglect of the AIDS crisis, which created mounting anger in the LGBT community.

Civil Rights for the Disabled

The Administration helped African Americans, whether straight or LGBT, when he pushed for the civil rights of the disabled – but only after they forced him to do so. They adopted Movement tactics such as legal action like the NAACP, and the sit-ins, demonstrations and boycotts of the SNCC, CORE, SCLC and SSOC. Their testifying at Senate hearings, like the anti-Vietnam veterans, had a major impact on political and public opinion. Judy Heumann, a polio victim confined to a wheelchair since childhood, 'reenacted dramas that the civil rights movement for blacks had charged with symbolism' (Berkwitz in Graham, 1984); like the Little Rock children she had been excluded from school. The reason? She was considered a fire hazard. Like James Meredith she had been denied a dormitory place at university and like Rosa Parks she was refused the right to travel by plane because she did not have her personal attendant. Their struggle overcame public resistance to government intervention. The 1990 Americans with Disabilities Act was signed at a ceremony on the White House lawn. The Act 'brought civil rights protections for people with disabilities to a level of parity with civil rights protections already enjoyed by racial minorities and women' (Berkowitz in Graham ed., 1994).

Bush had vetoed other civil rights laws and the question is why sign this one. The major reason was conservatives could not object. It benefited Vietnam veterans; was designed to rehabilitate people making them self-sufficient taxpayers; there was no reference to quotas or affirmative action; and it benefited not only the African Americans, overwhelmingly Democrats, but also many disabled Republicans in suburbia. 'The political strategy of playing on racial resentments did not have to affect civil rights for people with disabilities who, in many people's minds, represented the deserving poor, lived in suburbs, not in cities. They were the antithesis of the stereotypical, menacing members of the underclass' (Berkowitz in Graham, 1994). An estimated 50 million disabled people were the largest minority group in the United States. It was their actions and the Movement's methods that disarmed the vocal right wing and led many of the disabled to join the struggle to keep civil rights for all. It would be an important alliance and there were to be others.

8

A Third Way from Hope? Bill Clinton 1993–2001

George H. W. Bush, most of the media and many in both parties under-estimated the campaign skills of the Arkansas governor William Clinton. He had early political ambition reinforced as a teenager when he met JFK at the White House. After graduating from Yale Law School, he spent a short time teaching at the University of Arkansas. Despite joining anti-war demonstrations in London when a visiting student at Oxford University, he was confident on his return to Arkansas that he could defeat a conservative Republican incumbent congressman in the 1974 election. He lost. However, his challenge was almost successful and he was elected state Attorney General. He was a populist especially in his efforts to defend consumers against the giant utility companies. In 1978, aged 32, he became the youngest governor in the country but in his first term populism, in a time of mounting conservatism, resulted in defeat in 1982. He decided if he were to succeed he had to moderate his views.

In 1982 he was re-elected governor and advocated a 'Third Way'. This meant adopting many ideas from the conservative agenda, first advanced by Charles Murray in his book *Losing Ground*, which maintained that welfare programmes undermined the poor and unemployment should be replaced by so-called 'workfare' (Mayer, 2016). In 1991, as chair of the Democratic Leadership Conference, Clinton persuaded them to reject 'quotas' and when challenged said he supported affirmative action and civil rights (Klinkner and Smith, 1999; Clinton, 2004). Criticism of private enterprise and its abuses was toned down, if not entirely abandoned. Another central theme of his 'New Democracy' was the need for retribution against criminals who undermined social stability. Running for president in 1992, he unswervingly advocated the death penalty, the war on drugs with a national police force and the building of 'community boot camps' to discipline first-time non-violent offenders' (campaign literature).

He portrayed himself as a centrist: 'We can be pro-growth and pro-environment, we can be pro-business and pro-labor, we can make government work again by making it more aggressive and leaner and more effective at the same time, we can be pro-family and pro-choice' (campaign literature, 1992; *Time*, 2 November 1992; McAdam and Kloos, 2014). In a speech to Jesse Jackson's Rainbow Coalition, he attacked the rapper and activist Sister Souljah who said after the LA riots: 'If black people kill black people every day why not have a week and kill white people.' He insisted she was no better than David Duke, the white supremacist. 'By showing his toughness against African Americans, he hoped to impress Democrats who had voted for Reagan and other white conservatives' (*The Washington Post*, 30 November 2011). He not only adopted conservative policies on welfare and law and order but also sidelined traditional Democratic supporters in the AFL-CIO and to some extent minorities. In his election leaflets he did not use the words 'African American' or 'black'. However, he promised to create a national investment bank, pump an extra $20 billion into the economy (without specifying the amount for inner cities), encourage community investment by financial institutions and private business and support affirmative action (campaign literature, 1992).

Although as president he can be criticised for some of his policies and the adverse effect on the black and poor communities, as a southerner he realised that virulent racism prevented liberal reform. His bitter critics in Arkansas despised him not only for not fighting in Vietnam but also, perhaps mainly, for admiring JFK, supporting the integration of schools and even inviting the nine who had desegregated Little Rock Central High School to the governor's mansion and to the White House on the 40th anniversary in 1997. When he was governor he appointed the first ever African Americans to senior positions in the state government, the departments of Health, Human Services, and Finance and Administration (Wickham, 2002). His empathy for African Americans included their culture. His obvious pleasure when he attended their church services and played jazz saxophone won him widespread support in the black community but only deepened his opponents' hostility.

Like some African American beneficiaries of the Movement and liberals, he realised there were new coalitions of minority groups and women that would greatly influence national politics He responded and appointed women and the disabled to high positions. Critics denounced legislation to help women as a gimmick to win votes (Dye and Zeigler, 2000). But there were notable limits. After the Willie Horton campaign linked crime and race, he needed to be seen as tough on crime. As governor in 1992 he did not commute the execution of the African American Rickey Ray Rector even though Rector was severely brain damaged after an attempt to kill himself and unaware of his own crime. Clinton does not mention this in his autobiography.

Coming from the miniscule town called Hope, from a broken family with an alcoholic stepfather, for many Americans this made him a candidate who understood their problems – the hardship of single mothers in a society where many marriages ended in failure and where 'divorces, many initiated by women, soared' (Rowbotham, 1997). And after his nomination he did not balance the ticket in the conventional way by picking a northerner; instead he chose a fellow southerner, liberal Tennessee Senator Albert Gore Jr.

Unlike the man who chose him, Gore came from a very different background. Even though his father had known poverty, Gore Jr had had a stable loving family and a father who had been an outstanding senator and whose prescription for a southerner seeking the presidency was populism (see Chapter 6). His son adopted many of his father's views but did not fully share his populist beliefs. However, he defended civil rights and was a learned and passionate environmentalist. His service in Vietnam, something he always played up in his election fights, deflected criticism that he was unpatriotic because of his father's opposition to the war. This helped anti-war Clinton too but Gore's main appeal was the belief he would attract younger, wealthier, educated middle-class voters.

A difficulty Gore had with many younger voters was his wife's campaign against 'porn rock' after she heard their daughter listening to Prince's *Darling Niki*, and she organised the Parents' Music Resource Center (PMRC) to label recordings warning of sexually graphic lyrics. Others were more worried about rap artists who supported the Black Panthers and Black Power. Her husband participated in a Senate investigation into the music industry but disassociated himself from PMRC during the campaign. At first her campaign was not politically damaging. In 1984 Gore had demonstrated that he could win their votes and those of African Americans by defeating his Republican opponent, an unswerving Reagan loyalist, with over 60 percent of the vote, and in 1990 he defeated another ultra-conservative with 67 percent. This was despite attempts to link him with northern liberals such as Ted Kennedy. His response became the 1992 election theme: 'The old labels – liberal and conservative, have far less relevance to today's problems than the efforts to find solutions to these problems' (Russell, 2011).

Both Clinton and Gore stressed it was the end of the old liberal ideology. In 1991, as chair of the Democratic Leadership Conference, Clinton promised to 'end welfare as we know it' and told the poor: 'We will do with you. We will not do for you.' He wanted to win back the white working class but needed the support of African Americans, the poor, women and white liberals. Bush's hostility to many of these groups made him vulnerable. This was particularly true of the new very politically active and influential group: homosexuals. Clinton's coalition building, helped by the intervention of billionaire Ross Perot running as a conservative populist using a George Wallace platform, ensured Clinton's victory – not LGBT voters. Blue-collar workers did not accept 'Third Way' politics (Carter, 1995). Clinton only won 43 percent of the popular vote but a massive landslide in the Electoral College.

African Americans and the Campaign

The Clinton–Gore manifesto included general commitments to civil rights and assistance to minority business. Clinton's Third Way promised: 'Fight for civil rights, not just by protecting individual liberties, but by providing equal economic opportunity; support new and impor-tant initiatives that *move beyond the outdated answers of both major parties* and instead reflect the values most Americans share: work, family, individual responsibility, community' (campaign literature, italics added). He sidelined Jackson and his Operation PUSH (People United to Save Humanity) in Chicago, by claiming Jackson supported a rapper's call to kill whites (Klinkner and Smith, 1999). To head off crit-icism, he campaigned for a black woman, Carol Moseley Braun, to be an Illinois federal senator who was running because she was disgusted by the Democratic incumbent who had voted for Clarence Thomas. Campaigning for her and the EMILY's List, an attempt to ensure more women represented at the federal level, won him support from white and black female voters.

He pleased the black community when he persuaded Colin Powell to remain as head of the Joint Chiefs of Staff. Many minorities were appointed to senior positions. Ron Brown, Jesse Brown, Mike Espy, Hazel O'Leary, Alexis Herman, Rodney Slater and Lee Brown constituted the highest number of black Cabinet officers in the country's history. Thirty-six black women and men held high offices, including Terry Edmonds as the first speech writer and Maggie Smith as Hillary Clinton's chief of staff. Thirty-two served on the White House staff and 180 black men and women were executive appointees. Joseph Lowery, an Atlanta civil rights lawyer, maintained: 'Clinton made some very significant appointments. I think his appointment record will probably exceed the level of all pres-idents before him, maybe combined' (Wickham, 2002). Clinton was enthusiastically backed by the Congressional Black Caucus. But some say, too harshly, that few of his appointees 'had the inclination or stature to call for a strong agenda in support of racial equality' (Klinkner and Davis, 1999).

Although his first term promised much, his vacillation on civil rights can be seen in his failure to support three of his nominees. Jocelyn Elder's parents had been poor sharecroppers but, thanks to the GI bill, she graduated from medical school and taught at the state university. She was Governor Clinton's public health director and later US Surgeon General. She supported abortion, distribution of contraceptives in schools and legalisation of some drugs. Her views angered conservatives, many churches and moderate Democrats. At a conference on AIDS she promoted masturbation. 'I think that it is something that is part of sexuality ... something that perhaps should be taught. But we've not even taught our children the basics' (*New York Times,* 2 December 1994). Masturbating would limit AIDS and 'could end the crisis of single parent-hood and reduce crime' because 'children of unwed teenage mothers account for nearly all crime'. This latter statement was based on bad research and ignored issues such as poverty and homelessness (Males, 1996). Masturbation was logical but it outraged those who had fought for decades against any sex education. Clinton fired her.

Henry Foster met the same fate, and Clinton's attempt to win back African American and liberal confidence failed. Foster was a leading obstetrician who had been praised by Bush Sr Nominating Foster linked abortion and race and the Christian Coalition and Texas Senator Phil Gramm, a would-be Republican candidate in 1996, lobbied against him calling him an abortionist, ignoring the fact that abortion was legal. Foster helped them when he underestimated the number of abortions he had carried out. But many senators still supported him. Republican Bill Frist of Tennessee told *Time* reporters: 'I know he must have seen botched abortions.' He emphasised the impact of segregation on black doctors: 'I'm the only person on that panel who knows what it was like in the South in the 1960s' (*Time,* 15 May 1995). But Clinton capitulated and nominated African American Dr David Satcher.

But African Americans considered the greatest betrayal was of his friend and Yale classmate, Lani Guinier, for Assistant Attorney General. His black voter support fell from over 90 percent to 53 percent (Wickham, 2002). A staunch defender of affirmative action, she opposed strict racial quotas. Much more important was the undemocratic district system of the House of Representatives which resulted in over-representation of white people and which trapped Hispanic, Asian and African Americans into a permanent minority (Guinier, 1994). Ironically, her argument was similar to pro-slavery defender John C. Calhoun who attacked the tyranny of the majority and who campaigned for concurrent majorities between the North and South for all legislation. As John Safford argues, despite Calhoun's motive, 'that does not invalidate the minority veto as a democratic means of dealing with extreme or otherwise irreconcilable cases of majority tyranny' (Safford, 1995). Guinier cited the example of the city council of Birmingham, Alabama that devised a system that the federal court had ordered, requiring that blacks, a permanent minority, had at least one vote that counted (Berman, 2015).

Conservatives claimed that she was supporting a quota system and it was racist to believe white people would not vote for or fairly represent minorities. They said she did not consider black men elected with white support were truly black, and cited David Dinkins, elected mayor of New York City in 1989 (D'Souza, 1995). Another vocal and powerful critic was arch-conservative Abigail Thernstrom (McAdam and Kloos, 2014) who ignored the fact that states and cities in the North and West gerrymander districts to disenfranchise people of colour and that for over a century the South had ensured an all-whites 'quota'. Her argument enabled pressure groups and congressmen to dub Guinier 'the quota queen', parroting Reagan's language of 'welfare queen'. Clinton did not fight this assault and black attorney Johnny Cochrane asserted: 'I thought he ran away from her much too soon. He should have stood up for her' (Wickham, 2002). Others argue: 'When the Clinton administration has found itself linked with persons identified with strong civil rights activism, such as Lani Guinier, it has quickly severed those links' (Klinkner and Davis, 1999).

A 2001 report, assessing his Administration's civil rights achievements declared, for example, that the US Department of Agriculture (USDA) in 1996 had 'serious problems of civil rights enforcement … systemic [in] every major departmental civil rights mission', that minority farmers received 'little relief' and they cited USDA reforms that had not been implemented. Eventually black and Native American farmers sued and the latter settled for $375 million and, after two cases, African American farmers, 7 percent in the South, won $1.2 billion. The report also found 'an ever-present form of discrimination in the national school districts, health care and workplaces'. They conceded that the Reagan and Bush administrations had severely under-funded all aspects of enforcement and impeded the implementation of the law. Republican and court opposition to civil rights severely hampered Clinton's efforts and that is not fully explored in the report but it admits Clinton was often forced to rely on Executive Orders that could be overturned by the next president (US Commission on Civil Rights, April 2001). The Administration issued its own assessment. It pointed out that unemployment of African Americans fell from 14.2 percent in 1992 to 8.9 in 1998, poverty from 33.1 percent to 26.5, health provision had been improved, and extra benefits, lower taxes and more loans had helped minority businesses (clinton2.nara.gov). He also pointed out that he had raised the minimum wage (Piketty, 2014). However, this was not the perception of some disillusioned African Americans who met in Chicago June 1998 and established a Black Radical Congress.

LGBT: Reforms and Betrayals

Many gays saw Clinton as their champion. LGBT's had fought hard for his election and were delighted by his appointment of an openly gay man to his campaign staff and the first president to appoint lesbian and gay ambassadors. In September 1997 Vice President Gore said he believed in gay rights: 'It is time for all Americans to recognize that the issues that face gays and lesbians are not narrow special interests – they are matters of basic human rights.' But they did act as they outlined in their report 'A Record of Progress for Gay and Lesbian Americans'.

This shows how Clinton carefully linked their problems with others, such as discrimination against women and racial minorities, and the need for law and order – for example, making the Justice Department support prosecutions of hate crimes against LGBT people. He proclaimed a Gay and Lesbian Pride Month in 1999, increased AIDS research from $59 million to $461 million and care funding by 290 percent, and stopped insurance discrimination against people with some pre-existing conditions such as HIV/AIDS. He gave speeches at LGBT rallies and in his 1999 State of the Union Address demanded that discrimination in hiring and firing in employment should be outlawed. He was the first president to mention the gay community in his address to Congress. These and other actions educated many Americans and helped win wider tolerance.

But not all gay people were pleased. He signed the Defense of Marriage Act (1996) allowing states to ban same-sex marriages, under pressure from a Republican Congress, which the LGBT community saw as a betrayal. Equally infuriating was his failure to end discrimination in the armed services. World War Two ace, senator and former presidential candidate, Barry Goldwater, in 1993 wrote in the Washington *National Post Weekly*: 'Lifting the ban on gays in the military isn't exactly nothing, but it's pretty damn'd close … I think it's high time to pull the curtain on this charade of policy' (Miller, 1995).

But General Colin Powell opposed change and Clinton accepted the opponents' 'Don't Ask, Don't Tell' policy whereby gays and lesbians could serve but never admit their homosexuality. The military retained the right to dismiss those who spoke about their same-sex preference or who engaged in intercourse on or off base. His defence was that executive action would be overruled by the next president and the increasingly partisan Republicans would introduce an amendment to the Constitution which might be ratified. Clinton declared it 'an honorable compromise' that would also save millions of tax dollars by not persecuting those who honourably served the nation. The result was an unprecedented witch-hunt. A Human Rights Watch report found that by the end of 2001, 7793 service personnel were dismissed. In 1992 alone it was 730. The cost to the taxpayer to replace gays and lesbians was at least $218 million (www.hrw.org). For Clinton it had been 'a political disaster' (Faderman, 2015).

Homophobia was almost as powerful as racism and it was not confined to the white community. At the Black Radical Congress there were denunciations of gays and lesbians by male delegates even though they realised the need for coalitions with others to protect Movement gains. The stereotyping of black lesbians has a long history (National Public Radio, 17 March 2016). Despite the Black Radical Congress, there would be effective coalitions during Clinton's presidency. Gays' new-found authority had powerful voices in music that helped build acceptance of LGBT rights. African American Tracy Chapman explores a woman's love for a woman in *Baby Can I Hold You* and the continued revolution in sexual attitudes in *Talkin' 'bout a Revolution*. Folk/rock duo the Indigo Girls from Georgia embraced their lesbian identities in songs such as *Leeds* on their album *Shaming of the Sun*.

Million Man March

Millions of African Americans who were unemployed or underemployed by federal and state government and by business turned to community self-improvement or to Black Power. Cultural nationalist Ron Karenga in the 1960s had designated Kwanza a December holiday and an increasing number of African Americans adopted it as they did with using and inventing African names. The Nation of Islam's influence grew in the 1980s and 1990s because many were disillusioned by years of not so benign neglect. Louis Farrakhan, head of the NOI, organised a Million Man March on Washington DC on 6 October 1995. According to conservative critics, 400,000 listened to him 'indulge himself in lunatic numerology that went on for a mind-numbing two hours' (Thernstrom and Thernstrom, 1997). It was a message that conservatives should have admired. He denounced African Americans who lacked family values, verbally abused women and children, used drugs and engaged in men-on-men violence. For white folks these were almost exclusively inner city problems. The NOI commemorated the March in 2015 and Farrakhan said: 'Moses was not an integrationist and neither are we. Let me be clear. America has no future for you and me.' However, the Nation no longer considered white people devils and many attendees carried signs that read: 'Pro-black doesn't mean anti-white' (Iton, 2008; cnn.com, 10 October 2015).

The press attacked Jesse Jackson's presence at the 1995 rally but he knew if he had not attended 'it would have branded him as under the control of the white "they". Whatever the mainstream doubts ... he was one of the few political figures to communicate at all across racial lines' (Werner, 2000). But others opposed conventional politics and admired the Black Panthers, demanded socialism and denounced Farrakhan and cultural nationalists. For the Seattle Black Autonomy Collective, for example, capitalism had to be destroyed because it created racism and class division (*Black Autonomy*, January–February 1997).

Clinton and the Supreme Court

Clinton agreed with the Black Caucus that the balance of the Supreme Court needed to be changed. Reagan appointees Chief Justice William Rehnquist and Antonin Scalia, opponents of civil rights, had been joined by Clarence Thomas who all believed that the Fourteenth Amendment of the Constitution had been misconstrued. It was the start of a major assault on civil rights. They limited the federalisation of the Bill of Rights begun in 1925 and accelerated by the Warren court during the 1950s and 1960s. They accused liberal justices for their activism, and denied they themselves were activists inspired by right-wing beliefs. Rehnquist ignored precedents and limited the cases heard. In 1990 the court heard 150 cases, 107 in 1992–93 and 75 in 1995–96 (Lowi and Ginsberg, 2008). They upheld *Roe* allowing abortion but drastically limited its availability in *Webster v. Reproductive Health Services* (1989) and the 1992 case of *Planned Parenthood of South-eastern Pennsylvania v. Casey* (Riches, 2002).

Clinton's difficulties cannot be underestimated. A polarised Congress and the Supreme Court partly explain his problems promoting civil rights. In *Missouri v. Jenkins* (1995), a lower federal court decided that Kansas City's funded 'magnet schools' benefited white students because entrance tests were 'culturally biased' and the money should go to inner city schools where resources were below the national average. Thomas pronounced previous rulings, including *Brown*, had been misconstrued and the appeal judge had supported badly researched social science. He rejected 'the theory that black students suffered from any speci-fied psychological harm from segregation that retards their mental and educational development'. The lower court had ignored constitutional principle 'and based its ruling on the assumption of black inferiority' (Thomas, 2007). Thurgood Marshall would have been astounded that he had supported black inferiority in *Brown* and Thomas has been described as 'Uncle Tom Justice' (*Time*, 26 June 1995).

A 5–4 decision in *Adarand v. Pena* (1995) over-ruled affirmative action which required companies working on state contracts to use minority subcontractors. Clinton's review concluded he would support affirmative action but not unqualified companies or people, nor reverse discrimination against whites, and the programmes discontinued after their equal opportunity purpose had been achieved. 'In a phrase, my policy was, "Mend it, but don't end it"' (Clinton, 2004). This was better than the abolition wanted by Republicans but he gave no criteria to show equal opportunity had been achieved, how he would mend affirmative action or when it was time to end it. Phrases of support might have satisfied some African Americans but he did not address the issue and encouraged its opponents.

He was unable to alter the balance of the Court. In his first term he could only appoint two justices because, although seriously ill, Chief Justice Rehnquist refused to resign and kept a conservative majority. Clinton won the appointment of Ruth Bader Ginsberg, the first Jewish woman, and increased the number of women to two. An ACLU member, she consistently voted with the moderate justices, unlike Reagan appointee Sandra Day O'Connor who was 'very conservative on blacks if not on women's issues' (Shull, 1993). The second appointment was a white man. Stephen Beyer was a liberal among the conservatives who restricted the civil rights of African Americans, other minorities, the disabled and women. The Court's rightward nature meant that groups such as the NAACP avoided relying on it. It was no longer an ally in their struggle; it was considered the centre of resistance. Between 1995 and 1997, 12 rulings 'placed limits on affirmative action, school desegregation, voting rights, the separation of church and state, and the power of the national government vis-a-vis the states' (Lowi and Ginsberg, 2008). They refused to hear cases in which minority prisoners alleged extreme prejudice and inadequate court representation, a major cause of the excessive number of imprisoned black males. And it took until 2002 for the Supreme Court to rule that the execution of the learning disabled (the majority African American) was unconstitutional. Clarence Thomas dissented. The ruling, however, failed to define 'learning disabled' and executions continue.

Clinton tried to redress the balance of the federal appeal courts by appointing African Americans, including two women. But the lower courts were still dominated by Reagan and Bush appointees who opposed affirmative action. The University of Texas Law School version was declared unconstitutional in *Hopwood v. Texas* when a white woman claimed she had been refused admission although she had higher scores than black students. The 5th Circuit Court of Appeals ignored the fact that most applicants with lower scores were white students, accepted under the university's social diversity plan. Clinton could do nothing. *Hopwood* had a devastating effect on minority student enrolments in other states. Critics have argued that he encouraged opposition when he assured white America he would not do anything that created preferences for unqualified individuals and he would not restore preferences when equal opportunity was achieved (Klinker and Smith, 1999). In his memoir Clinton recalls a National Archives speech in which he said he was proud of his record but admitted there was a need for change. 'The speech was well received by civil rights, corporate, and military communities, but it didn't persuade everyone' (Clinton, 2004). African American historian and law professor Mary Lane Berry thought his defence of affirmative action was a positive feature of his time in office (Wickham, 2002). It has also been claimed that he went as far as possible in defending the programmes (Wadden, 2002).

The War on Crime

Death Sentencing

Although Clinton tried to moderate the courts with his appointments, it is also the case that he was enmeshed in the national fear of crime. Stephan and Abigail Thernstrom maintain that the criminal justice system is not biased against African and Hispanic Americans. They argue that more whites have been executed in Georgia and throughout the Deep South. However, they fail to explain why the number of southern and northern black men executed is disproportionate to their numbers in the states. If the explanation lies within the pathology of the black community, then why have there been so few executions for black-on-black murders and why in the sample years of 1996–1998 were only three whites executed for murdering blacks? When all-white juries found the murderers of Movement workers guilty, none was sentenced to death. The Supreme Court in 1976 ruled that the death penalty was not unconstitutional and it resulted in 589 executions with 3625 on death row. Although 55.6 percent awaiting death were white, 33.8 percent were black – a group that only makes up 12 percent of the national population. Many innocent people are executed and racism and class prejudice profoundly affect conviction rates (deathpenatlyinfo.org).

Private prisons were, and are, big business. Between 1994 and 1997 1.4 million Americans were incarcerated and between 1980 and 1990 this rate tripled for black people. Clinton could not control state legal systems but he signed the Violent Crime Control Law Enforcement Act (1994) which provided $30 billion allowing states and cities to increase police numbers and build more prisons. The 'three strikes' provision meant someone with a felony conviction had a mandatory sentence for a third offence. A California man's third strike was stealing $150 of tapes and he was sentenced to 50 years (findlaw.com). Federal prisons saw a dramatic increase in inmates under Reagan and Bush Sr but the greatest was during Clinton's office. A Center on Juvenile and Criminal Justice report (2002) pointed out that spending on environmental protection and energy was cut by 43 percent but the Justice Department received a 75 percent increase.

Cocaine and Racism

African Americans did not blame Clinton for the racism in the judicial system especially when it came to drugs but rather attributed it to the law-and-order policies of Reagan. Trading crack cocaine and the federal mandatory sentence meant that in 1994 those convicted for possessing the powdered form were 55.8 percent white with very few serving five years and 26.7 percent black who did. Over 84 percent of black people convicted got five years for crack and only just over 10 percent of whites (Jamison, 2002). Police reports were faked. The Dallas police claimed they had seized record amounts of cocaine and amphetamines but the cocaine was 'baggies of finely ground Sheetrock and powdered wallboard' (Houston *Chronicle,* 18 October 2002).

Clinton's African American 'drug czar', Lee Brown, wanted stricter drug enforcement. He wanted to change the image of marijuana to an 'addictive killer' and claimed that over 4000 emergency admissions of children aged between 12 and 17 were directly related to its use. He also reinforced the belief that crack was the drug of the ghetto. However, Department of Health and Human Services pointed out this was untrue and that those admitted had used more than one drug. 'African Americans [who] were only 13 percent of monthly drug users ... represent 35 percent of arrests ... 74 percent of prison sentences.' The arbitrariness of enforcement of drug laws can be seen in Texas in 1999. In the town of Tulia, population 4500 and 10 percent African American, 46 people were arrested on 23 July 1999 for selling small amounts of cocaine. Forty were black. The three whites were close to the black community, including Cash Love who had a black partner and child. Love was sentenced to over 300 years because 'they did not want to be seen as racist'. An undercover agent, Tom Coleman, who was responsible for the raids was trained by the Drug Enforcement Agency. A senior Texas officer said he was a 'compulsive liar'. Thirty cases were dismissed, the rest pardoned and Texas paid $6 million in damages. Coleman was convicted of perjury and given ten years' probation (*New York Times*, 7 October 2000; CBS Sixty Minutes, 4 July 2004). Drug-using pregnant women, virtually all women of colour, were frequently charged with endangering the life of their unborn children. In South Carolina Margaret Reyes, a heroin addict, was accused of endangering her twins because they suffered withdrawal symptoms after birth, and Selena Dunn was charged with second-degree criminal mistreatment because of her cocaine habit (Riches, 2002).

An Administration report warned that discriminatory sentencing was seriously affecting racial attitudes towards the judicial system and the policy's aims were ineffective. Clinton deplored this racial bias but defeat in mid-term elections and mounting rumours of impeachment meant he accepted Republican legislation that made matters worse. They increased the sentence for selling $225 of crack to the same as that of a person selling $50,000 of powdered cocaine. Michael Males argues: 'Drug laws and their selective enforcement represent the new Jim Crow laws' (Males, 1996). However, conservatives maintain that black popular opinion and their representatives supported tough action because drugs were widespread in their areas. Incarceration made their streets safer (Thernstrom and Thernstrom, 1997).

But they do not explain why marijuana sentences for use and possession were drastically cut and usually ignored when it became popular with the white middle class, especially their children; their understanding of popular beliefs that federal government conspires against black communities is non-existent. African Americans were certain that dramatic increases in cocaine imports was a US government plot to shore up friendly authoritarian governments and a CIA programme to control black lives. These conspiracy fears were not fanciful. Even though there was a cure in the 1940s, black men had died of syphilis in the federally funded Bad Blood 'research' that lasted into 1972 (Jones, 1993). A commission set up by Clinton in 1993 documented CIA experiments with radiation, LSD, torture and chemical weapons on black and other prisoners, and also mentally disabled children. Atomic testing and toxic waste had exposed unwitting civilians, especially Native Americans, to serious radiation resulting in cancers (Senate Select Committee Report on Intelligence Operations). No one was prosecuted and very few victims were compensated even by 2016.

Health Care Proposal

Despite valid criticisms of his civil rights achievements, Clinton tried to pass one of the great reforms that would benefit African Americans – indeed all Americans. Other presidents had tried and failed to solve the health care crisis. The United States spent more per person on health than any other advanced society but seven out of every ten dollars were administration costs. Although its defenders pointed out that 85 percent of people had health insurance, that meant 40 million had none and 30 million had inadequate coverage. These figures were not higher because the elderly and the acutely disabled, some 58 million in 2001, were qualified for LBJ's Medicare and Medicaid (us.gov/hhs). Women with children and who were on welfare and those with huge medical bills and no assets, a total of 36.3 million in 1997, benefited when these measures had been passed (US Census Bureau). The federal government paid 57 percent and the states 43.

Clinton promised to make health care more accessible and affordable. He established a commission in 1993 that was headed by his wife who did not want to play the traditional role of First Lady. But her appointment meant that opponents accused the president of nepotism and others remembered her role in Nixon's impeachment. The commission proposals required businesses to provide health plans for their workers and dependents. Corporations were supported by unions who believed the benefits would be inferior to those they had; the cover would include providing prescription drugs, immunisation and eye and dental care for children, as well as health care for drug users and the costs of some abortions. Clinton had introduced small tax increases on the rich which under Reagan had fallen from 70 to 28 percent by 1988. The plan would increase taxes. Insurance companies were certain profits would be cut and they spent huge sums to defeat the proposals.

Although initially popular, anti-government fears and individualism meant that the slow introduction of the plan galvanised Clinton's opponents and by the time he sought to act 85 percent opposed it. And there was the political factor. Republican Senator Bob Dole had praised Hillary's presentation, promised to offer reasonable amendments and generally favoured it. His colleagues warned him that if it succeeded it might recreate the Democratic coalition built by FDR (Clinton, 2004). Clinton became convinced Dole would not support him. Republicans, aware that Dole wanted to be president, told him that if he wanted to win, he must oppose it. He did. Also he was under pressure from right-wing forces such as William Kristol, former Vice President Dan Quayle's advisor. Lobbyists and the press insisted that people would lose their right to choose their own doctors. Clinton has been accused of kicking the reform into the long grass but he fought hard to get it through yet was realistic enough to know that Congress would never pass it. But as late as 1995 Dole insisted that universal coverage was a 'non-negotiable goal of reform' (*The Atlantic*, January 1995).

Bill Clinton admits that this failure constituted 'a good shellacking' but says that a consequence of their attempt was to make it an important part of the political agenda which resulted in Congress passing the Children's Health Insurance Program (1997) and measures to help women and diabetics, AIDS research, childhood immunisation, and for a 'patients charter' (Clinton, 2004).

Welfare Reform

Republicans were determined to pass policies set out by Representative Newt Gingrich in his 'A Contract for America', called 'A Contract *on* America' by liberals. Some of the proposed welfare reforms were draconian. The wealthy would benefit from tax cuts, and spending on the military would be greatly increased. What Gingrich and his supporters did not realise was that Clinton agreed with many of their objectives. As Clinton says in his autobiography: 'I agreed with many of the particulars of the contract.' He states that he was already 'pushing welfare reform and tougher child-support enforcement.' However, the Contract 'was, at its core, a simplistic and hypocritical document'. Their arguments for tax cuts and more military spending meant 'they were trying to abolish arithmetic' (Clinton, 2004). He undermined his opposition by stealing their clothing when he proclaimed 'the era of big government is over'.

Halfway through his second term in 1988 the national poverty rate was down to 13.7 percent, of which 28.4 percent represented black female-headed households and 29.4 percent Hispanic. Conservative welfare critics claimed that Clinton failed to reverse Bush's tax cuts for the rich and did not understand that there was a crisis with the welfare system. Social Security they claimed was on the brink of bankruptcy. They said nothing about benefits that were not means-tested and aided the wealthy. A Clinton defender says he was consistent and had ignored 'the forgotten middle class' and perpetuated dependency (Klein, 2002). And although he said he would oppose the Bill he had made it clear he would support radical reform.

In Memphis in 1993 he told black ministers that Martin Luther King Jr would have said he had not struggled 'for freedom of children to have children, and the father of the children to walk away and abandon them ... That is not what I lived and died for' (Klein, 2002). His middle-class African American audience stood and cheered him

(Clinton, 2004). But his was the same portrayal of black people and the poor as welfare-dependent that was exploited by Nixon and Reagan. He did not acknowledge that many were forced onto welfare because of low wages even though they often worked two or three jobs a day (Ehrenreich, 2001). And no white politician would have made a speech to white audiences using this language or blaming them for the problems in their communities.

Lobbyists for big business encouraged disparity of income and opposed all social reform to help the poor and minorities. They limited presidents who sought to help minorities. They followed the views of Supreme Court Justice Lewis Powell, a Nixon appointee, who expressed concern that capital was under attack and urged business to organise and pool financing – to act 'aggressively and with determination' and to be prepared to resist for years because achieving their interests was possible 'only through joint effort and ... political power ... through united action and national organization'. Some explain Clinton had not expected capital to act as it did or take into account the decline of organised labour. But business acted swiftly. Corporations with important government interests and numerous lobbyists have acquired enormous power since 1978. 'In 1971, there were just 175 such firms. Eleven years later the number had swelled to over 1200' (McAdam and Kloos, 2014). Conservative views dominated when they set up Political Action Committees (PAC) and funded think tanks such as the Business Enterprise Institute and the Heritage Foundation bankrolled by the billionaire Koch brothers. They have radically affected university programmes and employ ultra-conservatives such as Dinesh D'Souza (Mayer, 2016).

Their major targets were liberal programmes such as the Aid to Families with Dependent Children (AFDC) – essential for all poor women. The Republicans emphasised the pregnancy rates, particularly of black girls whose sons were allegedly twice as likely to commit crime; that welfare should be for the first child only; states should deny benefits to women between 18 and 20 but not fund birth control programmes; and penniless women would have their children put up for adoption. African American William Clay (D, Missouri) demanded: 'If that doesn't work what? Castration? Sterilization?' (Davis, 1994). Apparently he did not know that African American, Hispanic and poor women had been, and are, forcibly sterilised, that black schoolgirls were forcibly implanted with the Norplant contraceptive. The latter did not stop sexually transmitted diseases but was designed to prevent women's fertility. The proposals of the ultra-right measures were defeated. But left-wing critics also attacked welfare arguing that its goal was to pacify the poor and ensure a low-paid workforce. It shored up a patriarchal society, especially for women of colour, who were dependent on handouts from a white male elite.

But Clay was not the only Democrat appalled by the proposals and Clinton's willingness to make major concessions. Clinton could have fought harder because the Republicans had shut down Congress – a strategy that failed miserably and increased Clinton's popularity (salon. com, 1995). But he talked the Republican talk. At a meeting of African American journalists on 1 November 1995 Clinton assured them he would veto the Bill but crucially added: 'My belief is that we ought to have a reform bill that is pro-family and pro-work … [with] the possibility of ending welfare after a certain length of time if people have a job they can take.' He emphasised that it was the states that would run the system to protect young children.

In his compromise he accepted 'workfare', abandoned his plan to aid middle-class families and accepted he had to balance the budget knowing it was at the cost to the poor. Worse, he signed the Personal Responsibility Opportunity and Work Reconciliation Act (1996) that abolished the 31-year-old AFDC that supposedly only benefited promiscuous teenage black women. It 'embraced two of Reagan's central policy goals: the elimination of social programs and with it the "degrading" dependence of the poor on government largesse' (LA *Times*, 14 July 1995; Iton, 2008; McAdam and Kloos, 2014). When Clinton's economics team suggested cutting farm subsidies he reminded his 'urban budgeteers that farmers were good people who had chosen hard work in an uncertain environment' (Clinton, 2004). Presumably, poor black and white folks in rural and urban areas chose not to work hard and their environment was fine.

The link between welfare and race was reinforced at the signing ceremony when he was surrounded by overwhelmingly African American single parents (Neubeck and Cazenave, 2001). However, a May 2000 White House press release stressed how much had been done for black and Hispanic people and argued that 'the unemployment rates … are both at historic lows, while the unemployment rate for women is the lowest since 1953'. No figures are given for unemployed minority women or the low-paid jobs they were forced into because of the abolition of AFDC. The Administration boasted it had the lowest number on welfare since 1969. 'Welfare rolls are down by 7.2 million or 51 percent since 1993 after increasing by 22 percent from 1982 the years of Reagan and Bush.' Some African Americans defended him and believed, like Ben Johnson, head of the Institute for One America, that Clinton had had 'a bad rap on welfare reform' because the Republicans were intransigent (Wickham, 2002). But Clinton's appeasement had effectively undermined much of FDR's New Deal and LBJ's Great Society.

Voter Registration: The 'Motor Voter Act'

The majority of African Americans and Hispanics were unhappy with workfare but delighted when this southern president radically extended voter registration which had begun with the 1965 Voting Rights Act. He pushed through the National Registration Act of May 1993. Despite the 1965 Act, some states had failed to register African Americans and Hispanics and the Justice Department during the Reagan and Bush years had done little to ensure its enforcement; rather, it had sought to weaken it. Equally important was the assault on the Voting Rights Act by conservatives who denounced it as just another affirmative action measure, and the election of black officeholders was not 'an historic achievement but examples of pernicious social engineering' (Berman, 2015).

Clinton ignored the assaults and ensured the federal and state complications would be avoided. Voter registration would be completed easily in a motor vehicle department when a licence was renewed and the same when renewing other forms of identification. This was helped by groups such as ROCK THE VOTE who registered people on the streets.

At first, states were reluctant to comply but most had by 2000. Clinton had good reason to be proud of his achievement. Within the first year of its implementation over 11 million notified the authorities that they had changed address. Nine million of these were new voters and the League of Women Voters and the NAACP believed that another

6 million would register by the 2000 election. In a May 2000 press release the Administration emphasised that the Act was 'helping to eliminate historic disparities by registering citizens who have traditionally been left out – people with disabilities, minorities, young people, anyone who has recently moved, and people with lower incomes'. What he did not foresee was just how easy it was to get around this law. Jeb Bush, Governor of Florida, ensured this and it was crucial in the outcome of the presidential election in 2000, 2004 and also in 2016.

Clinton and Women of Colour

In 1992 Clinton won the overwhelming support of women. And this was especially true for African American women. Although many were churchgoing fundamentalists and opposed his pro-choice campaign, they supported him before and after his election. His ability to empathise with people, especially African Americans, was obvious in one of the election debates. An African American woman asked what the candidates would do to lower unemployment and aid the poor. Bush talked about the national debt. Silence. Trying to reach the audience he referred to a visit to an African Methodist Episcopal church ('you know, a black church'). Clinton moved down to the audience and asked the woman questions. He listened. He walked towards her, mike in hand, and spoke about the problems of friends and people he knew in Arkansas and he agreed that talk of economic theory was impractical and action was required and spelt out his plans. He was a tactile politician. Some sneered he was the Oprah Winfrey of politics – a man who had mastered the arts of TV talk-show hosts. But this empathy was genuine and his audiences knew it and were drawn to him. Bush had no answer (c-span.org/video).

And Clinton's many critics have a problem. If he was merely smoke and mirrors when it came to civil rights issues, why was he the most popular president ever as far as most African Americans were concerned? Toni Morrison, the Nobel prize winning author said in 1998:

> Years ago, in the middle of the Whitewater investigation one heard the first murmurs, that white skin notwithstanding, this is our first black

President. Blacker than any actual black person who could ever be elected in our children's lifetime. After all, Clinton displays every trope of blackness: single-parent household, born poor, working-class, saxophone-playing, McDonald's-and-junk-food-loving boy from Arkansas.'

(*New Yorker*, 5 October 1998)

Black businesswoman Gwen McKinney claimed Morrison's comment was 'partly tongue-in-cheek' but added that Clinton 'understands the psyche of oppressed people – black people – people who are on the outside looking in'. George Curry, a black political columnist, was more guarded: 'I have never bought the garbage about Bill Clinton being a black president. He is not black but was better than George Bush.'

Abortion

Even though most black men, and some women, believed abortion was a white conspiracy of ethnic cleansing, more and more black women supported pro-choice partly as a way to break away from male patriarchy. They and Clinton were aided by moderate Republicans such as Arlen Specter of Pennsylvania who wanted to stop 'abortion crazies' from controlling his Party. Specter became another victim of the Moral Majority and the right-wing Republicans who refused to condemn the harassment of women going to clinics, the bombings and even the murder of doctors.

Pro-choice women said men regarded white females as vessels and encouraged multiple births including the risky procedure of artificial reproduction techniques (ART). Meanwhile pro-life people did everything they could to limit black women having children. Bobbi McCaughey, a white working-class mother, used ART and despite doctors' warnings refused to abort some of the foetuses. Five of her septuplets had disabilities and all suffered delayed development. But she was rewarded. Supporters gave her a free house, two minivans and she was congratulated by the state governor and the president. A childless African American woman had healthy septuplets without using ART but was ignored. Linda Burg, head of a Washington DC pro-choice group, noted: '[T]he president did not even lean out of the window and holler, hello Mrs. Thompson' (Riches, 2002).

The Collapse of Consensus Politics

To get his way Gingrich had shut down the government twice and the intransigence of the Republicans made budget negotiations futile. Although the shutdown improved Clinton's popularity it demonstrated 'the growing influence of the extreme Republican right'. It is argued that there 'has been an evolution of a distinctive Republican politics of inequality haphazardly under Nixon, systematically by Reagan and "institutionalized" in the years since Reagan left office' (McAdam and Kloos, 2015). In a pamphlet published by Gingrich's action committee he suggested words to describe Democrats should include: betray, cheat, collapse, corruption, decay, destruction, incompetent, liberal, lie, permissive and traitors among others. 'It was not … an exaggeration … that in its divisive essence, the 104th Congress ushered in the brave new world of partisan politics we inhabit today' (McAdam and Kloos, 2015). Billionaire Ross Perot described a typical black man: 'I define what a man is from the rap music … A man is defined in this culture as a breeder who gets a woman pregnant and she goes on welfare' (Neubeck and Cazenave, 2001). Gingrich said: 'It's impossible to maintain civilization with 12-years-old having babies, 15-year-olds killing each other, 17-years-old dying of AIDS, and 18-year-olds getting diplomas that they can't even read' (Klinkner and Smith, 1999). Politicians who exploit racism 'need not say the words *Niggers* or *Nigras* as did the white southerner segregationists. They need only mention the word welfare' (Neuback and Cazenave, 2001, italics in original).

The economic gulf between the wealthy and the poor deepened even though Clinton won a modest tax increase on the rich, and free market conservatism and social libertarianism made sensible debate and compromise almost impossible (Piketty, 2014). Ironically, this income discrepancy can be seen after a US veteran's – a 'misguided revolutionary' according to the FBI (www.fbi.gov) – terrorist attack on a federal building in Oklahoma City on 10 April 1995 when 169 men, women and children were murdered. Black and white working- and middle-class victims shared $300,000 compensation. This is in stark contrast to the payout after the Twin Towers were destroyed by foreign terrorists in the 9/11 attacks. These housed stockbrokers, lawyers and corporations and a special compensation fund was established based on earnings lost. Of the $38.1 billion, 62 percent went to businesses. Service workers received a maximum of $250,000 whereas stockbrokers could get as much as $7 million. The head of the fund said it was mandated by Congress and 'it was the American way' (dailymail.co.uk, 6 September 2006). Oklahoma has been virtually forgotten but 9/11 is memorialised, its victims honoured and its first responders treated as heroes.

Clinton, like his predecessors and conservative opponents, can be held accountable for this economic disparity but, as Joe Klein of the *New Yorker* claims, Clinton fought to benefit many lower income people. The pre-school Head Start programme established by LBJ had its budget increased by $1.8 billion, childcare by $8.1 billion and Clinton's own domestic version of the Peace Corps, Americorps, an additional $100 million. Klein considers these were important achievements but they paled in comparison with LBJ's. Congress ensured he could do no more. Clinton's attempt to stymie his opponents by stealing their clothes had failed.

Clinton's problems multiplied. The small band of Republican moderates either left or were driven out of the Party by alienated right-wing Christians, white southerners and young radical conservatives. Centrists resigned and strengthened their adversaries. Wyoming Senator Alan Simpson, for example, quit because of the 'bug-eyed zealots' and others were purged by state activists (McAdam and Kloos, 2014). Although moderates opposed many of the president's policies, they believed Congress should reach a consensus. They understood, as Gingrich did not, that this was not surrender but they underestimated the visceral contempt that some of their colleagues had for Clinton and any support for civil rights for African Americans, LGBT people, the disabled, women and other minorities such as Hispanics and Native Americans.

From Clinton's first days in office he was accused of corrupt land dealing and forcing state troopers to procure prostitutes when he was governor, and his wife of murdering her lawyer after Clinton was elected president. Even though an independent investigation headed by a Republican lawyer found no corruption, this did not stop them. They appointed Kenneth Starr, a Nixon defence lawyer, to re-investigate. When this failed the Republicans spent $45 million on other investigations.

Starr intimidated witnesses and Susan McDougall was sentenced to two years in prison because she refused to lie (*The Washington Post*, 26 August 1996). He used the hearsay evidence of the state troopers who had previously been accused of perjury. Starr achieved one thing. Clinton had had consensual sexual activities with an adult White House intern, Monica Lewinsky. 'Nothing reflects the extreme partisanship that marked the scandal and impeachment process more clearly than the nearly straight party line voting in the House on the four articles of impeachment.' Only one Democrat voted with the unanimous Republicans. When Nixon was impeached the votes were bipartisan. 'Congress in 1988 bore little relationship to the substantially bipartisan institution in place a quarter of a century later' (McAdam and Kloos, 2014). But many Democrats did not want to accept that consensus politics was dead and buried. It was not until 2015 that Barack Obama admitted: 'The Republican vision has not moved to the right, but has moved to a place that is unrecognizable' (*Time*, 6 August 2015).

Home to Harlem? Popularity with African Americans

Despite accusations of symbolism, such as awarding Rosa Parks and many other civil rights activists with the Presidential Medal of Freedom, the highest award for an individual, this was not the perception of the majority of African Americans who saw this as an important recognition by the president of their struggle for justice, equality and democracy. Arson attacks on black churches were appropriated by the Christian Coalition as proof that Christians were victimised by liberal secularists (Watson, 1999). In 1993 Clinton signed the Church Arson Prevention Act although some said his tardiness was reminiscent of 1960s indifference (*Black Autonomy*, January–February 1997). The Act would not end terrorism (CNN, 1996) which was blamed on white diehard resisters (PRI's World, 2 July 2015). However, he had not implemented his high-level Civil Rights Commission proposals, headed by distinguished black historian John Hope Franklin. But African Americans blamed Congressional Republicans.

When he was impeached Clinton turned to African Americans, especially Vernon Jordan, a businessman and long-time friend to Jesse Jackson, whose help Clinton had spurned in 1992. Black church members supported him. The 2750-member Mount Carmel Baptist Church in Philadelphia was typically outspoken in his defence and their attacks on Republicans (philly.com, 21 December 1998). A black-owned polling company in 1998 reported that his approval rating was 91 percent, four points higher than the most popular African American, Jesse Jackson. They shared Clinton's hope that at every testing time for the nation: '[W]e have chosen union over division ... and in the sixties and seventies, while we were engaged in a struggle to define, defend and expand our union, powerful conservatives resisted, and as long as the outcome was in doubt, the political and personal conflicts were intense' (Clinton, 2004). But the resistance would get worse.

After leaving the White House Clinton moved his offices to Harlem and revelled in Morrison's remark that he was the 'first black president'. He had triumphed with the African American population who, for all his shortcomings, embraced him (Iton, 2008). His vice president, Al Gore, did not forgive Clinton's scandal with Lewinsky, and while he stood by the Third Way he did not want Clinton to campaign for him and this, it is suggested, cost him votes.

Republican campaign advisors urged the Party to soften its approach and chose the slogan 'caring conservatism'. Their choice of candidate surprised everyone because it was expected it would be Florida Governor Jeb Bush, but it was his brother, George W., Governor of Texas. Their father claimed he made sure his younger son was chosen (*Guardian*, 10 November 2015). The Gore–Bush campaign ended with a massive constitutional crisis. For historians of the African American experience there were disturbing similarities with the Hayes–Tilden election of 1876. For African Americans, Hispanics and other minorities it was alarming.

9

1876 and All That: George W. Bush
2001–2009

Why 1876? Because the November 2000 presidential election ended in much the same way as the earlier one. Both elections resulted in a furore over fraud. In 1876 Democrat Samuel Tilden needed one more Electoral College vote to defeat Republican Rutherford Hayes. Both parties claimed victory in the states of Florida, South Carolina and Louisiana, where both had been involved in vote rigging, and terrorist groups had intimidated and murdered black and white Republican officeholders and voters. As in 1876, Florida was crucial in deciding the 2000 election. In the compromise of 1877, Hayes was pronounced the winner and agreed to withdraw the last federal troops from the South. The Republicans abandoned the southern African Americans, especially those who had had the vote, and the long march of the Party away from the black community had begun. By 2000 many black citizens had regained their vote with the Voting Rights Act of 1965. Most white southerners, Democrats since the Civil War, aligned with the Republicans who chose to be a virtually all-white party and later even attracted ex-Nazis such as David Duke.

The Gore Campaign of 2000

It became a familiar refrain, especially among Clinton admirers, the press and network television, that Gore lost the election because he did not allow the former president to campaign for him. Most Americans forget that Gore *won* the election. Allegedly, he showed 'almost a pathological need to prove he could stand on his own outside the shadows of the political master [Clinton] – and perhaps outside his father's shadow, as well'. Clinton was 'frustrated' by Gore's 'mortal clunkiness as a campaigner' (Klein, 2002). He ignores Gore's role as a valuable and effective vice president and his support for Clinton's 'Third Way'. Gore's loyalty cost him votes.

Gore lacked the Oprah Winfrey touch but this did not cost him the election. The mess of the Lewinsky affair, and Clinton's lying about it, meant Gore believed he had to distance himself from Clinton but remain loyal to centrism. The claim that Gore wanted to escape 'his father's shadow' when he abandoned Clinton's 'Third Way' is wrong. Gore's campaign was effective when he later embraced his father's view that a southern aspirant had to be a progressive populist, and populism won him support from African Americans, LGBT people, women, the disabled and many traditional Democrats who had voted Republican. Clinton writes that: '[T]he populist edge sounded to some swing voters as if Al ... might change the economic direction of the party'. He was confined to making telephone calls to party supporters during the campaign (Clinton, 2004). However, liberal critics complained that Gore remained loyal to the 'Third Wave' even though he did not defend Clinton and embraced his father's populism for the rest of his presidential bid (*Esquire*, December 2000).

At a NAACP convention, Gore reminded his audience that he was a member and of his commitment to civil rights. 'I am not asking you *to read my lips*. I am asking you to read my heart' (italics added). He would defend public schools, affirmative action, pass a national hate crimes law and appoint Supreme Court justices who would defend civil rights. Like church ministers during the struggle, he quoted the Bible: 'Show me the faith without works, and I will show thee my faith BY my works. That is my text for today.' Bush, angered by this attack, promised 'compassionate conservatism' and claimed he had 'talked from the heart' (*North County Times*, 13 July 2000).

Bush visited Bob Jones University which had refused to admit African American and Catholic students and even in 2000 banned interracial dating because God had separated races and nations. One NBC TV moderator said these visits damaged Bush's claim to 'increase racial harmony' and another pointed out that African Americans were noticeably absent from Republican conventions. The only black Republican congressman, J. C. Watts of Oklahoma, defended him saying Bush was concerned about delegates regardless of their race (CNN, 10 July 2000).

But racism dogged his campaign; he had promoted Charles Williams to train Texas lawmen, a man who testified that calling a black person 'a porch monkey' was not racist (www.bushwatch.com, 12 January 2003). Democrats argued that Bush supported Republican welfare reforms that withheld benefits from legal Hispanic residents because of alleged fraud (CNN, 10 July 2000). His campaign website assured voters he opposed racial quotas but favoured a scheme of 'affirmative access'. He described Nixon and LBJ's affirmative action programmes as 'soft bigotry' (*Time*, 2000). He promised to aid small black-owned businesses with federal contracts but after the *Adarand* decision that preferential assistance was unconstitutional, it was uncertain how this would be possible. Additionally, he would legislate to benefit the poor and minorities still struggling for equality. This was perhaps deliberately vague, like his father's 'thousand points of light'. But Bush and later Republican presidential aspirants knew the party relied on its southern strategy and northern white male blue-collar workers.

Fraud and the 2000 Election

Gore surprised his critics. He led by 500,000 in the popular vote and all television stations reported he had won Florida and was president. But George Bush's cousin, reporting for Fox News, maintained Gore had not and this was accepted by all the other TV channels (Berman, 2015). Following a recount Bush 'won' by just over 1500 votes, eventually reduced to 537, and was declared the winner. At first the Democrats conceded but because of the narrow result filed for a hand recount of certain districts. But the Bush camp was not worried. A young Republican outside the Texas state house carried a prophetic sign: 'Don't Worry Jeb Will Deliver Florida.' Hendrik Hertzberg concluded: '[T]he votes of some citizens are more equal than the votes of others, and that the votes of the citizens of Florida are worth nothing, depending on who, if anyone, is doing the counting' (*New Yorker*, 18 December 2000).

Despite Bush's claims, only 8 percent of African Americans supported him (BBC News Online, 15 December 2000), whereas 12 percent had voted for Republican Bob Dole in 1996 (*New York Times*, 20 December 2002). In Florida, 92 percent of African Americans who were allowed to vote did so for Gore and the numbers would have been higher if the registers had not been purged after the 1997 fraudulent Miami mayoral election. The Republican-controlled state hired a private company, DBT, to cleanse the rolls of felons, duplicate registrations, people with the same surname and the deceased (Berman, 2015). Sixty-seven counties were 'investigated' and 'cleansed' of mostly black, elderly and Hispanic voters. DBT had warned that guidelines set by Katherine Harris, the state Attorney General appointed by Jeb Bush, would result in 'false positives'. Ex-felons had the right to vote in Texas and they could continue to do so if they had moved to Florida even though Florida's ex-felons could not. The Texas list was sent to Florida to deny former Texans the vote.

Wallace McDonald, an African American, who was guilty of a misdemeanour of 'sleeping on a bus-stop bench' in Texas in 1959, was listed as a felon in Florida (*Harper's Magazine*, 1 March 2002). A black man who had never been in Texas, Thomas Alvin Cooper, would commit his felony in 2007, move to Ohio, add a middle name and change his race! He was one of 300 with 'future conviction dates'. Thirty-one percent of black voters were listed as felons and although some registrars ignored the lists, most did not. DBT and Harris, who had co-chaired Bush's state election committee, disenfranchised Madison County election supervisor, African American Linda Howell, because she was listed as a felon and another supervisor because she shared the same name as a male criminal. The Florida law against felons dated from 1868 to prevent former enslaved people from voting and 'felony disenfranchisement laws have their roots in Jim Crow South' (Green, 2007). About 200,000 felons were disqualified between 1995 and 2005. Black men made up 50 percent of prison inmates – 90 percent of the disenfranchised (Florida Report on Felons 1995–2005, usccr.gov/2008).

Hillsborough County had a 15 percent error rate and: 'If that ratio held state-wide, no fewer than 7000 voters were incorrectly targeted for removal from voting rosters' (BBC News, 16 February 2001). '[P]recincts with more black, Hispanic and elderly voters had substantially more spoiled ballots' (*New York Times*, 12 November 2001). Harris lied when she denied responsibility for the inaccuracy of her information. A spokesman admitted it was 'a little embarrassing in the light of the election' but 'it was only a minor glitch.' And: 'It is under one-tenth of one percent of the electorate.' This 'glitch' was 15 times Bush's majority of 537.

The Republican House Speaker said elections should not mean everyone 'with two arms and two legs' had the right to vote, only those who are 'upholding the integrity and legitimacy of the society and culture'. Apparently this did not include African Americans. According to Abigail Thernstrom, appointed to the Civil Rights Commission by George W, 'The obvious explanation for a higher number of spoiled ballots among black voters is the lower literacy rates' (Berman, 2015). The problem was fraud by minorities, not discrimination. It was the opening shot in the campaign to destroy the Voting Rights Act (McAdam and Kloos, 2014).

The assertion that African Americans were illiterate was false and fails to explain why 9–10 percent of black votes were discarded compared with 2 percent of whites. In addition, the confusing ballot paper changed from one to two columns in some counties and 'the infamous butterfly ballot of Palm Beach' raises questions. The layout resulted in Jewish Gore supporters voting for the anti-Jewish Pat Buchanan who conceded that the ballot paper explained the error. The new systems were introduced in minority districts and over 18 percent of black votes were rejected – three times more than whites (*New York Times*, 12 November 2001). Democratic precincts had outdated voting machines which failed to punch through the ballot paper, resulting in so-called 'hanging chads'. These were not counted. Lani Guinier summed it up: 'This was not a robbery of the African American community. This was a robbery of democracy. It was not just black votes that weren't counted, there were also white people' (*American World*, February 2000).

The Florida Supreme Court in 2000 ordered a hand recount as Gore's legal team had requested and the Republicans asked the Supreme Court to overrule it. Their argument was drafted by John Roberts, a long-time opponent of civil rights and the Voting Rights Act, who was later rewarded by Bush. Roberts argued that a hand recount of some counties was discrimination. The majority of the Court decided they would hear the case although they did not have to.

The Court's ruling compounded the confusion. It seemed to be unanimous but it was not and reporters discovered that two justices had dissented. The Court publication stated that: 'The press of time does not diminish the constitutional concern. A desire for speed is not a general excuse for ignoring equal protection guarantees ... Having once granted the right to vote on equal terms the State may not, by later arbitrary and disparate treatment, value one person's vote over another.' (*Bush v. Gore*, caselaw.findlaw.com, 12 December 2000). Jeb Bush and Katherine Harris had valued 'one person's vote over another'. Justices who lauded the rights of states overruled the highest court in Florida. The press of time was the Court's fault because it was they who delayed prompt action. Justice Antonin Scalia wrote that a recount 'threatened irreparable harm to [George Bush] and to the country, casting a cloud over the legitimacy of the election'.

Opponents of Scalia and Thomas argued they should have recused themselves because of a conflict of interest: Thomas's wife worked for Bush and Scalia's son was a member of the law firm acting on Bush's behalf (Moore, 2001). They did not and the ruling was 5–4 not 7–2. The majority's claim was false. The conclusion: 'The election of 2000 was not stolen. Stealing after all is illegal and, by definition, nothing the Justices of the Supreme Court do can be outside the law. They are the law. The election was not stolen. It was expropriated' (*New Yorker*, 25 December 2000–1 January 2001). When law students complained, Scalia told them: 'Just get over it.'

Many saw Gore as a bad loser but Bush was awarded the presidency by five Republican-appointed justices – a majority of one. Bush only refers to the election in two and a half pages of his memoirs and says nothing about fraud (Bush, 2010). On 13 December Gore conceded but said: 'Let there be no doubt, while I strongly disagree with the court's decision,

I accept it.' He promised to support Bush: '[T]his belated broken impasse can join us on common ground, for its very closeness can serve to remind us that we are one people with a shared history and a shared destiny' (CNN Web Services, 13 December 2001). Bush proved him wrong.

2004: Another Questionable Election

In 2003 African Americans Reverend Al Sharpton and Carol Moseley Braun suggested they might run to remind politicians that civil rights issues had not been resolved (*The Washington Post*, 17 January 2003). However, a year later the presidential campaign followed the black arts of 2000. Senator John Kerry, the Democratic contender, was a Vietnam War hero while Bush had avoided military duty because his father's influence ensured his son joined the Air National Guard. George spent most of his time campaigning for southern Republicans. He needed to counter Kerry's war record. He did not repudiate ads by supposed Swift Boat veterans accusing Kerry of cowardice and being falsely awarded medals for bravery (Mark, 2007). Bush denied he was responsible for the ads and makes no reference to them in his book (Bush, 2010) but these were the same tactics he had used in 2000 against his Republican rival John McCain, another Vietnam War hero, who was accused of miscegenation, cowardice and homosexuality.

Again many lost their votes. After 2000 many states used Direct Recording Voting Machines which did not provide a paper record, making recounts impossible. Votes could be switched automatically and the machines could be hacked. Walden O'Dell, the head of the Ohio-based company Diebold which manufactured the machines, said in 2003 that he was 'committed to helping deliver its electoral votes to the president next year' (*Vanity Fair*, 4 April 2004). He did.

African American areas of Ohio and Florida especially had insufficient or broken voting machines and drastically reduced polling stations. In some Democratic districts voters waited nine hours to cast their ballot and in some barely 75 percent were able to do so. One black woman waited four hours to vote but her mother who lived in a white Republican suburb took only 15 minutes (Berman, 2015). In Lake County, Ohio a flyer sent to predominantly black precincts claimed that the NAACP and other registration groups possibly acted illegally, meaning 'you might not be able to vote in the next election'. The Ohio black secretary of state, Kenneth Blackwell, whose election had been financed by O'Dell (Green, 2007), discounted minority votes. John Conyers of the CBC reported his activities to the courts with little success. The number of people denied the vote in Ohio was greater than Bush's majority. Votes cast by African American and Hispanic people disappeared. In Illinois voting machines in black precincts were 'lost' and then discovered after polling had finished. Fraud was widespread in Florida (Berman, 2015). Not surprisingly, Bush barely mentions the 2004 campaign (Bush, 2010). Kerry did not challenge the result despite being urged to do so.

2001: Bush Takes Office

The exclusion of many African Americans, elderly and others put Bush in the White House. He told Jesse Jackson he understood 'the need to heal the nation'. The NAACP said he had to overcome 'a deeper belief in the minds of a lot of people that the nation did not care about them' (BBC News, 15 December 2000). The handful of liberal Republicans hoped to moderate his views and reach out to African Americans, Hispanics and the elderly and fight mounting homophobia. Republican Senator Lincoln Chafee wrote that vice president elect Dick Cheney outlined 'a shockingly divisive agenda' and that 'Bush displayed little interest in compromise and partnership and moderates in the Administration were humiliated at every turn' (McAdam and Kloos, 2014). Some claim that the terrorist attacks of 9/11 hardened Bush's conservatism and his indifference to the needs of the underprivileged. However, he was consistent. Despite verbal gestures, he opposed the achievements of the Movement and did not acknowledge other groups, certainly not gays. When same-sex couples wanted to adopt he opposed it, even though his sister and vice president's daughter were lesbians.

Clinton may have been motivated by his psychological needs (Renshon, 1988; Draper, 2007), but unlike Bush, he was genuinely interested in people and their problems, and had experienced childhood deprivation.

The NAACP and others soon discovered Bush was no Carter or Clinton. A senior aide announced that the offices on civil rights and AIDS set up by Clinton would be shut down (LA *Times*, 5 February 2001). It was denied. However, a spokesman admitted cuts in AIDS staff and no senior member of the White House staff would liaise with the Task Force for Uniting America (*The Washington Post*, 15 December 2000). In his Inaugural Address, Bush said he wanted to begin the 'healing process' and: '[I]n the quiet of American conscience, we know that deep, persistent poverty is unworthy of our nation's promise. And whatever its cause, we can agree that children at risk are not at fault. Abandonment and abuse are not Acts of God, they are failures of love' (presidency.ucsb.edu). For Bush and the New Right 'abandonment' and 'abuse' were parental failures, and had nothing to do with government policies.

Firstly, he appeased pro-life supporters by slashing aid to International Planned Parenthood because taxpayers should not 'pay for abortions or actively promote abortion' abroad. He knew *Roe* prevented similar restrictions in the United States. Critics accused him of ignoring the plight of foreign women, especially in Africa, where HIV/AIDS had reached pandemic proportions, and he supported pharmaceutical companies that set prohibitive prices for drugs designed to stop HIV spreading to pregnant women.

Appointments

His vice-presidential selection and appointments showed his support for corporations and individuals who had long opposed civil rights. Richard Cheney was former head of Halliburton Industries, an oil service company with which Bush and his Texas backers had had close business interests. Under Nixon and Reagan, Cheney and Defense Secretary Donald Rumsfeld had sought to dismantle Great Society programmes. As a congressman, Cheney voted against the Equal Rights Amendment (ERA), hate crimes proposals, federal funding for abortions (even in cases of rape and incest), funding Head Start and a resolution calling for Nelson Mandela's release. Typical appointments were Don Evans – former head of a giant oil and gas company – to Secretary of Commerce – and Tommy Thompson – a large investor in Philip Morris tobacco company – to Secretary of Health and Human Services.

The only moderate was the African American Secretary of State General Colin Powell who had shocked the convention when he defended abortion in some circumstances, urged inclusiveness and supported limited affirmative action. He failed to persuade black voters to vote Republican but he was more popular than Bush (Draper, 2007). He was isolated by the 'hard-assed' Donald Rumsfeld (Bush Sr, 2016) who set up his own foreign policy unit in the Pentagon. Powell faced persistent criticism from conservatives such as Newt Gingrich (*New York Times*, 26 November 2001). Powell argued passionately for the invasion of Iraq at the UN, a policy he had opposed, unaware he had been given false intelligence. He was not re-appointed in 2004. National Security Advisor, Condoleezza Rice, the only African American in the Administration, replaced Powell at the State Department.

In 2004 she told black academic Henry Gates about her childhood in Birmingham, Alabama, a city known as 'Bombingham' in the 1960s. She said nothing about terrorism and the murder of civil rights workers and argued faith-based Republican politics of an 'ownership society' would produce 'the pillars of the black community ... in my community Birmingham, Alabama, in the 1950s and 1960s there were black-owned businesses everywhere and everyone had their own homes. They made our community strong. We've got to get back to that again' (*New York Times*, 19 September 2004). Birmingham black folks had overwhelmingly fought so that those years would never return. Her shopowner father had thrived because segregation by white authorities gave him a monopoly. At her 2005 confirmation hearing she exploited the city's violence but said her appointment had nothing to do with colour or gender and she opposed affirmative action and feminism. In 2002 the NAACP executive director, Kweisi Mfume, awarded her their 'Image Award' (*Crisis*, March–April 2002). Yolanda White, black academic, poet and composer, wrote that Rice had done nothing to deserve it but 'only black men decided who was important within the community' (Baltimore *Chronicle and Sentinel*, 7 August 2002).

Bush selected black Texan Rod Page as Secretary of Education. Bush touted his 'No Child Left Behind' educational reform. Page claimed

Texas pupils had the best high school grades in the United States but the data excluded that Texas had the highest drop-out rate for black and Hispanic students (Ravitch, 2011). His support for federal funding of all-black colleges pleased black academics and white conservative segregationists. He opposed state university diversity programmes and affirmative action. He resigned in 2004. The black Assistant Secretary of Education Gerald Reynolds was in charge of civil rights only because his recess appointment avoided Senate approval. Such appointments can be made if they are essential and Congress is not in session. Reynolds controlled funding to prevent discrimination by schools and universities against minorities, women and gays. He did not. In 2005 Reynolds was made head of the Civil Rights Commission (*The Washington Post*, 17 January 2006).

The End of History and the Movement

In 1992 Francis Fukuyama wrote that the triumph of capitalism and Western democracy was the end of history. Conservatives embraced this absurd notion. The collapse of the Soviet Union re-enforced the belief that free markets, not central government, would mitigate social and economic problems. Dinesh D'Souza of the Business Enterprise Institute insisted there was a 'destructive stance that seems ingrained in African Americans, especially those in the middle class, who are too dependent on government' (D'Souza, 1995). Other conservatives admitted racism persisted but argued academic studies lacked 'intellectual rigor'. Interracial marriages had risen from 0.7 percent in 1963 to 12.1 percent in 1993 but until 1989 the census had counted children of these marriages as black, inflating the black population and perpetuating the 'caste system'. Poverty was 'a consequence of a huge rise in female-headed households among African Americans'. The answer was a colour-blind society (Thernstrom and Thernstrom, 1997) even though this had never existed. '[C]olor blindness was reconstituted from an oppositional weapon in the fight for racial justice to a conservative statement of American values ... The battle against inter-racial marriage came to be regarded as a mere ghost of America's troubled past' (Pascoe, 2009).

The troubled past was present. By 2004 'spitting and hitting interracial couples had virtually stopped but despite wider acceptance among younger people the racism in other forms remains' (Chicago *Tribune*, 19 June 2004). Lynching persisted. In Jasper, Texas in 1998 three white racists murdered James Byrd by chaining him behind their pick-up truck (Houston *Chronicle*, 19 June 1998). His grave was desecrated twice, the last time in 2013. The Minnesota *Daily* condemned the murder but linked African Americans and the KKK. 'With black militants and the Ku Klux Klan standing in the shadows ... each side [is] trading murder for murder' (17 June 1998). This reflects white people's growing indifference. Mississippi Governor Haley Barbour was asked what he remembered of the Movement replied: 'Not much' (AP, 20 January 2001). With this ignorance and indifference: 'It is not surprising that the Urban League's demand for a Marshall Plan, backed by civil disobedience, was ignored because this typified the early efforts ... based on traditional community institutions such as the church, the campuses, labor groups and women's groups' (Hudson and Davies, 2008).

Black Conservatism

The new conservatism had its black believers, converts and beneficiaries. Jesse Jackson 'took an active interest in black-owned businesses as an idealistic alternative to government dependence' and like them blamed poor African Americans for their plight (Chappell, 2014). The 'agenda reflects the priorities of the elite: equal access to white institutions and white neighborhoods ... to escape the black masses' (Iton, 2007). Clarence Thomas writes 'What I cared about more than anything else ... was the condition of blacks in Savannah and across America' (Thomas, 2007). Their own efforts would overcome poverty. At his confirmation, Thomas lied about his sister alleging she stayed at home and took welfare cheques when she was employed (Mayer and Abramson, 2002). Affirmative action has 'stigmatizing effects [that] perpetuate racism, averting what would otherwise be its natural death' (Tate and Randolph, 2002). But racism is deeply woven into the fabric of American society. Affirmative action ensured Thomas had been to

Yale and had worked for a Republican senator, a multi-national corporation, Reagan and Bush.

Alan Keyes, a black Harvard graduate and perennial Republican office-
seeker and Reagan appointee to the UN and State Department, opposed
South African sanctions and the funding of international family planning groups. He was homophobic, even attacking his lesbian daughter.
His three presidential campaigns (1992, 1998, 2004) were disastrous.
He challenged Barack Obama for the US Senate in Illinois, getting only
26 percent of the vote. He quit the Republican Party in 2008 saying it
was not conservative enough (BBC News, January 2008). The argument
that the black elite were pulling up the drawbridge has some merit. Like
corporations, they relied heavily on government help. Clinton's campaign manager sums it up: 'It is one thing to propose self-reliance, and
quite another to propose that the government has no responsibility for
the victims of discrimination. Republicans want to get rid of affirmative
action and return America to a meritocracy but America has never been
a meritocracy' (Carville, 1996).

Bush, Conservatism and the Supreme Court

Bush nominated John Roberts as Chief Justice and Samuel Alito as a
Justice to ensure conservative domination for years. The Court, it is
claimed, is not merely a battle between liberals and conservatives but
political ideology is important because presidents nominate those who
share their views and the Senate has to confirm them (Coyle, 2014).
Roberts testified to the Senate Judiciary Committee hearing he would
respect precedents, especially *Brown* and *Roe,* Congress's constitutional
role and ensure equality for all Americans. Some liberals accepted that
his previous criticisms of desegregation and affirmative action had been
presidential requests and not his views. And when Sandra Day O'Connor
retired, Bush nominated Alito. As with Thomas, the White House
campaigned vigorously for Alito who emphasised his deprived background and contrasted his time at Princeton 'with the good sense and
decency of the people in my community'. Senator Barack Obama voted
against Thomas and joined the filibuster against Alito who was narrowly

approved (Coyle, 2014). The NAACP argued that Alito would 'shift significantly ... jurisprudence relating to affirmative action, voting rights and criminal justice' (NAACP, January 2009). No one mentioned school desegregation.

The assault on *Brown* came in 2007. In a 5–4 decision, integration agreed by school boards in Seattle, Washington and Louisville, Kentucky was declared unconstitutional for violating the Equal Protection Clause of the Fourteenth Amendment – an amendment to protect emancipated slaves. The logic of Scalia, Thomas and Alito puzzled many. They declared: '[T]o achieve a system of determining admissions to public schools on a nonracial basis is to stop assigning students on a racial basis. The way to stop discrimination on the basis of race is to stop discriminating on the basis of race' (findlaw.com, 28 June 2007). The Justices reflected the determination to keep schools segregated. Although Jesse Jackson continued to fight to desegregate schools, most black people understood they would not prevail. Integrated schools dropped from 70 percent in the 1970s to 50 percent by the 1980s. Ninety percent of northern schools were segregated. 'As the nineties began ... massive white opposition to bussing ... and increasing residential segregation had quieted talk of integrated education' (Sugrue, 2008). Father Groppi's efforts in Milwaukee failed and he turned to improving inner city schools (Jones, 2009). As late as mid-2016, Cleveland, Mississippi was ordered by a federal court to desegregate its schools (*New York Times*, 17 May 2016). There was one exception. Fifty percent of Little Rock High School pupils were African American and over 40 percent were white. At a meeting honouring African American History Month, Bush claimed: 'We will continue to enforce the laws against racial discrimination in education and housing and public accommodation. We believe that every child can learn and we expect every school to teach. And we measure. And guess what's happening. Test scores are going up, there is an achievement gap for minority children that is closing in America' (AfricanAmericans.com, 1 February 2009).

All his talk of education did not help African Americans and their right to vote. Court conservatives upheld a 2008 Indiana law requiring voters to show identification papers before voting, a severe restriction of the Fifteenth Amendment of 1868 and the Voting Rights Act (1965).

If voters had provisional registration they had to present identification at the ballot if their vote was to be counted. Both the ACLU and the Democratic Party argued that many could not meet the arbitrary requirements owing to the costs and, although not a poll tax, many African Americans and Hispanics would be disenfranchised. Despite Roberts' promise to respect precedent, the ruling overturned *Harper v. Virginia Board of Elections* (1966).

Bush tried to pack federal appeal courts with conservatives and their rejection by Democrats allowed him to argue they opposed strict construction of the Constitution in favour of liberal activism. Nine out of eleven nominees were rejected. Bush chose Charles Pickering for the 5th Circuit Court of Appeals. In 1959 Pickering had advised the Mississippi legislature on how to tighten the ban on interracial marriage and in 1994 complained that sentencing a man who had burnt a cross on an interracial couple's lawn to a five-year mandatory sentence was too harsh. Pickering quit the Democratic Party because it insisted on integrated delegations and opposed the Supreme Court's ruling defending one-person-one-vote. Some supported him because in the 1960s he testified against a KKK defendant and protected Camp Sister Spirit, a Mississippi lesbian commune (Log Cabin Republicans, 5 March 2002). The Houston *Chronicle* dismissed these attempts to defend him (5 March 2002). The Detroit *Free Press* opposed his appointment because of his poor civil rights record, the failure to consult Mississippi black lawyers and NAACP objections (6 March 2002).

A Republican Apology: Trent Lott and Race

Republicans, increasingly reliant on the South and Midwest, embraced the race agenda (McAdam and Kloos, 2014). Senate leader Trent Lott (Mississippi) disagreed with the party minority urging accommodation with African Americans (GOPOutreach, 2 February 2002). At Dixiecrat-turned-Republican Strom Thurmond's 100th birthday celebrations in 2002, Lott proclaimed: 'When Strom Thurmond ran for president we voted for him. We're proud of it. And if the rest of the country had followed our lead, we wouldn't have had all these problems over all these years.' Lott praised Thurmond's campaign pledge that there would not be enough troops to end segregation. Colin Powell said: 'There was nothing about the 1948 Dixiecrat agenda that should have been acceptable in any way to any American at that time or now' (*New York Times*, 19 December). (At age 21 Thurmond had raped a 15-year-old servant in his house and fathered a black child. He funded his daughter's silence but continued his life-long denunciation of miscegenation.) In a speech to the Sons of Confederate Veterans, Lott had claimed: 'The spirit of Jefferson Davis lives in the 1984 Republican platform' (New York *Daily Post*, 12 December 2002). He defended tax exemption for Bob Jones University knowing its racist policies (findlaw.com, *Bob Jones University v. The United States*, 27 November 1981). Black Republican J. C. Watts defended him.

Eventually, Lott admitted his comments were 'terrible', regretted voting against King's birthday as a federal holiday, and now backed affirmative action and help for African Americans. He did not resign the Senate leadership. It was this apparent conversion, not praising Thurmond, that cost him the leadership (*New York Times*, 12 and 20 December 2002). Publicly Bush said he was 'a valued friend, and a man I respect. I am pleased he will continue to serve our nation in the Senate' (*New York Times*, 29 December 2002). Mississippians were too and re-elected him.

Bush and Affirmative Action

Bush welcomed the 1996 California referendum that effectively prohibited state universities' social diversity programmes, which had dire consequences for minorities. The Supreme Court struck down a University of Texas programme designed to benefit applicants regardless of race, gender, disability or sexual orientation. When the University of Michigan was accused of operating a quota system benefiting African Americans, the university countered that it was based on income only. General Motors supported the university saying that a true education required students to study with others from the widest background. When the case arrived at the Supreme Court Sandra Day O'Conner had the decisive vote.

Bush had no doubts. He said Michigan operated a 'quota system that unfairly rewards or penalizes prospective students based solely on their race'. He said: 'Race neutral policies have resulted in levels of minority attendance ... that are close to, and in some cases surpass, those under the old race-based approach.' He favoured 'affirmative access' without explaining what it meant. It was the politics of euphemism again. Critics pointed out that a quota system giving preference to children of former graduates got Bush Jr into Yale. Tom Daschle (D. South Dakota) observed: 'They have to decide whether they are for civil rights and racial diversity or not' (*USA Today*, 16 January 2003). Quotas mainly benefited women, and Representative Nancy Pelosi (D. California) denounced the Administration's intervention. 'If the Supreme Court agrees with President Bush and prohibits affirmative action in our colleges and universities, the dreams of countless young people will be crushed.' Her fears were allayed – O'Connor voted with the liberals in *Grutter v. Bollinger et al* in a 5–4 decision that upheld *Bakke*. Three of the majority said there should be a 25-year limit. Later, Reagan's practice of coaching nominated justices on how to answer Judicial Committee questioning would pay off (Coyle, 2013).

Despite this setback, Bush ordered the Attorney General to disband several civil rights committees and remove veteran lawyers. The appointment criteria favoured those who had 'strong conservative credentials' and preferably without experience in civil rights cases. In 2001, 77 percent of Civil Rights Division lawyers were experienced, by 2003 it was only 42 percent of new appointees, and from 2003 to 2006 only 19 out of 45. Additionally, '[T]he kinds of cases the Civil Rights Division is bringing has undergone a shift. The division is bringing fewer cases involving discrimination against African Americans, and more alleging reverse discrimination against whites and religious discrimination against Christians' (Boston *Globe*, 23 July 2006). The new Attorney General was forced to resign after he dismissed eight federal prosecutors because they were 'too liberal' (*New York Times*, 29 September 2008) as well as 34-year-old Monica Goodling at Justice for vetting prospective judges for their views on abortion and same-sex marriage (*The Washington Post*, 29 July 2008).

Gagging on the Donkey

At an Urban League meeting in July 2005 Bush quoted a Republican legislator: 'Blacks are gagging on the donkey [Democrats] but not yet ready to swallow the elephant [Republicans].' The President asked: 'How is it possible for Republicans to gain political leverage if the Democratic party is never forced to compete?' (*New York Times*, 10 September 2005). In truth he and his Party had no interest in the black vote and marched further to the right. Republican Senator Rick Santorum said: 'I don't want to make people's lives better by giving them someone else's money' (McAdam and Kloos, 2014). Bush shared Santorum's views.

During his first term he was the first president since Herbert Hoover who never spoke to the NAACP despite invitations and never disguised his dislike of the organisation. He said his relationship with the NAACP was 'basically nonexistent' and it was not until 2006 that he agreed to speak (Bush, 2010). The IRS had threatened the NAACP's tax-exempt status because they criticised his policies (*New York Times*, 10 March 2004). The National Republican chairman admitted at the NAACP convention that some in the party 'were trying to benefit from racial polarization' (Green, 2007). When Bush finally addressed them he promised: 'We'll work together, and as we do, so you must understand I understand that racism still lingers in America.' He said it was a tragedy that the Party had not fought hard enough for their votes. Many NAACP members credited him for coming but Kathy Sykes said: 'He waited until the 11th hour of his presidency to come to us with his great plans for working together' (*New York Times*, 21 July 2006).

The Rich Get Richer

The three women in his cabinet, Condoleezza Rice, Gale Norton and Elaine Chao, supported his economic policies. Families had sued over the health dangers of lead in paint products and Norton defended the manufacturers. Chao was a company board member fined for selling faulty heart catheters. They and Rice supported benefit cuts, a $60 million reduction in federal housing and $200 million in childcare and development grants forcing single parents into low-paid jobs. The $30 billion in tax 'relief that benefited the rich was, a reward not for effort, but simply for having been rich' (*New Yorker*, 5 February 2002). Bush cut disability allowances and veteran associations, natural Republican voters, demanded restoration of full funding (AMVETS letter to George Bush, 25 January 2003). He ignored them. He claimed his budget would revitalise the economy and over 92 million Americans would benefit on average by $1038. The *Financial Times* dismissed it as 'bogus' and Hendrik Hertzberg in the *New Yorker* wrote: '[A] typical taxpayer ... in the middle of the income range will get a couple of hundred dollars. And a worker in the bottom 20 percent will get next to nothing – at most a quarter or dime a week.'

In two terms Bush turned a large surplus into a massive deficit. His policies and the negligence of the Federal Reserve meant that stock market regulation was virtually non-existent and speculation in worthless stock was rampant. The budgets and Wall Street greed massively increased incomes of the top 1 percent (Piketty, 2014). The banking collapse and the selling of subprime mortgages ended the dream of house ownership for many African Americans seeking to escape the ghetto. 'If incarceration had come to define the lives of black men from impoverished black neighborhoods, eviction was shaping the lives of women. Poor black men were locked up. Poor black women were locked out' (Desmond, 2016). The plight of black and poor communities was made worse by the growing income, health and educational disparities (Piketty, 2014). And the government spent billions bailing out the banks.

Discrimination and the Law

In July 2002 a mentally disabled African American woman was sentenced to death for murdering her sister's newborn child; this was reduced to 15 years for manslaughter. She was innocent because her sister had been previously sterilised (*North County Times*, 18 July 2002). Later the Supreme Court in *Atkins v. Virginia* (2002) ruled that the death sentence was unconstitutional for 'mentally defective' persons. 'Mentally defective' was not defined and executions continued, especially of African

American men. Cecil Clayton who had 20 percent of his right frontal lobe destroyed in an accident was executed in Missouri in 2015 (*The Washington Post*, 18 March 2015).

The anti-death penalty campaign intensified. Law students of Northwestern University, Illinois proved that 13 innocent men had been executed since 1977. George Ryan, the Republican governor and a death penalty advocate, ordered a moratorium. On 19 December 2002 he pardoned three death row inmates and commuted the sentences of another 167 who were serving life (AP, 11 January 2003). He concluded the process was 'arbitrary and capricious and therefore immoral'. Evidence of racial discrimination in other states did not mean the governors followed suit. Ryan also stated: 'My concern is not just with the death penalty ... it's with the entire judicial system. If innocent people are sentenced to death – the cases that get all the scrutiny – what does that say about invisible lower cases – drug cases and so on (*Guardian*, 10 January 2003).' Despite his warnings about the racial disparity between crack and powdered cocaine sentencing, it hardly changed (ACLU, 20 May 2002). Children Requiring a Caring Kommunity (CRACK) offered $200 to some with alcohol and drug problems to agree to long-term contraception or sterilisation. Almost 50 percent of the women sterilised were African Americans (*The Washington Post*, 8 January 2003).

Hurricane Katrina

'Katrina had blown a hole through his presidency' (Draper, 2009) but Bush's apparent indifference to the 28 August 2005 hurricane was partly due to the African American mayor of New Orleans, Ray Nagin, and the Louisiana governor who had declared a state of emergency on the 26th. Bush knew in advance that a terrible storm was heading for the city. He did nothing. After completing his California golfing vacation he went to Florida and scheduled a return to Texas. Television showed dead bodies floating in the streets, families clinging to the rooftops with signs pleading for help that did not come and on the 30th Bush relaxed playing guitar with a country western singer.

The media claimed there was rioting, looting, murder and that firemen and police had been attacked and Bush repeats this slander in his memoirs (Bush, 2010). This is untrue. Rich city dwellers fled while the poor black and white residents of the 9th Ward tried to stay above the floodwaters from the broken levees. Bush's first sight of New Orleans was from Air Force One and it did not land. He claimed 'he had made the right decision in not burdening local officials with his presence'. He was accused of 'paralytic incompetence' (*Time*, 12 January 2009).

Bush believed small government was essential. But national outrage forced him to visit hurricane areas. He avoided the 9th Ward demonstrators, going to the Lower Garden District where he told community leaders that the city was 'a heck of place to bring your family. It's a great place to find the greatest food in the world some wonderful fun and I'm glad you got your infrastructure back on its feet' (Draper, 2007). As he was speaking, flood victims were crowded into the football stadium, dead bodies were stored in cupboards and there was only one white doctor. Families were separated and evacuated across the country. CNN television described African Americans as 'refugees'. Diane Watson said: 'Refugees calls up to mind people that come from different lands and have to be taken care of. These are American citizens' (Iton, 2008).

There was violence. It came from white police and white vigilantes. Four officers were later found guilty of murdering black people and given sentences ranging from 28 to 65 years. The judge complained that they were mandatory sentences and accused the prosecution of 'mendacity' (*New York Times*, 4 April 2012). The all-white residents of undamaged Algiers Point blocked the road, preventing black people from escaping and: 'They stockpiled handguns, assault rifles, shotguns and at least one Uzi.' This militia of 15–30 residents, mostly men, claimed they were looking for criminals or, as one member put it, 'anyone who simply didn't belong' (*The Nation*, 17 December 2008). They went free and later boasted about their killings in a Spike Lee documentary.

One year after the storm, CNN discovered that the small community of Pearlington, Mississippi was still devastated and contaminated with foul-tasting water. One family had a house with the rest in government-supplied trailers that had dangerous levels of formaldehyde. According to the Census Bureau, New Orleans was 36 percent smaller and increasingly white and middle class. Rapper Kanye West said: 'Bush doesn't care about black people'; and his words were made into a hip-hop recording. Bruce Springsteen released *How Can a Poor Man Stand Such Times and Live*, an indictment of Bush based on the 1929 blues of Blind Alfred Reed. In 2007 Brother Ali recorded *Uncle Sam Goddamn*: 'Welcome to the the United Snakes / Land of the the thief / And home of the slave.' The neglect following Katrina contributed to a revival of 1960s and 1970s protest music. In 1997 Bush had described the white rapper from Detroit, Eminem, as: 'The greatest threat to America's children since polio' (*Independent*, 14 February 2009).

Where Have All the (Male) Leaders Gone?

Abernathy's incompetence meant that some African Americans looked for a new charismatic leader and turned to Jesse Jackson. Others preferred to rely on community self-help under black male leadership. The NOI organised a Million Man March but its leaders appealed to machismo and lacked King's analytical understanding of the central role of poverty. For King the immorality of the Vietnam War was largely because the poor fought to enrich the few. Programmes to help America's disadvantaged and the poor Vietnamese were as starved as the people they were supposed to help. The economy needed radical restructuring. Foreign adventures meant imperialism, protecting capitalism and huge military expenditure. King had embraced Christian socialism to transform the nation (Jackson, 2007).

Although Jackson claimed King's mantle, he enthusiastically supported black capitalism and organised Operation Breadbasket and People United to Save Humanity (PUSH). PUSH raised $17 million in 2000. Critics claimed Toyota's $7.8 million for diversity and tolerance campaigns, like the threatened boycott of Wall Street firms, were 'shakedowns' (*New Yorker*, 22 October 2001). Toyota disagreed. They supported PUSH with training programmes, business funding and black-owned dealerships. Later they awarded scholarships for black students. Jackson's economic conservatism won him white votes during his Rainbow Coalition presidential campaigns (Chappell, 2014).

Other black aspirants denounced Jackson. After he left PUSH, Reverend Al Sharpton moved to New York City and established projects such as the Madison Avenue and the National Action Network. He said he was from Selma, Alabama but he was the son of a prosperous builder in New York City. Although he supported false claims by a girl who said she had been raped, he led effective campaigns against police brutality. He told Jackson 'to get a ringside seat and move over' (*New Yorker*, 25 February 2003). Other white critics were blunter: 'If Sharpton was a white skinhead, he would be a political leper' (Boston *Globe*, 16 January 2003). This feuding may have helped conservative efforts to dismantle the Movement's gains but some ignore the fact that although many black people revere King, it was his policies not his charisma they wanted. Self-proclaimed leaders were past their use-by-date. To defend gains and win more, African Americans knew they needed allies.

Power and Coalition Building

Jackson had proved a black presidential candidate could win white people's votes, primaries and might occupy the White House (Chappell, 2014), something that would have been impossible without the Movement's struggle and the goals of its leaders and grass-roots activists. Jackson took King's title 'Rainbow Coalition' for the Poor People's March as his campaign slogan.

Power at state and federal level saw dramatic gains for black politicians. The Congressional Black Caucus (CBC) had 13 members in 1971 and Nixon refused to meet them but Bush promised to work with them (*The Washington Post*, 31 March 200), but only after they picketed the White House (LA *Times*, 14 October 2004). John Conyers serves on the House Judiciary Committee. The CBC remains a powerful influence in the Democratic Party, increased by its cooperation with the Congressional Caucus on Women's Issues and the Hispanic Caucus.

After Reagan's refusal to impose South African sanctions, the CBC worked to win them working with the Free South Africa Movement (FSAM) who used Movement strategies – sit-ins, non-violent demonstrations and arrests. When George H. W. Bush vetoed the 1990 Civil

Rights Act the CBC were crucial in overriding it. They coordinated state causes and worked with professional organisations. Some claimed: 'the old lions give way to the younger generation of black politicians who do not want to be pigeonholed by race' (*International Herald Tribune*, 3 January 2009). This underestimates the CBC, and Democrats know it. It is too early to bring in the coffin.

African Americans in state legislatures formed caucuses and built coalitions with the local community and pressure groups. The National Black Caucus of State Legislatures had over 600 representatives in 42 states and Washington DC who, like the CBC, represented the poor regardless of colour, ethnicity, gender or sexual orientation. For example, Alabama elected 35 state House representatives, Georgia 53 and Mississippi 50 and 13 senators. African Americans, 13 percent of the national population, made up 9 percent in the state legislatures. This relative success as state representatives was not matched by election of state governors. In 1990 Virginians elected L. Douglas Wilder as the first black governor. Deval Patrick was the first black governor of Massachusetts, where black people constituted 7 percent of the population. Mayors and local administrators were elected in towns and cities in unprecedented numbers and black police officers and state troopers patrolled black and white communities. It was black power.

Doubts about white people supporting African Americans had a long life but success in the cities was only possible because of coalitions with white and Hispanic voters. Carl Stokes was narrowly elected mayor of Cleveland, Ohio but after rioting there did not seek re-election. In Chicago, Harold Washington defeated the Daley machine with a coalition of blacks and white liberals. Tom Bradley, a sharecropper's son, did this in Los Angeles from 1973 to 1993 where African Americans comprised only 15 percent of the population (*Christian Science Monitor*, 30 September 1993). Others included David Dinkins of New York City, Coleman Young of Detroit and Cory Booker of Newark, New Jersey. The problem for some of them was that coalitions were not of equals and white business had to be appeased. When black people sought 'community control of politics and economics [it] had unintended consequences. African Americans controlled cities that were haemorrhaging capital, population, and tax revenues (Sugrue, 2008).

Working Together

There are fierce debates over the benefits for African Americans' coalitions with other groups and: '[I]ntra-racial efforts were often hobbled by political infighting' (Sugrue, 2008). A scholar of the post-King years concludes: '[T]o the extent that a post 1960s economy allowed aspiring members of other minority groups, the disabled, and many kinds of white women to claim their rights, it did so in some ways at the expense of further rights for the black population and the poor' (Chappell, 2014). Coalitions failed African Americans, Hispanics and Native Americans. Critics seem to suggest that there were no black women and LGBT activists, no disabled, that unions deserted the struggle and that African Americans were not involved in the environmental movement.

The proposition that coalitions were harmful misses a major point. The Movement had never been a black people only struggle; it was made up of groups such as the NAACP, SCLC, SNCC and SSOC and this was recognised when they were united in the COFO in 1965 despite natural tensions. Without these intra- and interracial coalitions none of the great achievements such as the Civil and Voting Rights Acts would have been possible. Even if the Black Baptist Convention did not join the struggle, many of their ministers did. It is true that school desegregation and urban desegregation mainly failed, especially in the North. Most politicians have little sympathy for minorities but the plight of black people, LGBT people, Hispanics and environmentalists would have been worse if they had not fought together.

Trade Unions

It is true that union support weakened with the continued decline in industrial investment, opposition from white ethnic employees and capital flight to anti-union, 'right to work' laws of southern and midwestern states; nevertheless unions continued to benefit black workers and the struggle for equality and economic justice. The Steelworkers Union gave 98 percent of their campaign funding to the Democrats in 2012 although membership fell (Federal Election Commission Report, 2013).

Despite a drastic decline in UAW membership black workers benefited with victories in the Tennessee Volkswagen plants and union support for the auto bailout in 2009. The Memphis sanitation workers' strike of 1968 educated northern white union leaders on how to use tactics best suited to organising the black community (Honey, 2007). That success played a large part in strengthening public employee unions – such as the American Federation of State, and Municipal County Employees, a sector with many African American and Hispanic workers.

There were problems. JFK had signed the Equal Pay Act in 1963 but compliance was not good – certainly not for African American women who were paid 10 percent less than black men and 23 percent less than white men. Hispanic women were paid 21 percent less. The plight of all working women was highlighted in the experience of Lilly Ledbetter, a white woman, who had been a supervisor at the Goodyear Tyre Plant in Gadsden, Alabama. Her pay rises over 19 years resulted in her earning 15–25 percent less than her often inexperienced male colleagues. In the Supreme Court ruling, *Ledbetter v. Goodyear Tyre Company* (2007), the Republican appointees, Roberts, Scalia, Thomas and Kennedy, said that a Title VII complaint had to be filed in 180 days of the discriminatory action, regardless of the impact on the employee. They ignored evidence that companies kept pay information confidential which made it almost impossible to prove discrimination and litigation futile. Despite protestations that they would respect precedent, the Court majority overturned 20 years of federal court cases and Equal Employment Commission Rulings (NOW press release, 30 May 2007). Ledbetter had lost.

African Americans, Hispanics and women working with unions lobbied Congress and on 9 January 2009 the House of Representatives legislated to strengthen the ability of workers to fight discrimination. It passed two more bills that over-turned the 180-day deadline and another to make it easier to prove violations of the 1963 Act and to sue for compensatory and punitive damages. Employers' claims that superior education, market forces and previous experience justified pay differentials were severely limited. Bush threatened to veto both bills but could not because he was no longer president (*New York Times*, 10 January 2009). Earlier similar coalitions of the CBC with the Women's Coalition and Hispanic Congressmen saved the affirmative action programme that set aside 10 percent of Department of Transport contracts for small businesses mostly run by minorities and women, a programme vigorously opposed by conservatives (Lee, 1999).

Environmentalism

Groups united to fight environmental pollution. Contrary to the view of some scholars, this battle embraced all races and classes and remains a long-term struggle for improvements. It led to Obama's election in 2008, one of the greatest protectors of the environment in US history. It was and remains a long uphill struggle but that has not broken their determination. A 1997 study sponsored by the United Church of Christ proved that minority and poor neighbourhoods suffered the highest rates of pollution. Over 9 million poor people lived within a two-mile radius of 453 toxic waste sites, 56 percent predominantly minority communities. In 1998 ministers of the Missionary Baptist Convention toured sites in Louisiana in the chemical production area stretching from New Orleans to Baton Rouge known as 'Cancer Alley'. The ministers reported: 'Black, white, young and old are dying before their time' (National Council of Churches, 13 January 1998).

Residents of Convent told them that a Japanese PVC manufacturer wanted to build a plant that would produce 600,000 pounds of toxic chemicals, 8 million of air pollutants per year and pump 3 million gallons of toxic water into the Mississippi River every day. Carlotta Smothers, whose home was built on a landfill with 150 toxic chemicals said, 'the dream turned into a nightmare for us'. The churches, Greenpeace and Tulane University joined forces with local black and white women who participated in non-violent protest marches and, after a three-year court fight, defeated the company. There was a new generation, mainly women of all races, who united with environmental groups. Ronald Reagan had cited the Bronx, New York as proof that: 'The government fought a war on poverty, and poverty won.' Genevieve Brooks worked with others and restored thousands of apartments for low-income families. They received no federal or state aid (Hudson and Davis, 2008). Others in the Bronx struggled to end air pollution (*New York Times*, 14 December 2008).

Conservatives argued that environmental protection would reduce the United States to Third World status. Some local efforts were threatened by sponsors who tried to dictate community action but the persistence of African American and other low-income people led to significant improvements and, after 2009, federal government support.

Feminism and LGBT

The opposition of the black church, nationalists and some older African Americans to abortion and homosexuality has been emphasised to prove that unity with feminists and the LGBT community was impossible. Certainly, many black women had put male liberation first (see Chapter 3) and many minorities had serious religious doubts about abortion, believing it was a conspiracy to eliminate them. White Judge J. Pickering opposed abortion even in cases of incest and rape and Priscilla Owens argued that Texas abortion guidelines were lax while her critics argued they made access to abortion for poor and African American women almost impossible (NARAL Online Newsroom, 16 January 2003).

Many historians and others stress homophobia in the black community and that segregated lesbian communes in the 1970s prove the impossibility of joint action and that working with lesbians – the 'lavender menace' – was harmful. Some did fear that supporting LGBT people would be seen as encouraging sexual 'deviants' and would undermine gains made by the struggle. However, for most black women the need was 'to commit ourselves to the broader struggle against heterosexism in black communities'. A black lesbian argues: 'Because dominant gender norms define our common oppressions, the fate of the black lesbian, gay, bisexual and transgender people is inextricably joined to the fate of heterosexual black men and women' (Brandt ed., 1999). The linking of the LGBT with civil rights had its origins in the period after World War Two when gays adopted the same arguments and tactics of King and the Black Panthers (Faderman, 2015). Many African Americans, such as Pauli Murray, were founders of the feminist movement and others, such as lesbian poets Audre Lorde and June Jordan, opposed segregated relationships. Author James Baldwin never hid in the closet and Alice Walker is proudly bisexual.

However, many concluded that California's Proposition 8, banning same-sex marriage, passed because of African Americans (San Francisco *Chronicle*, 7 January 2009). What has been inadequately discussed is that many African Americans and Movement activists defended LGBT people. NAACP's Julian Bond pointed out that Hispanic, Native American and LGBT movements 'took their cues from the African American civil rights movement'. AIDS threatened everyone regardless of race or sexual orientation. He admitted that some, especially black preachers, were often homophobic which was 'disgraceful'. He wanted more openness by LGBT people in the black community and that they should be more active in the struggle. 'Their situation would be immeasurably helped if those said "Here I am"' (*The Advocate*, 12 October 2009). Congressman John Lewis was one of the most pro-gay legislators (think.progress.org, 3 July 2003). When Coretta Scott King addressed the AIDS quilt memorial initiative in Atlanta she denounced black homophobia, insisting that 'African Americans have suffered too long because of prejudice and bigotry to be parroting the words of the Ku Klux Klan and other hate groups who bash people for their sexual orientation' (gos.sbc.edu, 18 October 1999).

The Patriot Act

The 9/11 Patriot Act had widespread support from both political parties and the public, but it also strengthened coalitions and brought new recruits to the civil rights struggle because of abuses that followed its implementation. It allowed arrests without orders, search and seizure, wiretapping, email searches, library checkouts and deportation without legal protection for American Muslims. The FBI declared an orange alert in 2003 in Las Vegas which has 300,000 visitors a year, and collected data on all hired vehicles, storage points, airport and hotel check-ins and cross-matched this with utility bills, addresses and telephone numbers of alleged terrorists. Finding nothing, the alert ended in 2004. University of California, Berkeley faculty condemned the Act and its violation of civil rights (UC *Berkeley News,* 10 May 2004). Stanford University opposed the Act because of racial profiling. Marion Bray of the Stanford University Muslim Society recalled the firebombing of his grandparents' home when he stayed with them. 'That was my first experience with terrorism. Not September 11. And I was only 5-years-old' (*Cardinal Enquirer*, www.stanford.edu, 16 February 2005).

Non-violence and the struggle did not end during the conservative ascendancy. Coalitions brought together African Americans and many groups who suffered similar deprivation and discrimination and resulted in impressive victories with the help of sympathetic politicians. Old activists recruited new ones and they did not need a 'leader' either chosen by whites or one self-proclaimed. It was a community organiser who became a leader not of African Americans but of all Americans. For millions the 2008 election was a dream come true but for others it was what they had resisted for so long: their nightmare had become a reality.

10

'Post-Racial' America? Barack Obama
2008–2017

African Americans, Hispanics, liberals, women, LGBT people, unions and even some Republicans were certain 2008 would be the Democrat's year. For his loyalists, however, George Bush had defeated terrorism and won the 'crusade for democracy' in Iraq. Even though the mastermind of 9/11, Osama bin Laden, was free and there was a 'Great Recession', a Republican could win the election. Bush says he 'laid the foundations for recovery' (Bush, 2010). But he had ignored the plight of the low-income working and middle classes, especially African Americans, and for many the last months of his presidency were a rerun of Hurricane Katrina when African Americans and low-income white people had been left to drown. He floundered during the 2008 financial crisis caused by banks selling mortgages to low income African American and poor families wanting to live in suburbia. *Time* magazine's assessment of Bush was: 'He was less than a President and that is appropriate. He was never very much of one' (12 January 2009).

Republican Nominees: Race and Religion

Religion and race were crucial in the 2008 primaries. Arizona Senator John McCain, a war hero, was the Republicans' best chance but he had to placate evangelicals. In the 2000 primaries he had declared Pat

Robertson and Jerry Falwell (Welch, 2008) as an 'evil influence ... over the Republican Party' (Alexander, 2003). Now he embraced fundamentalist preachers such as Ohio's Rod Parsley who declared all Muslims were terrorists and that Mahomet's revelations came from demons (Thomas, 2009). These attacks fed old-fashioned racism that was all too familiar. Bush, however, was convinced McCain's problem was not with evangelicals; rather it was the generation gap (Bush, 2010).

Mitt Romney, former Massachusetts governor, was a Mormon and many voters believed Mormons were not Christian. He had supported a radical healthcare programme and defended abortion in cases of incest, rape and saving women's lives. He said nothing to appeal to minority or Hispanic voters. Romney and McCain's problems with evangelicals worsened when fundamentalist Mike Huckabee, governor of Arkansas, joined the race. Abortion, homosexuality and evolution were evil. He won the first primary.

A Democrat Revolution?

Hillary Clinton, former First Lady and New York senator, wanted to be the first woman president. Her husband's popularity with women, African Americans and most Hispanics made her nomination seemingly inevitable (Ellis, 2009; Thomas, 2009). However, she had problems. Some did not want Bill as a *de facto* president. And then there was her gender, her husband's scandals and conspiracy theorists' accusations she had murdered her lawyer. Others preferred the Hispanic New Mexico Governor Bill Richardson, and Hispanics were crucial in key states. Populists John Edwards and Joe Biden would take union and blue-collar voters.

Nobody expected a first-term US senator from Illinois would challenge this strong field. He was black, the son of a white woman from Kansas, an African father and had had an Indonesian stepfather. He was educated in Roman Catholic and Muslim schools. His name was Barack Hussein Obama and conservatives and talk-show hosts continually emphasised his middle name, the same as Iraqi dictator Saddam Hussein, or called him Osama, associating him with the terrorist Osama bin Laden. For them he was an African and a Muslim.

Others saw him as an elitist – editor of the *Harvard Law Review*, author and law lecturer at the University of Chicago. Some African Americans considered he was not black enough and he did not appreciate the Movement's achievements (Harris, 2012; Keller, 2015). When he challenged ex-Panther and congressman Bobby Rush, Rush said: 'Barack is a person who read about civil rights protests and thinks he knows all about them' (*New Yorker*, 17 November 2008). Obama was quintessentially the 'other' – racially, politically and socially.

He had made an impressive speech at the 2004 Democratic convention and praised Clinton's 'Third Way': government could not solve all people's problems, there were no liberal blue and conservative red states, minorities were not pitted against whites. Do we participate in a politics of hope? ... Hope in the face of difficulty ... The audacity of hope! His story exemplified American 'exceptionalism': '[I]n no other country on Earth is my story even possible' (*The Washington Post*, 27 July 2004).

Most black people supported Hillary partly because they were certain no black candidate could win. Obama needed to widen his appeal to them. At the Brown AME church in Selma, Alabama on 4 March 2007 he honoured 'the Moses generation' and described his as the 'Joshua generation'. 'I'm here because you all sacrificed – for me. I stand on the shoulders of giants' (*New York Times*, 17 November 2008; Ifill, 2009). Critics argue that he appealed to the prophets but abandoned the prophetic/activist theology of ordinary black people and opted for social gospel, believing that the new generation lacked 'the discipline and fortitude ... of the people who had participated ... in the Movement' (Harris, 2012). However, Obama's referring to the Moses generation converted some sceptics and he already had the endorsement of King's friend, Reverend Lowry.

Post-Racial Politics?

Those who see this campaign as post-racial politics have a serious problem reflected in the newspaper headline: 'How black can he afford to be before he alienates white voters?' A headline asking: 'How white can he be before he alienates black voters?' is unimaginable. The report quoted one black academic: 'Obama is the ideal middle way person – he is just as white as he is black' (Mendell, 2007; *New York Times*, 9 June 2008). '[T]he race test seemed peculiar to many of Obama's supporters who wanted to believe they did not see race when they looked at their candidate' (Ifill, 2009).

Obama maintained he had been misrepresented and the convention speech did not mean 'the fight for equality had been won' or that the problems of the African American community were 'self-inflicted' (Obama, 2008). Others believe Obama always advocated the 'politics of responsibility' to 'shore up support among white voters concerned ... [H]e was elevated ... to the rank of Mr. Respectability-in-Chief, a role that Obama was more than eager to assume on his trek to the White House' (Harris, 2012). Certainly, Obama did not want to be pigeon-holed as the black candidate, and meeting his advisors in 2006 they decided 'the tone of the campaign would not be defined by the color of his skin' (*International Herald Tribune*, 12 February 2008). And he was ambivalent about the Movement. It had made his career possible but too many, like his mother, were trapped into a romantic version of these years. In *The Audacity of Hope* he commends the constraints of monogamy and religion: 'The role of the victim was too readily embraced as a means of shedding responsibility.' Like Reagan, he said people were longing for order and the need to rediscover 'the traditional values of hard work, patriotism, personal responsibility, optimism and faith' (Obama, 2008). Most whites saw it as criticism of African Americans, for others it was for both white and black, but a significant number of black people considered it was a valid criticism of their community (Chappell, 2014). But as a black man he had, more than white politicians, to avoid favouring one race. The question was, if he became president, to what extent would it marginalise concerns of African Americans, Hispanics and other minorities? Would his goal to work with environmentalists, feminists, LGBT people worsen the plight of racial minorities? Some think it did (Keller, 2015).

The Democratic Primaries

The first contest came in virtually all-white Iowa. The state selects delegates by caucus and Obama became a serious contender when he overcame Clinton's lead of 30–40 points by exploiting the IT revolution to recruit and register more young voters and raise campaign money. He combined this with old-style stump politics, and canvassing, establishing 35 field offices and winning endorsements from senior politicians and trade unionists. Clinton's team expected a small caucus but on a snowy night more than expected numbers participated, 25 percent of them young and only 5 percent of them voted for her. In a virtually all-white state, Obama won 37.6 percent of the votes and Clinton came third with 29.5 percent. The 2000 and 2004 elections proved registration alone meant nothing and he used the internet to recruit thousands of volunteers to ensure registrants met all state requirements. Lawyers were hired to prevent fraud.

Clinton's New Hampshire landslide and winning New Jersey rescued her and convinced many Obama would not carry eastern white voters (Thomas, 2009). Virtually everybody believed she would win South Carolina, only needing 25 percent of the black vote but Bill, 'the first black president', cost her African American support (Thomas, 2009). Clinton alienated the press and increased personal attacks on Obama, claiming he was only appealing to black voters. Clinton said Obama 'played the race card on me' (Ifill, 2009). Obama carried the state. Congressman John Lewis, a Movement veteran, switched his allegiance to Obama.

Hillary Clinton was accused of racism. A primary TV ad showed three sleeping children and then a telephone rings. Immaculately dressed Hillary Clinton picks it up and a voice-over asks who would they want to answer it at 3 a.m. during a crisis. Harvard professor Orlando Patterson saw 'symbols of racism and slavery'. Clinton would save them because Obama is 'the danger, the outsider within'. The ad represented 'the darkest messages of a twisted past' (*New York Times*, 11 March 2008). Whatever one's view of this interpretation, it demonstrated the racial minefield she had to negotiate.

Her campaign was revived by Obama's pastor Jeremiah Wright who had officiated at his wedding and baptised his children (Ifill, 2009). Obama's campaign heads forgot to check Wright's sermons. ABC news did. They found a video in which Wright asks his congregation what their children have and shouts: 'The government gives them drugs, builds bigger prisons ... and then wants them to sing "God Bless America." No, no, no. God damn America' (ABC News, 13 March 2008). The sermon was in the black church prophetic tradition and 'those with deep familiarity of black religious culture could recognize the historical foundations of Reverend Wright's prophetic message of damnation against the nation' (Harris, 2012). Millions lacked that necessary 'deep familiarity' and for them it proved black people hated the United States and it proved their 'otherness'.

Obama could not avoid the race issue. At the Constitutional Hall speech in Philadelphia he said the media saw his campaign through a racial prism. Wright's anger was 'divisive at a time when we need to come together to solve monumental problems ... that are neither black or white or Latino or Asian ... I can no more disown him than I can disown the black community. I can no more disown him than I can disown my white grandmother.' Wright and his generation had had to overcome rage and discrimination and they had made Obama's candidacy possible. He sympathised with whites who saw their dreams 'drop away' in an uncertain world, who were told to bus their children to school, who heard that affirmative action only benefited blacks and that this resentment could result in prejudice. But, 'America can change. That is the true genius of this nation' (ABC News, 18 March 2008). The speech turned a potential disaster into a triumph. Wright's fury with Obama underscored Obama's moderation. Obama left Wright's church.

Clinton exploited race when she said she was the only Democrat who could win and mentioned a report 'that found out that Senator Obama's support among working, hardworking Americans, white Americans, is weakening again, and whites ... who had not completed college were supporting me. There's a pattern emerging here' (*USA Today*, 7 May 2008). A *New Yorker* editorial warned her 'to avoid this sort of demographic analysis – and, more importantly, to abandon the dishonorable political strategy that lies behind it' (19 May 2008). Clinton conceded on 7 June.

The divisions at the 1968 convention about violence, racism, poverty and the cultural wars were buried. Senator Ted Kennedy, dying from brain cancer, told convention delegates: 'Barack Obama will close the book on the old politics of race, gender and group against group and straight against gay.' Hillary Clinton said they would achieve 'deep and meaningful equality – from civil rights to labor rights, from women's rights to gay rights' (ABC News, 26 August 2008). Although he has been accused of having 'messianic ambition' (Keller, 2016), Obama was more cautious. There were differences about same-sex marriage but gays should not suffer discrimination; disputes about abortion should not affect everyone's agreement that there should be fewer unwanted pregnancies (Obama, 2008).

Pressing the Self-destruct Button

Arizona Senator John McCain was the Republican candidate. His hero was Robert Jordan from Hemingway's *For Whom the Bell Tolls*, a republican fighter who carries out a mission he knows is 'doomed to failure'. It was McCain's story in 2000 and 2008. Journalists accepted he was 'maverick' (Welch, 2008). He started well, dismissing Obama as a former Chicago community worker, a political novice unfit to be commander-in-chief. But then he pushed the self-destruct button by selecting Alaska Governor Sarah Palin as his running mate.

Ultra-conservatives wanted her because they hoped she would win women's votes (Thomas, 2009). Palin? She espoused fundamentalist opposition to abortion, even in cases of incest or rape, and it alienated many moderate and all liberal women. Her rallies became uglier as she fought for blue-collar votes. Obama was un-American and often she asked: 'Who is the real Barack Obama?' (Ellis, 2009). Obama was willing 'to work with a former domestic terrorist who targeted his own people'. In Florida she said: 'I am just so fearful that this is not a man [Obama] who sees America the way I see America' (Thomas, 2009). Crowds yelled 'Kill him', 'Treason', and a man called him 'a one-man terror cell'. Obama was a Muslim schooled at a 'civilian madrassa' and, if elected, would take the oath on the Qur'an (Thomas, 2009). Obama's health care plan would mean 'death camps' for old people. She claimed Obama was not an American citizen and could not be president; he was an African and his birth certificate was a forgery. It was the start of the birther movement. He was the ultimate other (Grunwald, 2013). It was a lie that persisted through his terms in office, ardently promoted by 'the demagogue Donald Trump' (Skocpol and Williamson, 2013) and throughout the campaign of 2016.

Sixty-three percent of voters thought Palin was unfit compared with 12 percent who thought she was and 36 percent of independents who considered her the wrong choice (Todd and Gawiser, 2009). McCain sometimes worried about her crowds' reaction and he reassured one woman that Obama was Christian, American and a family man (Keller, 2015). Others considered McCain just as guilty as she was in exploiting Obama's willingness to associate with a former terrorist and continually questioning Obama's citizenship (Parlett, 2014). Palin's legacy? She started to make overt racism respectable again.

After Obama's victory, many Republicans said the Party faced a long-term problem. They had lost African American, most Hispanic, women and young voters and were too reliant on a declining white population of older women, most blue-collar men and people with lower educational attainment. A black American won the majority of white voters in 17 states and the Republicans lost every state on the eastern seaboard except Georgia and South Carolina. Some suggest the persistence of a plantation culture explains the low turn-out of African American voters in Deep South states (Asch, 2008).

An African American President

After centuries of slavery, segregation and lynching and 44 years after the Voting Rights Act, a black man was the 44th president. Jesse Jackson and millions of Americans cried and wept with joy. Obama wept. His beloved grandmother had died on election day not knowing he was president. His victory was more than the symbolism that some maintain (Harris, 2012); rather it was a revolution in itself with thousands of Movement people and their children cheering his victory speech in Grant Park, Chicago. Again he appealed for a tolerant society: 'Let us resist ... partisanship and pettiness and immaturity that has plagued our politics for so long' (American Presidency Project, accessed 2012). Bush was magnanimous: 'This moment is especially uplifting for a generation of Americans who witnessed the struggle for civil rights with their own eyes – and four decades later see their dream fulfilled' (Bush, 2010).

The day before the inauguration 90-year-old Pete Seeger, the minstrel of the struggle, performed with Bruce Springsteen and Stevie Wonder and the next freezing day 2 million people came to hear one of the founders of the SCLC, Reverend Joseph Lowery, give the invocation and cheer as their president denounced torture and pleaded for unity. They were optimistic and shared a reborn faith in the American Dream (Parlett, 2014).

But bloggers and internet users refused to share Obama's vision. The desperate continued to weep and curse that a black man would occupy the White House (Blog, 'Barack Hussein Obama is Antichrist', 12 February 2009). The so-called alt-right exploited virulent racism and bizarre conspiracy theories thrived – Obama was a reptile from outer-space and a homosexual mass murderer (Grunwald, 2013; Parlett, 2014). The idea that he was a gay prostitute and a drug pusher persisted throughout his years in office (*New York Times*, 12 August 2016). Michelle was his male lover. The multi-billionaire Koch brothers, David and Charles, financed Dinesh D'Souza who exploited the trope of the angry black man, someone who did not share the American Dream, but rather sought to foist his father's dream of 'African-style socialism and anti-imperialism' on the country (D'Souza, 2011).

Welcome to the Tea Party

Americans have long feared strong central government. The Kochs were horrified that a 'socialist' black man was in the White House. The Tea Party people gave the rich 1 percent the popular audience they had lacked, and the Kochs secretly funded the Tea Party through tax-free Super Political Action Committees (Mayer, 2016). Supported by Fox News, they ensured that the overwhelmingly white, older Tea Party supporters had maximum publicity. The participants espoused racist notions about African Americans and Hispanics. '[T]he strongest single predictor of Tea Party support is fear and antipathy toward the first African American president in US history' (McAdam and Kloos, 2014). This populist movement embraced alt-right goals to slash programmes that benefited black and poor people while cutting taxes that benefited the super-rich.

It was Reaganism on steroids. The aim was to push the Republican Party to the far right aided by sympathetic academics, and Senate and House Republicans who, even before the inauguration, agreed to vote against everything proposed by the Administration. 'The Republicans were determined … to limit, humiliate, and defeat Barack Obama and other Democrats … majority democracy be damned' (Skocpol and Williamson, 2013). Most liberal Republicans did not survive the Tea Party cleansing (McAdam and Kloos, 2014). Ironically, the Tea Party faithful wanted a smaller federal government but no cuts in the programmes such as social security, Medicare and farm subsidies that benefited them (Skocpol and Williamson, 2013).

First Days in the White House

A president can act swiftly through executive orders but they can be as quickly overturned by an incoming president. Obama disliked their use and only at the end of his second term, stymied by recalcitrant Republicans, did he resort to them more frequently (*New York Times*, 13 August 2016). However, in his first day in office he signed orders that abolished the use of torture, ordered the closure of the Guantanamo prison in Cuba (that failed because of widespread opposition) and extended civil rights to accused terrorists (*Guardian*, 15 May 2009). He angered political opponents by lifting the ban on family planning groups that provided contraceptive and abortion advice overseas (ABC News, 8 March 2009). A New Jersey Republican denounced him as 'the abortion president' (*New York Times*, 9 March 2009) and Catholic bishops said any relaxation of abortion restrictions would be an 'attack' on the church (Chicago *Tribune*, 17 November 2008).

In another order he established the Commission on Women and Girls to ensure that all federal agencies checked appointments to prevent discrimination. His African American personal advisor and chief of staff, Valerie Jarrett, and Asian American, Tina Tchen, chief of staff to Michelle Obama, headed the commission (www.whitehouse.gov, 9 March 2011). A press release was issued claiming the gains made for women in his first year in office (www.whitehouse.gov, 10 March 2010). Certainly, the Movement and the experience of women who worked in it helped ensure the greatest presidential action to overcome discrimination against women.

The impact of coalition politics can be seen also in his environmental orders. He signed two to control emissions for the auto industry and set higher standards than had been passed in California. Additionally, he established a commission on climate change that ensured savings would be used for jobs in new energy production and that promised lower energy costs for poorer families. He was the greatest environmental protector, more than any other president in the history of the United Sates – establishing 19 national monuments and granting protection to 260 million acres of land and waters (*Christian Science Monitor*, 10 June 2016). He fought to ensure his legacy (*Guardian*, 24 November 2016). Also in 2016 he signed the Paris Climate Change Agreement which was ratified by 133 countries but not by Congress.

Bush had twice vetoed Medicaid bills designed to benefit 4 million children in low-income families (*New York Times*, 4 February, 2008). Obama signed the legislation eight days after taking office. In February he signed the Lilly Ledbetter Fair Pay Act which sought to end discrimination on pay for workers regardless of gender, race or disability. Although not mentioned in recent studies on Obama, it gave workers a longer time to bring cases against companies (for the Supreme Court ruling see Chapter 9). To many civil rights workers it was proof that coalitions continued to pay with groups such as labour. Mrs Ledbetter, a white working-class woman from Alabama, travelled in the presidential train to the inauguration ball and danced with the Yale-educated African American from Chicago. It captured the hope and optimism of 2009.

Consensus Appointments?

Despite conservative fears that he was an angry socialist (D'Souza, 2011), he followed his stated goal to reach across to Republicans and others. But the first thing was to heal wounds from the primaries and he selected Hillary Clinton as Secretary of State which also pleased feminists and black women. However, other senior posts went to Republicans or former Republican officeholders (Republicans for Obama, 25 November 2008) and the only major African American appointee was Eric Holder, who had had disputes with Jesse Jackson but was a first-class civil rights lawyer. After his confirmation, he angered conservatives when he said that the United States was 'a nation of cowards' because people did not talk frankly about race and, despite progress, on every Saturday and Sunday America was as segregated as it had been 50 years earlier (*New York Times,* 11 February 2009). Susan Rice was appointed ambassador to the United Nations and African American Lisa Jackson proved the value of the coalition with environmentalists when she was appointed head of the Environment Agency. But not all were pleased with Obama's appointments at first. The Black Caucus were disappointed. Brent Walker of the League of United Americans was worried that there were few Latinos in the Cabinet and the president of NOW criticised the predominance of white men (San Fransisco *Chronicle,* 15 December 2008). LGBT blogs were full of complaints even though by autumn of 2010 Obama had appointed 150 LGBT people to office, more than Clinton had in eight years. He tried to keep alive the outreach built by the coalitions but did not want to be a black issue president alone but rather to push through legislation that would benefit everyone as well as African Americans. Obama consulted with Jewish leaders, Latinos and gays about specific issues that centred on them but he preferred to lecture blacks on personal responsibility (Harris, 2012; Cornell West interview, BBC Newsnight, 10 November 2016).

The Economic Crisis and African Americans

Obama had to solve the worst economic collapse since the 1929 Great Depression. If it had happened two years into Bush's second term he would not have been blamed for the bank bailout agreed before he came into office. But Obama had to act quickly to stop rising unemployment which by 2010 was almost twice as high for blacks (16 percent) as for whites at 8.7 percent; Hispanic unemployment was 12 percent (Bureau of Labor Statistics Report, December, 2011). This data disguises the highest unemployment which was among 19- and 20-year-olds, especially people of colour and women. The question was whether Obama would target economic policies to tackle this persistent generational discrepancy.

The anger of the Occupy Wall Street activists was directed at Obama even though the bank bailout had been drawn up by the Bush Administration, and Obama felt bound to implement it to prevent economic depression with its massive unemployment, to save private pensions and the social security system. What motivated the Occupy groups? One analyst writes that 'The civil rights movement provided some inspiration' but allegedly it 'drew most heavily on the counter culture of the 1960s' (Keller, 2015). For other critics, white and black, Obama's plan lacked coherence and that his stimulus programme was dictated by long-term, low employment creation schemes such as renewable energy, high-speed trains and a national grid. Unlike FDR, there were no pick and shovel public works programmes. They said he failed, unlike previous presidents faced with recessions; he gave too much power to state governments and lacked the ability to negotiate with Republicans in Congress. Even his bailout of the auto industry has been criticised (Keller, 2015). The election of a black president made African Americans proud but his actions did nothing to challenge structural inequality (Harris, 2012). Others have been more positive in the assessment of his help to the black community. For example, his efforts to control excessive mortgage arrangements helped not only the black middle class but others escaping the ghetto and this was combined with financial aid to help reduce foreclosures. His training programmes on federal contracts helped all disadvantaged people. In addition, he won $1.2 billion for job training, and one week's paid leave for sick workers. Because of Republican intransigence he resorted to executive orders to raise the minimum pay for federal workers to $10 per hour benefiting 45 percent of working mothers and that influenced 17 states and DC to increase it still further. There had been no increase in the minimum wage for 12 years. His effort to improve overtime protection was not even discussed by Congress. Obama's long-term proposals would have benefited African Americans – indeed everyone. The high-speed transit and national grid proposals would have created many jobs quickly but they were opposed by many even moderate conservative Republicans. Ironically, these opponents touted the latter projects in 2016.

And to compare this financial meltdown with other recessions is fatuous. The president and his staff did negotiate with the opposition. It is difficult to square the accusations that Obama did not seek the support of Congress for reasonable agreements. He did reject 'porkbarrel' schemes – projects designed to benefit certain politicians and ensure their re-election. The bailout of General Motors and Chrysler carmakers saved thousands of jobs across the country despite the rejectionists. When they failed to defeat his efforts, opponents eagerly sought political credit for job-creation schemes. To say that Republicans in Congress did not cooperate is an understatement. As soon as he won the election they were determined to obstruct every proposal and guarantee the minimum amount of legislation to ensure Obama's defeat in 2012 (McAdam and Kloos, 2014).

It is true that Obama failed to challenge structural inequality but no president had achieved this – even FDR's New Deal or LBJ's Great Society. In the mounting conservatism any effort would have failed. At least others understood that his Affordable Care Act and increased Medicare funding benefited every race by vastly expanding health insurance for everyone. This had been the goal of presidents of both parties since 1945. However Tea Party activists attacked it and the Republican Party tried 50 times to overturn it and their Party control of many states meant that the reform was not fully implemented.

Action for the LGBT Movement

From the start he had defended women's right to choose an abortion and to equal pay by legislation and a raft of executive orders p. 262. He assuaged the concerns of many when he vigorously defended *Roe v. Wade*. His commitment was not doubted. Despite early criticism that gays and lesbians were overlooked in appointments, Nancy Sutley and Elaine Kaplan joined the Administration (*New Republic*, 10 December, 2008; *New York Times,* 11 February 2009) and Kaplan was made a federal judge in 2013. The LGBT community rightly accused him of allowing the military to dismiss gays under Clinton's 'Don't Ask, Don't Tell'. He had said 18 days after taking office that the policy should be ended only to meet fierce opposition from the military, his Secretary of Defense and the Justice Department, led by Holder, who filed briefs supporting the Defense of Marriage Act. Obama was willing 'to be educated' on same-sex marriage and he stopped defending the Marriage Act. It was not repealed until December 2010 (Faderman, 2015). But it excluded transgender people and this was only corrected in 2016 when openly gay Secretary of the Army Eric Fanning ordered it (BBC News, 25 June 2016). Military service was dismissed by radical gays as assimilationist and they opposed anti-gay hate crimes legislation because 'hate crime laws most often hurt people of color and poor people' (Faderman, 2015).

However, bigotry mounted against transgender people. Between 2008 and 2010 there were four reported murders and by 2015–2016 it was 45, nearly all African Americans. Other crimes, including violent assaults, are not known. 'Trans women of color suffer from the effects not only of transphobia and racism but also xenophobia, poverty and homelessness' (*The Advocate*, 19 November 2016). However, Obama could not prevent states harassing gay people which continued even after the Supreme Court ruled in *Lawrence v. Texas* (2003) that same-sex relationships were lawful. For example, despite the influence and wealth of many gays in Knoxville, Tennessee, police continued arresting gay men accused of cruising in Tyson Park as late as 2006 (WLTV-Knoxville.local 8news.com, 21 December 2006). Despite continued harassment and discrimination more gays, even among minorities, left the closet. Texas, for example, had 600,000 gay adults and 46,000 same-sex couples, 15 percent African Americans and 38 percent Hispanics (williamsinstitute law.ucla.edu, April 2011).

His critics condemned his lack of concern for AIDS victims. Although he continued funding for overseas projects and set up a national strategy committee, a leading gay newspaper argued that George W. Bush had done far more than Obama (Washington *Blade*, 19 July 2012). But such criticism is not justified. Considering the large number of African American gays and lesbians working in federal posts, his actions were significant. Just as important he provided extra funding for black gays with HIV, a group that had been seriously neglected, and also focused on ten cities that had virtually no funding for minority HIV sufferers. He prevented dismissal of federal employees because of their sexual orientation and made it very clear that he supported their right to civil contracts even if he did not publicly argue for the right of same-sex marriage until the middle of his second term. His actions, despite shortcomings, encouraged the growing sympathy for gay rights among Republican and Democratic voters. For example, the LGBT commune on Short Mountain in rural Tennessee was integrated into a local fundamentalist county before 2015 (*New York Times* magazine, 6 August 2015). It was now easier for Obama to appoint LGBT staunch gay activists, such as Chai Feldblum, as head of the Equal Employment Opportunity Commission. Obama made the Stonewall Inn, where gays had fought the New York police in 1969, into a National Monument in 2016 to honour LGBT rights (CNN. com, 25 June 2016). One assessment is: 'During his eight years as president, Obama created a revolution in LGBT equality' (*The Advocate*, 8 November 2016).

'Obamacare'

The goals of Movement people such as A. Philip Randolph and Bayard Rustin were not just to end Jim Crow segregation. Those who joined the struggle also understood this from King to Malcolm X and the students in the SNCC. One of the greatest problems afflicting African Americans and millions of other Americans was no, or inadequate, health insurance – by 2009 this meant people under the age of 65 numbering 43.3 million or 16 percent of the population. The President's 2010 proposal included important reforms. It proposed people with previous conditions and HIV should be insured and that 18–25 year olds would be covered by their parents' insurance, something Republicans, such as Richard Nixon and Bob Dole, had supported. The bill also required state insurance centres as well as private providers. Those who refused to buy insurance could be fined. Additionally, Medicaid was increased by 138 percent for African Americans and others who lived below the poverty level – but 24 states refused the funding offered.

But for many the Affordable Care Act was proof of central government tyranny (D'Souza, 2011). The Tea Party movement appealed to white voters who felt betrayed by the federal government bailout of big business. They were determined to punish this black president and the Democrats. Many were racist, and militia movement extremists and the KKK easily joined their ranks. Obama did not realise – or perhaps accept – that opposition would be fuelled by racism and that most Tea Party members believed that blacks and Hispanics were shiftless, unintelligent and untrustworthy (Skocpol and Williamson, 2013). In 2009 Jimmy Carter had warned: '[M]any people, not just in the south ... believe that African Americans are not qualified to lead this great country' (*Guardian*, 16 September 2009). He was right. The conclusion must be that: 'Far from the imagined post-racial society Obama's election was supposed to herald, we find ourselves living through the period of greatest racial tensions and conflict since the 1960s and early 1970s' (McAdam and Kloos, 2014). The Affordable Care Act was seen as a socialist conspiracy by an un-American black president to benefit 'lazy' black people all at the expense of hardworking white folks. Republicans who supported the bill were purged and Republican state governors and legislatures opposed it and whipped up Tea Party opposition. Welfare was a racist euphemism again.

Opponents looked to the Supreme Court, confident that Chief Justice Roberts would support them. In *The National Federation of Small Businesses v. Sibelius* (2013) the plaintiffs maintained the Act was unconstitutional because individuals who did not buy health insurance would be fined. However, Roberts, reluctantly supported by the liberal justices, ruled that the mandatory requirement to buy health insurance was not interstate commerce but a tax, and Congress alone had the taxing power (Coyle, 2013). Roberts has been seen as a jurist in the mould of Warren (Keller, 2015). But it was a dramatic limitation of hundreds of precedents since the 1930s – even admitted by Roberts' admirers.

Since the New Deal of the 1930s, it was accepted that interstate commerce was a federal government duty and that clause of the Constitution granted it wide powers. Conservatives had not challenged this as it benefited them in many ways, such as agricultural subsidies. Their enthusiasm waned when it was used to end segregation, disenfranchisment of black people, and supported affirmative action. Roberts' ruling that health care was not interstate commerce but a tax not only made Obamacare more unpopular but also what conservatives and liberals never appreciated was the consequences of limiting federal powers. Instead Obama's opponents believed they had been betrayed. From its passage in March 2010 up to 2016 there were 50 attempts to repeal the Act.

Massive Resistance Continues

The Republicans never hid their determination to fight every measure introduced by Obama regardless of its need or even if they agreed with it. It is legitimate for the opposition to challenge legislative proposals of any administration but it became a weapon to undermine the presidency with attempts to block the Recovery programme they agreed with, and persisting in raising issues they could not win, such as repeal of the Affordable Care Act and limiting abortion rights. The House was considerably more conservative than the traditional wing of the Republican Party. The witch-craft practising Christine O'Donnell of Delaware beat her Republican opponent in the primary because he had supported limited gun control, the economic stimulus and health programmes that benefited the poor. Media outlets such as Fox News and Tea Party activists supported her and forced the National Republican Committee to do so as well. She, and others like her, lost their elections but they successfully defeated moderate Republicans willing to compromise (Skocpol and Williamson, 2013). Their objective was the same as that of the weakened Christian Coalition attacking African Americans, Hispanics, pro-choice feminists and LGBT people. Conservative Republicans seeking re-election to Washington had a choice: scramble on the bandwagon or be swept out of office. They scrambled.

2012 Re-election

Republican state governments were determined to disenfranchise the Democratic voters, especially African Americans, the elderly and students (*New York Times*, 30 August 2016). Nineteen states introduced ID and other restrictions specifically to disenfranchise people. The ID card requirement was, according to a North Carolina Republican, to curtail voting by 'a bunch of lazy blacks that wants the government to give them everything' (McAdam and Kloos, 2014). If Obama thought he might face reckless opposition after he was elected, he did not foresee the 'rightward plunge' of the Republican Party after the 2010 mid-term elections (Skocpol and Williamson, 2013). The newly elected representatives had the backing of far-right pressure groups that had demonstrated their power in state elections where their adherents wanted to restrict African American, Latino and other Democrat voters, deport Muslims and illegal immigrants, cut taxes on corporations, and attack labour rights. They passed 'religious freedom' bills to drastically reduce abortion rights and passed laws permitting discrimination against LGBT people. Extreme obstructionism got worse after 2012. The public did not blame them for the dysfunction in Washington but rather the president and the Democrats.

In 2000 and 2004 the abuse of the electoral system by state authorities guaranteed Bush's election, but voter fraud personation by voters in the inner cities (read African American) was virtually non-existent – unlike state government manipulation and gerrymandering. The anti-labour governors such as Scott Walker in Wisconsin followed other states in voting restrictions in the belief that it would ensure Obama's defeat. Movement leaders such as African Americans fought back. Congressman John Lewis, who had suffered a fractured skull on the Selma voting rights march, rallied support but could not overcome the claims of voter fraud and lost repeated efforts to renew the Voting Rights Act. Lewis led a sit-in in the House of Representatives. The NAACP launched court challenges to the new restrictions, and there were marches and voter registration drives. 'The activists of the past had inspired the activists of the future' (Berman, 2015). Another who joined the long march away from moderation was Mitt Romney, former liberal Republican governor of Massachusetts. Having lost the nomination in 2008, he 'plunged to the right'. He campaigned on a promise to introduce a federal constitutional amendment to prohibit same-sex marriage (Faderman, 2015). He opposed the Affordable Care Act, promised to appoint judges to overturn *Roe* and cut welfare, and to continue the war on crime and drugs (i.e. black people). In a closed-door meeting he told a group of wealthy donors he had a problem.

> [T]here are 47 percent who will vote for the president no matter what. They are dependent on government [and] believe they are victims who believe that government has a responsibility to care of them, who believe they are entitled to health care, to food, to housing, to you name it ... These people pay no income tax ... [M]y job is not to worry about these people. I'll never convince them that they should take personal responsibility for their lives.
>
> (Skocpol and Williamson, 2013)

Unfortunately for Romney his remarks were recorded and leaked to the media. Conceding defeat, he did not congratulate Obama on his re-election. He complained Obama's victory was because of Obama's 'gifts' to the 'victims' and named 'the beneficiaries' – 'especially the African American community, the Hispanic community, and young people' (McAdam and Kloos, 2014). What had always been coded was officially stated and encouraged people, who had denounced 'political correctness', to openly disparage African Americans, gays and other groups.

Obama: A Pyrrhic Victory?

Obama continued to believe that the electorate shared his views of a post-racial, tolerant America, even though he knew that he would face bitter opposition from Republicans in Congress and the states they controlled. His slim victory in 2008 in North Carolina turned into a narrow defeat in 2012 and ended Democratic hopes that they might win more southern states. The *Shelby* ruling paid dividends for the Republican Party. With the support of massive unregulated political funding, following the *Citizens United* decision, Republicans controlled state government, redrew (gerrymandered) districts, reduced Democrat representation at all levels of government and ensured that most future Republican presidential nominees could count on at least 180 votes in the Electoral College (Berman, 2015). They believed this would result in the repeal of Obama's 'socialist' schemes. To their cost Democrats ignored the anger of the middle-class, suburban and blue-collar workers and they paid dearly in the congressional elections of 2010 and 2012 and would continue to do so in 2016.

Some claim that regional identity played little part in the 2008 and 2012 elections but rather that Obama was more popular than his opponents (Keller, 2015). It is difficult to square this with the Republican long-term southern strategy and, according to all the polls, the unpopularity of Obama and the Affordable Care Act. Even though he won re-election he faced Republican obstructionism from states and Congress. Every Congress resulted in near refusal to consider budget proposals, social reform and even the most junior appointments for the Administration and the courts. They even voted against their own proposals such as immigration reform because the president supported it (McAdam and Kloos, 2014). Indeed, throughout his terms in office and in the election campaign of 2016, they used Mexicans, Islam and refugees as additional euphemisms for racism.

The Supreme Court: Marching Backwards

The conservative Supreme Court justices were part of the resistance movement. Roberts not only undermined the interstate commerce clause in the ruling on the Affordable Care Act but led the conservative majority in the biggest assault on civil rights since *Plessy v. Ferguson* (1896) that held separate but equal was constitutional. Movement activists who had been murdered and others who had been tear-gassed, beaten with electric cattle prods and fire-hosed in the Selma march to demand the vote were forgotten. Knowing the consequences of his action, losing the South to the Republicans, LBJ in 1965 chose the moral high ground and demanded that Congress ensure the enfranchisement of African Americans. Joined by liberal Republicans, the Voting Rights Act had prohibited devices such as literacy tests and poll taxes. Pre-clearance enabled the federal authority to oversee the states' voting procedures to prevent discrimination. Congress in 2006 overwhelmingly had renewed the Act for another 25 years.

At his confirmation hearing Roberts had said he would respect the rights of the legislative branch of government and specifically the Voting Rights Act when he said he had 'no issue' with its renewal or to the prior rulings that the Act was constitutional (Berman, 2015). In deciding the case of *Shelby County, Alabama v. Holder* (2013), the conservative majority declared that the renewal of the Act contravened states' rights and ignored the evidence that conditions had dramatically changed. Congress had relied on outdated information. In addition, he seemed to ignore the provisions of the Reconstruction amendments. He admitted the Voting Rights Act had been valuable and cited several improvements but the conservative majority took no account of the fact that this was because the Act had been successfully enforced. They declared it was now redundant. It turned triumph into defeat. Roberts wrote: 'Our country has changed, and while any discrimination in voting is too much, Congress must ensure that the legislation it passes speaks to current decisions' (supremecourt.gov/opinions, 25 June 2013). They did not overturn the Voting Rights Act but sent it back to Congress knowing that the Republicans would never amend it. Ultra-conservative Abigail Thernstrom came to the bizarre conclusion: 'The court's ruling Tuesday will benefit black America.'

The voting restrictions passed in several northern and southern states before *Shelby* were ignored and the decision opened the floodgates for even harsher voter denial. Leading the way was North Carolina (McAdam and Kloos, 2014; Berman, 2015). There were mass protests on Moral Monday. A march from Shaw University, made up of all races, was described by William Barber: 'Just like Dr. King sent out the call and said come to Selma in 1965, we're saying come to Raleigh' (Berman, 2015). Efforts by John Lewis, who led a sit-in in the House of Representatives, and other Democrats to amend the Voting Rights Act failed when Republicans, who had promised to do so, voted against this. One of the greatest achievements of the Movement had rendered the Voting Rights Act useless.

However, it was not all reverses. Seven states, including Michigan and Tennessee, were alarmed by the growing sympathy for gay marriage and legislated that only heterosexual partners could marry, passing legislation that this was protected by the Freedom of Religion Amendment of the Constitution. Same-sex marriages performed in other states would not be recognised. In *Obergeffel v. Hodges* (2016) Justice Kennedy joined the liberals declaring that state laws prohibiting same-sex marriages were unconstitutional and such marriages in other states had to be recognised. Obama responded by lighting up the White House in the Rainbow colours of the gay Movement. State laws that seriously restricted a woman's right to choose were struck down. *Whole Women's Health v. Hellerstedt* (2016) went further than *Roe* when Justice Kennedy wrote that Texas laws limiting choice denied women's equality under the Fourteenth Amendment (SCOTUS.blog, June 2016). A unique feature at that hearing was that Clarence Thomas asked his first question after serving ten years on the Court! Thomas persisted in his role of opposing all that the Movement and Thurgood Marshall had achieved. In a 7–1 ruling in *Foster v. Chatman* (2016), he stood alone. Foster had served 30 years in prison for the rape and murder of a 79-year-old woman after being found guilty by an all-white jury in Georgia and sentenced to death. The prosecution had deliberately prevented any black person from serving on the jury. Even Alito reluctantly supported his colleagues but Thomas argued that defence lawyers should not go on fishing trips for new evidence long after the prosecutors had retired (*New York Times*, 8 June 2016). Republican refusal to consider criminal justice reform forced Obama to use his powers of clemency and pardon.

Justice Antonin Scalia died in February 2016. Obama, who had nominated the first Hispanic judge Sonia Sotomayor in March 2016, chose Judge Merrick Garland to fill the vacancy left by Scalia's death. Garland, a liberal Republican who had conducted the investigation into the bombing of a federal building in Oklahoma City by white domestic terrorists, was widely respected by members of both parties – initially that is – until Obama named him for the Court. Proof of the obduracy of the Senate was their refusal to hold hearings on Garland or meet with him, claiming that the vacancy could only be filled by the next president after the 2016 election. This was unprecedented. The remaining eight could only fulfil their duty if there was a majority vote, no split decision was valid. Senate Republicans ensured he would not be appointed if they won a majority of Senate seats which was almost certain.

This was a repeat of their battle against the first-ever African American woman, Loretta Lynch, as Attorney General to replace Eric Holder who was retiring. Lynch, a highly respected and successful district attorney in New York, was forced to wait 167 days before being approved by a vote of 56–43, with 10 Republicans joining the Democrats. Democrat Dick Durbin compared her experience to that of Rosa Parks: 'And so Loretta Lynch is asked to sit in the back of the bus.' (*Guardian*, 23 April 2015). It was pure obstructionism because the Republicans hated Holder but the delay had kept him in office.

Drugs: The Continuing War

The War on Drugs started by Richard Nixon cost nearly one trillion dollars by the end of George W. Bush's administration and it had had no effect except to incarcerate many males, overwhelmingly African Americans. At the end of Obama's first year in office 58 percent of those imprisoned for drug offences were black and Hispanic. One-third of these groups used crack but they made up 80 percent of the arrests and they were ten times more likely to be jailed (naacp.org/report, no date) even though African Americans constituted only 12 percent of monthly drug abusers. The federal government spent $15 billion on the 'war' in 2010 and the states and local governments a further $25 billion. Obama's expenditure on anti-drug law was the same as that spent by George W. Bush (Reuters, 6 April 2016). African American men had a one in six chance of being imprisoned and women one in 100. If the sentencing was the same as that of white users, the prison population, the highest in the advanced countries in the world, would fall by 50 percent. To be fair to Obama he did try to get the sentencing of crack users and sellers, mostly black, to be the same as that of the predominantly white users of powdered cocaine. This initiative was opposed by the Republicans on the Judiciary Committee and Obama signed the Fair Sentencing Act that narrowed sentence disparities from 100 to one to 18 to one and ended the mandatory sentences for crack possession. Before he left office he commuted the heavy sentences of 1014 people, many of them black crack users and dealers and white sellers of opioids.

The abuse of drugs was not confined to the inner cities as politicians had argued; rather, it had always been a serious problem that politicians had ignored and local law enforcement officers often profited from. Opioids, Oxycontin for example, were pushed by drug companies as painkillers. Native American deaths from opioid use rose by 263 percent (*Huffington Post*, 29 February 2016) and their use had quadrupled since 1999 (Baltimore *Sun,* 29 April 2016). The greatest problems were in the seven states that made up Appalachia. The war against opioids by the states and aided by the federal government only resulted in a dramatic increase in the use of heroin (Voice of America, 26 January 2016).

The strange case of marijuana grew even stranger in the years Obama was in office. It was widely used by all ethnic groups and all classes. Between 2008 and 2016 seven states had legalised it for recreational and medicinal use and 28 others and DC did so for medicinal use – and some states' regulations did not make it difficult to obtain (*Rolling Stone*, 9 October 2016). Despite growing acceptance of pot the federal government insisted on listing it as a Class A drug, no different from heroin or cocaine.

Black Lives (Don't) Matter

Just as the Democrats had encouraged violence against freed African Americans since 1865, now the rhetoric of the Republican Party was unleashing bigotry. As in the past, from the white race riots after World War One to the southern and northern police riots in the 1960s, the danger from racists had not gone away and indeed became more evident. It was nothing new. It was not captured by the press or television; they only disseminated what they found on Facebook. It was the technological revolution and smartphones that captured police oppression of unarmed, innocent black men, just as technology had in the beating of Rodney King in 1991, when the acquittal of the officers involved had inflamed black opinion. The LA riot that followed changed nothing. And King's was not the worst case. Following the numerous killings of unarmed African American men after 2013, it was revealed that Chicago police from 1972 to 1981 had had a torture chamber using suffocation and electric shock techniques to illicit 167 'confessions' for serious crimes. The officer who set it up, Jon Burge, and those who worked with him were never charged. The city was forced to pay $5.5 million in compensation but President Obama never condemned what had happened (*The Atlantic*, 26 October 2016). Between 2004 and 2008 in Oakland, California police killed 45 men, 37 black and no whites (*Mother Jones*, 15 August 2014).

However, it was not police killing unarmed black men that first sparked protests. Unarmed teenager Trayvon Martin was walking through a white community when he was shot in the back and killed by a self-styled neighbourhood watchman, George Zimmerman. Although he was charged with manslaughter Zimmerman was acquitted. He caused national outrage when he later auctioned the gun he had used, allegedly getting at least $120,00 for it (*Guardian*, 18 May 2016). Martin's death and Zimmerman's acquittal resulted in two black women setting up a website entitled Black Lives Matter (BLM) which became the message of a Movement-like non-violent protest movement at the death of Michael Brown in Ferguson, Missouri.

Ferguson is a suburb which is 67 percent black and 27 percent white but whose police force is 94 percent white and is equipped with military weapons. The officer responsible for Brown's death was later acquitted of manslaughter. This and the protests led to a Department of Justice investigation which uncovered wholesale discrimination and brutality by the police. Such arrests were heard at a Municipal Court and were revealed to be not only a question of racism but also a means of raising revenue for the area (justice.gov, 4 March 2015).

The police killings continued. In Madison, Wisconsin Tony Robinson was unarmed and innocent (NBC News, 6 March 2015). In Cleveland, Ohio a black man and woman were shot dead when an officer leapt on the hood of their car firing 49 times. No weapons or drugs were found and no officer was charged. Two days later 12-year-old Tamir Rice was in a playground with a BB gun and was shot and, like the others, with no verbal warning. In so many cases the family had to rely on civil courts for compensation. Rice's mother was aided by the Justice Department and Cleveland had to pay her $6 million in damages. In Milwaukee, one of the most racist cities in the United States, Dontre Hamilton who was mentally ill, homeless and not guilty of anything, was shot 17 times (NPR, 22 December 2014). A married man with four children was called a 'bad dude' before he was stopped in his SUV. The video taken by the police shows he had his hands the air when a female officer killed him (*Independent*, 19 September 2016). A man selling cigarettes in New York City was killed in an illegal stranglehold and no charges brought; a woman in South Carolina was stopped for careless driving, beaten and committed suicide in jail; a handcuffed prisoner in New Orleans was face down on the floor and shot twice in the back; and a black woman used her smartphone to show the horrific killing of her boyfriend. There are too many innocent black people killed to give all of the accounts.

Many white people, especially the young, LGBT and others who had formed alliances with African Americans, joined the demonstrations held by BLM but many others did not. Republican Governor of New Jersey and presidential aspirant Chris Christie accused BLM of advocating 'the murder of police officers'. Admittedly he did not go as far as another presidential hopeful, former governor of Arkansas Mike Huckabee, who declared on 3 October 2015 that the 1857 *Dred Scott v. Sandford* ruling that had asserted that black people were not human was 'still the law of the land'. These views encouraged racists who set up White Lives Matter (WLM), founded by Rebecha (*sic*) Barnette, of Tennessee, a leading member of Aryan Strikeforce (*sic*) and the National Socialist Movement. WLM sought the preservation of white rule and culture. These and other groups such as the Council of Conservative Citizens (CCC) were the 'respectable' face of the KKK. A growing number of white supremacist groups, such as California's Noble Breed Kindred, fed off the bitterness and frustration of the Great Recession (Southern Poverty Law Center, splcenter.org, 3 August 2013). The worst incident was the killing of nine black people at a Bible study class in the historic black Emanuel AME church in Charleston, South Carolina by white supremacist Dylan Roof on 17 June 2015. President Obama called it 'a dark moment in our history' while attending a memorial service and where he gave an impassioned address on racism in the United States and sang *Amazing Grace*.

Not all shared his grief. Liberal commentators pointed out that the nation felt greater outrage at the deaths of people killed by foreign terrorists than by those who were domestic terrorists. The CCC called a conference in Nashville to defend Roof's use of the Confederate battle flag which had been removed from the state house after widespread protests

(NBC News, 20 August 2015). And Breitbart News, an alt-right online site run by Steve Bannon, who blasted the ultra-right as feeble, published a defence of the South and its flag urging people to 'Fly it High and Fly it Proud' (breitbart.com, 1 July 2016). The National Rifle Association announced that the tragedy was due to laws that regulated weapons – if the church members had been armed they would not have died (*Mother Jones*, 19 June 2015). Racists in Georgia demonstrated and shouted slogans demanding that the flag should be kept flying as a symbol of southern honour (NPR, 13 October 2015). For the far right it was 'an alleged mass shooting'. Obama was bent on 'cleansing white America' (americanfreepress.net, 13 July 2015). The extremist groups' conspiracy theories were in large part shared by a much wider audience as demonstrated by the black church bombings between 2008 and 2015 in states as far apart as Massachusetts and Texas (*Mother Jones*, 18 June 2015). The bitterness and anger many white people felt towards African Americans, Hispanics and LGBT people was cynically exploited by politicians, especially by those seeking the presidency.

Obama and the Nation's Fear

In his State of the Union Address on 13 January 2016, Obama still asserted his belief that the American people could escape from political social and race identity and cited King's belief 'that as Americans we are bound by a common creed'. This was his deeply held belief but he knew that he had faced constant obstruction. His first plea was for criminal law and justice reform that had been blocked, especially the laws on prescription drug and heroin abuse. The nation had faced changes – immigration, depressions, wars, workers fighting for a fair deal and movements to expand civil rights:

> Each time, there have been those who told us to fear the future; who claimed that we could slam the brakes on change; who promised to restore past glory if we just got some group or idea that was threatening America ... And each time we overcame those fears.
>
> (whitehouse.gov/, 13 January 2016)

Obama was one of the most intelligent and articulate presidents of the United States and one with a sharp wit and sense of humour. Critics blame him for not fulfilling his promises but no president, not even FDR, had faced such bitter intransigence. Despite this he dragged the country out of its worst recession since the Great Depression of the 1930s; even if he did not effect structural economic reform he did pass laws to control Wall Street; he revolutionised health care provision with his Affordable Care Act; he helped families facing home foreclosure; he halved African American unemployment; he increased federal workers' wages that particularly benefited black workers; and he encouraged and fought for LGBT rights and voter protection. Thanks to the coalitions built by former Movement people and their young admirers he did all this in an effort to drag America into the 21st century. All the time he knew his achievements were threatened. It would remain to be seen in the coming elections if his critics from the right and the left would rise to the challenge and overcome the fear and paranoia he had fought against.

Epilogue

The Great Divide: The Election of 2016

There was fraud and violence in the 1876 election but the presidential election campaign of 2016 was probably the most bizarre in American history. Democrats hoped it would be the year of the woman and Hillary Clinton would be certain to win the nomination; her campaign managers and the Party establishment never foresaw she would have to fight for it and face a major struggle against Bernie Sanders – a democratic socialist – the first since union leader Eugene Debs of Indiana fought five times between 1900 and 1920, in 1920 as federal prisoner number 9653 for violating the Sedition Act of 1918 (Salvatore, 2007). In 2015–16 there were constant calls that Hillary too should go to jail.

Many Democrats were confident that Hillary would lead the Party to success. As First Lady she was an advisor during Bill's presidency, had been a successful Secretary of State and a New York senator. She was the most experienced candidate ever. Even more, women, a major bloc favouring the Democrats, would vote for her, especially feminists and those who feared that the Supreme Court would overturn *Roe*; Toni Morrison had called Bill Clinton the 'first black president' and she would seal the black vote from the ever-growing popularity of Barack Obama and the consistent popularity of his wife Michelle; and LGBT people believed Clinton would protect all the gains they had made (*The Advocate*, 26 July 2016). She promised to defend Obama's directive that protected US-born children of illegal immigrants and this would guarantee the Hispanic voter. She believed that climate change was real and action was urgently needed (www.clinton.com/issues, no date). She was criticised for only hinting about free college education and how she would significantly close the income gap (*The Atlantic*, 26 May 2015). Although Sanders could not be ignored, the divisions in the Republican Party and their 17 would-be challengers would ensure a triumph if not a coronation.

But she had problems. At the State Department she had used a private server for some of her emails which was against all the regulations because of security concerns. The problem haunted her campaign. She had had to face 11 hours of tough questioning from a congressional committee and the issue was handed over to the FBI which eventually reported that she had been 'extremely careless' in her email use of classified information but that the evidence was not strong enough to 'support a criminal indictment' (FBI National Press Release, 5 July 2016). The FBI would make another dramatic intervention in the closing days of the campaign that some believe influenced the outcome. Another concern among voters was that she and Bill were too close to Wall Street bankers and financiers, earning millions from speaking engagements at a time when many were still furious about the bank bailouts. While in the State Department and as a senator she had allegedly pressured wealthy people to give donations to the Clinton Foundation – a charitable trust. And in a media-saturated society, she was not a good speaker and seemed cold and distant. She followed Michelle Obama's advice: 'When they go low, we go high' (Los Angeles *Times*, 25 July 2016). That is an admirable sentiment but she should have known from her experience as First Lady that this is not good strategy in US elections.

Everybody dismissed Vermont Senator Bernie Sanders' entrance with benign amusement; even his democratic socialism was portrayed as mere populism. The media especially treated Sanders in the same way they had reported on Obama's announcement in 2007. Sanders eschewed dirty politics as promised – his socialist message finding widespread appeal with younger voters. His radical manifesto promised jobs with $1 trillion to be spent on infrastructure; he would change the tax code to force the rich to pay more and close what he called the 'obscene' economic inequality. He would legislate so that big money would not corrupt politics, and appoint Supreme Court justices who would overturn what he saw as the reactionary rulings of the current Court. The United States should lead the world in the battle against climate change. His defence of abortion rights and feminism also challenged Clinton (pbsnewshour, 30 April 2015). His great advantage was his fiery speeches which appealed to young voters and those who believed that Obama had not fulfilled their dreams. Packed audiences shouted his slogan, 'Feel the Bern' (*Observer*, 9 February 2016).

He had problems. Many did not know of his role in the Movement, and the fact that he was a leading defender of African American civil rights was not widely appreciated even though old Movement people like John Lewis and Jesse Jackson did. Black Lives Matter (BLM) protesters disrupted his Seattle rally and he was accused of being racist (*Time*, 9 August 2015). An early poll showed that only 29 percent of non-white voters sympathised with him (*Politico*, 10 August 2015). Also, how could he succeed with such a radical agenda as an outsider and as a new member of the Democratic Party (previously an Independent) when faced with ultra-conservative Republican opposition?

During the hard-fought primary campaign, Sanders attacked Clinton's close ties with Wall Street, especially the exorbitant fees she charged bankers for her speeches. How could she regulate powerful Wall Street financiers? While acknowledging her past work in civil rights, women's rights, health care and for the LGBT community, he said it was no longer time for the old elite's agenda no matter how liberal. It was time for a revolution. His vision harked back to the days of the Movement and, as then, the young responded and dared to dream that anything was possible.

His enthusiastic primary audiences were not only the young. He carried states such as Indiana and Oregon that all the polls predicted Clinton would win. It was not the same for the nomination. The Democratic Party uses proportional representation in its primaries and although, for example, he crushed her in Kentucky, she still won delegates (Los Angeles *Times*, 18 March 2016). He needed a massive win in California but did not get it. However, if the Democrats had had the winner-take-all system, like the Republicans, she would have had 1000 delegates more than Sanders. Her share of the popular vote was 55 percent to his 43 (fivethirtyeight.org, 27 July 2016).

The question was whether he would endorse her and if he did would it persuade his ardent supporters to work and vote for her. His apparent reluctance increased the hope of his supporters that enough delegates at the Convention would switch to him. He knew that was hopeless. Eventually endorsing her and claiming Clinton and the Party had adopted many of his policies, he saw her nomination as the first step to the revolution. And the idea that a Republican would be president, appointing ultra-right Supreme Court judges, horrified him. At the Convention he declared the nation did not want 'leadership [that] insults Latinos and Mexicans, insults Muslims, African Americans and women'. He praised coalition politics. 'Yes, we are stronger when blacks and, Latino, Asian American, Native American, when all of us stand together' (*The Washington Post*, 26 July 2016).

The Republican Scramble

The Republicans had 17 suitors and it seemed Jeb Bush, brother of George, was the favourite while others admired Florida Senator Marco Rubio. Black neurosurgeon Ben Carson described 'Obamacare' as 'the worst thing that has happened to this nation since slavery', that in the Boston ghetto he had seen 'people dying on the street with bullet holes and stab wounds' (*New Yorker*, 30 November 2015) and that LGBT people chose to be gay because, like Hillary, they were part of a Satanic cult. Texas Senator Ted Cruz had filibustered for 12 hours in a futile attempt to block the Affordable Care Act. He was a homophobic, anti-evolution Christian fundamentalist from Texas and was unpopular in the Party.

Virtually no one expected a self-described real estate billionaire, Donald Trump, to enter the race, a man who had never held elective office. But he intuitively grasped how to exploit people's fears that the world they had known – a utopian land etched by Europeans when they 'discovered the New World' and carved out when they occupied it – had been stolen by a ruling elite. Trump told them the African Obama did not share their dream. In fact, there was no longer an American Dream – Obama had destroyed it. He channelled the righteous anger of the embittered white folk – their longing for a resurrected nation, for work and the promise they would dream again. Trump fought the most extraordinary campaign for the presidency ever.

In the primaries he ignored the Party machine and abused his colleagues while claiming he was a billionaire outsider who would 'drain the swamp' in Washington. In a ghostwritten book, *The Art of the Deal*, he asserted he had never lost. Success meant never admitting anything and always taking ruthless revenge against any opponent or critic. You were always right (Johnston, 2016). Fear and racial hate were his weapons. The politics of euphemism was thrown out. He knew his audience fed on cable TV and 'socialised with friends' on Twitter and Facebook. He was a reality TV star who had sole authority in which every episode ended with 'You're fired'. Newspapers were losing their audience and reporters seemed helpless dealing with a man who broke all the rules that had governed political campaigning. They had never dealt with a presidential candidate who would say anything that came into his head, blatantly dispense with the truth and who made promises that were considered impossible by some in the Party and by most conservative commentators and economists (Johnston, 2016). His very unconventionality destroyed his opponents.

Trump benefited because the Republican establishment and its major donors did not want a loser. Virtually every newspaper, magazine and TV station considered his candidacy a joke. Why would voters choose someone whose fame was chairing a reality TV show, *The Apprentice*? When he declared he was a candidate he told the waiting press at Trump Tower in New York: 'I will be the greatest President God has ever created' (abcnews.com, 16 June 2016).

Publicly, Nixon wrapped his racism in coded slogans; Reagan angrily denied he was racist. As for George H. W. Bush, the Willie Horton advertisement had nothing to do with him and Romney had deliberately not mentioned race in his complaints about the 47 percent welfare dependent. These evasions were not for Trump. He embraced the racism that had come to dominate Republican politics. Trump led the birther campaign from 2008 which declared Obama was an African and asserted that the short and long birth certificates Obama released were forgeries. Trump said he had evidence to prove it. None of it was produced. It was not until September 2016 that he conceded Obama was a US citizen. Under pressure to explain the campaign tactics from many senior Republicans, his campaign managers assured them that much of what Trump said was just part of the battle.

And African Americans were an obvious target. Trump has a history of racial prejudice as did his father Fred. Woody Guthrie wrote a song in 1950 about one of Fred's developments that Donald later managed. It was entitled *Old Man Trump*: 'racial hate / He stirred up that blood-pot of human hearts / When he drawed that color line.' In 1973 Trump and his father were sued by the Justice Department for racial discrimination in renting. The Trumps countered, demanding $100 million for defamation. They lost and had to pay $20 million but Donald never admitted his guilt. Three years later they were sued again (Johnston, 2016).

He encouraged violence. During his campaign he said a BLM protestor 'should have been roughed up' and said his supporters' 'passion' explained why they beat up a homeless man (*Huffington Post*, 29 February 2016). He asserted: 'I could stand in the middle of 5th Avenue and shoot somebody and I wouldn't lose voters.' Gun ownership under the Second Amendment was a right but there was no way to ensure it was safe if Clinton was elected. He added: 'Although [with] the 2nd Amendment people maybe there is' (cnn.com, 24 January and 9 August 2016). Many assumed he was advocating her assassination.

Obama was a 'foreigner' but now it was other immigrants. To roars of approval he described undocumented immigrants from Mexico: 'They're bringing drugs. They're bringing crime. They're rapists.' But Americans need not worry because: 'I will build a wall, a great wall on the southern border. The Mexicans will pay for it.' These 'illegals' not only stole jobs from true Americans but US companies were moving factories to Mexico. What was the response of his Republican rivals? Total silence. Jeb Bush, married to a Mexican American, and Cuban-American Senator Marco Rubio did not demand a retraction. Only one Party official said 'it was not helpful' (usnewstoday.com, 24 June 2016). They understood that anti-immigrant prejudice was Trump's winning card.

Trump's assertion that Obama was a Muslim was shared by many Republicans and Democrats. As early as 2011 he implied that the Qur'an taught hate. But in 2015–2016 he went further. Eleven million Muslims in the United States should be deported and a special force would ensure they were. He called for a 'total and complete shut down' of Muslims entering the country (cnnpolitics.com, 7 December 2015). Syrian refugees should be excluded because they were a terrorist threat. As for Obama: 'He's the founder of ISIS.' Adding: 'I would say the co-founder was crooked Hillary Clinton' (*New York Times*, 10 August 2016). Jeb Bush said religion should not be used as a requirement to settle in the country and Democratic contender Martin O'Malley said Trump was running as a 'fascist demagogue' (abcnews.com, 17 December 2015).

At the Democratic Convention on 28 July 2016, Khizr Khan told how his son, a captain in the army, was killed when saving his platoon while serving in Iraq. He denounced Trump's attacks on Muslims and, pulling a copy of the Constitution from his inside pocket, he asked Trump if he had ever read it and if not he would lend him his copy. The families whose children die in combat are known as 'gold star families' and their patriotism has never been doubted – that is until Trump. On his favourite means of communication, Twitter, he wrote that Khan had been 'very emotional' and claimed Clinton's speechwriters had 'concocted' the address. Mrs Khan was silent because, 'She probably wasn't allowed to say anything' (*The Washington Post*, 30 July 2016). Although Republican leaders praised the Khan family they did not mention Trump and it was left to Senator John McCain to declare he 'deeply disagreed' with Trump (nprpolitics.com, 1 August 2016). Trump said he did not consider McCain a war hero. It was discovered that on a TV talk show Trump had spoken about *his* Vietnam – avoiding venereal disease. 'It is a dangerous world out there … It is my personal Vietnam. I feel like a great and brave soldier' (cbsnews.com, 7 October 2016).

As his campaign swept on, some alarmed Republicans and their donors started a Stop Trump campaign. Mitt Romney called Trump a 'fraud' and a 'phony' and in the closing stages Cruz was left to battle Trump alone in a desperate effort to block him. Trump calmly asserted that Cruz's father was part of a conspiracy to murder JFK (usatoday.com, 3 May 2016). His source? The notorious scandal sheet known as the *National Enquirer*. With Trump's victory unstoppable, his opponents hoped he would tone down his rhetoric.

Trump: Paranoia and Fear on the Campaign Trail

Trump had claimed he loved the punk band Green Day. Although he pirated songs from Madonna, Springsteen and others for his rallies, he did not choose Green Day's 2016 recording. They had amended an earlier version of their *American Idiot,* responding to Trump's primary campaign. 'Don't wanna be an American idiot / Don't want a nation under the new media / Can you hear the sound of hysteria? / The subliminal mind-fuck America.' But fear and paranoia were central to his campaign. Former rivals and the Party central organisation endorsed him. They never questioned his policy to exclude Mexicans, his equating Muslims with terrorism or his assertion that Obama and Clinton were founders of ISIS. He constantly denounced Clinton as a criminal, and said as president his first act would be to imprison her; and he repeated accusations that BLM protestors conspired to murder the police. He said it was 'outrageous' that five black and Hispanic men, found guilty in 1989 of raping a white woman in Central Park, New York City had been released – even though DNA evidence proved their innocence and another man had confessed (*New York Times*, 17 October 2016). But he still continued to claim as he always did: 'I will get 95 percent of the African American vote' (*Guardian,* 20 August 2016).

His paranoia spread to the 'lying media'. He promised a new libel law that would enable people to make millions if they were slandered. When students of Trump University sued him for fraud it was another conspiracy. After the judge Gonzalo Curiel ruled that their case could proceed, Trump publicly denounced Curiel's Mexican heritage saying he could not be impartial. Curiel was born in Indiana. As before, Trump swore he would fight the case and win. He settled for $26 million.

He stirred up the fury of unemployed white workers. For desperate coal and steel workers he promised jobs. They did not know he had employed illegal Polish migrants who worked 84 hours a week without safety equipment on his construction sites. It took years of legal action before he eventually paid them. His admirers ignored his many bankruptcies, failed promises to revive Atlantic City with his casinos, and were unaware of his fraudulent apartment and resort projects in Azerbaijan, Mexico and Florida (Johnston, 2016; Kranish and Fisher, 2016). They saw him as a brilliant businessman whose acumen would make the nation great again. They believed him when he said the Chinese stole their jobs by dumping cheap steel, and they had invented the job-losing, global warming conspiracy. Free trade deals would be torn up.

The America of the 21st century would be rediscovered in the 1950s – when the nation was at peace with itself, God-fearing and a beacon of hope to the world. Christian fundamentalists loved his early promise to punish women who had abortions (*The Washington Post*, 3 April 2016). They ignored his divorces and his virtual total absence of church attendance. For them he shared their family values. They could trust him. Clinton was a liar who had destroyed the American Dream and only Trump would make 'America Great Again'.

And then it seemed his campaign had fallen apart. A video was released:

Trump: 'I moved on her and I failed … I tried to fuck her. She was married … I moved on her like a bitch but I couldn't get there … Then all of sudden I see her, she's got big phony tits and everything.'

[On beautiful women] 'You know I start kissing them. It's like a magnet. I don't even wait … And when you're a star. You can do anything … Grab them by the pussy.'

(*The Washington Post*, 7 October 2016)

Suddenly the failed contenders and several Republican governors demanded he step down and be replaced by his vice-presidential nominee, Michael Pence. They were conspicuously silent on his other crude statements and encouraging violence but this was beyond the pale (*Huffington Post*, 7 October 2016). They did not sympathise with the abused woman but talked about their own wives and daughters. He counter-attacked and after 12 women testified he had assaulted them his response was typical: he threatened to sue them.

He dismissed the video as merely locker room talk and said he was sure Bill Clinton had said much worse and now he would take the gloves off. Before the second debate with Hillary he held a press conference with women who claimed Bill Clinton had abused them and one who said she had been raped by him – even though she had years earlier given a sworn affidavit saying she had not been. Trump's campaign staff went on the attack too. Hillary had condoned Bill's activities and internet users claimed she had acted as his pimp. At every opportunity Trump raised it and it was as if he was running against her husband and not her. But there were different responses. Evangelicals such as Jerry Falwell Jr continued to endorse him (politco.com, 27 October). They accepted Trump's behaviour was youthful indiscretion, that he was a changed man and the Clintons had done far worse. Clinton did not respond but supporters, of all races, religions and genders, turned to Movement-style mass demonstrations and sit-ins waving placards declaring 'Pussy Power'.

Seeking to Shatter the Glass Ceiling

At the Democratic Convention in 2008 Hillary Clinton said she had put cracks in the glass ceiling and this time it would shatter. But what she did not realise, or could not accept or acknowledge, was that she would never be trusted. Many Americans did not just distrust her; they hated her.

In 1994, as First Lady, she was accused of killing her lawyer Vince Foster to cover up an alleged scandal and this fake news was repeated on every conservative website as well as by Donald Trump. In 2015 alt-right sites reported that she had murdered an FBI agent investigating her time at the State Department. Dressing in pantsuits during the campaign proved she was a lesbian (*Huffington Post*, 2 February 2016) and her lovers included John Lennon's widow Yoko Ono and her personal assistant Huma Abedin. Abedin should be investigated because she was probably connected to extremist Muslims (Breitbart News, 18 January 2016). Not untypical are the bizarre stories exemplified by a book, *The Occult Hillary*. The author fantasies that a powerful elite led by Clinton engaged in child abuse, blood sacrifices and, among other things, in league with the Forces of Darkness, threatened all human life. This nonsense not only appealed to those locked into the world of alt-right websites and conspiracy theorists but influenced others who doubted her.

All polls predicted Clinton would win and so what went wrong? A negative, no matter how bizarre, is very difficult to disprove and attempts to do so can be treated as an admission of guilt – as is ignoring them. Attacking the opponent merely underscores the untruth and ensures its repetition in the mainstream news – like the Willie Horton campaign.

When two previous Republican presidents, George H. W. and George W. Bush, and Jeb Bush publicly stated they would not vote for Trump, for his believers it only proved that Clinton's long service in Washington made her part of the old elite, those who were responsible for the nation's malaise. Sanders' attacks on her Wall Street connections helped Trump by showing she was corrupted by the associations. Trump supporters did not care that he associated with the same people and he had depended on Wall Street bankers five times to escape bankruptcy (Kranish and Fisher, 2016). Trump's refusal to release his tax returns and his pride in not paying federal taxes only increased their admiration for him.

There has been widespread speculation about her failure to win the working-class vote. This is exaggerated but she did not spend enough time in important states such as Michigan, believing Obama's rescue of the auto industry and the state's traditional Democratic support would ensure success. However, she only lost the state by just over 10,000 votes. A recount demanded by the Green candidate revealed irregularities in the overwhelmingly Democratic areas of Wayne County and the city of Detroit, but they made no difference to the Electoral College vote.

With Trump's campaign in trouble because of his misogyny, Clinton believed that there was a large disaffected group of moderate Republicans, especially women, who would abandon their traditional allegiance. They did not. Her campaigning in solid Republican states, such as Arizona, was a waste of time and money. Trump concentrated on safe Democratic states, a plan that was derided by the media, but conservatives' loyalty has been well documented (Aughey et al., 1992). His treatment of women upset them, and a few voted for two independent conservatives, but the majority did not vote for Clinton. Evangelicals not only voted for Trump; they were enthusiasts. It was the 19- to 25-year-olds who did not want him and who were disgusted by his predatory behaviour. Trump sought to turn defence into attack. He hired 'white nationalists' (white supremacists) Roger Stone and also Stephen Bannon of Breitbart News – the latter as his campaign manager – who constantly reported fake news against Clinton as fact.

Moderate Republicans were horrified by Bannon's appointment as campaign manager but members of the National Committee were not. And extreme right-wing groups were delighted to see Bannon was central to the Republican campaign. David Duke, a former Klan leader, and the KKK endorsed Trump (*The Washington Post*, 1 November 2016). Trump's reaction was to deny he knew Duke and did not know what white supremacy meant (npr.org, 26 February 2016). It is also the case that many of his admirers were racists as evidenced by the unfiltered recordings of people chanting against African Americans, Hispanics, LGBT, Muslim and Jewish people (*New York Times*, 3 and 5 August 2016) after his rallies.

Additionally, the African American vote was down but that was to be expected considering the very large turn-out for Obama and the subsequent gerrymandering; but the Democrats did overestimate Hispanic sentiment in Florida which was affected by Obama's reconciliation with Cuba. Also it is not certain how many of Sanders' supporters refused to vote for Clinton but chose the Green Party. Exit polls showed her voter share was not as good as Obama's with younger voters and Trump did as well as Romney in 2012 with women voters (edisonresearch. com, 9 November 2016). Two other reasons for her defeat, according to Democrats, were the public announcement by the FBI eight days before voting, and against all precedent, that they were reopening the State Department server investigation (bloomberg.com, 28 November 2016). Russian intelligence, according to 17 government agencies, had hacked the Democrats' office computers hoping to help Trump's campaign. The Bureau refused to support these findings (*New York Times*, 10 and 14 December 2016). The Democrats overestimated their support from the Latino community, especially in border states where it was believed that Trump's deportation threats would result in a massive swing to their Party.

But Clinton, to Trump's fury, won the popular vote by over 2.9 million, the largest margin ever, and it was only the Electoral College, where 48 states have a winner-takes-all system, that ensured his victory. He returned to Twitter and declared that three million votes had been fraudulently cast for Clinton (npr.org, 27 November 2016) and as usual he had no evidence. Angry voters gathered in several cities from Portland, Oregon to Houston, Texas declaring 'HE'S NOT MY PRESIDENT'. At 2.19 a.m., 11 November he tweeted that 'professional protestors, incited by the media, are protesting. Very unfair' (*The Washington Post*, 11 November 2016).

'The protests continued. Congressman John Lewis, the SNCC member who had had his skull fractured in 1965 on the Selma to Montgomery march fighting for a voting rights act, questioned Trump's election on 24 January 2017 because of alleged Russian intervention. Trump launched a bitter assault on one of the most admired members of the struggle just two days before the Martin Luther King federal holiday and six days before his inauguration Trump wrote that Lewis 'should spend more time in fixing and helping his district, which is in horrible shape and falling apart, not to mention crime infested ... All talk, talk, talk – no action. Sad!' (cbsnews.com, 15 January 2017). The bipartisan outrage was overwhelming. Republican Senator Ben Sasse responded: 'John Lewis and his "talk" have changed the world.' And Democrat Donald Wolfson pointed out: 'John Lewis did more to make America great again in one day on the Edmund Pettus Bridge than Donald Trump ever will.' Many believed Trump had played the race card with his attack on a man they saw as a black icon. His assault mirrored Richard Nixon who had claimed that Abernathy and the Movement leaders were only interested in talk not action. One thing is certain: Trump did not respond.

Proposed Appointments

After the results were in there were still hopes that the president-elect would seek to heal a bitterly divided people and moderate his views on issues of race, environment, the LGBT community, Muslims and Hispanics. And he said he 'wanted to govern for all' and his critics, Republicans, Democrats and independents, waited to see if his nominations would match his promise. But far from reaching out to the majority who did not want him in the White House, he surrounded himself with people like Stephen Bannon, the racial supremacist, as his strategic advisor.

And African Americans, Hispanics, immigrants and gays had particular reason to be alarmed. One of his first nominees was Alabama Senator Jeff Sessions as Attorney General. Sessions had been nominated by Reagan in 1986 as a federal judge and the Senate Judiciary Committee, controlled by Republicans, rejected him because of evidence of racism.

He admitted saying he thought the KKK was all right until he heard they smoked pot. He denied he had told a white lawyer that representing black clients was a disgrace, that a black lawyer should be careful about what he said to white people, or that he used the 'N' word. He admitted at the 1986 hearing to saying that the NAACP, SCLC, ACLU, Operation PUSH and the National Council of Churches were 'not working in the best interests of the country'. However, he denied he had called them un-American, communist-inspired or that he was tired of the ACLU forcing 'civil rights down our throats'. There is no evidence to support his claims to have supported the civil rights movement in Alabama. And Sessions also passionately opposed women's right to abortion and frequently criticised the Supreme Court's approval of gay marriage. In the Senate he did everything in his power to limit the rights of legal immigrants and enthusiastically endorsed forced deportation of illegal aliens, especially Hispanics and Muslims. He opposed legislation designed to amend the Voting Rights Act.

Trump nominated one African American, Ben Carson, as head of Housing and Urban development. Carson had grown up poor but his concerns for urban betterment and improved housing were unknown and he had never made a statement about the issues except for his stories on violence. His only recorded remark on housing was his assertion that Joseph had built the Egyptian pyramids for grain storage. Government programmes for the disadvantaged are 'not helping these people, all you have to do is look at what happened since the Great Society programs of Lyndon Johnson'. His contention was that over $19 trillion spent resulted in ten times more people on food stamps, more broken homes, single parents, crime and imprisonment. 'Everything is not only worse, it's much worse' (politico.com, 9 October 2015).

Retired Lieutenant General Michael Flynn was nominated as the National Security Advisor. Flynn had declared at the Republican Convention that Islam was not a faith but a 'political ideology' and 'a cancer'. His rhetoric was exactly the same as that of Donald Trump and criticisms from the NAACP and Muslim American civil rights groups were simply proof that he was right. Flynn followed the alt-right site Infowars. On 2 November Flynn tweeted: 'U decide-NYPD Blows Whistle on New Hillary Emails: Money Laundering, Sex Crimes w

Children etc .... MUST READ' (bbc.news.com, 7 December 2016). Other typical appointments were fast-food chain owner Alan Pudzer as Secretary of Labor who opposed the minimum wage, better opportunities for overtime pay and workers' safety regulations in an industry that unions said relied on illegal immigrants who forced down wages for all workers in the sector. He was forced to withdraw because Republicans opposed his support for immigration reform and for employing undocumented domestic staff (*The Washington Post*, 15 February 2017).

In a ploy recommended in *The Art of the Deal*, Trump would call in people who bitterly opposed his views. Trump knew every politician has his price. Power. The president-elect kept Romney and others waiting for weeks to see if they would get appointments. Romney took the bait of the possibility of becoming Secretary of State and told the press Trump would be a good president. He did not get it. Former vice president and passionate environmentalist, Al Gore Jr accepted an invitation to talk with Trump and said he was pleased that his views were seriously considered and he looked forward to further meetings. But environmentalists were not part of the government for all Americans. A few days later it was announced that the nominee to head the Environmental Protection Agency was the Oklahoma Attorney General, Scott Pruitt, who believed that global warming was a Chinese conspiracy and that virtually all environmental safety regulations and the Agency should be scrapped.

Trump had done the same with Obama. At their first meeting he promised he would keep large parts of the Affordable Care Act but in weeks reneged on his promise. Obama hit back. Because Republicans opposed law reforms he had pardoned and commuted more sentences than all previous presidents. To protect his environmental legacy he had used an obscure 1953 act of Congress to permanently prohibit oil drilling in hundreds of millions of acres of the Arctic and Atlantic (*The Washington Post*, 20 December 2016).

The late 19th century is known as the 'Gilded Age' when big business magnates controlled the government. Trump, the candidate who said he would protect the little man and who had attacked big business, bankers and Wall Street operators, nominated the wealthiest group of Cabinet officers in the history of the United States (*New York Times*, 11 December 2016). None of them showed the slightest interest in philanthropic work.

They were the men who promised more tax cuts for the richest 1 percent (themselves), and to slash corporation taxes while supporting Trump's view that the worker's minimum wage should be abolished and welfare virtually wiped out.

The Land of Dixie

George Wallace had always portrayed white folks as the carriers of the burden of lazy and shiftless black people who eagerly held their hands out for free government gifts provided by hardworking, over-taxed white people. Trump proved that a campaign based on blatant racism and violence could make a President. When BLM protested the killing of an unarmed black man in Charlotte, North Carolina, Republican Robert Pittinger said: 'They hate white people because white people are successful and they're not' (Charlotte *News & Observer*, 22 September 2016). Maine Governor Paul LePage called black people 'the enemy' and the state was being overrun by black and Hispanic drug pushers from New York who also came to 'impregnate white girls' (*Guardian*, 27 August 2016). Asked what he wanted to happen in 2017, Cal Paladino, Trump's campaign manager in New York, said Obama engaged in bestiality and he hoped Obama would die of mad cow disease and Michelle would stop pretending to be a woman and go back to Africa and live with an ape in a cave. When there was widespread disgust, he said his critics 'can go and fuck themselves' (*Guardian*, 24 November 2016).

Some people believed they had voted for the 'idyllic' 1950s. It was everything the Movement people had fought to overcome. Those who believed in the struggle were determined to fight on, understanding the urgent need to work together. With at least three new Supreme Court Justices to be appointed and the capitulation of all Trump's opponents in the Republican Party, such as Mitt Romney, it was seen as essential that sympathetic state legislatures and their Attorney Generals should challenge the Administration.

Before Trump's inauguration on 20 January 2017, the opposition organised using Movement tactics and the day after a Women's March on Washington for civil rights, with an estimated 500,000 people participating, followed the example of the Jobs and Freedom March of 1963. Marches took place in all 50 states and in over 600 countries. Millennial activists set up a Freedom House in Washington DC, copying the Freedom Houses of the Movement, which enabled activists to rally quickly. The NAACP, and other legal activists such as the ACLU, would rely on the earlier strategy of the Courts, and in Congress the record number of 48 African Americans, 15 Asians and the majority of the 39 Hispanic Representatives formed a coalition in December 2016 to fight all Republican legislation that threatened the gains from the 1960s (*Guardian*, 20 December 2016). Hispanic American Ruben Gallego (D. Arizona) said they were united 'to protect the most vulnerable'. He said the United States was not a racist, bigoted nation (*Guardian*, 22 December 2016).

However, in his Farewell Address given in Chicago, Obama warned:

> After my election, there was talk of a post-racial America. And such a vision … was never realistic. Race remains a powerful and often devisive force in our society … If every economic issue is framed as a struggle between a hardworking white middle class and an undeserving minority, then workers of all shades are going to be left to fight for scraps, while the wealthy withdraw further into private enclaves.
>
> (text on whitehouse.gov, 9 January 2017)

He argued for a coalition of all minorities to protect and ensure further progress and to acknowledge 'the middle-aged white guy who has seen his world upended by economic and cultural and technological change' (*Mainichi* [Japan's national newspaper], 11 January 2017).

Trump in his inauguration speech said the opposite. He talked about the neglected middle class and workers (read white) and his determination to wage war on drugs and crime (read black). He painted a bleak picture. The single parents of the inner cities (read black) were left in poverty with well-funded schools failing to educate their children. Workers (read white) were neglected and 'rusted out factories are like scattered tombstones' across the nation (cnn.politics.com, 20 January 2017).

However, Trump's first weeks in office were troubled by continued failures. He said he was 'calling for a total and complete shutdown of Muslims entering the United States' (donald.trump.com, 7 December 2015).

On his first day in office he signed an Executive Order banning Muslims from seven Middle East countries entering the United States (*Guardian*, 28 January 2017). Mass demonstrations and airport picketing to defend Muslims entering the country was followed within days by a New York federal court ruling that the Order discriminated against people with valid entry documents. Trump hastily issued a second Order which did not include an ally like Iraq and did not exempt Christians. A Hawaiian judge blocked the Order for 90 days, citing Trump's numerous campaign promises to exclude Muslims. The injunction was renewed because 'the Executive Order was issued with a purpose to disfavor a particular religion' violating the First Amendment (cnn.com, 15 March 2017). But despite the setback, the Administration launched a sweeping deportation programme targeting Latino communities who had no terrorist involvement. Critics argued that this was always the intention, to keep America white and English-speaking.

The Administration's troubles had only just begun. General Flynn was the shortest serving appointee ever, lasting only 24 days before submitting his resignation on 13 February. He admitted he had 'misled' the vice president when he failed to disclose meetings and telephone conversations with the Russian ambassador in December 2016. They had discussed lifting sanctions imposed by Obama. It was seen as proof that the Russian government had infiltrated the 2016 presidential campaign and aided Trump's victory (*The Washington Post*, 14 February 2017). It was later claimed that the president had sacked Flynn (npr.com, 24 March 2017). Trump tweeted that Obama was a 'sick' and a 'bad guy' because he had wiretapped Trump Tower – a felony (*Guardian*, 4 March 2017). This was seen as a diversionary tactic but did not stop the FBI investigations and lead to Congressional probes. The questions about Russia meant that Trump's efforts to overturn Obama's achievements were seriously affected.

His major promise at every campaign stop was to 'repeal and replace the disastrous Obamacare' on day one (nbc.com, 17 October 2016). No one was surprised that this did not happen but they had expected the Republicans, who had voted 60 times to repeal it and asked the Supreme Court to strike it down, would be prepared to act. The Affordable Care Act enabled millions of Americans such as those who were poor, members of minority groups, especially African Americans, unemployed white working and lower income people of all ethnic groups to gain medical insurance. Defunding Planned Parenthood would have meant that women would be denied a whole range of health care such as cancer screening, contraceptives, adoption, pre-natal care, abortion facilities and counselling.

The president and the Republicans had stressed that with the American Health Care Act they had a better alternative that would cover all Americans, be cheaper and ensure lower premiums. But it did not. Instead the party that controlled Congress and the White House failed and so why did they? The House speaker, Paul Ryan, and a chosen few drew up the Act without consulting their own party or the Democrats. When it was published a Republican coalition of ultra-conservatives of the Freedom Caucus, centrist conservatives, the Tuesday Group, refused to vote for it. For conservatives it was not repeal but what they called Obamacare Lite. Moderates rejected it because of the swingeing cuts in Medicaid (20 percent by 2018), abolition of maternity care and higher premiums, especially for those over 50 – concessions to the Freedom Caucus that were totally unacceptable. To the moderates, according to the Congressional Budget Office, the Ryan proposals would have meant an increase of 4 million uninsured by 2018 and 24 million by 2026 (AP Fact Check, pbs.com, 14 March 2017).

A bitterly divided party meant that the proposal lacked 24 Republican votes as well as public support – only 17 percent approved of it. The two wings of the Republican party, along with the Democrats, forced the Administration to withdraw the Act before a vote. Trump had not even read the proposal, only made concessions to the ultras and totally ignored the Democrats. According to an MSNBC commentator the Administration retreat was 'a victory for Obama and a complete disaster for the current president' (MSNBC, 24 March 2017). But the defeat was not total. Funding restrictions from the federal government and obstruction by state governments and other means would severely limit coverage available under Medicaid and Obamacare.

With mounting criticism, the Democratic Party and the opposition were reinvigorated. Groups, many led by feminists, started to mobilise and reach out to coordinate their action against the new president and to encourage people to run for office at all levels (*Guardian*, 30 March, 2017). Patrisse Cullors, the black lesbian cofounder of BLM, warned it was not enough to shout 'We Hate Trump' but rather urgent action was needed to ensure the new administration would not pursue goals that would hurt marginalized communities.

In her 2017 song, *Freedom Highway*, Rhiannon Giddens links enslaved peoples' flight for freedom with the blues of Mississippi John Hurt, and the Birmingham Baptist Church bombing. She and other African Americans hope that the majority of popular votes will be translated into a majority in the Electoral College in the 2020 election and that they will still be singing *We Shall Overcome* as they did outside Trump Tower in New York City and at other protests across the country. They believe that the struggle is not over and fighting the resistance might be as dangerous as the Freedom Summer of 1964.

Glossary

Alt-right A recent expression of right-wing views that rejects the ideology of other conservatives – the ultra-right – and preaches 'white nationalism' and defence of 'white culture'. They almost exclusively rely on social media and are racists. In 2016 the movement has millions of followers and its leading advocates have been included in the current administration.

Baby boom A commonly used expression that describes the generation born after World War Two, a period that saw a dramatic increase in childbirth in the United States.

Bossism A form of corrupt government, primarily in urban centres, used by politicians to enable parties to control local government using patronage, e.g. Mayor Daley in Chicago.

Bussing After World War Two bussing was used, especially in southern states, to consolidate schools to eliminate inferior rural institutions seeking to improve educational standards. However, the school bus was a means to ensure separation of white and black pupils – segregation – in schools. The Supreme Court ruled in 1971 that the bus should be used to ensure desegregation. This spread massive resistance to the civil rights movement nationally.

Carpetbagger A name given by southerners to black and white Republican politicians who moved to the South after the Civil War and who were active in state and federal government. According to southern whites they had come to rob the defeated Confederacy and their only belongings were carried in a carpetbag.

Dixie The name given to the 11 states that made up the Confederacy. The exact origin of the term is unknown but a popular belief is that it came from the 1859 popular song *Dixie* which became a marching tune for the southern army.

Filibuster A method used to prevent or delay legislation at federal and state legislatures by prolonging debate or using parliamentary procedures to prevent passage of legislation.

Gerrymander To divide electoral districts for political gain named after Elbridge Gerry who devised it when he was Governor of Massachusetts in 1810.

Governor Title of the head of the executive in a state.

Great Society Lyndon Baines Johnson's social and economic reform programme to tackle racism and poverty and to complete the New Deal policies of his hero Franklin Delano Roosevelt.

Impeachment Article 2, Section 4 of the Constitution stated: 'The President, Vice President, and all Officers of the United States, shall be removed from Office on Impeachment for, and Conviction of, Treason, Bribery, or other high Crimes and Misdemeanors.' A serious problem with the clause was that it failed to define 'misdemeanors'. At the federal level the House of Representatives hears the charges and if approved the process proceeds to the Senate where two-thirds of the Senators must vote for conviction. Impeached people may not hold any office again and are liable for trial in criminal courts. Two presidents, Andrew Johnson (1868) and William Clinton (1998), were impeached by the House but found innocent by the Senate. President Richard Nixon (1974) and his Vice President, Spiro Agnew were both impeached – Nixon for high crimes but he resigned before impeachment went to the Senate; Agnew pleaded no contest to bribery and resigned in 1973 before his impeachment began.

Interposition The southern contention before the Civil War and against the abolition movement that every state was sovereign and should interpose its authority between the people of the state and the Federal Government to prevent the enforcement of federal laws that state governments deemed unconstitutional.

Jim Crow Laws The system of segregation of the races imposed in the South and in bordering states after the Civil War. The origin of the term Jim Crow is not known.

Ku Klux Klan A paramilitary terrorist organisation formed in Pulaski, Tennessee after the Civil War. Describing themselves as Knights of the Invisible Empire, they were in effect the terrorist wing of the Democratic Party and were largely responsible, along with other terrorists, for the overthrow of southern Reconstruction governments. The modern KKK was launched in Georgia exploiting anti-Jewish and anti-Catholic bigotry as well as racism and claimed 5 million members in 1925. It became, and remains, a national terrorist organisation but is smaller in the 21st century because other terrorist groups have been formed.

New Deal The title given to the wide-ranging social and economic reforms intro-duce by Franklin Delano Roosevelt after 1932 which were designed to resolve the crisis of the Great Depression by regulating the capitalist economy and introducing a limited welfare state. It revolutionised the Democratic Party and is the basis of modern liberalism.

Nullification The southern argument that every sovereign state had the right to call a convention and decide that federal legislation should be declared null and void if the people deemed it unconstitutional.

Peculiar Institution This was the euphemism used by southerners before the Civil War to describe the institution of slavery. In the North it was used to indicate that slavery was a peculiar (exclusively) southern form of forced labour.

Sharecropper A southern tenant farmer who paid his rent and his supplies by giving a share of his crop to the landowner. It was a means to ensure debt peonage.

Solid South Following the defeat of the South in the Civil War, the region was governed by the Republican Party. Defeated by terrorism and fraud, the South became an undemocratic one-party region ruled by the Democrats.

Territories Land acquired by the United States and held by the federal government until it reached a certain population, adopted a republican form of government and then was admitted to the Union by a vote of Congress. As with other states, the membership of the House of Representatives was based on the size of population and the state had two senators.

Bibliography

Abernathy, Ralph David. *And the Walls Came Tumbling Down*. Harper and Row, New York, 1989.

Adams, Frank T. *James Dombrowski: An American Heretic, 1897–1983*. The University of Tennessee Press, Knoxville, 1992.

Allen, James, *et.al*, *Without Sanctuary: Lynching Photography in America*. Twin Palms Publishers, Santa Fe, New Mexico, 2000.

Alexander, Paul. *Man of the People: The Life of John McCain*. John Wiley & Sons, Hoboken, New Jersey, 2003.

Ambrose, S. *Eisenhower the President*. Simon and Schuster, New York, 1984.

——-*Nixon*. 3 vols. Simon and Schuster, New York, 1989.

Anderson, Terry. *The Movement and the Sixties: Protest in America from Greensboro to Wounded Knee*. Oxford University Press, New York, 1995.

Arsenault, Raymond. *Freedom Riders: 1961 and the Struggle for Racial Justice*. Oxford University Press, New York, 2006.

Asch, Chris Myers, *The Senator and the Sharecropper: The Freedom Struggle of James O. Eastland & Fanny Lou Hamer*. The New Press, New York, 2008.

Aughey, Arthur, A. G. Jones, W. T. M Riches. *The Conservative Political Tradition in Britain and the United States*. Pinter Press, London, 1992.

Barnet, Richard and Larry Burriss. *Controversies in the Music Industry*. Greenwood Press, Westport, 2001.

Bass, Jack, *Taming the Storm: The Life and Times of Judge Frank M. Johnson and the South's Fight Over Civil Rights*. Doubleday, New York, 1993.

Beals, Melba Patillo. *Warriors Don't Cry*. Pocket Books, New York, 1994.

Berkowitz, Edward D. 'A Historical Preface to the Americans with Disabilities Act,' in B. J. Berstein. *Politics and Policies of the Truman Administration*, Quadrangle Books, Chicago, 1997.

Berman, Ari. *Give Us the Ballot: The Modern Struggle for Voting Rights in America*, Farrar, Straus and Giroux, New York, 2015.

Bernstein, I. *Promises Kept: John F. Kennedy's New Frontier*. Oxford University Press, New York, 1991.

Beschloss, Michael R. *Taking Charge: The Johnson White House Tapes, 1963–1964*. Simon and Schuster, New York, 1997.

Blackmon, Douglas A. *Slavery By Another Name: The Re-enslavement of Black Americans from the Civil War to World War11*. Anchor Books, 2008.

Blight, David W. *Race and Reunion: The Civil War in American Memory*. Harvard University Press, Cambridge, 2001.

Blum, J. M. *Years of Discord in American Politics and Society, 1961–1974*. W.W. Norton, New York, 1991.

Bovard, James. *Attention Deficit Democracy*. Palgrave Macmillan, New York, 2005.

Boyarsky, Bill. *Ronald Reagan: His Life and Rise to the Presidency*. Random House, New York, 1981.

Boyer, Paul. *When Time Shall Be No More: Belief in Modern American Culture*. Harvard University Press, Cambridge, 1992.

Boyer, Peter J. 'Man of Faith Can Jesse Jackson Save Himself, *The New Yorker*. 26 November 2001, 48–53.

Bracey Jr J.H. and August Meier and Elliott Rudwick. *The Afro-American: Selected Documents*. Allyn and Bacon, Boston, 1972.

Branch, Taylor. *Parting the Waters: Martin Luther King and the Civil Rights Movement, 1954–1963*. Simon and Schuster, New York, 1989.

—— *Pillar of Fire: American in the King Years, 1963–1965*. Simon and Schuster, New York, 1999.

—— *At Canaan's Edge: America in the King Years 1965–1968*. Simon and Schuster, New York, 2007)

Brand, Neil. *BBC Arts – The Sound of Song: The Recording Revolution*. BBC 4, January 16, 2014.

Brandt, Eric. *Dangerous Liaisons: Black Gays and the Struggle for Equality*. The New Press, New York, 1999.

Bryant, Nick. *The Bystander: John F. Kennedy and the Struggle for Black Equality*. Basic Books, New York, 2006.

Buell, Frederick. *From Apocalypse to a Way of Life: Environmental Crisis in the American Century*. Routledge, New York, 2004.

Burner, Eric R. *and gently he shall lead them: Robert Moses and Civil Rights*. New York University Press, New York, 1994.

Burns, James M. *Roosevelt: The Soldier of Freedom*. Harcourt Brace Janovich, New York, 1970.

Bush, George W. *Decision Points*. Crown Publishers, New York, 2010.

Cannon, Lou. *President Reagan: The Role of a Lifetime*. Touchstone, New York, 1991.

Carbado, David. Dwight McBride and Donald Weise, eds., *Black Like Us: A Century of Lesbian and Gay and Bisexual African American Literature*. Cleis Press, San Francisco, 2002.

Caro, Robert A. Lyndon. *The Passage of Power*. Bodley Head, London, 2012.

—— *The Years of Lyndon Johnson*. Bodley Head, London 2012.

—— *The Years of Lyndon Johnson: Master of the Senate*. Jonathan Cape, London 2002.

Carson, Clayborne ed. *The Student Voice.1960–1963*. Mekler, Westport, 1990.

—— *In Struggle: SNCC and the Black Awakening of the 1960s*. Harvard University Press, Cambridge, 1981.

Carter, Dan T. *The Politics of Rage: George Wallace and the Origins of New Conservatism, and the Transformation of American Politics*. Louisiana State University, Baton Rouge, 1995.

Carter, David C., *The Music Has Gone Out of the Movement: Civil Right and the Johnson Administration. 1965–1968*. University of North Carolina Press, Chapel Hill, 2009.

Carter, Jimmy. *Keeping Faith: Memoirs of a President*. Collins, London, 1992.

—— *A Full Life: Reflections at Ninety*. Simon & Schuster, New York, 2015.

Carville, James. *We Were Right, They're Wrong: A Handbook for a Spirited Progressive*. Random House, New York, 1996.

Chafe, William H. et all, *Remembering Jim Crow. African Americans Tell About Life in the Segregated* South. The New Press, New York, 2001.

Chalmers, David M. *Hooded Americanism: A History of the Ku Klux Klan*. Quadrangle, Chicago, 1965.

Chappell, David. *Waking from the Dream: The Struggle for Civil Rights in the Shadow of Martin Luther King Jr* Random House, New York, 2014.

Clinton, Bill. *My Life*. Hutchinson, 2004.

Cleaver, E. *Soul on Ice*. Delta, New York, 1991.

Coates, Ta-Nehisi. *Between the World and Me*. Text Publishing, Melbourne, 2015.

Cobb Jr Charles E. *This Nonviolent Stuff'll, Get You Killed: How Guns Made the Civil Rights Movement Possible*. Basic Books, New York, 2014.

Cockburn, Alexander and James St. Clair. *White Out: The CIA, Drugs and the Press*. Verso, London, 2001.

Cohen, Michael J. *American Maelstrom: The 1968 Election and the Politics of Division*. Oxford University Press, New York, 2016.

Cooper, William Jr and Thomas Terrill, *The American South: A History*. Rowman and Littlefield, Lanham, Maryland, 2009.

Cone, James H. *Martin & Malcolm: A Nightmare or a Dream?* Fount Paperbacks, London, 1995.

Cose, Ellis, *Color-Blind: Seeing Beyond a Race Obsessed World*. Harper-Collins, New York, 1998.

Countryman, Matthew J. *Up South: Civil Rights and Black Power in Philadelphia*. University of Pennsylvania Press, Philadelphia, 2006.

Coyle, Marcia. *The Roberts Court: The Struggle for the Constitution*. Simon & Schuster, New York, 2014.

Crawford, Vicki, et al. *Women in the Civil Rights Movement: Torchbearers and Trailblazers*. Indiana University Press, Bloomington, 1993.

Crespino, Joseph. *In Search of Another Country: Mississippi and the Conservative Counterrevolution*. Princeton University Press, Princeton, 2007.

Crosby, Emilye. *A Little Taste of Freedom: The Black Freedom Struggle in Claiborne County, Mississippi*. University of North Carolina Press, Chapel Hill, 2005.

Cunningham, David. *Klansville, U. S. A.: The Rise and Fall of the Civil Rights Era Ku Klux Klan*. Oxford University Press, New York, 2013.

Dalleck, Robert. *John F. Kennedy: An Unfinished Life, 1917–1963*. Allen Lane, London, 2003.

—— *Lone Star Rising: Lyndon Johnson and his Times 1908–1960*, Oxford, New York, 1991.

—— *Ronald Reagan: The Politics of Symbolism*. Harvard University Press, Cambridge, 1984.

Daniel, Pete. *In the Shadow of Slavery: Peonage in the South 1901–1969*. University of Illinois Press, Urbana, 1972.

—— *Lost Revolutions: The South in the 1950s*. University of North Carolina, Chapel Hill, 2000.

—— *Standing At the Crossroads: Southern Life in the Twentieth Century*. Hill & Wang, New York, 1986.

D'Souza, Dinesh. *The End of Racism: The Principles for a Multicultural Society*. Free Press, New York, 1995.

—— *The Roots of Obama's Rage*. Regency Publishing Inc., 2011.

—— *Obama's America. The Unmaking of the American Dream*. Threshold Editions (reprint) New York, 2014.

Davis, Angela. *An Autobiography*. Random House, New York, 1988.

—— *Women, Race & Class*. Vintage, New York, 1983.

—— 'Civil Liberties and Women's Rights Twenty Years On,' *Irish Journal of American Studies*. Vol.3, 1994, 17–30.

Davis, David Brion. *The Problem of Slavery in the Age of Revolution, 1770–83*. Cornell University Press, Ithaca, 1975.

—— *In Human Bondage: The Rise and Fall of Slavery in the New World*. Oxford University Press, New York, 2006.

Dawley, Alan. *Struggle for Justice: Social Responsibility and the Liberal State*. Belknap Press, Cambridge, 1991.

D'Emilio, John D. *Lost Prophet: The Life and Times of Bayard Rustin*. Free Press, New York, 2003.

Desmond, Matthew, *Evicted: Poverty and Profit in the American City*. Crown Publishing, New York, 2016.

Divine, Robert ed. *The Johnson Years*. University of Kansas Press, Lawrence, 1994.

Dittmer, John. *Local People: The Struggle for Civil Rights in Mississippi*. University of Illinois Press, Champagne, 1995.

Dorr, Lisa, *White Women, Rape & the Power of Race in Virginia 1900–1960*. University of North Carolina Press, Chapel Hill, 2004.

Douglass, Frederick. *Life and Times of Frederick Douglass*. Collier Macmillan, London, 1962.

Draper, Robert. *Dead Certain: The Presidency of George W, Bush*. Free Press, New York, 2007.

Du Bois, *The Souls of Black Folk*. Bartlby Press, New York, 1999. Reprint of 1903 ed.

Duberman, Martin. *Paul Robeson*. Pan Books, New York, 1989.

Du Bois. *The Souls of the Black Folk*. Reprint of 1903 edition Bartlaby Press, New York, 1999.

Dye, Thomas and R. Zeigler. *The Irony of Democracy: An Uncommon Introduction to American Politics*. Cengage Learning, Boston, 2002.

Dyson, Michael E. *Making Malcolm: The Myth and Meaning of Malcolm X*. Oxford University Press, New York, 1995.

Dunaway, David and Molly Beer, *Singing Out: An Oral History of America's Folk Music Revivals*. Oxford University Press, 2010.

Early, Gerald, ed. *Lure and Loathing: Essays on Race, Identity, and the Ambivalence of Assimilation*. Allen Lane, Viking Penguin, New York, 1993.

Egerton, John. *Speak Now Against the Day: The Generation Before the Civil Rights Movement in the South*. University of North Carolina Press, Chapel Hill, 1995.

Ehrenreich, Barbara, *Nickel and Dimed: Undercover in Low Wage USA*. Granta Books, London, 2001.

Ellis, Ian. *To Be President: Quest for the White House*. Politico's, London, 2009.

Ely, James C. *The Crisis of Conservative Virginia: The Byrd Organization and the Politics of Massive Resistance*. University of Tennessee Press, Knoxville, 1976.

Emery, Fred. *Watergate: The Corruption and Fall of Richard Nixon*. Johnathan Cape, London, 1994.

Engelhardt, Tom. *The End of the Victory Culture: Cold War America and the Disillusionment of a Generation*. BasicBooks, New York, 1995.

Essien-Udom, E. U. *Black Nationalism: A Search for Identity in America*. Dell, New York, 1964.

Faderman, Lillian. *Old Girls and Twilight Lovers: A History of Lesbian Life in The Twentieth Century American*. Penguin, London, 1992.

—— *The Gay Revolution: The Story of the Struggle*. Simon & Schuster, New York, 2015.

Fairclough, A. *Race and Democracy: The Civil Rights Struggle in Louisiana 1915–1972*. University of Georgia Press, Athens, 1999.

—— *Better Day Coming: Blacks and Equality, 1890–2000*. Penguin Books, New York, 2001.

—— *To Redeem the Soul of American: The Southern Christian Leadership Conference and Martin Luther King Jr* University of Georgia Press, Athens, Ga., 1987.

Faludi, Susan. *Backlash: The Underground War Against Women*. Chatto & Windus, London, 1992.

Fannin, Mark. *Labor's Promised Land: Radical Visions of Gender, Race and Religion in the South*. University of Tennessee Press, Knoxville, 2003.

Faust, Drew Gilpin. *James Henry Hammond and the Old South: A Design for Mastery*. Louisiana State University Press, Baton Rouge, 1982.

Ferris, William. *Blues from the Delta*. De Capo Press, New York, 1978.

Fleming, Cynthia Griggs. 'Black Women Activists and the Student Nonviolent Corordinating Committee: The Case of Roby Doris Smith Robinson.' *The Irish Journal of American Studies*. 1994, vol. 3, 31–54.

Foner, Eric. *Free Soil, Free Labor, Free Men: The Ideology of the Republican Party Before the Civil War*. Oxford, New York, 1970.

—— *Reconstruction: America's Unfinished Revolution, 1863–1877*. Harper & Row, New York, 1988.

Fosl, Catherine. *Subversive Southerner: Anne Braden and the Struggle for Racial Justice in the Cold War South*. Palgrave Macmillan, New York, 2002.

Fraser, Tom. 'Two American Presidents and Israel: Studies in Ambiguity,' *Irish Journal of American Studies*, vol. 3 1994, 93–114.

Freidenburg, Daniel M. *Sold to the Highest Bidder: The Presidency from Dwight D. Eisenhower to George W. Bush*. Prometheus Books, Amherst, New York, 2002.

Furgurson, Ernest. *Hard Right: The Rise of Jesse Helms*. W. W. Norton, New York, 1986.

Garrow, David. *Bearing the Cross: Martin Luther King Jr and the Southern Leadership Conference*. Jonathan Cape, London, 1988.

—— *Liberty and Sexuality: The Right to Privacy and the Making of Roe v Wade*. Macmillan, New York, 1994.

Garson, Robert A. *The Democratic Party and the Politics of Sectionalism, 1941–1948*. Louisiana State University Press, Baton Rouge, 1974.

Gates, Jr *Colored People*, Viking, London, 1995.

Giddings, Paula. *When and Where I Enter: The Impact of Black Women on Race and Sex in America*. Bantam, New York, 1984.

Gilmore, Glenda E. *Defying Dixie: The Radical Roots of Civil Rights, 1919–1950*. Bantam, New York, 2008.

Glad, Betty. *Jimmy Carter: In Search of the White House*. W. W. Norton, New York, 1980.

Goodwin, Doris Kearns. *Team of Rivals: The Political Genius of Abraham Lincoln*. Penguin Books, London, 2005.

Gore, Albert. *The Eye of the Storm: A People's Politics in the 1970s*. Herder & Herder, New York, 1970.

—— *Let the Glory Out: My South and its Politics*. Viking Press, New York, 1972.

Graham, Hugh Davis. *The Civil Rights Era: Origins and Development of a National Policy 1960–1972*. Oxford, New York, 1990.

Graham, Hugh Davis ed. *Civil Right in the United States*. Pennsylvania State University Press, University Park, 1994.

Green, James R. *Grassroots Socialism: Radical Movements in the South West*. Louisiana State University Press, Baton Rouge, 1978.

Green, Mark. *Losing Our Democracy: How Bush, the Far Right and Big Business Are Betraying America and How to Stop It*. Source Books, Naperville, Illinois, 2007.

Greenburg, Jan C. *Supreme Conflict: The Inside Story of the Struggle for Control of the Supreme Court*. Penguin Books, London, 2008.

Greene, John R. *The Limits of Power: The Nixon and Ford Administrations*. Indiana University Press, Bloomington, 1992.

Greene, Lee S. *Lead Me On: Frank Goad Clement and Tennessee Politics*. University of Tennessee Press, Knoxville, 1982.

Greene, Melissa Fay, *Praying for Sheetrock*. Secker and Warburg, London, 1992.

Grimshaw, William J. *Bitter Fruit: Black Politics and the Chicago Machine 1931–1991*. University of Chicago Press, 1992.

Grubbs, Donald H. *Cry from the Cotton: The Southern Tenants Farmers Union and The New Deal*. University of North Carolina Press, Chapel Hill, 1971.

Grunwald, Michael. *The New New Deal: The Hidden History of Change in the Obama Era*. Simon & Schuster, New York, 2013.

Guiner, Lani. *The Tyranny of the Majority: Fundamental Fairness in Representative Democracy*. Free Press, New York, 1994.

Guralnick, Peter. *Last Trains to Memphis: The Rise of Elvis Presley*. Little Brown, 1994.

Hahn, Steven. *A Nation Under Our Feet: Black Political Struggles in the Rural South from Slavery to the Great Migration.* Harvard University Press, Cambridge, 2003.

Halberstam, David. *The Fifties.* Fawcett Columbine, New York, 1993.

Halpern, Rick. *Down on the Killing Floor: Black and White Workers in Chicago's Packinghouses, 1904–54.* University of Illinois Press, Urbana, 1997.

Hamby, A. L. *Beyond the New Deal: Harry S. Truman and American Liberalism.* Columbia University Press, New York, 1973.

Harris, Frederick. *The Price of the Ticket: Barack Obama and the Rise and Decline of American Politics.* Oxford University Press, New York, 2012.

Hodes, Martha. *White Women, Black Men: Illicit Sex in the Nineteenth Century South.* Yale University Press, New Haven, 1997.

Holsaert, et al., *Hands on the Freedom Plow: Personal Accounts by Women in SNCC.* University of Illinois Press, Urbana, 2012.

Honey, Michael J. *Going Down Jericho Road: The Memphis Strike, Martin Luther King's Last Campaign.* W.W Norton, New York, 2007.

Howard, G. *The Sixties,* Washington Square Press, New York, 1982.

Houston, Benjamin. *The Nashville Way: Racial Etiquette and the Struggle for Social Justice in a Southern City,* University of Georgia Press, Athens, 2012.

Hudson, Cheryl and Gareth Davies, eds. *Ronald Reagan and the 1980s: Perceptions, Policies, Legacies.* Palgrave Macmillan, Basingstoke, 2008.

Hughes, Langston. *Ways of the White Folks.* Vintage Classics Edition, New York, 1999.

Ifell, Gwen. *The Breakthrough: Politics and Power in the Age of Obama.* Doubleday' New York, 2009.

Issel, William. *Social Change in the United States, 1945–1983.* Macmillan, Basingstoke, 1985.

Iton, Richard. *In Search of the Black Fantastic: Politics & Power in the Post-Civil Rights Era.* Oxford University Press, New York, 2008.

Jackson, K. T. *The Ku Klux Klan in the City, 1915–1930.* Macmillan, Basingstoke, 1992.

Jackson. Thomas F., *From Civil Rights to Human Rights: Martin Luther King Jr and the Struggle for Economic Justice.* University of Pennsylvania Press, Philadelphia, 2007.

Jamison, Ross. *Too Little Too Late: President Clinton's Prison Legacy.* The Center on Juvenile Crime and Criminal Justice, San Francisco, 2002.

Johnson, Haynes. *Sleepwalking Through History: America in the Ronald Reagan Years.* W. W. Norton, New York, 1991.

Johnston, David Cay. *The Making of Donald Trump.* Melville House, London, 2016.

Johnson, Lyndon Baines. *The Vantage Point: Perspectives of the Presidency, 1963–1969*. Popular Library, New York, 1971.

Jones, James H. *Bad Blood: The Tuskegee Experiment*. The Free Press, New York, 1993.

Jones, Leroi (Imiri Baraka), *The Autobiography of Leroi Jones*. Freundlich Books, New York, 1984.

Jones, Patrick D. *The Selma of the North: Civil Rights Insurgency in Milwaukee*. Harvard University Press, Cambridge, 2009.

Joseph, Peniele E. *Stokeley: A Life*. Basic Books, New York, 2014.

Kaplan, Carla. *Miss Anne in Harlem: White Women of the Harlem Renaissance*. Harper Collins, New York, 2013.

Kaufman, Burton I. *The Presidency of Thomas Earl Carter Jr* University of Kansas, Lawrence, 1993.

Kearns, Doris. *Lyndon Johnson and the American Dream*. Signet, New York, 1976.

Keller, Morton. *Obama's Time: A History*. Oxford University Press, New York, 2015.

Kerber, Linda and Sharon de Hart. *Women's America: Refocusing the Past*. Oxford University Press, New York, 1991.

Kessler, Glenn. *The Confidante: Condoleezza Rice and the Creation of the Bush Legacy*. St. Martin's Press, New York, 2007.

King, Coretta Scott, 'Keynote Address – AIDS Memorial Quilt,' www.GiftsofSpeech.com 1991.

King, Martin Luther, *Chaos or Community*. Hodder and Stoughton, London, 1967.

Klein, Joe. *The Natural: The Misunderstood Presidency of Bill Clinton*. Hodder & Stoughton, London, 2002.

Klibaner, Irwin, *Conscience of a Troubled South: The Southern Conference Education Fund, 1941–1966*. Carlson Publishing, New York, 1989.

Klinkner, Philip A. with Rogers W. Smith, *The Unsteady March: The Rise and Decline of Racial Equality in America*. University of Chicago Press, Chicago, 1999.

Knight, Thomas M. *Street of Dreams: The Nature and Legacy of the 1960s*. Duke University Press, Durham, 1989.

Kolbert, Elizabeth, 'Putting a Value on Three Thousand Lives,' *New Yorker*, 25 November 2002, 42–29.

—— 'The People's Preacher: Al Sharpton would Rather Walk Naked than Wear Your Wretched Dress,' *New Yorker*, 18 and 25, November, 2002.

Kotlowski, Dean. *Nixon's Civil Rights: Politics, Principle, and Policy*. Harvard University Press, Cambridge, 2002.

Kutler, Stanley L. ed., *Abuse of Power: The New Nixon Tapes*. Simon & Schuster, New York, 1998.

Karnish, Michael and Marc Fisher. *Trump Revealed: An American Journey of Ambition, Ego, Money and Power*. Simon & Schuster, London, 2016.

Lamis, Alexander, P. *The Two Party South*. 2nd ed. Oxford, New York, 1990.

Lasky, M. J. *The Hungarian Revolution*. Secker & Warburg, London, 1957.

Laue, James H. *Direct Action and Desegregation, 1960–62. Toward a Theory of the Rationalization of Protest*. Carlson Publishing, New York, 1989.

Lee, Chana Kei. *For Freedom's Sake: The Life of Fanny Lou Hamer*. University of Illinois Press, Urbana, 2000.

Leslie, Ian. *To be President: The Quest for the White House 2008*. Politico's, London, 2008.

Lewis, John. *Walking with the Wind: A Memoir of the Movement*. Simon & Schuster, New York, 1998.

—— 'Brief History of Prince Edward County Desegregation Fight,' www.civil-rights-memorial (accessed 9 January 2009).

Lewis, George. *Massive Resistance: The White Response to the Civil Rights Movement*. Hodder Arnold, London, 2006.

Litwack, Leon. *Trouble in Mind: Black Southerners and the Age of Jim Crow*. Alfred Knopf, New York, 1998.

Lowi, Theodore J. and Benjamin Ginsburg. *American Government*. W. W. Norton, New York, 1998.

Loevy, Robert D. 'To Write in the Book of Laws: President Johnson and the Civil Rights Act of 1964,' in Bernard Firestone and Robert Vogt, eds. *Lyndon Baines Johnson and the Uses of Power*. Greenwood, New York, 1980.

McAdam, D. R. *Freedom Summer*. Oxford, New York, 1988.

McAdam, Doug and Karina Kloos *Deeply Divided: Racial Politics and Social Movements in Postwar America*. Oxford University Press, Oxford, 2014.

McCullough, David. *Truman*. Simon & Schuster, New York, 1992.

McCoy, D. R. *The Presidency of Harry S Truman*. University Press of Kansas, Lawrence, 1984.

Males, Mike. *The Scapegoat Generation: America's War on Adolescents*. Common Courage Press, Monroe, 1996.

Marable, Manning. *Malcolm X: A Life of Reinvention*. Allen Lane, New York, 2011.

—— *Race, Reform and Rebellion: The Second Reconstruction in Black America 1945–1982*. University Press of Mississippi, Jackson, 1991.

Mark, David. *Going Dirty: The Art of Negative Campaigning*. Rowman & Littlefield, New York, 2007.

Matusow, A. J. *The Unraveling of America: A History of Liberalism in the 1960s.* Harper & Row, New York, 1986.

Mayer, Jane and Jill Abramson. *Strange Justice: The Selling of Clarence Thomas.* Houghton and Miflin, New York, 1994.

Mayer, Jane. *Dark Money: How a Secretive Group of Billionaires is Trying to Buy Control in the US.* Scribe Publications, London, 2016.

Meier, August and Elliot Rudwick. 'The Bus Boycott Against Jim Crow Streetcars in the South,' in David Garrow, ed. *We Shall Overcome: The Civil Rights Movement in the United States in the 1950s and 1960s.* Carlson Publishing, New York, 1989.

—— *From Plantation to Ghetto.* Hill and Wang, New York, 1970.

Mendell, David. *Obama: From Promise to Power.* Amistad, Harper-Collins, New York, 2008.

Menifield, Charles E. and Edward Shaffer, eds. *Politics in the New South: Representation of African Americans in Southern State Legislatures.* State University New York Press, New York, 2002.

Merl, E. *Seedtime of the Modern Civil Rights Movement: The President's Committee On Fair Employment Practice, 1941–1946.* Louisiana State University Press, Baton Rouge, 1991.

Miller, Loren. *The Petitioners: The Story of the Supreme Court and the Negro.* Meridian, New York, 1967.

Miller, Merle. *Plain Speaking: Conversations with Harry S. Truman.* Victor Gollancz, London, 1974.

Miller, Neil. *Out of Our Past: Gay and Lesbian History from 1869 to the Present.* London, 1995.

Milligen, Stephen. *Better to Reign in Hell: Serial Killers Media Panics and the FBI.* Headpress, London, 2006.

Mills, Kay. *This Little Light of Mine: The Life of Fanny Lou Hamer.* University Press of Kentucky, Lexington, 2007.

Moore, Michael, *Stupid White Men: … and Other Sorry Excuses for the State of the Nation.* Penguin, London, 2001.

Moraga, C and Gloria Anzaluda, *This Bridge Called My Back: Racial Writings of Women of Color.* Kitchen Table, Women of Color Press, New York, 1983.

Morris, Aldon, *The Origins of the Civil Rights Movement: Black People and Communities Organizing for Change.* Free Press, New York, 1984.

Morrison J and R. K. Morrison, *From Camelot to Kent State: The Sixties Experience in the Words of Those Who Lived It.* Times Books, New York, 1983, rev.1988.

Myrdal, Gunnar. *An American Dilemma.* McGraw Hill, Toronto, 1964.

Murray, Pauli. *Pauli Murray: The Autobiography of a Black Activist, Feminist, Lawyer and Priest.* University of Tennessee Press, Knoxville, 1989.

Navasky, Victor. *Kennedy Justice.* Atheneum, New York, 1971.

Neubeck, Kenneth J. and Noel Cazenave. *Welfare Racism: Playing the Race Card Against America's Poor.* Routledge, New York, 2001.

Nightingale, C. H. *On the Edge: A History of Poor Black Children and Their American Dreams.* Basic Books, New York, 1993.

Nixon, Richard. *The Memoirs of Richard Nixon.* Sidgewick and Jackson, London, 1978.

Oates, Stephen. *Let the Trumpet Sound: A Life of Martin Luther King Jr* Harper Perennial, New York, 1994.

Obama, Barack, *Dreams from My Father.* Cannongate, Edinburgh, 2007.

—— *The Audacity of Hope: Thoughts on Reclaiming the American Dream.* Cannongate, Edinburgh, 2007.

Ogbar, Jeffrey O. G. *Black Power: Radical Politics and African American Identity.* Johns Hopkins University Press, Baltimore, 2005.

Olson, Lynne. *Freedom's Daughters: The Unsung Heroes of the Civil Rights Movement 1830–1970.* Touchstone Press, New York, 2002.

O'Reilly, Kenneth. *Black Americans: The FBI Files.* Caroll & Graff, New York, 1994.

Pascoe, Peggy. *What Comes Naturally: Miscegenation Law and the Making of Race in America.* Oxford University Press, New York, 2009.

Parish, Peter. *The American Civil War.* Eyre Metheun, London, 1975.

Parlett, Martin. *Demonizing a President: 'Foreignization' of Barack Obama.* Praeger Publishers, New York, 2014.

Patterson, James I. *Great Expectations: The United States 1945–1974.* Oxford University Press, New York, 1996.

Payne, Charles. *I've Got the Light of Freedom: The Organizing Tradition and the Mississippi Freedom Struggle.* University of California Press, Berkley, 1996.

Perlstein, Rick. *Nixonland: The Rise of a President and the Fracturing of America.* New York, 2008.

Piketty, Thomas, *Capital in the Twenty-First Century.* Belknap Press of Harvard University, Cambridge, 2014.

Philpott, Thomas Lee, *The Slum and the Ghetto: Immigrants, Blacks, and Reformers in Chicago 1880 – 1930.* Wadsworth Publishing, Belmont, 1991.

Pinkney, Alphonso. *Red Black and Green: Black Nationalism in the United States.* Cambridge, 1976.

Portis, Larry. *Terror and its Representations: Studies in Social History and Cultural Experience in the United States and Beyond.* Presses Universitaire de la Mediterranee, Montpellier, 2008.

—— *Soul Trains: A People's History of Popular Music in the United States and Brittan.* Virtual Bookworm.com College Station, 2002.

Powell, Colin (with J. E. Perisco). *My American Journey.* Ballantine Books, New York, 1996.

Prelinger, Rick. *Ephemeral Films.* Voyager CD Rom, New York, 1997.

Proudfoot, Merrill. *Diary of a Sit-in.* University of Illinois Press, Urbana, 1990.

Quarles, Benjamin. *The Negro in the American Revolution.* University of North Carolina, Chapel Hill, 1961.

Raines, Howell. *My Soul Is Rested: Movement Days in the Deep South Remembered* New York, 1977.

Ralph, James R. *Northern Protest: Martin Luther King Jr Chicago and the Civil Rights Movement.* London, 1993.

Rankin, Annie James, 'Autobiography.' Handwritten document in the Mississippi Digital Archive, Tougaloo College.

Ransbury, Barbara. *Ella Baker & the Black Freedom Movement: A Radical Democratic Vision*: University of North Carolina Press, London, 2003.

Ravitch, Diane. *The Death and Life of the Great American School System: How Testing and Choice Are Undermining Education.* Basic Books, New York, 2011.

Redkey, Edwin S. *Black Exodus: Black Nationalism and Back to Africa Movement, 1890–1910.* Yale University Press, New Haven, 1969.

Reed Jr Adolph L. *The Jesse Jackson Phenomenon.* Yale University Press, New Haven, 1986.

Reed, Merl E. *Seedtime of the Modern Civil Rights Movement: The President's Committee on Fair Employment Practice, 1941–1946.* Louisiana State University Press, Baton Rouge, 1991.

Renshon, Stanley A. *High Hopes: The Clinton Presidency and the Politics of Ambition.* Routledge, New York, 1998.

Republic of New Africa archive, Mississippi Digital Collection, Tougaloo College.

Rhea, Joseph T. *Race Pride and American Identity.* Harvard University Press, Cambridge, 1997.

Riches, Julia, 'Fetal Attraction': The Politics of Fetal Protection in the Law.' unpublished PhD dissertation, Georgetown University, 2002.

Riches, W. T. M., 'White Servants and Black Servants and the Question of Providence: Servitude and Slavery in Colonial Virginia'. *The Irish Journal of American Studies.* Vol. 8, 1999, 1–33.

—— 'Remembering and Appropriating the Civil Rights Movement: Mississippi,' in Zitomersky, Joseph and Michael Bellesiles, eds. *Conspiracy and Consent.* Universite de Montpellier, (2017).

—— 'Three Portraits of a Native Son,' Deutsch Englische Jarbucker 8, 1980, 28–37.

Roberts, Gene and Hank Klibanofff, *Race Beat: The Press, the Civil Rights Struggle and the Awakening of a Nation.* Alfred Knopf, New York, 2006.

Rogers, Mary B. *Barbara Jordan: American Hero.* Bantam, New York, 1998.

Rowbotham, Sheila. *A Century of Women: The History of Women in Britain and the United States.* Penguin Books, London, 1997.

Rudwick, Elliott M. *Race Riot in East St. Louis, July 2 1917.* Southern Illinois, University, Press, Carbondale, 1964.

—— *W. E. B. Du Bois: Propagandist of Negro Protest.* Atheneum, New York, 1968.

Ruiz, Vicki and Ellen Carol DuBois, eds. *Unequal Sisters: A Multi-Cultural Reader in Women's History.* Routledge, New York, 1994.

Safford, Joel, 'John C. Calhoun, Lani Guinier and Minority Rights,' *Political Science and Politics.* June 1995, 211–26.

Salvatore, Nick. *Eugene V. Debs: Citizen and Socialist.* University of Illinois Press, Champaign, 1982.

Sandweiss, Martha A. *Passing Strange: A Gilded Age Tale of Love and Deception Across the Color Line.* Allen Lane, New York, 2009.

Savage, Jon. *Teenage: The Creation of Youth 1875–1945.* Chatto and Windus, London, 2007.

Schlesinger Jr Arthur. *Robert Kennedy and His Times.* Futura, London, 1979.

Seeger, Pete and Rob Reiser, *Everybody Says Freedom: A History of the Civil Rights Movement in Songs and Pictures.* W. W. Norton, New York, 1989.

Seale, Bobby. *Seize The Time: The Story of the Black Panther Party and Huey P. Newton.* Vintage, NewYork, 1980.

Shilts, Randy. *And the Band Played On: Politics, People, and the AIDS Epidemic.* St Martin's Press, New York, 1987.

Shull, Steven. *A Kinder, Gentler Racism? The Reagan-Bush Legacy.* M. E. Sharpe, New York, 1993.

Signorile, Michelangelo, *Queer Nation: Sex, the Media and the Closets of Power.* Abacus, 1993.

Sitkoff, Howard. *The Struggle for Black Equality, 1945–1992.* Hill and Wang, New York, 1993.

Skocpol, Theda and Vanessa Williamson. *The Tea Party and the Remaking of Republican Conservatism.* Oxford University Press, New York, 2013.

Smith, Lillian. *Killers of the Dream*. W. W. Norton, New York, 1994 (1st ed., 1946).

Smith, Rogers. *Civic Ideals: Conflicting Visions of Citizenship in US History*. Yale University Press, New Haven, 1997.

Smith, Therese. *'Let the Children Sing': Music and Worship in a Black Mississippi Community*. University of Rochester Press, Rochester, 2004.

Spotswood, D. et al. *Goodbye, Babylon*. Dust-to-Digital, Atlanta, 2003.

Stein, Judith. *The World of Marcus Garvey: Race and Class in Modern Society*. Louisiana State University Press, Baton Rouge, 1986.

Springsteen, Bruce. *Born to Run*. Simon & Schuster, London, 2016.

Stockman, David. *The Triumph of Politics: The Inside Story of the Reagan Administration*. Avon, New York, 1987.

Stokes, Melvyn and Rick Halpern. *Race and Class in the American South Since 1890*. Berg, Oxford, 1994.

Stoper, Emily. *The Student Nonviolent Coordinating Committee: The Growth of Radicalism in a Civil Rights Organization*. Carlson Publishing, New York, 1989.

Sugrue, Thomas J., *Sweet Land of Liberty: The Forgotten Struggle for Civil Rights in The North*. Random House, New York, 2008.

—— *The Origins of the Urban Crisis: Race and Inequality in Postwar Detroit*. Princeton University Press, Princeton, 2005. (new preface 2015).

Summers, Anthony. *The Arrogance of Power: The Secret World of Richard Nixon*. Victor Gollanz, London, 2000.

Tate, Gayle T and Lewis Randolph eds. *Dimensions of Black Conservatism in the United States*. Palgrave, New York, 2002.

Theoharis, Jeanne. *The Rebellious Life of Mrs. Rosa Parks*. Beacon Press, Boston, 2013.

Thernstrom, Stephan and Abigail Thernstrom. *America in Black and White: One Nation Indivisible*. New York, 1997.

Thomas, Clarence. *My Grandfather's Son: A Memoir*. Harper Collins, New York, 2007.

Thomas, Evan. *'A Long Time Coming:' The Inspiring Combative 2008 Campaign and the Historic Election of Barack Obama*. Public Affairs, London, 2009.

Thornton, J. Mills, 'Challenge and Response in the Montgomery Bus Boycott of 1955–1956' in David Garrow ed., *The Walking City: The Montgomery Bus Boycott 1955–1956*. Carlson Publishing, New York, 1989.

Thrasher, Sue. Unpublished interview with Anne Braden. 18 April 1981.

Todd, Chuck and Sheldon Gawiser, *How Barack Obama Won: A State-by-State Guide To the Historic 2008 Election*. Vintage Books, Vintage Books, New York, 2009.

Topping, Simon. *Lost Legacy: The Republican Party and the African American Vote, 1928–1952*. University Press of Florida, Gainesville, 2008.

Truman, Harry S. *Memoirs: Years of Trial and Hope*. Doubleday, New York, 1956.

Tuck, Stephen, 'African American Protest', in Cheri Hudson and Gareth Davies eds., *Ronald Reagan and the 1980s: Perceptions, Policies and Legacies*. Palgrave MacMillan, Basingstoke, 2008.

Tuttle, William. *Race Riot: Chicago in the Red Summer of 1919*. Oxford University Press, New York, 1980.

Wadden, Alex. *Clinton's Legacy? A New Democrat in Governance*. Palgrave Macmillan, Basingstoke, 2002.

Walker, Samuel. *Presidents and Civil Liberties from Wilson to Obama: A Story of Poor Custodians*. University of Cambridge Press, New York, 2012.

Ward, David. *Just My Soul Responding: Rhythm and Blues, Black Consciousness and Race Relations*. UCL Press, London, 1998.

Washington, James. *A Testament of Hope: The Essential Writings and Speeches of Martin Luther King Jr* HarperCollins, New York, 1991.

Watson, Justin. *The Christian Coalition: Dreams of Restoration, Demands for Recognition*. Macmillan, Basingstoke, 1999.

Watters, Pat. *Down to Now: Reflections on the Southern Civil Rights Movement*. W. W. Norton, New York, 1990.

Weisbrot, Robert. *Freedom Road: A History of the American Civil Rights Movement*. W. W. Norton, New York, 1991.

Welch, Matt. *McCain: The Myth of the Maverick*. Palgrave Macmillan, New York, 2008.

Werner, Craig. *A Change is Gonna Come: Music, Race and the Soul of America*. Cannongate Books, London, 2000.

West, Cornell. *Keeping Faith: Philosophy and Race in America*. Routledge, New York, 1993.

White, John. *Black Leadership in America, 1895–1968*. Longman, London, 1985.

Whitfield, Stephen. *A Death in the Delta: The Story of Emmett Till*. Collier Macmillan, London, 1988.

Wickham, DeWayne. *Bill Clinton and Black America*. Ballantine Publishing, Group, New York, 2002.

Weidner, Donald. *A History of Africa South of the Sahara*. Vintage Books, New York, 1962.

Wilkerson, Isabel. *The Warmth of Other Suns: The Epic Story of America's Great Migration*. Random House, New York, 2010.

Wilson, Midge and Kathy Russell. *Divided Sisters: Bridging the Gap Between Black and White Women*. Anchor Books, New York, 1996.

Wirt, Frederick M. '*We Ain't What We Was': Civil Rights in the New South*. Duke University Press, Durham NC, 1997.

Wolters, D. *The New Negro on Campus: Black College Rebellions of the 1920s*. Princeton University Press, Princeton, 1975.

Woods, Randall B. *LBJ: Architect of American Ambition*. Harvard University Press, Cambridge, 2006.

Wynn, Neil A. *The Afro-American and the Second World War*. Paul Eleck, London, 1976.

Yarborough, Tinsley. *Judge Frank Johnson and Human Rights in Alabama*. University of Alabama Press, Tuscaloosa, 1981.

Young, Andrew. *An Easy Burden: The Civil Rights Movement and the Transformation of America*. Harper Collins, New York, 1996.

Zinn, Howard. *A People's History of the United States*. Harper & Row, New York, 1980.

Index